Human Response to
CROWDING

Human Response to CROWDING

EDITED BY

ANDREW BAUM
Trinity College

YAKOV M. EPSTEIN
Rutgers University

 LAWRENCE ERLBAUM ASSOCIATES, PUBLISHERS
1978   Hillsdale, New Jersey

DISTRIBUTED BY THE HALSTED PRESS DIVISION OF

JOHN WILEY & SONS
New York   Toronto   London   Sydney

Lawrence Erlbaum Associates, Inc., Publishers
62 Maria Drive
Hillsdale, New Jersey 07642

Distributed solely by Halsted Press Division
John Wiley & Sons, Inc., New York

Library of Congress Cataloging in Publication Data

Main entry under title:

Human response to crowding.

Includes indexes.
1.   Crowding stress.   I.   Baum, Andrew.   II.   Epstein,
Yakov M.
BF 353.H855   155.9'2   78-6875
ISBN 0-470-26374-1

Contents

3   Crowding and the Developmental Process
Gary W. Evans

4   Crowding: Methods of Study
Yakov M. Epstein and *Andrew Baum*

5   A Setting-Specific Analysis of Crowding
Robert A. Karlin, Yakov M. Epstein, and *John R. Aiello*

PART II
MODELS OF CROWDING AND DENSITY-RELATED STRESS

Preface

The purpose of this volume is to describe theoretical developments, examine research methods, and consider evidence of human response to crowding. Although interest in crowding and environmental influences on behavior has been emerging for the past decade, the study of human response to crowding has only recently gone into high gear. The reasons for this are many and varied, but it may generally be said that until recently the literature on crowding was inconsistent and fraught with contradictions. Indeed, despite one's intuitive feelings about crowding, it was difficult to conclude from published findings as late as 1974 that crowding had a significant impact on human behavior. Recently, however, more definitive theoretical and methodological statements have appeared, revealing causes for the inconsistency of empirical findings. By gathering papers from those who have contributed much of what we know about crowding, we hope to further this growth and facilitate the development of more sophisticated, predictive models of crowding.

This book does not present empirical research in the usual sense, but ultimately these data form its core. One characteristic of the study of crowding has been a rather large base of experimental findings relative to the development of theory. One of the more important developments over the period in which this book was being written has been an acceleration in conceptual analysis and theory building. As a result, we present three general categories of recent work in this area. The first group of papers deals primarily with the mass of data generated between 1970 and 1976, reviewing them in different ways in an attempt to integrate seemingly divergent findings. Altman reviews the evolution of the field as an area of scientific investigation, and Sundstrom considers the findings of many studies, summing them into a sequential perspective. Evans interprets previous research in light of developmental processes, and Epstein and Baum discuss some of the methodological characteristics of crowding research. Finally, Karlin, Epstein, and Aiello consider this research in terms of the differences in settings in which it has been conducted. Thus, the papers in this section attempt to deal with seeming contradictions in the experimental literature, both by reviewing findings in terms of how well they fit different conceptual frameworks and by evaluating specific techniques that have been used.

Part II is also concerned with reconciliation of divergent findings, but these papers are more concerned with the advancement of theory. After a quick look backward, Stokols extends his taxonomic analysis of crowding, distinguishing between *personal* and *neutral* crowding in *primary* and *secondary* environments. Knowles discusses crowding in the context of social influence models, linking different analyses of crowding to social physics. By briefly reviewing related studies, he begins to demonstrate how, in a manner analogous to the force of gravitational attraction, factors such as strength of arousal, emotional involvement, and friendship vary as an exponential function of the distance between people. Saegert discusses the many ways in which crowded situations involve a loss of control. Reviewing potential consequences of large numbers of people and of spatial constraint, she discusses control-relevant problems associated with congestion, interference, lack of privacy, and an inability to limit or avoid interactions with others. As a consequence of these problems, individuals are stressed and they experience cognitive deficiencies and negative affect. However, she also points out that there are conditions under which high-density experience is pleasurable, considering arousal as a possible "intensifier" of pre-existing affect. Evans also discusses the role of arousal in the crowding process, deriving support from studies of crowding, social behavior, and physiological arousal. He points out that the strengths and weaknesses of his approach lie in its rather mechanistic nature, providing very specific predictions but lacking in sensitivity to psychological and social mediation of crowding.

The third group of papers is theoretical in varying degrees, but most important, they begin to test theoretically derived hypotheses and to evaluate applications of different models of crowding. Worchel provides another explanation of Freedman's (1975) intensification hypothesis, using Schachter and Singer's (1962) discussion of emotion as a starting point. In developing his perspective, Worchel suggests that crowding is arousing but that the consequences associated with arousal depend on the label attached to it. By discussing an experiment conducted to evaluate some aspects of this view, Worchel provides an interesting perspective on the effects of spatial density and proximity. Davis reviews the findings of research on architecture and architectural mediation of density in identifying design variables that affect crowding and suggesting strategies to counter consequences of high-density living. His effort is an important attempt to apply behavioral data to the design process, and it provides an interesting analysis of naturalistically induced crowding stress. Loo discusses the impact of spatial density on children, noting that what we may experience as crowding may be manifested in children's responses but that they may not label their experience as such. Rodin and Baum consider the role of density in evoking reactance and in conditioning learned helplessness, assuming a control-related perspective similar to Saegert's.

Clearly, there is overlap across these sections, and our editorially imposed structure should not prevent integration of many of these papers. Many, for example, are concerned with reconciliation of discrepant findings, and most of them begin to establish linkages with more traditional theories of social behavior. Many have implications for policy and planning decisions, and all have implications for theoretical developments in the study of crowding. As Altman notes in his paper, the improvement of theoretical underpinnings of research on crowding and the generation of specific hypotheses that can be tested are crucial to the field. Many of the papers in this volume can be thought of as attempts to conceptually restructure the field of crowding. In light of the wisdom of years to come, these statements may appear simplistic. Yet we hope that they will lay the groundwork for increasingly more sophisticated theoretical statements and that they will stimulate the consideration of theoretically derived research problems.

Our hopes for this volume are many. Reconciliation of divergent findings and facilitation of theoretical development are just two of them. A third is that this book will be useful to students of behavior *and* environment, to students of psychology *and* architecture, for example. We have tried to provide information for designers and planners as well as for behavioral scientists and lay people concerned with the impact of high density and crowding. Although the papers are technical at times, we hope that they can be of use to a variety of people and that they can stimulate dialogues among researchers, practitioners, and the public that they serve.

A related question is one of "Why now?" What are the reasons for this surge of interest in crowding? The answers are not altogether clear. In his chapter, Altman suggests that recent concern with the environment and ecology of our planet has spurred interest in deriving solutions to environmental problems. A second impetus to the study of crowding is the growing fear of overpopulation of the planet. Despite gains in population control through reduction of the birth rate, high-density living in cities seems inevitable. Already a fact in many regions, it seems apparent that the density of high concentrations of people will increase before it decreases. As a result, people want to know about the effects of crowding, and designers and planners want to determine ways of minimizing the negative impact of high density. Another reason for this book, then, is to explore the mechanisms by which high density and crowding cause stress and to facilitate the generation of data that can be used to reduce these effects.

Altman also points out that the typical student of crowding was educated during the late 1960s and early 1970s. During this period of turbulence, many students sought increased relevance and were concerned with the applicability of behavioral science to the solution of social problems. Crowding seems to be a topic that fulfills these needs, providing a problem largely social in nature that should be better understood. Crowding has also been an area of study in which contradictory findings and divergent theoretical statements have been common, and another impetus to the study of crowding has been the controversy it has generated. Lay accounts of urban crowding and initial animal study provided frightening descriptions of the impact of density and led to gloomy predictions of dire consequences. Other studies underscored the "infinite" adaptability of people, suggesting that we could adapt to crowding with minimal difficulty. The vast majority of opinion lies between these extremes, and by compiling this collection we have sought to present the most current research, theory, and speculation about the impact of density and crowding. We have asked the contributing authors to discuss the results of their research and to extend the boundaries of current models. Happily, we think that they have risen to the occasion and have developed some interesting and exciting new positions.

We are fledgling editors, and as such we may have failed to adhere to some of the traditional editorial norms. In our role as editors, we have found that at times we exercised a heavy hand in making decisions about style and continuity. We would like to thank our contributors for cooperating with our requests. We encouraged the use of the first person to make the book more informal and to have the authors assume responsibility for their research. To avoid repetition in reviews of the literature, we asked authors to omit portions of their papers. Finally, we asked that authors discuss research findings rather than reporting them in traditional fashion. Thus, papers by Worchel, Davis, Loo, and Rodin and Baum, for example, do not present tests of significance or great details about the results of the research.

Over the course of the year and a half that we have worked on this book it has changed its form several times. Originally, we had intended it as a vehicle for the presentation of papers read at a 1975 Eastern Psychological Association symposium. We then decided that a more comprehensive volume, including theoretical statements and discussion of research from those active in the field, would be far more useful. It is hoped that the student of crowding or the concerned layperson can gain a better understanding of the complexities and consequences of high-density living. The book has already stimulated what we feel has been an exciting interchange of ideas among contributors. We can only hope that this interchange will continue and grow.

Our work on this book was facilitated by research grants by the National Institute of Child Health and Human Development (#HD–08546–01 to Yakov M. Epstein, and #HD–07545–01 to Stuart Valins and Andrew Baum). We would like to thank Jerome E. Singer and Stuart Valins for their advisory assistance and our wives, Carlene S. Baum and Ellen W. Epstein, who encouraged and supported our endeavors. We are also grateful to Carole Heeren, Hilda Streiber, and Heidi Holstein for their excellent secretarial assistance and remarkable patience.

ANDREW BAUM
YAKOV M. EPSTEIN

PART I

CONCEPTUAL AND METHODOLOGICAL ISSUES

1

Crowding: Historical and Contemporary Trends in Crowding Research

Irwin Altman
University of Utah

INTRODUCTION

This chapter presents an historical and sociological perspective on the research and theory of crowding and human behavior, which is in a period of accelerated growth, especially in psychology and sociology. For me, an interesting problem is how to characterize present-day activity in the field and how to project what it is that we are likely to do in the future. As historians sometimes state, it is difficult, if not impossible, to write a history of the present. Nevertheless, there are several directions and philosophies of research that I would like to describe in order to sensitize us to emerging trends and to assist us in making decisions about how to spend our energies in researching and theorizing about crowding.

The first section of the chapter briefly reviews the history of research on crowding, beginning in the 1920s and continuing into the 1970s. The main part of the chapter deals with contemporary trends in methodological, theoretical, and substantive aspects of crowding research. The last section of the chapter considers prospects for the future.

A CAPSULE HISTORY OF RESEARCH ON CROWDING[1]

Three traditions have historically dominated crowding research: a sociological tradition centered around urban analysis, which began in the 1920s; studies of animal crowding, which emerged in the 1950s and 1960s; psychological research,

[1]See Freedman (1972), Lawrence (1974), Altman (1975), and Michelson (1970) for more detailed historical overviews.

which came on the scene for the first time in the late 1960s and early 1970s. Although I will describe "early" and "late" phases of research, the future-shock quality of our existence will sometimes mean, especially for psychological research, that "early history" can be as recent as 1970.

The Sociological Tradition

Sociological research emerged in the 1920s during the heyday of the early urban sociologists. Among other features of urban life, these researchers examined the concomitants of life in high population areas. Their approach was correlational, with the basic strategy being to relate measures of population concentration (people per neighborhood, people per census tract, etc.) to various outcomes, especially social pathology indicators such as crime and juvenile delinquency, physical and mental illness, mortality rates, and the like. Many such studies yielded moderate relationships between population concentration and social pathology, which led to the conclusion that crowding was harmful to human well-being.

These studies were criticized on several grounds. The correlational nature of the research made interpretation difficult, that is covariation did not necessarily mean that population density "caused" social pathology. Many other explanations could have accounted for the results, such as economic, social, educational, health, and ethnicity factors that often paralleled differences in population density. Also, these sociological analyses used different indicators of population density such as people per acre, people per census tract, buildings per geographical area and so on, all of which reflect relatively large geographical units. Only infrequently were measures based on people or families per dwelling unit or per room, or on other molecular indicators of population concentration. And there were few conceptual analyses of different density indicators in this research, nor were there any systematic attempts to compare them in terms of social pathology.

Another characteristic of this early research was its emphasis on long-term outcomes, rather than on ongoing social processes. Crime rates and mental and physical illness are probably long-term results of a history of crowding. Early sociological research did not directly examine social processes that occurred in high and low density environments so as to identify how people coped with crowding. Finally, this early tradition dealt with crowding as a societal level problem, not as an individual, family, or small group problem.

The volume of sociological research on crowding declined in the 1950s and 1960s but it recently has gained new momentum. Although it is difficult to pinpoint the reasons for this decline, I suspect that the preceding factors played some role. That is, having documented over and over moderate correlations between population concentration and social pathology, but being unable to clearly ascertain underlying dynamics, not having a clear conceptual framework of the concept of density, and not being able to track social processes could well have led to the belief that continued research along the same lines could only be redundant. However, with more sophisticated analytic techniques and theoretical models now available, there is a growing body of sociological research on crowding.

The Animal Ethological Tradition

Beginning in the late 1950s students of animal behavior began to report research and naturalistic observations on population control in various animal species.[2] The dramatic description of the lemmings' migration to the sea (DuBos, 1965), the die-off of an apparently healthy herd of deer on an island in Chesapeake Bay (Christian, Flyger, & Davis, 1960), and Calhoun's research program on crowding in rats and mice, which spanned two decades (Calhoun, 1962a, 1962b, and is summarized in Calhoun, 1971), had considerable appeal to the research community. One could telescope in time the analysis of population density because animal life expectancies were shorter than that of humans; one could study ongoing social processes and reactions to crowding; one could do detailed autopsies and histological analyses; one could experimentally vary living conditions in ways that would be impossible with humans, and so on. Although there is controversy about the effects of population concentration on animal behavior, this research tradition generally confirms the idea that excessive population density is associated with problems of social and physiological functioning in animals.

This line of research stimulated lay and scholarly thinking, with many persons being quick to claim that it indicated the negative effects of population concentration on humans. However, many researchers discounted such claims on the grounds that generalizing from animals to humans was unwarranted, that animal studies themselves were not always consistent, and that it was necessary to do research on humans to understand the issue of crowding and population density. Under the influence of such logic, social psychologists and others soon entered the scene, bringing their own unique stamp to the study of human crowding.

The Social Psychological Tradition

Although there was an occasional study in the 1960s, psychological research on human crowding began to appear with any frequency only in the early 1970s, some 50 years later than the original sociological analyses and almost two decades following early ethological studies. However, psychologists have made up for lost time, with many studies now available and innumerable ones under way.

It may be myopic to talk about "early" and "later" psychological research on crowding, but there are some differences in substance, style, and philosophy

---

[2]See DuBos (1965), Davis (1971), Eibl-Eibesfeldt (1970), and Wynne-Edwards (1972) for detailed reviews of this work.

of initial and more recent studies. Although it is perhaps a straw-man argument, and certainly not typical of every study, there were several common features of this early research. First, the tradition of the laboratory was applied to the study of crowding, with an emphasis on control, manipulation, use of only a few variables, and so on. Groups were formed under conditions of crowding (large and small numbers of people in the same size space, or the same group in small and large spaces) and were studied largely in terms of task performance and various feelings. Furthermore, group members were strangers, were knowingly gathered for temporary periods of time (varying from minutes to a few hours), and often worked on tasks designed for the laboratory rather than on activities from their everyday lives. In general, the ecology of the laboratory setting was the one that had been used for two decades of work on other social psychological problems.

Another feature of this work, also harking back to 20 years of laboratory-oriented research, was to manipulate that which could be clearly manipulated, and to measure "simple" outcomes of those manipulations, without giving much attention to intervening social processes. The goal was to narrow the range of variables to a manageable number, to measure and manipulate what could be done so clearly, and to deal with only a limited number of questions. On the antecedent variable side, little systematic attempt was made to conceptualize about differences in spatial versus social density, the effect of length of time of crowding, the nature of the task, and so on. On the dependent variable side, the tone of the times was to measure performance on a variety of tasks and/or subjective feelings of comfort and tension.

The result of a few years of research in this tradition was equivocal. Crowding did not seem especially debilitating, results were weak in terms of psychological states and performance outcomes, and all in all, one had the feeling that, somehow, we were not grasping the problem very well. Yet the history of research in sociology and ethology and the starkly evident plight of crowded cities and overpopulated nations stood in contrast to the results of these laboratory demonstrations. Somehow, applying the tried and true methods of the past had not been very illuminating.

The Present Period of Transition:
New Researchers and New Strategies

I believe that we are now in a stage of transition in research on crowding that involves the appearance of a new breed of researchers and a cultural milieu that fosters different approaches to research and theory. In the next section of the chapter I will describe this transition period in terms of the methodology, theory, and content of crowding research. I will propose that we have progressed quite far in regard to methodological issues, that we have made somewhat less progress in theoretical developments, and that we have not yet clearly defined the appropriate range of substance that should be studied. This analysis fits with Kuhn's

(1970) notions that drastic changes in science often first involve shifts in methodology approaches, which are then followed by theoretical and substantive changes.

A key feature of the present transition period is a newly emerging type of researcher. In earlier articles (Altman, 1973, Altman, 1976), I describe environmental designers and social/behavioral scientists who came together in the 1960s partly because of discontent with their parent disciplines. On the environmental side, the traditional design professions were accused of ignoring people and their needs whereas in the social sciences the alienated felt that their field had ignored the role of the environment in human affairs. For social scientists, especially social psychologists, their dissatisfaction also centered around the apparent lack of "relevance" of traditional research to important social problems, the seeming inappropriateness of the laboratory method, the comfortable, establishment quality of journals, organizations and content of the field, the minute and static quality of questions that were being researched, and so on.

The typical crowding researcher probably fits one of two "clinical" profiles. First, there is a group of relatively senior people who have been in the field for at least 10 years. My guess is that these people were never in the mainstream of their parent field and were not especially attached to the traditions of the 1950s and 1960s, that is, cognitive consistency theory, laboratory methods as the sole path to truth, and so on.

The second type of crowding researcher is the relatively young person who received professional training during the late 1960s and early 1970s. This group constitutes the bulk of contributors to this volume. These people were for the most part educated during the time of the societal turbulence of the 1960s and largely under the tutelage of senior people who held traditional values about the content and methods of their field. The cross-pressures of strong traditionalism and mounting discontent both in society at large and in social psychology probably had many interesting effects on these neophytes that are beginning to be reflected in research on crowding.

Generally speaking, I would bet that many of these young people tried to apply the methods, content, and theory of traditional social psychology to the study of crowding in their dissertations and in research with their mentors. I also suspect that they quickly experienced a sense of dissatisfaction. Somehow, the study of crowding in a short-term laboratory setting, where groups of strangers were gathered together for the sake of a requirement in introductory psychology to work on an artificial task, probably seemed inadequate to the magnitude of this complex problem. And, furthermore, the then-dominant theoretical framework in the field—cognitive consistency—probably could not quite be tailored to the phenomenon of crowding.

During this period these younger researchers sought one another out, formed ad hoc groups, struggled with new directions that could incorporate their past experiences (or rejected them), and have at this writing established a sense of identity and direction. To me, they are at once a tough- and tender-minded group of people. They understand data and the need for scientific rigor, whether it be in the laboratory or elsewhere. They are also genuinely concerned with social issues and want their research to contribute to the solution of such problems. They also interact easily with people from other disciplines, especially those in the environmental design field, and they are active in interdisciplinary groups. Moreover, present-day researchers are activists in the sense of reaching out to do things—engaging in applied research projects, forming interdisciplinary work groups, organizing conferences, writing books, and so on. They are, in short, good organizers and good "movers," and they are not always concerned with social amenities or their "proper place" in the scientific establishment. They are also not afraid to take gambles in their research, as illustrated later, and to take on difficult field studies, longitudinal projects, and so on. They are brash and confident and hardheaded in their scientific values. There is an energetic quality to this newer breed of researchers that often tempts one, especially a senior person, to say "Wait for me, I'm your leader."[3]

DEVELOPMENTS IN RESEARCH METHODOLOGY

In my opinion, progress in methodology is the most dramatic feature of recent research on crowding, far more so than advances in content and theory. Methodological developments center around the following topics: broadly based eclecticism, multilevel analysis of behavior, a social process orientation, and time-linked strategies.

Broadly Based Eclecticism

The earliest social psychological studies of crowding were largely laboratory-oriented, whereas traditional sociological studies were correlational. However, scanning of this volume and of research in the field reveals that no single methodological strategy predominates any longer. Laboratory studies still appear but so do field experiments and observational analyses where data are collected in naturalistic everyday settings. In addition, there is now a greater willingness to use quasi-experimental designs. Furthermore, traditional sociological analyses are still being conducted, although more sophisticated concepts of density and more sophisticated statistical techniques are employed.

Consider some examples of the broad spectrum of methodology now in use. The laboratory tradition continues in force as evidenced, for example, in a study

---

[3]This description probably best fits the social psychological researcher and may not be appropriate to sociolgy or other disciplines. My impression is that sociologists have not struggled as much with the laboratory-field issue, although the newer breed of sociologist interested in crowding is quite concerned with social processes, is well tuned into potentially confounding variables, and has a sophisticated battery of analysis techniques that permits unraveling complex correlational relationships.

by Sundstrom (1975a), who examined the impact of spatial density, personal space intrusion, and goal blocking on self-disclosure and subjective feelings of stress (see cell 1, Fig. 1). Consider also Marshall and Heslin (1975), who experimentally examined the joint impact of spatial and social density and the sex composition of groups on feelings of attraction and other psychological states; Rohe and Patterson (1974), who studied the effect of density and availability of resources on childrens' aggressive behavior; Aiello, Epstein, and Karlin (1975), who investigated physiological arousal in groups in large or small rooms; Epstein and Karlin (1975), who examined the social behavior and task performance of crowded and uncrowded groups. Many similar studies are currently in the literature, so that the laboratory tradition continues in good health, as it should.

Perhaps more dramatic is the growing number of naturalistic and field studies of crowding. Here, researchers have gone into the everyday life settings of people, not merely for the sake of ecological validity and realism but because they recognize that crowding effects are probably not always easy to create in short-term laboratory settings. Several studies illustrate field analyses of crowding (see cell 2, Fig. 1). For example, Stokols, Smith, and Prostor (1975) varied architectural features of a waiting line at a motor vehicle bureau through the use of partitions or rope separator arrangements. Mackintosh, West, and Saegert (1975) worked in the shoe section of a department store and in Grand Central Railway Station in New York. In the first study, people were administered various recall cognitive tasks during high or low density crowding conditions. In the second study, people were exposed to high and low densities in Grand Central Station, and some were also taken on a familiarization tour of the station. They were then asked to perform certain tasks appropriate to being in the railroad station, such as finding seating areas, locating the ticket counter, and so on, as well as working on traditional cognitive tasks. In another field study in a prison, Paulus, Cox, McCain, and Chandler (1975) compared the behavior on a figure placement

Response Formats
(Dependent Variables)

		Researcher Structured Responses	*Naturally occurring Responses*
Situational conditions (Independent Variables)	Experimentally created conditions	Laboratory experiment I	Field experiment II
	Naturally occurring variations	Field experiment III	Observational studies IV

FIG. 1   Methodological strategies used in crowding research.

task with feelings of crowding of inmates who lived in single occupant cells versus dormitory arrangements and of inmates with short-term versus long-term stays in prison.

These examples of field research are interesting in several respects. In the Stokols et al. (1975) study, the researchers experimentally created different conditions in the environment and measured ongoing naturalistic behaviors that were not "imposed" on the subjects (see cell 2, Fig. 1). In the Mackintosh et al. (1975) and Paulus et al. (1975) studies, the researchers took advantage of naturally occurring variations in the environment (varying population concentration) but structured the behaviors performed by people (see cell 3, Fig. 1).

In still another strategy (cell 4, Fig. 1), Munroe and Munroe (1971, 1972, 1973) worked in a cross-cultural setting. Three African tribal groups who lived under different conditions of population density were compared in terms of infant care practices, content of folk tales, affiliation customs, and the like. In this strategy, the researchers worked with naturally occurring variations in crowding and examined naturally occurring responses. This approach is analogous to traditional sociological analyses, which examined variations in population concentration as related to social pathology. Other studies adopting this strategy include D'Atri (1975), who investigated the relationship between living arrangements in prisons and blood pressure; Dean, Pugh, and Gundersen (1975), who examined the relationship between population density on U.S. Navy ships and accident rates, illness, and so on; and by Wolfe (1975), who studied the relationship between room and group size and the behavior of children in a psychiatric hospital.

Thus, we begin to see a mix of strategies, even in field situations, with elements from traditional laboratory settings and from naturalistic observations pieced together in various combinations. One type of study worked with naturally occurring variations in crowding. Within each type of independent variable strategy we also see two possible dependent variable strategies: (1) use of naturally occurring responses appropriate to the situation and (2) use of restructured and improved responses such as questionnaires, simulation tasks, and cognitive and performance tasks.

Two programmatic efforts illustrate well the theme that present-day researchers on crowding are eclectic and willing to use a variety of methodological strategies. In one program, Valins and Baum (1973), Baum and Valins (1973), and Baum, Harpin, and Valins (1975) used a mixed strategy of field and laboratory methods. They compared residents of a traditional college dormitory with those who lived in uncrowded four-to-six-person suites. Questionnaire data indicated that corridor residents felt equally crowded and perceived themselves as having too much undesired contact with others. And crowded students placed fewer stick figures in a model of a room, suggesting less tolerance for too many people. When asked to work on problem-solving tasks, corridor residents performed best under a competitive versus cooperative set and in the presence of others. Still other data indicated that suite residents worked in a more cooperative fashion with their roomates on a group problem-solving task. These data reflect different aspects of the relationship between naturalistic variations in density and structured responses. Valins and Baum also worked with naturalistic, freely occurring responses. For example, unobtrusive observation in a waiting room indicated that corridor residents chose seats more distant from a confederate, looked less often at him, and interacted less frequently with the confederate, suggesting avoidance of interactions.

A similar approach is now underway by Epstein, Aiello, and their associates (see Chapter 5, and Aiello et al., 1975). Because of inadequate dormitory space, students sometimes lived in three-person groups in two-person rooms, or in two-person groups in two-person rooms. Epstein and Aiello mounted a longitudinal study in which a variety of data were collected, including questionnaires tapping feelings and interpersonal ratings, medical and health information, biochemical data, task performance, activity logs, and so on. As with the Valins and Baum program, they examined both naturalistic and structured responses and also undertook longitudinal analyses to track changes in response as experience in different living arrangements cumulated.

These examples of the methodological range of present-day research on crowding illustrate several points. There is a breadth of methodological perspective that permeates the field. Laboratory and field strategies, and combinations of both, are clearly evident, and there is general acceptance of the value of such eclecticism. Researchers also are willing to use elements from several different strategies, Valins and Baum and Epstein and Aiello being notable examples. Underlying these features is a sense of pragmatism and willingness to reach out to new methods as the situation warrants. Instead of using a single strategy, researchers on crowding now seem willing to let the problem guide their methodological choices, rather than working only on problems for which methods seem appropriate. Sometimes, as I think about traditional social psychological research, I have the feeling that many researchers previously were "method bound"—specialists in one type of procedure, task, and setting who researched only those problems their favorite   method could handle. This does not appear to be the case in present-day research on crowding where we see problems defined first and researchers using any and all methods they can muster. Thus, the same researcher may use laboratory simulations alongside naturalistic observations, and self-reports coupled with biochemical analyses. I consider this to be a healthy trend and a dramatic turning of the corner with regard to methodology. I believe that major advance in knowledge of crowding may now be possible by breaking a "method bound" set. If this analysis is correct, then we will have taken a first step toward a change of scientific paradigm (Kuhn, 1970), with problems now studied according to an expanded methodological perspective.

Multilevel Analysis of Behavior

Another methodological aspect of present-day crowding research is what I have termed elsewhere a "multilevel analysis" of dependent variables (Altman, 1973; Altman, 1975; Altman, 1976, 1977). Simply put, such a strategy involves the measurement of multiple dependent variables, with an important consideration being that they come from several behavioral domains, for example verbal behavior, feeling states, nonverbal bodily mechanisms, and environmentally related behavior such as territory and personal space. In addition, this approach calls for identification of patterns of behavior in which verbal and nonverbal behavior, for example, may complement, substitute, or compensate for one another. One end product of such a strategy is a better understanding of how behaviors link together in relation to such issues as crowding. Another result is a better understanding of intact "social units"—people, groups, families, and so on. By piecing together behaviors from different domains one eventually can learn more about holistic social systems. Thus the focus of analysis can include an understanding of behaviors taken one at a time, a better appreciation of how behaviors fit into patterns, and an understanding of how different people and groups use various mixes of behaviors (see Altman, 1976, 1977 for an extended discussion of this issue).

Aspects of this strategy appear in studies and in programs of research on crowding. For example, using an anthropological perspective, Munroe and Munroe (1971, 1972, 1973; Munroe, Munroe, Nerlove, & Daniels, 1969) examined the relationship between population density in three East African tribal groups and various aspects of cultural norms, behavior, and literature. They worked with the Logoli, who have a population density of 1,440 people per square mile, the Gussi with 692 people per square mile, and the Kipsigis with 253 people per square mile. Based on content analyses of folk tales, behavioral observation of child rearing, questionnaire and psychological test responses about customs, they came up with a profile that distinguished highly crowded and uncrowded groups. Among the crowded Logoli there is a general pattern of avoidance of contact with others. For example, the Logoli had norms against holding hands with friends, had the worst recall for interpersonal affiliation words, and also evaluated other family members less favorably than did the less crowded groups. In addition, analyses of folk tales indicated more symbolic attempts to leave interpersonal situations among the most crowded group, as reflected in physical movements of the body through space. Finally, among the Logoli, the more densely populated the home, the more rapid the response to young children's crying (not always by the mother), and, in general, the crowded Logoli devoted less and less time to children as they grew older so that by the age of three the child was more or less on its own during most of the day. Thus, by tapping into several levels of behavior from different facets of a group's life, one begins to discern a pattern of functioning that is far more revealing than the study of a single behavior.

Another example involves work by Booth (1976), conducted within a sociological framework. Several hundred families in Toronto, Canada, were studied in terms of actual household and neighborhood crowding. Data were collected on aggression (arguments within and outside families, physical violence), health and disease (psychiatric and physical illness, weight, height, urine analyses), school performance stress responses, feelings about marital relationships and parent-child relationships, social participation and withdrawal (group membership, attendance at religious services, TV watching, etc.), activity analyses, and the like. In general, household and/or neighborhood crowding was associated with aggression, some forms of withdrawal from social contact, feelings of deterioration of the marital relationship, problems with children, some stress reactions, some deterioration in school performance, and so on. Thus Booth tapped into many facets of people's lives, with the goal of identifying patterns of behavior that related to various types of crowding.

Another example of a multilevel approach is the dormitory studies of Valins and Baum, partially described earlier. They examined many facets of student behavior such as perceptions and feelings of satisfaction, responses in waiting room situations, verbal and nonverbal behavior, performance on simulated personal space tasks, group problem solving, group cohesion, and group formation. From this variety of measures a pattern of behavior of crowded and uncrowded students emerged that included withdrawal from social interaction and individualized functioning by crowded students, feelings of stress and dissatisfaction, and more attempts to develop formal groups. Withdrawal was evident in several respects: Crowded students avoided eye contact and were less socially interactive, they placed fewer stick figures in a simulated room setting, they felt more crowded, performed better under competitive versus cooperative arrangements, adopted more individualistic strategies of problem solving, knew less about their neighbors and shared less information about themselves, often did not achieve group consensus in problem solving, and so on.

In summary, recent research on crowding has adopted the methodological strategy of multiple dependent measures, tapping several levels of behavior, which can be examined in terms of patterns or profiles. In my opinion this is an important advance over traditional dependent variables. I predict that one result of this strategy will be a better understanding of crowding, as well as a more holistic understanding of the impact of crowding on intact individuals and social groups.

Social Process Orientation

Several writers have proposed a sequential model of crowding (Altman, 1975; Sundstrom, 1975b; Stokols, 1972b) in which distinctions are made between *psychological states* such as stress, anxiety, feelings of overcrowding; *interpersonal states* such as feelings of attraction or hostility toward others; *social processes* or ongoing behaviors such as nonverbal responses of gaze aversion or eye contact, changes in posture, or verbal responses such as content and form of interaction, problem solving processes. Finally, these models also address issues of short- and long-term *outcomes,* including accuracy of performance on tasks, indicators of health, crime, and so on.

Traditional sociological research on crowding was directed toward under- standing relatively large gaps in the preceding sequential chain, with such questions posed as "What is the relationship between population concentration and long- term outcomes of crime, mental and physical health, and so on?" These studies did not examine intervening psychological states and the social processes by which people reacted to population density. So it was with the early psychologi- cally oriented studies of crowding, where emphasis was placed on the impact of density on outcomes such as performance effectiveness and feeling states with relatively little attention given to problem-solving processes or other intervening events. Such intervening processes are critical, for they provide information about how people cope with crowding, their preventive and reactive responses, and the ways in which they regulate their interaction with one another.

Recent work in the sociological and psychological traditions suggests that another methodological corner has been turned, with efforts now being directed toward understanding social processes. For example, Mitchell (1971) examined crowding in Hong Kong and collected data on marital interaction, contacts with neighbors, and the like along with traditional long-term measures of social pathology. Booth and his associates, cited earlier, not only examined long-term effects of population concentration but also studied marital and family interac- tion, child-rearing processes, neighborhood interactions, and so on. Similarly, the anthropological analyses by Munroe and Munroe, also cited earlier, examined cultural styles of social interaction that accompanied different degrees of popula- tion density. A similar strategy has evolved in psychological research. For example, Ittelson, Proshansky, and Rivlin (1970) and Wolfe (1975) examined social and individual behavior in hospital situations as a function of number of room occu- pants, that is, active versus passive and individual versus social behaviors. The work cited earlier by Valins and Baum and by Epstein and Aiello places heavy emphasis on processes that mediate between population density and longer term outcomes. Other examples include studies of physiological arousal (Aiello et al., 1975) and analyses of nonverbal responses such as self-manipulation, leaning and turning away from others, and willingness to disclose to others (Sundstrom, 1975a).

This emerging focus on social processes sets the stage for theoretical analyses that deal with the mediating links between density or crowding and ultimate outcomes. Many things intervene between antecedent and consequent outcomes, and unless research pursues such mediating processes, little detailed understand- ing of crowding will occur. It now appears that crowding researchers have made a commitment to penetrate these social processes, which complements the other methodological principles of eclecticism and multilevel analysis.

Time-Linked Methodological Strategies

Underlying the matter of social processes is another philosophical and methodological issue—the temporal aspects of crowding. Early sociological research seemed to assume that crowding would have a cumulative long-term impact on outcomes such as disease and crime. Research in this tradition therefore looked at *long-term effects*. Early research in the psychological tradition, however, seemed to assume that there were also *short-term* effects of crowding, which would appear quite rapidly. Thus, studies were conducted on the effect of brief periods of crowding on psychological states and on performance effectiveness. As we have previously stated, early studies in both traditions typically yielded ambiguous, weak, or enticing results. One contributor to unclear results was perhaps too little emphasis on crowding and its outcomes as a *time-linked* process in which events unfolded in a sequential, time-bound fashion, so that time-dependent processes may need to be studied along with short- and long-term consequences.

I believe that this attitude has now permeated newly emerging research. For example, Sherrod (1974) examined both immediate and delayed effects of crowding on performance and demonstrated that subjects showed no performance decrement when tested immediately after crowding but did deteriorate on tasks performed at a later time. This suggests a short-term adaptive process and a possible accumulation of effects over the longer run, similar to research by Glass and Singer (1972) on noise. Thus to look only at either short- or long-term effects alone may obscure the time-linked aspects of crowding. A recent study by Sundstrom (1975a) illustrated the same point in a different context. Subjects who were intruded upon showed early stress reactions and a variety of nonverbal and verbal withdrawal behavior—a kind of adaptive coping to the stresses of crowding. By the end of a one-hour experiment, however, they exhibited much lower stress and reactive behaviors, suggesting successful coping with the situation. If one had looked only at the early or at the later reactions, an incomplete picture would have emerged, suggesting again the importance of considering crowding as a time-linked process. By adopting such a methodological strategy we stand to learn about crowding as a sequential and dynamic process, and we will avoid the conceptual error of viewing it solely as either a short- or long-term process.

Summary

This section examined the current methodological status of research on crowding. I concluded that significant advances have been made in the last few years in regard to (1) increased breadth of methodological perspective—a kind of eclecticism that now seems to pervade crowding research, (2) a multilevel analysis strategy in which behaviors from different levels of functioning are examined in terms of patterns and profiles, (3) a greater emphasis on analysis of intervening social processes, along with psychological and interpersonal feeling states and long-term outcomes, and (4) methodological strategies that recognize the time-linked qualities of crowding, with an examination of short- and long-term effects and direct and indirect outcomes. I am encouraged by these methodological directions, for they can have an important role in theoretical analyses of crowding, to which I turn next.

THEORETICAL DEVELOPMENTS

My view is that theoretical progress in crowding research has been less substantial than methodological developments, but I do believe that some important theoretical groundwork has been laid for the future, especially in regard to definitional issues.

Theoretical advances can occur in several ways. The most basic level is definitional and taxonomic, where one identifies basic concepts, defines and differentiates among them, identifies dimensions, and establishes standard and consensual meanings. In the case of crowding, this level of theorizing has centered around the meaning of the terms "crowding" and "density." A second level of theorizing involves specification of relevant variables, sometimes in the form of a listing and sometimes in terms of directional links between variables. My view is that theoretical efforts have largely centered around definitional issues and preliminary statements of variables relevant to crowding. A third level of theorizing involves fuller theoretical statements, including assumptions, explicit hypotheses and derivations, and directions and chains of relationships among key variables. I do not believe that theorizing about crowding has progressed very far at this third level.

Definitional Issues: Density and Crowding

Until just a few years ago the terms *density* and *crowding* were not clearly defined nor were they well differentiated from each other. Stokols (1972a) provided an articulate analysis that cut through part of the confusion by sharply distinguishing between density and crowding in terms of a physicalistic-psychological distinction. Density (or population concentration) was, according to Stokols, best conceived of as a physical concept devoid of direct psychological meaning and reflecting number of people per unit of space. Crowding, according to Stokols, was a psychological state, a subjective and experiential process. Although density could produce feelings of crowding, it was in no way *equal* to crowding and was merely one of several antecedent conditions that could precipitate feelings of crowding. This distinction broke a log jam in our thinking about crowding and set the stage for the next level of theorizing—taxonomic analyses of the concepts of crowding and density.

The concept of density.   Until recently density was treated in a relatively undifferentiated way. Early sociological analyses used a variety of density indicators such as number of people per city, per census tract, per neighborhood, and so on without giving systematic attention to differences among indicators. However, effort has recently been devoted to distinguishing between varieties of density and to their relationship with crowding outcomes.

One general approach was offered by Zlutnick and Altman (1972), who distinguished between "inside" dwelling unit density and "outside" dwelling unit density, which generates four situations:

1. High inside and high outside density, (e.g., many people living in a dwelling that is in a highly populated neighborhood such as an urban ghetto)

2. Low inside and high outside density (e.g., a luxury apartment in an urban setting)

3. High inside and low outside density (e.g., a rural situation with many people living in a dwelling)

4. Low inside and low outside density (e.g., a suburban setting)

This type of analysis implies the importance of day-to-day interpersonal contacts within dwelling units and of general stimulation in the environment.

Recent sociological analyses have also dealt with different types of density. For example, Galle, Gove, and McPherson (1972) examined different levels of density—people per room, rooms per apartment, apartments per building, and so on, and found the strongest relationships between people-per-room measures of density and indicators of social pathology, which emphasizes the importance of interpersonal levels of population concentration. Similar approaches have been taken by Booth (1976), Marsella, Escudero, and Gordon (1970), and others. Also, Day and Day (1973) called for greater attention to geographic factors in defining types of density. For example, coastal versus strip versus dispersed concentrations of people may make for quite different situations even though the overall density per area is equivalent. Thus there is increasing awareness that all densities are not equal and that different distributions and patterns of population concentration may have strikingly different effects.

A similar view has evolved in psychologically oriented research. Several writers quickly came to the realization that a distinction was possible between *social density* and *spatial density* (Hutt & McGrew, 1967; Hutt & Vaizey, 1966; Loo, 1973a, 1973b). Spatial density refers to comparisons of same sized groups in different sized spaces, and social density involves different sized groups in the same space. Most researchers appreciate this distinction and specify which type of density variation is emphasized in their research. However, information about the impact of such differences is cumulating only sporadically.

A perceptual element recently has been added to theorizing about the nature of density. Rapoport (1975) reasoned that we must include perceptual components in our analyses of density because perception is an intervening link between physicalistic features of density and psychologically negative states of crowding. He calls for an analysis of how people perceive physical densities and for a better understanding of how spatial layout, organizational, associational, and symbolic meanings, and temporal features of physical density mediate perceptual reactions. Rapoport has set the stage for a discussion of how density bridges to crowding, and he has also opened up a link between the topic of crowding and research on environmental cognition and perception (Downs & Stea, 1973). It remains to be seen how this line of thinking will be pursued.

In summary, not only has present-day research on crowding distinguished between the central concepts of "density" and "crowding," but there has begun to be more systematic definitional and taxonomic analyses of the concept of density itself. Most important, there is now consensus on some general distinctions between density and crowding, and research can now proceed within a generally agreed-upon definitional framework.

The concept of crowding.   Researchers have begun to deal with crowding as other than a simplistic, unitary concept. Most of them agree that crowding deals with psychological, subjective states that typically have a stress component. Some researchers reason that such feelings are associated with perceptions of too little physical or psychological space (Stokols, 1976): others emphasize feelings of loss of control over interaction and undesirable or excess contact with others (Altman, 1975; Desor, 1972; Rapoport, 1972); others discuss disharmonious psychological and biological processes (Esser, 1972).

Distinctions about crowding sometimes relate to variations in density. For example, Stokols (1972a) distinguished between social crowding (feelings of crowding deriving from the presence of others) versus nonsocial crowding (feelings stemming from physical factors alone) and between molecular versus molar crowding (feelings derived from interpersonal versus mass population factors). These distinctions illustrate that one could potentially map between varieties of feelings of crowding and could examine the nature, similarities, and differences among such linkages. This has not yet been done in a systematic fashion.

In viewing the taxonomic/definitional state of affairs regarding crowding, I believe that there is basic consensus about density and crowding. We are now at a stage where finer distinctions can be made, and as this happens there will be better integrations of definitional and theoretical statements. Definition and taxonomy are important first steps in the development of general theory (Proshansky, 1973), and I believe that we have generally succeeded in this task, although finer distinctions are still necessary.

CONCEPTUAL FRAMEWORKS AND THEORIES

The level of sophistication of formal theories of crowding is not very high. Historically, researchers have devoted most of their energies to the generation of basic facts about crowding, to the development of research methods, and to definitional issues. But with methodological and definitional questions partly resolved, the time now seems appropriate to develop theoretical constructs to integrate existing knowledge and to guide future research.

To say that there has been no conceptual work is, of course, an overstatement, for theoretical notions about crowding are implicit in much present-day work. For example, several writers offered *stimulus overload* explanations of crowding, beginning with the early sociological observations of Wirth (1938) and Simmel (1950), who noted that city life typically involves a high level of physical and social stimulation, which has both positive and negative features. On the one hand, city life provides excitement, availability of resources, and access to cultural opportunities. However, there is also intrusion, stress, lack of privacy, and stimulus overload in urban living. More recent versions of the overload approach appear in Milgram (1970), who described a series of coping mechanisms used by city dwellers to deal with overstimulation. Others have adopted variants of this overload model, For example, Altman (1975), Desor (1972), Booth (1976), and others speak of unwanted stimulation, overstimulation, and so on. These overload approaches to crowding all presume a homeostatic, equilibrium underpinning to human functioning, in which deviations from some optimal level of stimulation are undesirable. Thus overstimulation presumes a deviation in a particular direction—more stimulation than desired—and often results in coping processes designed to reestablish an optimal level of functioning (see Wohlwill, 1974 for a review of this type of model).

I think it is accurate to state that the overload and homeostatic/equilibrium style of theorizing dominates present conceptualizations about crowding. There are variants to this approach, but they are simply variations and not "new" or alternative conceptual models. For example, Stokols (1976) refers to ecological and confinement modes of theorizing about crowding. The latter is represented by Proshansky, Ittelson, and Rivlin (1970), who described crowding as involving a loss of behavioral options. Although this way of thinking emphasizes freedom of choice, it also presumes some optimal level of functioning that has been temporarily interfered with, resulting in a state of disequilibrium. Similarly, the ecological orientation of Barker (1968) and his associates (see especially Wicker, McGrath, & Armstrong, 1972) considers crowding to be a problem of "overmanning" of a behavior setting, in which the capacity of a setting is exceeded by the number of people available to perform. Again, the notion of an ideal match of capacity and participants assumes a homeostatic/equilibrium process.

Another feature of contemporary theorizing about crowding, which is also a derivation from an equilibrium/homeostasis model, is the emphasis on "stress" (physiological and/or psychological) as an accompaniment of disequilibrium. From earliest thinking to the present, practically every conceptualization assumes some sort of stress, anxiety, tension, or discomfort as a correlate or result of overload, confinement, and loss of freedom. The stress concept is pervasive throughout psychology and biology, whether it involves cognitive dissonance or cognitive inconsistency, overload of biological systems, or whatever. Furthermore, stress is presumed to act as a motivating force that results in adaptive coping reactions.

Perhaps raising this issue seems elementary, but it is interesting to see how a homeostasis/equilibrium and stress-coping model is central to many areas in the social and behavioral sciences. It also highlights the fact that, although many researchers in the environment and behavior field feel that they are treading new ground, their basic theoretical constructs are permeated by traditional thinking in their parent and related diciplines.

Although most researchers presume a homeostatic process, some theoretical analyses also include notions of sequence and time, interpersonal and situational control, and cognitive/emotional assessments. Altman (1975), Sundstrom (1975b), and Stokols (1972b) emphasize sequential and time-linked aspects of crowding. In response to density and its concomitants (e.g., social interference, intrusion, and blocking access to desired resources), these models hypothesize a time-linked sequence of events involving stress, coping responses designed to alleviate the undesired state of affairs, assessment of outcomes, and readjustments in the form of feedback loops. Although these approaches contain the stress/ equilibrium concept, they attempt to lay out a sequence of events and place the phenomenon of crowding in a temporal perspective.

Another direction of thinking, still within a homeostatic framework, was offered by Altman (1975) and Proshansky et al. (1970). It emphasizes "control" in relationship to social and physical enviornment. Altman (1975) developed a theoretical framework to integrate the concepts of crowding with privacy, personal space, and territory. Privacy was the central construct, and it was related to the regulation of interpersonal interaction through a boundary control process. The regulation of contact with the external environment was hypothesized to involve the use of personal space and territory, along with verbal and nonverbal control mechanisms. Breakdowns in the system occurred when boundary regulation mechanisms did not function well. One type of breakdown, "crowding," occurred when there was more interaction than desired. Thus, for Altman (1975) the stress/equilibrium concepts are overlaid with the notion of loss of control or failure of boundary regulation mechanisms. So it is with Proshansky et al. (1970), who see crowding as a loss of behavioral options, choice, or control.

Another direction of current theorizing, still cast within a homeostatic model, emphasizes subjective and cognitive processes in relationship to control of the environment (Stokols, 1976). In this approach, crowding involves a perception of insufficient control over events and subjective assessments of the direction and intentionality of thwarting. Sources of thwarting involve people or the environment, and they vary in motivational intent. For example, neutral thwartings are not specifically directed at a person, do not necessarily derive from a specific other, and are not perceived as being intentional. Personal thwartings have the opposite quality. This approach is important because it highlights the role of cognitive, information processing and expectancy processes in crowding phenomena, a direction of thinking that is beginning to assume prominence in other fields.

In summary, the present state of theorizing about crowding has the following features: (1) traditional homeostatic/equilibrium model; (2) stress as a correlate or resultant and a motivating force that arises from disequilibrium; and (3) goal-directed behaviors designed to restore equilibrium. Newer directions of thinking include notions of control expectation, and other cognitive concepts. Although many write about developing new concepts, the current directions of theorizing about crowding seem to involve direct application and translation of older notions. To use the metaphor of an earlier section, unlike methodology and definitional work, we have not yet "turned the corner" in regard to theory development but have merely "peeked" around that corner, tentatively and with caution.

THE SUBJECT MATTER OF RESEARCH ON CROWDING

Although the volume of crowding research has increased in the last few years, my opinion is that we have not yet decided on the central content areas to be explored. Specific variables and topics are only gradually emerging, with research being done in a variety of topics. There is consensus on definitional issues regarding crowding and density and some general, if only implicit, consensus on homeostasis/equilibrium theoretical models. However, there is little agreement in regard to specific content areas of research. This is not to say that there is strong disagreement; rather, the tone is one of uncertainty or of waiting for a compelling direction to emerge.

Early research in the sociological tradition was based on the view that crowding resulted in harm in the form of physical and mental disease, crime, and deterioration in human functioning. Perhaps driven by this line of reasoning, content variables emphasized indicators of such pathology. With the emergence of the psychological tradition, the same line of thinking was pursued, with analyses of task performance, subjective stress, aggression, and withdrawal, on the assumption that these would reflect deterioration in functioning under conditions of crowding. With the advent of new methodologies and the clarification of the concepts of crowding and density, there has been an expansion of content areas. One facet of newer research is an emphasis on social events—what goes on among people in crowded settings. There seems to be recognition that crowding

is a social and interpersonal phenomenon and that the effects of population concentration may be ameliorated or exacerbated by social interaction. For example,
in recent work by Galle et al. (1972) and others in the sociological tradition,
there is an attempt to understand interpersonal events in families living in crowded conditions, including husband and wife, parent and child, and between neighbors. Thus research has moved toward understanding social interaction as a
likely mediator between population concentration and various outcomes.

Recent psychologically oriented research has followed a similar path, and
even more directly. For example, Sundstrom (1975a), Aiello and Epstein (Chapter 5), and others measured willingness to disclose about the self under conditions
of crowding; Stokols, Rall, Pinner, and Schopler (1973) examined social behaviors of laughing, nonverbal movements, and so on; Baum (1975) studied feelings
of group cohesion, as did Griffit and Veitch (1971) and others.

In addition, recent research has begun to analyze physiological reactions to
crowding. For example, Aiello et al. (1975), D'Atri (1975), and Paulus et al.
(1975) measured autonomic arousal, including blood pressure and skin conductance. Such work is motivated by homeostatic concepts, which assume adjustment processes in psychological and physiological levels.

There is little more that can be said about general content areas of research
on crowding, which may reflect the fact that there is, as yet, incomplete consensus on the most fruitful lines of research. This is a period of groping, whereas in
regard to methodology and certain aspects of theory, there is consensus about
how to proceed. Put in another way, the early years of research on crowding
involved development of tools and terms, with content and theory being secondary in importance. With methodological and definitional foundations now reasonably well established, the time is ripe to begin exploring alternative theoretical
models and associated content areas of study. I predict that the coming decade
will yield important theoretical and substantive advances. Whether the homeo-
stasis/equilibrium model and its associated dynamics of stress and coping will
continue to hold sway is a question for the future.

SOME FURTHER QUESTIONS

I have discussed the current status of research on crowding in terms of methodological, theoretical, and substantive issues. I view the future with optimism and
predict that major steps in research on crowding will occur in the next decade.
As indicated earlier, we have witnessed a "quantum" change in approaches to
research methodology, which is the necessary backdrop for theoretical and substantive advances. In the area of theory development I also believe that we have
surmounted issues of taxonomy and definition and have begun further to dimen-
sionalize key terms. Although further theoretical and substantive advances have
not been dramatic as of this writing, the seeds are sown and the next few years

should show important advances. However, there are still several important issues that need to be addressed which, although philosophical, bear closely on methodological and theoretical issues.

A Systems Orientation to Crowding

A "systems" orientation is a popular idea about which everyone nods positively but often without mutual sharing of meaning. Most people will agree that a systems approach involves multivariate analysis of a phenomenon and treatment of variables as part of an interrelated conceptual framework. For our purposes, several other features of a systems orientation are important. First, this perspective implies that the traditional notions of "linear causation" may be overly constricting. That is, many have come to think of science as involving the statement of linear, one-way sequential chains of causation among variables (e.g., antecedent or independent variables). A systems view raises questions about the limited perspective of such reasoning (Altman, 1976, 1977) and argues that, in a broader sense, *all* variables may at one time or another serve as causal agents of other variables. Thus, environmental variations affect behavior, but so does the reverse occur; stress may result from population density, but so do changes in population density derive from stress, however indirectly. Perhaps models of crowding should be presented as circular rather than chainlike (see Altman and Chemers, in press, for an analysis of this issue in relation to culture and the environment), with directions of causation proceeding in all directions. This does not mean that one cannot study specific cause-effect links, only that one should not become seduced into thinking that the demonstration of a particular directional bond is, in fact, the only direction of causation. This way of thinking is not new; rather, it has become more and more salient, I believe, because we have begun to break out of a monolithic laboratory orientation in social psychology. The laboratory, with all its strengths, has also fostered a strictly linear perspective because of its features of control and manipulation. A nonlinear approach to crowding will permit us to examine a greater spectrum of variables in relationship to one another, thereby paving the way for more comprehensive theory.

As a derivative of the nonlinear perspective, a systems orientation permits a more *descriptive* approach to a phenomenon. That is, if the analysis of multiple directions of association is a legitimate goal, then one is gradually led to a tolerance of description as an appropriate research enterprise, without the necessity always to specify which variable "causes" changes in other variables. Furthermore, if one adopts a multiple level, social process orientation, as described earlier, then the establishment of causal links among variables becomes an overwhelming task that is perhaps not even especially fruitful as the sole goal of research. Detailed descriptions of associations among variables, statements of covariation, and identification of patterns of relationships eventually can yield understanding of a descriptive type. Obviously, this is an old philosophical issue, and we have opted in the past few decades for a nondescriptive, cause-effect route to understanding (there are exceptions to this, especially in the work of Barker, 1968, and his associates). Frankly, I question the appropriateness of using any singular strategy alone to understand a phenomenon such as crowding, and I hope that the methodological directions unfolding in the field will stimulate us to work with both descriptive and cause-effect orientations. Thus, I welcome this revival of descriptive analysis as a legitimate research enterprise, not as a substitute but as a philosophical complement to present approaches.

There is another derivative of a social systems orientation, which I have termed elsewhere a *social unit* orientation (Altman, 1976, 1977). Emphasis in the social and behavioral sciences has traditionally been on behaviors such as stress, performance, and social interaction, usually taken one at a time. If the newer directions of research strategy implied in this paper are carried through, then I predict that our emphasis will be expanded to include both the study of "behavior" and of intact "social units" such as teams, families, couples. That is, our conclusions will not only deal with, for example, "stress reactions to crowding," but will begin to deal with "family" reactions to crowding, poor and rich people's handling of density, and so on. Thus complex measurement techniques, the search for patterns of behavior, and the like will lead to better understanding of whole organisms—people and groups—not just segmented behaviors exhibited by "subjects." With an expanded perspective I predict a shift toward more holistic organismic analyses. For example, the work by Valins and Baum and by Aiello and Epstein on crowding in dormitories begins to describe "types of residents," not simply single behaviors. Such studies will eventually provide descriptions of how types of people cope with residential situations along with analyses of particular behavior. This social unit orientation can be considered in any piece of research and, as I have stated elsewhere (Altman, 1976, 1977), it is not an issue of laboratory versus field, basic versus applied research, or any of the other issues we commonly address. It is more a philosophical question that is independent of method, theory, or variable. I believe that our understanding of crowding can be considerably expanded by adopting such a complementary orientation.

The New and the Old: What is the Appropriate Balance?

In the earlier discussion I described a homeostatic/equilibrium philosophy and a stress/coping sequence as central to current theorizing about crowding. This philosophical model is a long-standing one in the social and biological sciences, and it assumed a powerful drive in people to establish order and balance. My question is (and I have no real answer at present) whether theory in regard to crowding should break away from this model and develop ideas unique to the phenomenon. Or, conversely, to what extent should there be integration of thinking about crowding with other, already well-established bodies of knowledge and theory? The latter is clearly happening in regard to crowding, as witnessed by studies of competition-cooperation, cognitive and information processing, arousal and physiological processes, self-disclosure and group processes, and the like. Although I do not have the answer, I believe that the question is quite important. There are obvious values to integration, including theoretical parsimony, breadth of understanding, unity of knowledge, guides for research, and so on. But there are also limitations, such as constriction of alternatives, possibly inappropriate levels of analysis, and elimination of alternative directions of analysis. Lewin (1964) helped social psychology out of a potential quagmire by calling for levels of analysis and for theoretical and empirical directions appropriate to the phenomena of the field. Where is the balance in the case of crowding?

Relationships to Other Environmental Concepts

The study of environment and behavior is, at present, somewhat fragmented. Many lacunae exist with only minimal interaction among them. Although there are innumerable interdisciplinary conferences, one wonders about the reality of communication among disciplines. The study of crowding is currently dominated by psychologists and sociologists, with only marginal involvement by anthropologists, geographers, economists, and others. Note, for example, that the contributers to this volume are primarily psychologists. If one did a tally of bibliographic citations, it would probably reflect an even greater degree of insularity. Although I do not necessarily call for interdisciplinary work of a team type, there is a need to view the problem of crowding from the perspective of several disciplines and to incorporate other viewpoints into our thinking. The environment and behavior field in general and a topic like crowding in particular are ripe for such a perspective.

A similar insularity needs to be dealt with at even more specific levels. For example, research knowledge is accumulating about environmental cognition and perception, personal space, privacy, and territory. Up until the present time we have acted as if these were unrelated areas, each to be pursued in its own light, with its own methods, theories, and content areas. With few exceptions, there has been little bridging among concepts. Researchers on environmental cognition and perception largely ignore and are ignored by the personal space, crowding, and territorial researchers (and the latter often ignore one another). The time has come in these and other areas to explore integration of knowledge and concepts. Although knowledge must be pursued in delimited areas, there must also simultaneously be a search for broader integrations.

To summarize this chapter, I see research on crowding as having made in the past few years important methodological advances that anchor around the following points: an expanded methodological capability and philosophical eclecticism, analysis of social processes in a time-linked fashion, in the context of multiple levels and patterns of behavior. In addition, some central definitional and taxonomic problems involving the distinction between density and crowding have been solved, although each concept needs further dimensional analysis.

By establishing such consensus at a general level, the stage is now set for systematic empirical work and for the development of theory. Theoretical work is just beginning, and a clear direction has not yet emerged although a homeostatic/ equilibrium model seems to underly present thinking. It is likely that theoretical and substantive advances will be made in the coming years, now that methodological and definitional issues are temporarily resolved.

Finally, I pointed to a number of issues that need to be addressed in the coming years. These issues include questions of nonlinear causation, social unit analysis, and other features implicit in a "systems" orientation. In addition, I raised the knotty questions of an appropriate balance between development of new lines of thinking about crowding versus integration with existing concepts, the need for an interdisciplinary perspective, and the desirability of lessening the insularity among several areas of research on environment and behavior. I conclude on a note of optimism, believing that we are well beyond the crude beginnings of past research and hopeful that the present freshness of attitude and approach will not too quickly become a new provincialism.

REFERENCES

Aiello, J. R., Epstein, Y. M., & Karlin, R. A. Effects of crowding on electrodermal activity. *Sociological Symposium,* 1975, *14,* 43-58.

Altman, I. Environmental psychology and social psychology. *Personality and Social Psychology Bulletin,* 1976, *2,* 96-113.

Altman, I. Research on environment and behavior: A personal statement of strategy. In D. Stokols (Ed.), *Psychological perspectives on environment & behavior: Conceptual and empirical trends.* New York: Plenum, 1977.

Altman, I. Some perspectives on the study of man-environment phenomena. *Representative Research in Social Psychology.* 1973, *4,* 109-126.

Altman, I. *The environment and social behavior: Privacy, personal space, territory and crowding.* Monterey, Calif.: Brooks/Cole, 1975.

Altman, I., & Chemers, M. M. Cultural aspects of environment-behavior relationships. In H. Triandis (Ed.), *Handbook of cross cultural psychology.* Boston: Allyn & Bacon, in press.

Barker, R. G. *Ecological psychology.* Stanford, Cal.: Stanford University Press, 1968.

Baum, A., & Valins, S. Residential environments, groups size and crowding. *Proceedings of the 81st Annual Convention of the American Psychological Association,* 1973, 211-212.

Baum, A., Harpin, R. E., & Valins, S. The role of group phenomena in the experience of crowding. *Environment and Behavior,* 1975, *7* (2), 185-199.

Booth, A. *Urban crowding and its consequences.* New York: Praeger, 1976.

Calhoun, J. B. A behavioral sink. In E. L. Bliss (Ed.), *Roots of behavior.* New York: Harper & Row, 1962. (a)

Calhoun, J. B. Population density and social pathology. *Scientific American,* 1962, *206,* 139-148. (b)

Calhoun, J. B. Space & the strategy of life. In A. H. Esser (Ed.), *Environment and behavior: The use of space by animals and men.* New York: Plenum, 1971.

Christian, J. J., Flyger, V., & Davis, D. E. Factors in the mass mortality of a herd of silka deer cervus nippon. *Chesapeake Science,* 1960, *1,* 79-95.

D'Atri, D. A. Psychophysiological responses to crowding. *Environment and Behavior,* 1975, *7* (2), 237-253.

Davis, D. E. Physiological effects of continued crowding. In A. H. Esser (Ed.), *Behavior and environment: The use of space by animals and men.* New York: Plenum, 1971.

Day, A. T., & Day, L. H. Cross-national comparison of population density. *Science,* 1973, *181,* 1016-1023.

Dean, L. M., Pugh, W. M., & Gunderson, E. K. E. Spatial and perceptual components of crowding: Effects on health and satisfaction. *Environment and Behavior,* 1975, *7* (2), 225-237.

Desor, J. A. Toward a psychological theory of crowding. *Journal of Personality and Social Psychology,* 1972, *21,* 79-83.

Downs, R. M., & Stea, D. *Image and environment: Cognitive mapping and spatial behavior.* Chicago: Aldine, 1973.

Dubos, R. *Man adapting.* New Haven, Conn.: Yale University Press, 1965.

Eibl-Eibesfeldt, I. *Ethology: The biology of behavior.* New York: Holt, Rinehart & Winston, 1970.

Epstein, Y. M., & Karlin, R. A. Effects of acute experimental crowding. *Journal of Applied Social Psychology,* 1975, *4* (1), 34-53.

Esser, A. H. A biosocial perspective on crowding. In J. F. Wohlwill & D. H. Carson (Eds.), *Environment and the social sciences: Perspectives and applications.* Washington, D. C.: American Psychological Association, 1972.

Freedman, J. L. The effects of population density on humans. In J. Fawcett (Ed.), *Psychological perspectives on population.* New York: Basic Books, 1972.

Galle, O. R., Gove, W. R., & McPherson, J. M. Population density and pathology: What are the relationships for man? *Science,* 1972, *176,* 23-30.

Glass, D. C., & Singer, J. E. *Urban stress.* New York: Academic Press, 1972.

Griffitt, W., & Veitch, R. Hot and crowded: Influence of population density and temperature on interpersonal affective behavior. *Journal of Personality and Social Psychology,* 1971, *17,* 92-98.

Hutt, C., & McGrew, W. C. *Effects of group density upon social behavior in humans.* Paper presented at the meeting of the Association for the Study of Aminal Behavior, *Symposium on Changes in Behavior with Population Density,* Oxford, England, July 1967.

Hutt, C., & Vaizey, M. J. Differential effects of group density on social behavior. *Nature,* 1966, *209,* 1371-1372.

Ittelson, W. H., Proshansky, H. M., & Rivlin, L. G. A study of bedroom use on two psychiatric wards. *Hospital and Community Psychiatry,* 1970, *21,* (6), 177-180.

Kuhn, T. S. *The structure of scientific revolutions* (2nd Ed.). Chicago, Ill.: University of Chicago Press, 1970.

Lawrence, J. E. Science and sentiment: Overview of research on crowding and human behavior. *Psychological Bulletin,* 1974, *81* (10), 712-721.

Lewin, V. *Field theory and social science.* New York: Harper & Row, 1964.

Loo, C. M. The effect of spatial density on the social behavior of children. *Journal of Applied Social Psychology,* 1973, *2* (4), 372-381. (a)

Loo, C. Important issues in researching the effects of crowding on humans. *Representative Research in Social Psychology,* 1973, *4* (1), 219-227. (b)

Mackintosh, E., West, W., & Saegert, S. Two studies of crowding in urban public spaces. *Environment Behavior,* 1975, *7* (2), 159-185.

Marsella, A. J., Escudero, M., & Gordon, P. The effects of dwelling density on mental disorders in Filipino men. *Journal of Health and Social Behavior,* 1970, *11* (4), 288-294.

Marshall, J E., & Heslin, R. Boys and girls together: Sexual composition and the effect of density and group size on cohesiveness. *Journal of Personality and Social Psychology,* 1975, *31* (5), 952-961.

Michelson, W. *Man and his urban environment: A sociological approach.* Reading, Mass.: Addison-Wesley, 1970.

Milgram, S. The experience of living in cities. *Science,* 1970, *167,* 1461-1468.

Mitchell, R. Some social implications of higher density housing. *American Sociological Review,* 1971, *36,* 18-29.

Munroe, R. H., & Munroe, R. L. Household density and infant care in an East African society. *Journal of Psychology,* 1971, *83,* 3-13.

Munroe, R. H., & Munroe, R. L. Population density and affective relationships in three East African societies. *Journal of Social Psychology,* 1972, *88,* 15-20.

Munroe, R. H., & Munroe, R. L. Population density and movement in folktales, *Journal of Social Psychology,* 1973, *91,* 339-340.

Munroe, R. H., Munroe, R. L., Nerlove, S. B., & Daniels, R. E. Effects of population density on food concern in three East African societies. *Journal of Health and Social Behavior,* 1969, *10,* 161-171.

Paulus, P., Cox, V., McCain, G. E., & Chandler, J. Some effects of crowding in a prison environment. *Journal of Applied Social Psychology,* 1975, *5,* 86-91.

Proshansky, H. M. Theoretical issues in environmental psychology. *Representative Research in Social Psychology,* 1973, *4* (1), 93-109.

Proshansky, H., Ittelson, W. H., & Rivlin, L. G. (Eds.), *Environmental psychology.* New York: Holt, Rinehart & Winston, 1970.

Rapoport, A. Toward a redefinition of density. *Environment and Behavior,* 1975, *7* (2), 133-159.

Rapoport, A. *Some perspectives on human use and organization of space.* Paper presented at the meeting of the Australian Association of Social Antropologitsts, Melbourne, Australia, May 1972.

Rohe, W., & Patterson, A. H. *The effects of varied levels of resources and density on behavior in a day care center.* Paper presented at the meeting of the Environmental Design Research Association, Milwaukee, Wisconsin, April 1974.

Sherrod, D. R. Crowding, perceived control, and behavioral aftereffects. *Journal of Applied Social Psychology,* 1974, *4* (2), 171-186.

Simmel, G. The metropolis and mental life. In K. W. Wolff (Ed.), *The sociology of George Simmel.* New York: Free Press, 1950.

Stokols, D. On the distinction between density and crowding: Some implications for future research. *Psychological Review,* 1972, *79* (3), 275-278. (a)

Stokols, D. A social psychological model of human crowding phenomena. *American Institute of Planners Journal,* 1972, *38,* 72-83. (b)

Stokols, D. The experience of crowding in primary and secondary environments. *Environment and Behavior,* 1976, *8,* 49-86.

Stokols, D., Smith, T. E., & Prostor, J. J. The perception of crowding as a function of architectural variations in a naturalistic setting. *American Behavioral Scientist,* 1975, *18,* 792-814.

Stokols, D., Rall, M., Pinner, B., & Schopler, J. Physical, social, and personal determinants of the perception of crowding. *Environment and Behavior,* 1973, *5* (1), 87-117.

Sundstrom, E. A study of crowding: Effects of intrusion, goal blocking and density on self-reported stress, self-disclosure and nonverbal behavior. *Journal of Personality & Social Psychology,* 1975, *32,* 645-654. (a)

Sundstrom, E. Toward an interpersonal model of crowding. *Sociological Symposium,* 1975, *14,* 129-144. (b)

Valins, S., & Baum, A. Residential group size, social interaction and crowding. *Environment and Behavior,* 1973, *5* (4), 421-440.

Wicker, A. W., McGrath, J. E., & Armstrong, G. E. Organization size and behavior setting capacity as determinants of member participation. *Behavioral Science,* 1972, *17,* 499-513.

Wirth, L. Urbanism as a way of life. *American Journal of Sociology,* 1938, *44,* 1-24.

Wohlwill, J. F. Human adaptation to levels of environmental stimulation. *Human Ecology,* 1974, *2* (2), 127-147.

Wolfe, M. Room size, group size, and density: Behavior patterns in a children's psychiatric facility. *Environment and Behavior,* 1975, *7* (2), 199-225.

Wynne-Edwards, V. C. *Animal dispersion in relation to social behavior.* New York: MacMillan (Hafner Press), 1972.

Zlutnick, S., & Altman, I. Crowding and human behavior. In J. F. Wohlwill & D. H. Carson (Eds.), *Environment and the social sciences: Perspectives and applications.* Washington, D. C.: American Psychological Association, 1972.

2

Crowding as a Sequential Process: Review of Research on the Effects of Population Density on Humans

Eric Sundstrom
University of Tennessee

This chapter presents a review of empirical findings on crowding among humans. Such an undertaking has become increasingly complex during the recent period of intensive research (Altman, 1975). In an attempt to provide broad coverage of current research findings, this review deals not only with published papers but with as many unpublished papers as could be obtained for primary reference (detailed abstracts were used in six cases). As an indication of the pace of research on crowding, a tally indicated that 16 of the 83 empirical papers cited in this review were published during 1975. Another 39 papers are unpublished as of this writing.[1] Assuming a publication lag of around 12 to 18 months, it is probably safe to say that over half of the empirical papers reviewed here were completed during the last two years.

The review is organized around a model of crowding as a *sequential process* that involves (1) high population density, (2) aversive events that may or may not accompany high density, (3) stress and other subjective responses, (4) immediate behavioral responses, and (5) aftereffects or cumulative effects (see Sundstrom, 1975a). The basis for the review is a series of tables, presented as an appendix, in which the findings of each study are summarized and separated to correspond with components of the hypothetical sequence. A section of the review describes findings related to each component of the sequence; each section

---

[1]This chapter was completed in February, 1976. It is certainly not exhaustive in coverage of unpublished research and may have missed published work. The tally included the studies abstracted in the appendices of Freedman's book (1975) as separate, unpublished studies unless they appeared elsewhere as journal articles. Dissertations and theses were treated as unpublished. Articles reporting several studies were counted only once.

31

ends with a table that summarizes the empirical support for the major hypotheses. The review of research findings begins after a brief discussion of the concept of crowding and an overview of current strategies of research.

THE CONCEPT OF CROWDING

For purposes of discussion, *crowding* may be defined as a state of psychological stress that *sometimes* accompanies high population density. *High density* refers to the concentration of a relatively large number of people into a single area, producing a shortage of space. The subjective experience of crowding is distinguished from the physical condition—high density (Stokols, 1972a, 1972b).[2] As detailed here, the bulk of empirical evidence indicates that crowding often does accompany conditions of high density. As a form of stress, crowding involves *subjective discomfort* and *physiological arousal* (Lazarus, 1966). However, the simple definition of crowding as a stress response to high density ignores the fact that *high density* refers to many different situations, each involving different conditions that could produce stress. Galle, Gove, and McPherson (1972) distinguished four independent components of *gross density,* or the number of persons per acre. These consisted of (1) the number of structures per acre, (2) the number of dwellings per structure, (3) the number of rooms per dwelling, and (4) the number of persons per room. The first two components, structures per acre and dwellings per structure, partly define *neighborhood density* by determining the number of residences in an area. The remaining components, rooms per dwelling and persons per room, define *household density* (or inside density). These types of density involve different experiences (Zlutnick & Altman, 1972). High density in neighborhoods can mean large numbers of people on sidewalks and streets, in parks, in shopping areas, in schools, and in other public or semipublic areas. In apartment buildings, outside density also refers to the number of dwellings within a structure and the consequent number of people a resident meets in the building containing his or her dwelling (see Bickman, Teger, Gabriele, McLaughlin, Berger, & Sunaday, 1973). High household density, on the other hand, means a large number of people within a single residence, where individuals may not have physical means of separating themselves. High density in a dwelling can even mean that several persons live in a single room.

The definition of crowding as a stress response to high density clearly needs to take account of the various *types* of high density. However, a second problem

---

[2]An alternative definition of crowding presents it as purely a physical condition, equivalent to high population density (e.g., Freedman, 1975). This conception is unsatisfactory for several reasons (see Stokols, 1976) but primarily because it ignores the variety and complexity of conditions that may be called "high density" (Rapoport, 1975).

in defining the concept of crowding stems from the fact that high density may not always produce stress (Altman, 1975; Freedman, 1975; Stokols, 1972b; Sundstrom, 1975b). Instead, interpersonal or physical conditions that *accompany* or *result from* high density may mediate crowding (see Rapoport, 1975; Stokols, 1972a). For example, stress in high density might stem from such aversive conditions as heat or noise, from *overload of social stimulation,* close interpersonal proximity or too many interaction partners (Milgram, 1970; Stokols, 1976). "Social interference," thwarting, or "behavioral constraint" in high density may also produce stress (Saegert, 1973; Stokols, 1972a, 1972b, 1976). The importance of aversive physical and social conditions for crowding is underlined by studies that found no signs of stress in response to high density (e.g., MacDonald & Oden, 1973). In brief, a central problem in the definition of crowding is the specification of conditions that lead to stress in high density.[3]

Consistent with the idea that stress does not always accompany high density, theorists have suggested modifying factors that could influence crowding. The main ones are as follows.

1. *Duration of exposure.* An individual may easily tolerate a brief exposure to conditions of high density such as a ride on a crowded elevator, but prolonged exposure may increase the likelihood of crowding.[4] Another important element of crowding may be an individual's advance knowledge of the duration of exposure. Even prolonged high density conditions can be tolerable if a person knows how long they will continue.

2. *Predictability.* Research on stress suggests that aversive conditions are more stressful when they are unpredictable (Averill, 1973).

3. *Current desire for social stimulation.* Altman (1975) theorizes that a person sometimes needs solitude and at other times desires intensive social interaction, depending on recent experience and personality characteristics that derive from past experience. A person who has recently been isolated may have a temporarily elevated threshold for crowding. Someone raised in a crowded household may establish a high *adaptation level* for social stimulation (Helson, 1964; Wohlwill, 1974) and may prefer relatively crowded quarters.

4. *Primary versus secondary environment.* Stokols (1976) distinguishes two types of environments: Primary environments are places where a person spends large amounts of time, relates to others on a personal basis, and performs personally important activities. Examples include homes, apartments, and places of

---

[3]If crowding is seen as a kind of stress linked to certain conditions that accompany high population density, the term *crowding* may be appropriately viewed as a label for an area of research on stress.

[4]The term *crowded* refers to physical conditions characterized by any type of high population density (see Stokols, 1976).

work. Stokols proposes that when overload or thwarting occurs in these settings, they pose a greater threat to "psychological security" than in other settings. Therefore, crowding in primary environments is expected to be more intense and difficult to resolve than in secondary environments where a person spends little time and relates to others on an impersonal basis. By this reasoning, crowding in dwellings is more difficult to resolve than crowding produced by high neighborhood density.

5. *Perceived origin of interpersonal events.* Stokols (1976) posits that if social interference or thwarting by other people is *personal* (emanating from a single person, deliberate, and personally directed), crowding is experienced as being more intense than in response to *neutral* thwarting. Similarly, a violation of norms of interpersonal distance may be more stressful if it appears intentional and not due to the physical constraints present in a situation (Sundstrom, 1975a).

In general, crowding refers to a form of stress that derives from several antecedents. When crowding occurs, it may motivate several types of behavior, including coping behaviors designed to reduce aversive conditions (cf. Altman, 1975; Stokols, 1976; Sundstrom, 1975b; Valins & Baum, 1973). For example, field experiments with children have shown that increased room density resulted in withdrawal from interaction (e.g., Hutt & Vaizey, 1966; Loo, 1972).

Crowding may also diminish over time because of *adaptation,* or a decrease in responsiveness to aversive conditions mediated by internal processes such as reappraisal of the conditions (Wohlwill, 1974). However even though an individual may neutralize aversive conditions through coping or adaptation, *aftereffects* or *cumulative effects* may follow. In a study modeled after research on the aftereffects of noise (Glass & Singer, 1972), Sherrod (1974) showed that exposure to high room density produced decrements in persistence on a task *after* subjects had left the high density conditions. At least three kinds of negative aftereffects can be distinguished: (1) costs of mere exposure to the aversive conditions (see Glass & Singer, 1972); (2) costs of coping or of adaptation, such as fatigue; and (3) costs incurred when coping or adaptation does not eliminate stress. If crowding is prolonged, it may lead to *cumulative effects* that represent negative aftereffects or habitual modes of coping. Thus, some researchers have investigated relationships between density and "social pathologies" such as crime and illness (e.g., Booth, Note 4). (It is conceivable that crowding could produce positive aftereffects, but none of the studies reviewed here have looked for such effects.)

In brief, crowding may be seen as a *sequential process* (Sundstrom, 1975a): (1) Conditions of high density produce or are accompanied by aversive physical or interpersonal events; (2) crowding may occur, depending on personality and situational conditions; (3) coping behaviors are performed with the goal of reducing stress; and (4) negative aftereffects or cumulative effects may follow.

A conception of crowding as a sequence of events emphasizes (1) the role of high density as a *source* of aversive conditions, and (2) the resulting processes of coping and adaptation. Figure 1 presents a schematic model of crowding based on the sequence just outlined. The model represents an attempt to extend earlier models (Altman, 1975; Stokols, 1972a; Sundstrom, 1975a) and reflects several assumptions:

1. The various types of high density *do not necessarily produce aversive conditions* that result in crowding. (High density can also lead to neutral or positive responses.)

2. Effects of high density on individual experience are mediated by conditions that either accompany high density or are produced by it. In other words *high density only indirectly produces stress.*

3. Psychological events that accompany crowding may include changes in attitudes toward other people (e.g., decreased attraction and changes in perceptions of others).

4. Under some conditions, cognitive or perceptual processes of *adaptation* may diminish crowding. People may also reduce crowding through *coping,* or alteration of conditions through interpersonal behavior, task performance, or physical environment.[5]

5. Negative aftereffects and cumulative effects of crowding may result from (a) stress, (b) the effort expended during coping, or (c) the effort spent in adaptation.

One important limitation of this model is its linear construction, which de-emphasizes the cyclical nature of the processes (see Altman, 1975). For example, in prolonged, high density living conditions, stress may not only motivate coping behaviors, but its aftereffects may downgrade a person's ability to cope. Similar cyclic processes may characterize other aspects of crowding.

For purposes of reviewing the research, the sequential model provides categories for organizing the findings. Antecedents of crowding include (1) *physical conditions* such as small room size, noise, heat, and complex settings; (2) *interpersonal conditions* such as the social climate, interpersonal distance and interference; (3) *individual characteristics* such as sex, a preference for large interpersonal distances, or a history of crowded surroundings; and (4) *modifying factors* such as the duration of exposure. Consequences of crowding include (1) *psychological responses* to stress, such as adaptation and altered attitudes toward other people; (2) *behavioral responses,* such as changes in performance of tasks or coping responses designed to reduce interpersonal interaction; and (3) *aftereffects and cumulative effects,* which include changes in health or performance that occur after crowding. These categories form the outline for the review of research findings.

[5]*Coping* refers here to deliberate, active attempts to reduce the impact of aversive conditions. Coping is an overt response, whereas *adaptation* refers to changes in a person's perception or appraisal of the situation.

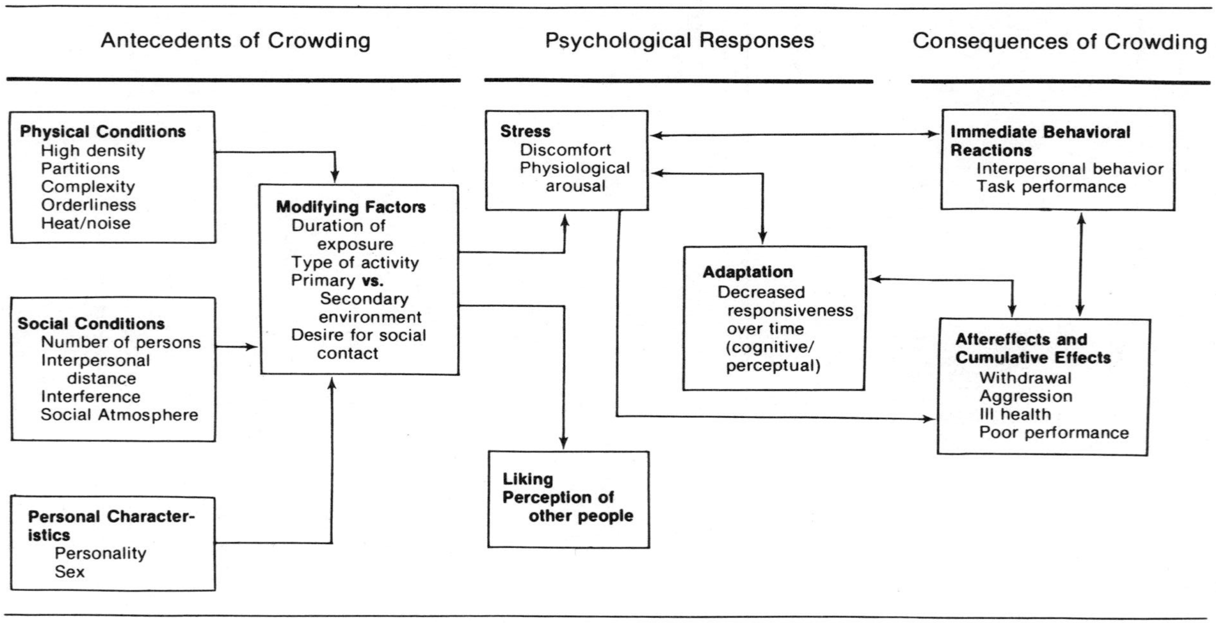

FIG. 1 Crowding as a sequential process.

STRATEGIES OF RESEARCH ON CROWDING

One characteristic of research on crowding is the diversity of techniques used to study it (cf. Ch. 1, this vol.). A frequently used technique is the traditional *laboratory experiment;* of the 83 studies reviewed here, 34 were conducted in laboratories. They usually varied social or spatial density and asked groups to work on various tasks. Many laboratory studies are extremely complex, involving up to five independent variables and multiple measures based on physiological reactions, responses to questionnaires, performance of tasks, placement of miniature figures, nonverbal behaviors, and other responses (e.g., McClelland, 1974; Saegert, 1974). All the steps in the sequential model of crowding have been examined in the laboratory, especially antecedents and immediate behavioral consequences. However, only a few studies have looked at aftereffects (e.g., Sherrod, 1974).

A second, more prevalent class of techniques involves the *field study;* 41 of the 83 studies observed people in more or less "natural" settings. Researchers have taken advantage of natural variations in density (e.g., Aiello, Epstein & Karlin, Note 2; Wolfe, 1975) or have varied density in natural settings (e.g., Loo, 1972; Price, 1971). Some researchers carried complex measurement apparatus into field settings (e.g., Aiello & Capriglione, Note 1); others used simple techniques of observation (e.g., Hutt & Vaizey, 1966). Although most field studies are based on the comparison of groups that experienced different conditions of density (27 out of 41), a few (14) are based on correlational techniques.

Most of the field studies examined behavioral consequences of high density or of crowding. In many studies, conditions of density were prolonged, as in a crowded dormitory room (e.g., Baron, Mandel, Adams, & Griffen, 1976). On the other hand, some field studies of children used only brief exposures to different densities (e.g., Loo, 1972). Reactions to brief exposures to high density can be classified as behavioral responses to crowding. However, responses to prolonged high density may reflect reactions to current conditions, or the cumulative effects of earlier conditions.

A third type of study employs *sociological* methods and examines aggregate data from census tracts, city blocks, and other urban land areas. Such studies comprise only eight of the 83 in the review; they provide indirect evidence on the cumulative effects of crowding. In brief, diverse methods supply evidence related to all of the components of the crowding process, although some data may show a combination of immediate responses and cumulative effects.

The remainder of this chapter reviews the findings of the studies of crowding and/or density among humans. For purposes of the review, "finding" means a result with a statistical significance of 0.05 or better. (A few marginal findings are mentioned as such.)

ANTECEDENTS OF CROWDING: PHYSICAL CONDITIONS

Spatial Density in Rooms

Perhaps the most often tested hypothesis in the literature on crowding links high spatial density in a single room with stress, discomfort, dissatisfaction, restriction, crowdedness, or a similar psychological reaction. Several studies compared groups of four to 10 people in spacious rooms with similar groups in smaller rooms with densities of around four to eight square feet per person. Groups in high room density reported greater discomfort or crowdedness (Aiello & Capriglione, Note 1; Emiley, Note 9; Epstein & Karlin, 1975; Evans, 1975; Freedman, Heshka, & Levy, 1975b; Joy & Lehmann, Note 13; McClelland, 1974; Poe, Note 16; Ross, Layton, Erickson, & Schopler, 1973; Sundstrom, 1975b). Similar results appeared in studies that led people to believe they were about to experience high room density (Baum & Koman, 1976; Greenberg, Lichtman, & Firestone, Note 10; Rall, Stokols, & Russo, Note 17). One study obtained parallel results by asking people to rate the crowdedness of miniature "rooms" containing clothespin figures (Cozby, 1973).[6] Another study asked people to rate pictures of settings showing varying numbers of people and amounts of space; ratings of crowding were higher when space was limited (McClelland & Auslander, Note 15). In brief, spatial density was associated with crowding, discomfort, or a similar reaction in 18 studies. On the other hand, a few studies varied spatial density and found no simple effects on discomfort. For some studies, the lack of a simple effect was due to an interaction between spatial density and another factor or factors (Freedman et al., 1975b; Freedman, Levy, Buchanan, & Price, 1972, Study #2; Smith & Haythorn, 1972; Worchel & Teddlie, 1976). A few studies that found a simple effect of density on one measure of stress found an interaction effect on another (McClelland, 1974; Poe, Note 16; Saegert, 1974). At least three studies found *no* effect of spatial density on comfort (Freedman et al., 1972, Study #3; Marshall & Heslin, 1975; MacDonald & Oden, 1973). And one study found *lesser* anxiety under conditions of high spatial density (Freedman & Staff, 1975). These last four studies that found either no effect or a positive effect of high spatial density on comfort employed groups of mixed sex.

---

[6]Studies using miniature figures in manipulating density or in measuring crowding must be interpreted with extreme caution. Findings based on similar methods in the literature on personal space have shown little consistency with findings based on actual interpersonal distances (see Sundstrom & Altman, 1976). And at least one miniature-figure study of crowding (Desor, 1972) contradicts a study that placed people in life-sized rooms (Stokols, Smith, & Prostor, 1975).

In brief, the evidence suggests that high spatial density in a single room for short periods of time tends to produce discomfort, except in groups of mixed sex. A few studies also found evidence of physiological arousal as a function of high spatial density (Aiello & Capriglione, Note 1; Aiello, Epstein, & Karlin, 1975; Evans, 1975; Saegert, 1974). Thus, brief exposures to high spatial density seem to produce at least mild stress. This conclusion raises an obvious question: What specific aspect(s) of high spatial density produced the stress? Other types of physical conditions have been examined with this question in mind.

Complexity of Physical Surroundings

A conception of crowding based on an "overload model" (cf. Milgram, 1970; Stokols, 1976) predicts that complicated or disorderly settings create demands on a person's capacity to assimilate information; such settings are expected to produce greater stress than simple, orderly ones. Consistent with this idea, Wohlwill (1968) reported evidence that people tend to prefer moderate degrees of complexity over highly complex displays. McClelland and Auslander (Note 15) asked students to rate the degree of crowding depicted in several photographs. Ratings of crowding were positively correlated with complexity and negatively correlated with orderliness, consistent with the "overload" hypothesis. A study using miniature figures found that a high degree of complexity intensified crowding in dark rooms but only for certain activities (Baum & Davis, 1976). On the other hand, a laboratory experiment by Worchel and Teddlie (1976) found evidence that the presence of pictures tended to *reduce* discomfort that accompanied close interpersonal proximity in groups of males. Similarly, McClelland and Auslander (Note 15) found that ratings of crowding varied inversely with the number of "visual escapes" in a situation. Schiffenbauer, Brown, Perry, Shulack, and Zanzola (1977) reported that ratings of crowding in dormitory rooms were inversely related to the "floor" (ground floor, second floor, third floor, etc.). Perhaps the higher floors provided better views of surrounding areas, hence more visual escapes. The implication is that the visually complex features of a crowded setting can sometimes provide a diversion from conditions that would otherwise produce discomfort. However, complexity may also contribute to stress. The conditions that determine whether diversion or stress will occur remain to be specified.

Lightness Versus Darkness

At least two studies have shown that well-lit or light colored rooms tend to be perceived as larger than comparable, darker rooms (Baum & Davis, 1976; Schiffenbauer et al., 1977). Ratings of crowding were lower in lighter rooms.

Partitions Within Rooms

One study employed miniature figures (Desor, 1972) to show that crowding was lower in a room divided by partitions (a larger number of figures was "comfortable" in the partitioned room). This finding agrees with the overload hypothesis; the partitions may be seen as reducing the amount of social stimulation received by each individual, thus reducing demands on their capacities for processing information. Stokols, Smith, and Prostor (1975) examined the effects of partitions in a field experiment in a waiting room at the California Department of Motor Vehicles. The results *contradicted* Desor's findings: Nonverbal signs of tension were most frequent *with* partitions. Crowding was also higher with the partitions (a marginal effect). This finding may be interpreted in terms of the "behavioral constraint" model of crowding (Stokols, 1976); the partitions may be seen as infringements on individual freedom. In the absence of other evidence, it appears that partitions may not prevent overload and may instead be seen as constraining individual behavior.

Variations in Architecture

A program of research by Baum and colleagues (Baum & Valins, 1973; Baum, Harpin, & Valins, 1975; Valins & Baum, 1973) has shown that students who live in dormitory rooms arranged along double-loaded corridors report greater crowding than do students who live in suites of two or three rooms arranged around a common lounge. One explanation derives from the concept of overload: Students who live on corridors tend to meet a greater number of people in the vicinity of their rooms than students who live in suites.

Noise and Heat

Both noise and heat may be seen as aversive, arousal-producing stimuli. They may produce stress, and they may intensify the stress produced by other aversive conditions. This hypothesis presumes that arousal sensitizes people to their environments. However, research evidence generally has failed to support the idea that heat or noise intensifies crowding. Griffitt and Veitch (1971) placed students in an environmental chamber in groups of three to five or 12 to 16 at either a normal or "hot" temperature; high social density *and* heat each produced discomfort but did not enhance each others' effects. In an experiment by Freedman et al. (1972), people worked on mock jury deliberations in a large or small room. Half were exposed to white noise, but it affected none of the dependent measures. Thus, it remains to be demonstrated that aversive physical conditions can intensify crowding. (These two studies did use constant, *predictable,* aversive stimuli. Had the aversive conditions been unpredictable and uncontrollable, crowding may have been more intense. See Averill, 1973; Glass & Singer, 1972, 1973.)

Summary of Physical Antecedents of Crowding

As shown in Table 1, crowding seems to occur in brief exposures to small rooms; complex settings may provide diversion from aversive conditions. Architectural features that increase the number of potential interaction partners also increase crowding. Other physical antecedents were not consistently related to crowding or were not studied enough to allow firm conclusions.

ANTECEDENTS OF CROWDING: SOCIAL CONDITIONS[7]

Social antecedents of crowding may originate from two sources: (1) One of the types of high density may produce aversive conditions, such as close proximity or limited privacy (Sundstrom, 1975a). (2) High density may be accompanied by aversive social conditions independent of the space supply, for example, a competitive task. Few researchers have attempted to identify interpersonal events that accompany high density, but Loo (1972) reported that children in high room density tended to interfere with one another's activities (a marginal trend).

A typical strategy for investigating social antecedents of crowding has involved variation of density along with variation of social conditions thought to affect crowding. These have included the number of people present or expected, interpersonal proximity, interference, the necessity for interaction, the social atmosphere, and the structure of the group task.

Social Density and Group Size

McClelland and Auslander's (Note 15) study indicated that the number of people depicted in a photograph was the strongest of several predictors of perceived crowding. Variation of "social density" was common in research on crowding; such variation usually confounds the amount of space per person with *group size* (e.g., Griffitt & Veitch, 1971). A few studies varied social density in a single room for brief periods of time and found that crowding, discomfort, or other forms of stress were greater in large groups than in small ones (Griffitt & Veitch, 1971; Joy & Lehmann, Note 13; Saegert, 1974; Dooley, 1974). Studies that varied the size of *expected* groups also found greater crowding with higher social density (Baum & Greenberg, 1975; Baum & Koman, 1976).

Other laboratory studies found more complicated effects in which stress depended on interactions of social density and other variables. Marshall and Heslin (1975) reported finding relatively positive emotion in mixed-sex groups exposed to high social density. Poe (Note 16) found relatively high scores on

---

[7]The categorization of certain antecedents of crowding as "social" instead of "physical" was sometimes arbitrary. For example, high social density is as much a physical condition as a social one; the same argument could be made for interpersonal distance.

TABLE 1
Summary of Research on
Physical Antecedents of Crowding

	Research Findings			
Hypothesis	Supportive Findings	Interactions with Other Factors	No Effects	Contradictory Findings
1. Small room size (high spatial density) produces crowding, discomfort, or other negative moods/states.	18(3)	7 (3)	3	1
2. Highly complex or disorderly settings produce crowding, discomfort, or negative moods/states.	1(1)	1	0	4(1)
3. Well-lit or light colored rooms appear larger and elicit less crowding than darker rooms.	2	0	0	0
4. A partitioned room is associated with less crowding than nonpartitioned room.	1	0	0	1
5. Architectural features that increase the likelihood of interactions with large numbers of people tend to produce crowding.	3	0	0	0
6. Noise or heat intensifies the effects of high density.	0	0	0	2

Note: If a study showed effects on more than one measure, its findings may fit into two columns. The number of such cases is shown in parentheses after each entry containing a study that counted twice. (For example, studies related to Hypothesis 1 included three that reported both supportive findings and interactions with another factor.) "No effects" means no differences on any relevant measure, except when the hypothesis calls for an interaction; in such cases, "no effects" means no interaction effects.

anxiety for large groups (eight people) in large rooms and small groups in small rooms. These last two studies may be seen as contradicting the general tendency for high social density to produce stress. In another brief laboratory study, Bergman (1971) found no effects of social density on reports of crowding.

Several field studies examined variations in social density that continued over *prolonged periods* in such settings as dormitory rooms, naval vessels, prisons, and classrooms. Results generally indicate greater stress with larger groups (Aiello, Love, & Epstein, Note 3; Baron et al., 1976; Dean, Pugh, & Gunderson, 1975; Eoyang, 1974; Paulus, Cox, McCain, & Chandler, 1975; Saegert, Mackintosh, & West, 1975; Sommer & Becker, 1971). On the other hand, D'Atri (1975) reported no differences in crowding as a function of social density in prisons. Smith and Haythorn (1972) reported that during a 21-day study, two-man groups showed more stress than three-man groups. However, the majority of studies indicate that stress increases with group size, at least when space is limited. This conclusion applies to brief laboratory experiments *and* to prolonged exposures. These findings agree with a social overload hypothesis: A large number of actual or potential interaction partners may tax a person's capacity for processing information.

Another way of looking at social density is based on Barker's (1960) theory of "undermanning," which uses the behavior setting as a unit of analysis. The theory asserts that individuals experience discomfort when the number of persons exceeds personnel requirements of a setting. Two experimental tests of this idea (Wicker & Kirmeyer, 1977) showed that in groups with more people than tasks, subjects reported feeling more marginal and less involved than in "adequately staffed" groups. But *understaffed* groups reported greatest crowding, perhaps because they required more physical movement and coordination of members' activities (see Stokols, 1976).

Excessive Proximity or Immediacy

Some researchers (e.g., Ross et al., 1973; Sundstrom, 1975b; Worchel & Teddlie, 1976) have hypothesized that crowding results from excessive interpersonal proximity, citing evidence that "personal space invasion" produces discomfort (see Sundstrom & Altman, 1976). A more general version of the hypothesis holds that stress follows from excessive stimulation from other people, that is, *immediacy,* which includes physical proximity, eye contact, directness of body orientation, forward lean, intimacy of conversation topic, and other cues (see Argyle & Dean, 1965; Mehrabian, 1972; Patterson, 1973).

To test the idea that excessive immediacy in a group leads to stress, Bergman (1971) varied interpersonal distance in groups of three, six, or twelve males and asked them to work on a task. For all the group sizes, the "close" groups were more uncomfortable and had higher palmar sweat, an indicator of stress. Another experiment (Sundstrom, 1975a) varied spatial density in groups of six males that included three confederates who were either intrusive (touching; too much eye gaze) or nonintrusive. Intrusion produced discomfort in both a large room and a small one. A recent experiment by Worchel and Teddlie (1976) also varied interpersonal distance in groups and found crowding at close proximity. In summary, it appears that excessive immediacy in a group may produce stress. This finding suggests that crowding may follow from excessive immediacy, because high density necessitates relatively close proximity. An alternative hypothesis holds that excessive immediacy *intensifies* a person's response to a situation, either positive *or* negative (see Hall, 1966). Schiffenbauer and Schiavo (1976) varied the distance between people and reported just such an "intensification effect" of distance.

Social Interference

Few studies have examined social interference as a source of crowding. In the experiment by Sundstrom (1975a), males talked with confederates who either interrupted and appeared inattentive or who listened during an impression formation task. This manipulation of "goal blocking" produced reports of discomfort, along with irritation that increased over time (compared with a decrease over time in no goal-blocking conditions). The stress that followed goal blocking appeared in high *and* low room density. Another laboratory study by Joy and Lehmann (Note 13) included procedures that made interference likely in conditions of high room density; discomfort was greater in high density, but the contribution of interference is unclear. McClelland (1974) showed that groups whose task required interpersonal interaction reported more interference than groups doing a noninteractive task; crowding was greater during the interactive task. In brief, available evidence, some of it indirect, suggests that stress may follow from interference by members of a group.

Necessity for Interaction

Three studies using miniature figures suggested that crowding occurs at lower densities when the task is solitary than when it is social (Cohen, Sladen, & Bennett, 1975; two studies by Desor, 1972). A similar study found that crowding was higher in high density "rooms" regardless of the nature of the situation (Cozby, 1973).

In a laboratory experiment, McClelland (1974) found that groups reported greater crowding when it was necessary for them to interact. However, subjects acquainted with one another were "upset" by interactive tasks in a small room and by noninteractive tasks in a large room. In the large room, the acquaintances may have experienced less than their optimal level of social interaction. This finding underlines the importance of the concept of an optimal amount of social contact (see Altman, 1975; Sundstrom, 1977; Wohlwill, 1974).

Social Atmosphere

Researchers have examined many conditions related to cohesion, liking, cooperativeness, and warmth in a group. Such conditions seem to affect crowding. Usually, the hypothesis holds that high room density intensifies the effect of the social atmosphere (e.g., the so-called "density-intensity" hypothesis of Freedman, 1975) or that the social atmosphere intensifies the effect of high room density (see Stokols & Resnick, Note 21). Both versions of this *intensification hypothesis* seem to assume that arousal, produced by high density or social conditions, sensitizes a person to his or her situation and makes its effects more pronounced.

Consistent with the intensification hypothesis, Stokols and Resnick (Note 21) found in one of two studies that when subjects were placed in high density conditions and asked to evaluate one another, they reported more crowding than did groups asked to "get acquainted." Another study showed that crowding in residence was strongly correlated with evaluations of social environments (Stokols & Resnick, Note 22). Freedman, et al. (1975b) manipulated positive versus negative feedback and room density. Results showed that the positive feedback group in high room density had highest scores on "would participate again." Lowest scores occurred in the negative feedback, high density condition. Another study by Freedman et al. (1975c) showed similar results: Scores on "would participate again" were highest for task success in high room density and lowest for task failure in high room density.

In contrast, several studies failed to find the intensification effect of social atmosphere and room density. Stokols, Rall, Pinner, and Schopler (1973) found that groups working on a competitive task showed higher scores on crowding than did groups who cooperated, but the effect was not intensified in high density. Bergman (1971) manipulated success versus failure in a group; failure produced stress, but stress did not differ as a function of group size of proximity. Freedman and Staff (1975) varied room density and positive versus negative feedback and failed to show the intensification effect on reports of crowding or discomfort. Emiley (Note 9) varied attraction and room density in groups of males; results showed no effects of attraction on crowding. Smith and Haythorn (1972) conducted a 21-day study of men isolated in groups of two or three in large or small quarters. The compatibility of the group members was also varied, but it had no effects on stress. Schopler and Walton (Note 18) varied the expected pleasantness of a group task in conditions of high room density but found no effects of this manipulation or reports of crowding. Rall et al. (Note 17) varied the expected threatening or nonthreatening nature of an interview in a large or small room; subjects anticipated greater crowding in the "threat" condition, but crowding was not intensified by small room size.

In summary, the intensification hypothesis has not received consistent support. It appeared in four studies but failed to appear in seven studies. *Possible explanations* for the inconsistencies are as follows:

1. Interpersonal proximity or immediacy intensifies the effects of the social atmosphere, and manipulations of density sometimes failed to introduce strong differences in immediacy. This explanation is not plausible in the case of Bergman (1971) where close proximity led to crowding, but crowding was not intensified under conditions of task failure.

2. The effect may appear only among people or groups with certain characteristics, although at present, explanations based on sex or the sex composition of groups appear untenable.

3. Some types of social atmosphere are more apt to show the intensification effect than others.

Structure of Group Activities

Schopler and Walton (Note 18) placed groups of males in high room density and varied the amount of structure they expected in their task; results indicated greater crowding in anticipation of the unstructured task. Similar results appeared in another study of anticipated crowding by Baum and Koman (1976). However, these studies provide only suggestive evidence for the hypothesis that a high degree of structure *during* an actual group task under conditions of high density would make for less stress than would a low degree of structure.

Summary of the Effects of Social Conditions on Crowding

As shown in Table 2, research evidence supports the following hypotheses: (1) Increased social density leads to stress, in brief *or* extended exposures; and (2) excessive immediacy in groups leads to stress. The idea that high room density

TABLE 2
Summary of Research on Social
Antecedents of Crowding

	Research Findings			
Hypothesis	Supportive Findings	Interactions with Other Factors	No Effects	Contradictory Findings
7. In *brief exposures* to a constant sized area, increases in group size are associated with crowding, stress, or discomfort.	6	2	1	0
8. In *prolonged exposures* to a constant sized area, increases in group size are associated with crowding, stress, or discomfort.	7	0	1	1

(continued)

TABLE 2 *(continued)*

	Research Findings			
Hypothesis	*Supportive Findings*	*Interactions with Other Factors*	*No Effects*	*Contradictory Findings*
9. Overstaffing in a behavior setting (too many people for available jobs) produces crowding or stress.	2(1)	0	0	1(1)
10. Excessive immediacy (close proximity, eye contact, etc.) in groups leads to crowding or stress.	3	0	0	0
11. Interference by members of a group with one another's activities produces crowding or stress.	2	0	0	0
12. Crowding is more likely when a group works together or interacts than when members work alone.	4(1)	(1)	1	0
13. (a) The effects of social atmosphere, positive or negative, are intensified under conditions of high room density. (b) The effects of high room density are intensified by a negative social atmosphere.	4	0	7	0
14. When a group works on a task in conditions of high room density, crowding is greater with low task structure than with high task structure.	2	0	0	0

Note: If a study showed effects on more than one measure, its findings may fit into two columns. The number of such cases is shown in parentheses after each entry containing a study that counted twice. (For example, studies related to Hypothesis 12 included one that reported supportive findings and interactions with another factor.) "No effects" means no differences on any relevant measure, except when the hypothesis calls for an interaction; in such cases, "no effects" means no interaction effects.

intensifies the effect of social atmosphere was not well supported. The remaining hypotheses regarding the social antecedents of crowding either failed to receive consistent support or received support in only two or three studies.

ANTECEDENTS OF CROWDING: CHARACTERISTICS OF INDIVIDUALS

Personality

Two studies reported that persons with relatively large "personal space zones," measured by "comfortable approach distance," tend to have a low threshold for crowding (Cozby, 1973; Dooley, 1974). These studies add weight to the hypothesis that crowding stems in part from the immediacy of other persons.

Another trait associated with a low threshold for crowding is an "external locus of control" (Schopler & Walton, Note 18). This finding fits with the idea that crowding is a kind of loss of control over social stimulation (see Altman, 1975).

Other attempts to relate crowding and personality have found no relationships. Evans (1975) used regression analysis to examine several personality variables; none were significant predictors of crowding. Joy and Lehman (Note 13) also reported no relationships of crowding and personality.

Sex

Most effects related to sex seem to appear on measures of liking, but a few sex differences appear in measures of crowding. In examinations of *brief exposures* to high room density, one field study and 13 laboratory studies varied sex and room density and measured crowding or discomfort. Three of them (Baum & Koman, 1976; Freedman et al., 1972; Rall et al., Note 17) reported that in same-sex groups, males showed greater discomfort in high room density (or in anticipation of high room density) than did females. Saegert (1974) found the opposite result for reports of anxiety. Marshall and Heslin (1975) found a complicated interaction of sex, sex composition, and group size. The remaining nine studies reported no sex differences in crowding or discomfort as a function of room density (Aiello & Capriglione, Note 1; Aiello et al., 1975; Baum & Greenberg, 1975; Epstein & Karlin, 1975; Evans, 1975; McClelland, 1974; Ross et al., 1973; Schopler & Walton, Note 18; Stokols et al., 1973).

As for studies of long-term exposure to high room densities, one study reported that females experienced greater discomfort than did males (Aiello et al., Note 2). Studies by Baum and Valins (1974), Baum et al. (1975), Valins and Baum (1973) and McDonald & Oden (1973) reported no sex differences. As shown in Table 3, research evidence provides only limited support for hypotheses that relate crowding to characteristics of individuals.

TABLE 3
Summary of Research on Individual
Characteristics Related to Crowding

| | Research Findings | | | |
Hypothesis	Supportive Findings	Interactions with Other Factors	No Effects	Contradictory Findings
15. Individuals with large personal space zones are more susceptible to crowding than individuals with small personal space zones.	2	0	0	0
16. Individuals with an external locus of control are more susceptible to crowding than individuals with an internal locus of control.	1	0	0	0
17. In *brief exposures* to high room density, all-male groups experience greater discomfort than do all-female groups.	3	1	9	1
18. In *prolonged exposures* to high room density, all-female groups experience greater discomfort than do all-male groups.	1	0	4	0

ANTECEDENTS OF CROWDING:
MODIFYING VARIABLES

The duration of exposure to high density was varied in only one brief laboratory study (Ross et al., 1973), without producing any effects on crowding. Stokols' (1976) concepts of *primary versus secondary environments* and *personal versus neutral* character of interpersonal events have not been examined in empirical studies. The *type of activity* has been examined in studies that employed miniature figures. Results suggest that crowding is more likely (1) during work than recreation (Cohen et al., 1975), (2) with strangers than with acquaintances (Cohen et al., 1975), and (3) when people are seated than when they are standing (Desor, 1972). Needless to say, many questions about the factors that modify crowding remain unanswered.

PSYCHOLOGICAL RESPONSES ASSOCIATED WITH CROWDING

As indicated in the sequential model, crowding may involve at least two psychological responses besides stress: (1) changes in *liking* for others or in perceptions of their characteristics, and (2) *adaptation*, or cognitive and perceptual adjustments that lead to decreased responsiveness to aversive conditions.

Liking for Other People and Perception of Their Characteristics

In many laboratory experiments and field studies, participants completed questionnaires about other members of the group or the group as a whole. The questionnaires usually contained bipolar adjective scales such as "good-bad," "friendly-unfriendly," or "like-dislike." The simplest relevant hypothesis holds that high density (or crowding) leads to a tendency to see other people in negative terms and/or dislike them. For example, Griffitt and Veitch (1971) showed that high social density was associated with relatively low attraction to an anonymous stranger. Only two other studies of both males and females in brief exposures to high room density (or expectation of high room density) found a similar effect (Baum & Greenberg, 1975; Saegert, 1974). Evans (1975) reported greater hostility in groups in a small room than a large one. On the other hand, Aiello and Capriglione (Note 1) reported that elderly people liked each other more during a brief stay in a small room than in a large one.

One of the most frequently reported findings in research on brief exposures to high density is an interaction of sex and room density: In high room density, members of all-female groups like one another better than do members of all-male groups; in low room density, members of all-male groups like one another better than do members of all-female groups. This effect appeared in six studies (Baum & Koman, 1976; Epstein & Karlin, 1975; Freedman et al., 1972; Ross et al., 1973; Saegert et al., 1975; Stokols et al., 1973). The five studies that found simple effects of room density on liking can be seen as failures to find this Sex X Density effect. Rall et al. (Note 17) found the opposite effect. Three studies using all-male groups found more negative reactions to others in high than in low room density (Dooley, 1974; Joy & Lehmann, Note 13; Worchel & Teddlie, 1976). These studies are consistent with the Sex X Density effect, but they can also be seen as supporting the hypothesis of a simple, adverse effect of high density on liking. One study by Sundstrom (1975a) found no effects of room density on liking among males. Two studies found complicated three-way interactions of sex, room size, and another factor (McClelland, 1974; Marshall & Heslin, 1975), but Marshall and Heslin's findings run opposite the usual Sex X Density effect. In summary, about as many studies failed to find the Sex X Density effect on liking as found it (see Table 4). One explanation for the effect is based on the finding that males prefer larger interpersonal distances than do females (see Altman, 1975). High room density may sometimes force males closer than their comfortable distance while ensuring that females are not too far for comfortable interaction. On the other hand, high density may place males at more or less optimal distance while making females too far apart.

A few studies looked at both sex and room density in long-term exposures. MacDonald and Oden (1973) did not find the Sex X Density effect that often occurred in short-term studies. Bickman et al. (1973) found that male and female residents of high density dormitories rated other people more negatively than in low density dormitories. Baron et al. (1976) reported that male students who lived in "tripled" rooms liked each other less than did students who lived in "doubled" rooms. Smith and Haythorn's (1972) study of Navy men indicated *less* reported hostility in high density than in low density. In summary, only the Baron et al. (1976) findings were consistent with the Sex X Density effect, and these findings were based on all-male groups. A hypothesis consistent with two of the four studies is that in prolonged conditions of high room density, people dislike one another.

Adaptation

Glass and Singer (1973) define adaptation as ". . . a cognitive process involving one or another mechanisms designed to filter out of awareness certain aspects of an aversive event, or in some other way reappraise it as benign [p. 181]." Adaptation refers to a kind of *habituation* to aversive conditions and excludes alteration of the conditions. To study adaptation, it is necessary to examine an individual's responses at different times. However, the use of repeated measures has been uncommon in research on crowding, and the findings have often been inconsistent.

In laboratory research based on *brief exposures* to high density, adaptation effects have appeared in one study. Poe (Note 16) found that in groups of males reports of comfort and liking showed an increase over time. Sundstrom (1975a)

TABLE 4
Summary of Research on Psychological Responses
Associated with Crowding

	Research Findings			
Hypothesis	Supportive Findings	Interactions with Other Factors	No Effects	Contradictory Findings
19. In *brief exposures* to high room density, people like others less than in lower density.	7	9	1	1
20. In *brief expsoures* to high room density in same-sex groups, males react more negatively to others in low density than in high room density, but females react more positively to others in high room density than in low room density.	9	2(1)	5	2(1)
21. In *prolonged exposures* to high density, people react more negatively to others than in low density.	2	0	1	1
22. In *brief exposures* to high density, people show *adaptation*, i.e., stress decreases over time.	1	2(2)	0	4(2)
23. In *prolonged exposures* to high density, people show *adaptation*, i.e., stress decreases over time.	0	(1)	1	(1)
24. A person with a history of intense or frequent social stimulation shows greater toleration for high density than a person with a history of relative isolation (*adaptation-level effect*).	4	0	0	1

Note: If a study showed effects on more than one measure, its findings may fit into two columns. The number of such cases is shown in parentheses after each entry containing a study that counted twice. (For example, studies related to Hypothesis 20 included one that reported findings and interactions with another factor.) "No effects" means no differences on any relevant measure, except when the hypothesis calls for an interaction; in such cases, "no effects" means no interaction effects.

found a decrease over time in crowding and discomfort in both high and low room density. However, decreases in crowding were accompanied by nonverbal coping behaviors, and the results may not represent adaptation but successful coping. The same study found an increase over time in irritation produced by a manipulation of goal blocking, despite coping behaviors. However, irritation decreased over time with no goal blocking. Sundstrom's findings thus do not clearly support the idea of adaptation. Aiello et al. (1975) reported that when college students were enclosed in a very small room in groups of six, their skin conductance (a measure of arousal) *increased* over time, indicating the *opposite* of adaptation. A second study of isolated individuals showed increases over time in skin conductance that depended on the room size and the order of exposure to a large and small room. A similar study in a field setting among elderly people showed parallel findings (Aiello & Capriglione, Note 1). The trend toward the opposite of adaptation in these three studies might be due to the fact that the subjects were not allowed to talk or were alone, whereas subjects could talk in the one study that did find adaptation (Poe, Note 16). Evidence related to adaptation during brief exposures to high room density is limited, but it seems to indicate that: (1) stress may *increase* over time under some circumstances; and (2) what appears to be adaptation could actually be successful coping.

Only two studies used repeated measures to examine responses to *prolonged* high density; neither showed adaptation. Smith and Haythorn (1972) found that among sailors isolated for 21 days in groups of two or three in large or small quarters, anxiety increased over time. Stress was highest during the last 11 days for large groups in small quarters. Anxiety increased over time in two-man groups during the same period.

Aiello et al. (Note 2) examined students in dormitory rooms designed for two. "Tripled" students reported greater crowding than "doubled" students, but there was no change over time in reports of crowding, and thus no sign of adaptation.

Another approach to adaptation relates a person's current toleration for high density to his or her previous living conditions. One line of reasoning is that individuals establish an *adaptation level for social stimulation* on the basis of cumulative experience (see Wohlwill, 1974). The adaptation level hypothesis holds that people with a history of intense or frequent social interaction are less likely to experience crowding at a given level of density than are people with a history of relative isolation. Consistent with this idea, Wohlwill and Kohn (1973) found that migrants to Harrisburg, Pennsylvania, were more likely to report crowding if they had come from a smaller town than if they had come from a larger one. The same authors reported similar findings in a second study of migrants to New York City. Also consistent with the adaptation-level hypothesis, Eoyang (1974) found that ratings of identical housing units in a trailer park were related to the number of people per unit, and to the size of the individual's family—people from large families rated their housing in more positive terms. Herrenkohl and Egolf (Note 11) reported that when individuals rated photos of various types of dwellings, perceptions of crowding were inversely related to familiarity with the types of dwelling. The same study reported that having lived in a high-rise apartment (versus not having done so) was associated with relatively low levels of crowding, and having lived in single-family unit was associated with relatively high levels of crowding. In contrast with these four studies, a field study by Paulus et al. (1975) among prison inmates showed that the longer an inmate had been imprisoned, the lower was his threshold for crowding, as indicated by placement of miniature figures. Thus, four of five studies related to a person's previous living conditions are consistent with the adaptation level hypothesis.

The adaptation level hypothesis also predicts that a person's threshold for crowding remains relatively constant in different settings. Consistent with this idea, Stokols and Resnick (Note 22) reported that students' ratings of crowding in a single classroom were positively related to their ratings of crowding in their residences.

In summary, as shown in Table 4, research based on repeated measurements of responses to high density, in brief *and* prolonged exposures, failed to show adaptation. But the research related to a person's living conditions points toward the development of an *adaptation-level* for social stimulation based on cumulative experience.[8] This apparent contradiction may reflect two different responses to high density: (1) immediate stress that increases slightly over several months; and (2) gradual increases in a person's toleration for intense social contact.

CONSEQUENCES OF CROWDING: BEHAVIORAL REACTIONS

In studying the outcomes of exposure to conditions of high density, researchers have usually examined two types of behavior: (1) *performance of tasks,* and (2) *interpersonal behaviors* such as the frequency of interaction, aggression, altruism, and behaviors related to immediacy (e.g., proximity and eye contact). For purposes of discussion, such responses during exposure to high density are labeled "behavioral reactions"; if they occur immediately *after* exposure to high density, they are called "aftereffects." Responses observed after prolonged exposure to high density are labeled "cumulative effects" because it is not clear whether they are immediate responses or aftereffects or both.

---

[8]One corollary of the adaptation-level hypothesis holds that persons with a history of frequent, intense social contact develop personality traits related to the seeking of interpersonal interaction. Cozby (1973) found a positive relationship between "personal space" and family size, suggesting that toleration for close proximity was *lower* for subjects from large families. This finding contradicts the adaptation-level hypothesis.

Performance of Tasks During Exposure to High Density

In a series of studies cited in most research on crowding, Freedman, Klevansky, and Ehrlich (1971) hypothesized that the performance of complicated tasks would be adversely affected by high room density. Such a prediction follows from the overload hypothesis, or from hypotheses related to the concept of arousal. Freedman et al. (1971) also predicted that performance of simple tasks would be best under conditions of high density (provided that initial "drive level" is low). This prediction follows from the concept of *social facilitation* (Cottrell, 1972). However, three separate experiments involving up to seven different tasks failed to support either prediction.

Several subsequent studies involving the performance of *simple tasks* during brief exposures to high or low density found a similar lack of differences (Bergman, 1971; Evans, 1975; Sherrod, 1974; Stokols et al., 1973). The tasks typically involved simple arithmetic, crossing out letters, or answering simple, historical questions. Other studies employed slightly more complex tasks involving the formation of words from collections of letters or other words. (A version of this task was the most complex task used in the three experiments by Freedman et al., 1971, which found no effects.) Poe (Note 16) also found no effects, but Freedman, Heshka, and Levy (1975c) found better performance in high than in low room density. Saegert (1974) also found better performance of a simple word-association task in high than in low room density. In contrast to these two findings that suggest social facilitation in high density, Saegert et al. (1975) found that high density in a public place had a detrimental effect on the performance of simple tasks that involved getting from place to place. In summary, the evidence has generally not shown that brief exposures to high density affect performance of simple tasks.

A few studies that used relatively *complex tasks* suggest that high room density can have a detrimental effect on performance. Evans (1975) found that when students worked on two tasks at once, performance of the secondary task suffered in high density. Evans also found lower performance of another complex task in high density. McClelland (1974) reported that the performance of a task involving assembly of a bibliography suffered in high room density. Similar results appeared in a study by Saegert (1974). On the other hand, two studies by Emiley (Note 9) and one by Dooley (1974) found no effects of room density on complex tasks.

In summary, high room density seems to have a detrimental effect on the performance of complex tasks under some circumstances. One possibility is that high density sometimes creates excessively "immediate" arrangements, which produce arousal and create distractions from a complicated task. Consistent with this idea, Worchel and Teddlie (1976) found that task performance in groups was poorer at close proximity than at moderate proximity. Perhaps high density affects the performance of tasks when it is not possible to avoid excessive immediacy or to compensate for it through coping behaviors.

A variant of the overload hypothesis holds that in high density the capacity for processing information is taxed, and therefore a person obtains less residual information in high density than in low density. This effect may be seen as a kind of decrement in performance. Findings consistent with this idea appeared in studies by Joy and Lehmann (Note 13) and Saegert et al. (1975), in which people exposed to high density showed less "incidental learning" than those exposed to lower densities. Similarly, Evans (1975) found that performance of a secondary task suffered in high density.

Interpersonal Behavior During Exposure to High Density

Many types of interpersonal behavior have been examined in research on crowding, but most studies seem to reflect one of two lines of reasoning:

1. Hypotheses that derive from an *overload model* hold that in high density the degree of social stimulation is higher than optimal, and a person *copes* by reducing social stimulation. Such coping can involve avoidance of or withdrawal from interaction or decreases in immediacy.

2. Hypotheses based on the *behavioral constraint* model assume that high density involves interference with a person's activities, and the accompanying frustration leads to antisocial behaviors.

1. *Responses to social overload: Withdrawal or decreased immediacy.* Several field studies of children in large or small rooms, or in large or small groups, have reported lower frequencies of interaction under conditions of high density (Hutt & Vaizey, 1966; Loo, 1972; Price, 1971; Slosnerick, Note 19). Similarly, an observational study of psychiatric patients indicated that the larger the number of patients housed in a single bedroom, the less frequently they interacted (Ittelson, Proshansky, & Rivlin, 1972). Another study in a psychiatric population by Wolfe (1975) found that the frequency of isolated passive behavior was relatively high among children who shared a four-bed room with three others. Although Wolfe's study suggests that withdrawal from interaction may occur for several reasons, it is consistent with the other five studies that found withdrawal from interaction as a response to high density. One study by Hutt and McGrew (Note 12) reported higher interaction in high than in low density.

Another version of the overload hypothesis predicts that when people perceive themselves as too immediate with another person, they compensate by decreasing signs of immediacy. Such compensatory reactions (see Argyle & Dean, 1965; Patterson, 1973) are designed to restore an optimal level of immediacy, called equilibrium. One laboratory experiment by Sundstrom (1975a) found that males in groups of six in high *or* low room density showed lowered facial regard (looking at another's face) in response to "intrusions" in which a confederate attempted 80 percent eye contact and touched the subject. Similarly, Ross et al. (1973)

reported in a marginal trend less facial regard in high density than in low density among males but more facial regard among females in high density than in low density. This effect resembles the Sex X Density effect on ratings of other people and suggests that compensatory reactions accompanied negative feelings toward others, but not positive feelings. The idea that such coping actually reduces stress has yet to be tested directly, but Sundstrom (1975b) showed that discomfort in response to intrusion declined over time, whereas facial regard remained at low levels. This indirect evidence that compensatory reactions can reduce stress suggests that crowding may reflect aversive conditions *and* the inability to neutralize them through coping responses.

Another line of research has examined what might be called *anticipatory coping responses*. In studies of people "waiting for a crowd" (e.g., Baum & Greenberg, 1975), the participants believed they soon will work with a group in a small or large room. The researchers observe their responses to one or two confederates posing as participants. Consistent with the overload hypothesis, people waiting for a crowd tend to avoid interaction. Their responses have included lower facial regard and head movements away from the confederate (Baum & Greenberg, 1975; Baum & Koman, 1976; Greenberg et al., Note 10), choice of less central seating position (Baum & Greenberg 1975; Baum & Koman, 1976), greater interpersonal distance (Baum & Greenberg, 1975; Rall et al., Note 17), and indirect body orientation (Rall et al., Note 17). Such responses occurred not only in anticipation of high density but in anticipation of an unstructured task (Baum & Koman, 1976) or a threatening interview (Rall et al., Note 17). As in other studies of density, these nonaffiliative responses can probably be linked to *specific aspects* of density such as excessive immediacy.

2. *Response to interference: Aggression and competition.* A person may respond in constructive ways to interference, for example by coordinating activities with others or by cooperating (see Stokols, 1976). However, most studies of crowding implicitly or explicitly predict aggressive or antisocial responses to interference that accompanies high density. This prediction may derive from the "frustration-aggression hypothesis" (see Berkowitz, 1969) or from generalizations of findings based on nonhumans (e.g., Calhoun, 1962).

One line of research involves the observation of children at play in high or low spatial or social density. Studies by Hutt and McGrew (Note 12) and by Hutt and Vaizey (1966) found increased aggression along with increased density in groups of children in nurseries. However, Price (1971) found no effects of spatial density on aggression in classrooms. And Loo (1972) reported a *decrease* in aggression with increased spatial density among preschool children. The apparent inconsistency of these three studies may be understood in light of an experiment by Rohe and Patterson (1974), who varied both spatial density and the number of toys available to groups of children. Aggression was greatest in the high density, low toys condition. Perhaps a shortage of a valued commodity is not easily amenable to the coping responses that children could use to circumvent social interference under most conditions.

TABLE 5
Summary of Research on Immediate Behavioral
Responses to High Density

	Research Findings			
Hypothesis	Supportive Findings	Interactions with Other Factors	No Effects	Contradictory Findings
25. Performance of *simple tasks* is better during brief exposures to high room density than low room density.	2	0	8	1
26. Performance of *complex tasks* is poorer during brief exposures to high room density than low room density.	3	0	3	0
27. During brief exposures to high room density, a person obtains less incidental information from the setting than in low room density.	3	0	0	0
28. Under conditions of high room density, children show less social interaction than in low room density.	5(1)	(1)	0	1
29. Among adults in groups, excessive immediacy (close proximity, eye contact, etc.) leads to decrease in other signs of immediacy.	1	1	0	0
30. Among adults who believe they will soon be exposed to high room density, affiliative behavior is less prevalent than among those who expect low room density.	4	0	0	0

(continued)

TABLE 5 *(continued)*

	Research Findings			
Hypothesis	Supportive Findings	Interactions with Other Factors	No Effects	Contradictory Findings
31. Under conditions of high room density, children show more aggression than in low room density.	2	1	1	1
32. Adults are more competitive and hostile during brief exposure to high room density than low room density.	1	2	2	0

Note: If a study showed effects on more than one measure, its findings may fit into two columns. The number of such cases is shown in parentheses after each entry containing a study that counted twice. (For example, studies related to Hypothesis 28 included one that reported supportive findings and interactions with another factor.) "No effects" means no differences on any relevant measure, except when the hypothesis calls for an interaction; in such cases, "no effects" means no interaction effects.

In studies of adults, the closest approximations of aggressive responses in high density have been hostile comments, competitive choices in games, or punitive decisions in a mock jury task. Freedman et al. (1972) found in two studies that in high density, males were more competitive and gave harsher sentences in a mock jury deliberation than in low density. The reverse was true for females; this is the familiar Sex X Density effect. Emiley (Note 9) examined groups of males and found more negative comments in high density than in low density. Stokols et al. (1973) reported no effects of density on the occurrence of hostile comments. Poe (Note 16) found inconsistent responses in five different mock jury cases, although the first case drew harsher sentences in high density. For the hypothesis that adults react immediately to high density with antisocial behavior, there is only limited and inconsistent evidence, as shown in Table 5.

One study attempted to isolate the effects of social interference, or goal blocking among adults. Sundstrom (1975b) placed groups of males in high or low spatial density and asked them to work on a task in which confederates interrupted and were inattentive (goal blocking). Irritation in response to goal blocking increased over time, and subjects in high *and* low density showed relatively low levels of affiliative behavior (facial regard, gesturing, head nodding). Such reactions to interference may represent partial withdrawal from interaction.

In summary, the behavioral constraint model of crowding may apply only to children under certain circumstances (e.g., a shortage of toys). Evidence regarding responses to interference by adults is too limited and inconsistent to draw conclusions.

CONSEQUENCES OF CROWDING: IMMEDIATE AFTEREFFECTS

Researchers have recently begun to study effects that appear *immediately after* exposure to high room density (or after crowding). The typical experiment exposes people to high or low room density and then observes their responses in a different room, either in isolation or in a group. This line of research represents an extension to work by Glass and Singer (1972). Their studies showed that when people were exposed to unpredictable, uncontrollable noise and taken to a separate room, performance of a proofreading task and persistence in solving puzzles were lower than that of people not exposed to noise. Glass and Singer had thought that the negative aftereffects of noise represented "costs" of adaptation, but their data indicated that negative aftereffects were unrelated to adaptation. So the negative aftereffects of noise may have been costs of stress.

Sherrod (1974) attempted to produce the same negative aftereffects with high room density as the stressor. Results did show a decrement in persistence on problem solving but not a decrement in proofreading. Since Sherrod's study, several other researchers have used similar techniques to examine three kinds of aftereffects: (1) decrements in the performance of tasks; (2) tendencies to avoid interaction or seek relatively nonimmediate positions; and (3) tendencies toward hostility or competition.

Decrements in the Performance of Tasks

Besides the experiment by Sherrod (1974), seven studies compared the performance of people who had been in high room density with the performance of others who had been in low room density. Dooley (1974) and Evans (1975) both found poorer performance after exposure to high density. However, the results of other studies have not been as simple. Epstein and Karlin (1975) found no effects of density on subsequent performance of complex tasks, but performance of simple tasks was actually *better* after high density. (The effects were greater among people who had been seated between two others than people who sat near walls.) Poe (Note 16) found that after exposure to high *or* low spatial density, groups of eight showed poorer performance. Joy and Lehmann (Note 13) found that in groups of males, proofreading scores were poorest in large groups after exposure to a small room. Saegert et al. (1975) found that after performing tasks in a crowded or uncrowded train station, females did better on subsequent tasks after low density than after high density, but males did *better* after exposure to *high* density. McClelland (1974) found no aftereffects of density on performance of two different tasks, but on one task, groups who had been required to interact did more poorly than groups who had less interaction. Dooley (1974) reported a decrement in proofreading scores among males with "far" personal space after either high or low density.

In summary, as shown in Table 6, three studies found the expected decrement in performance; one found improved performance of a simple task; there were four complex findings in which aftereffects depended on group size or sex; two studies found simple, negative aftereffects of variables other than density. Exposure to high density clearly does not always bring decrements in performance and can even lead to improved performance. The same argument that applied to the antecedents of crowding also applies here: It is not high density *per se* that brings negative aftereffects but the aversive events that *sometimes* accompany high density. Available evidence suggests that among the critical factors may be: (1) the degree of social interaction (McClelland, 1974); and (2) the immediacy of the people involved (Dooley, 1974; Epstein & Karlin, 1975). Under some conditions, it appears that the same factors can bring *positive* aftereffects.

Avoidance of Interaction or Immediacy

A variant of the social overload hypothesis predicts that if a person's need for interaction is exceeded, then later he or she avoids interaction in order to overcome fatigue or restore equilibrium. Consistent with this idea, Dooley (1974) found that after exposure to high density, groups of males were less likely to volunteer for another session than after low density. Joy and Lehmann (Note 13) found that after exposure to high density, groups of males preferred larger personal spaces and recalled fewer names than after exposure to low density. Epstein and Karlin (1975) found the familiar Sex X Density effect as an aftereffect on dispersion of seating positions. Males who had been exposed to high density and females who had been exposed to low density were more distant. All three of these studies indicate that males become less inclined toward interaction after exposure to high density. Females may respond differently, but female subjects appeared in only one of three studies.

One study showed that avoidance of interaction varied as a function of the social atmosphere of the group. Stokols and Resnick (Note 21) exposed groups to high density and told them either to get acquainted or to evaluate one another. In another room, people in the evaluative groups sat farther apart. (This effect appeared in only one of two separate studies.) The implication is clear: Aftereffects involving the avoidance of interaction may follow from interpersonal conditions that occur independently of high density.

TABLE 6
Summary of Research on Aftereffects and Cumulative Effects
of Exposure to High Density

Hypothesis	Research Findings			
	Supportive Findings	Interactions with Other Factors	No Effects	Contradictory Findings
33. Immediately after an exposure to high room density, a person shows poorer performance of tasks than after an exposure to low room density.	3	4(1)	1	(1)
34. Immediately after exposure to high room density, a person avoids interaction more than a person who has been exposed to low room density.	2	1	0	0
35. Prolonged exposure to high household density is associated with:				
a. withdrawal from interaction among males	2	0	2	1
b. withdrawal from interaction among females	3	0	0	1
c. poor health	11(3)	(1)	1	(2)
d. crime or aggression	4	0	0	1
e. poor performance	2	1	1	0
36. Prolonged exposure to high neighborhood density is associated with:				
a. withdrawal from interaction among males	4	0	0	1
b. withdrawal from interaction among females	3(1)	0	0	(1)
c. poor health	0	0	3	2
d. crime or aggression	2	(1)	4	2(1)

Note: If a study showed effects on more than one measure, its findings may fit into two columns. The number of such cases is shown in parentheses after each entry containing a study that counted twice. (For example, studies related to Hypothesis 33 included one that reported contrary findings and interactions with another factor.) "No effects" means no differences on any relevant measure, except when the hypothesis calls for an interaction; in such cases, "no effects" means no interaction effects.

Hostility and Competition

Only one study reviewed here included competition as an immediate aftereffect of high density. Epstein and Karlin (1975) reported that responses to a prisoner's dilemma were more competitive among males who had been exposed to high density and among females who had been exposed to low density.

In summary, Table 6 indicates that neither of the two hypotheses related to immediate aftereffects of exposure to high density received support in more than three studies, and there were inconsistent findings. These hypotheses deserve further investigation.

CONSEQUENCES OF CROWDING:
CUMULATIVE EFFECTS

Integral to popular conceptions of crowding is the idea that prolonged exposure to crowded conditions brings adverse effects such as disease, crime, and mental illness (Zlutnick & Altman, 1972). What might be called the *social pathology hypothesis* is one of the oldest in research on crowding. The hypothesis may have appeared to gain support from simple correlations between measures of *gross density*, such as the number of persons per acre, and such forms of pathology as crime and mental illness (see Zlutnick & Altman, 1972, for a review). However, early sociological research typically overlooked the fact that both high density and social pathologies such as crime and illness tend to occur among poor people. Using aggregate data from Chicago, Winsborough (1965) showed that the relationship between gross density and various types of pathology disappeared or turned negative when variables related to socioeconomic status were statistically controlled. Therefore in studies of crowding based on data from aggregates, it is essential to employ procedures that control for the effects of socioeconomic status.[9] But even when such controls are used, data based on aggregates create difficulties for interpretation.[10] Fortunately, a majority of studies related to the social pathology hypothesis examined data from individuals; a few were experi-

[9]The review deliberately excluded correlational studies if the results were confounded by socioeconomic status. These studies include much of the pre-1960 research reviewed by Zlutnick and Altman (1972) and a few recent studies (Collette & Webb, Note 7; Kahn & Perlin, 1967; Schmitt, 1963).

[10]When a study based on aggregate data fails to show a relationship between some form of density and another variable (e.g., gross density and crime rates) it is possible that the use of group scores obscured a relationship that would be present in data from individuals. When a relationship between gross density and crime rates appears (after controlling for socioeconomic factors) it is always possible that one set of people within each aggregate was primarily responsible for the value of the density variable, and separate segments of the aggregate were the main contributors to the crime rate. For example, in Honolulu, residents of the beach-districts may be very crowded and crime-ridden, but high crime rates in those districts could be attributable to tourists or residents of other areas.

ments that involved relatively high degrees of control over the conditions of density (e.g., Aiello et al., Note 2).

Evaluation of the evidence related to social pathology is complicated by its extreme heterogeneity. Five types of diversity in the data are important:

1. Many *types of density* have been examined, including four varieties of household density (persons per room, persons per dwelling, proportion of dwellings with more than one person per room, and household size). These studies have seldom made the important distinction between density and crowding.

2. *Populations* have been tremendously varied, including groups in the continental United States, Canada, Hong Kong, Holland, and Manila. One study used data from 65 countries.

3. The *duration of exposure* to conditions of high density varies from weeks to years.

4. Researchers seldom have data on the availability of "escapes" from high density.

5. Many *types of pathology* have been studied.

The result is a motley collection of studies, the results of which are difficult to compare. When the findings disagree, there are many explanations. When they agree, it is seldom apparent why they do.

There are several theoretical rationales for the social pathology hypothesis. The simplest derives from the uncritical extrapolation of data from studies of nonhumans (e.g., Calhoun, 1962) to humans. The prediction of social pathology in response to prolonged crowding can also be derived from the overload and behavioral constraint models. The overload model predicts fatigue from prolonged stress, from the efforts required to avoid stress, or from the energy expended in adaptation. It also predicts a syndrome of avoidance of interpersonal interaction and reluctance to form social ties as an habitual way of coping that minimizes social overload. The behavioral constraint model might predict fatigue from the coordination of one individual's activities with the activities of others. The model also might predict an aggressive reaction to cumulative or repeated frustration that occurs because of high density. The present discussion distinguishes four categories of cumulative effects: (1) withdrawal or avoidance of interpersonal interaction; (2) antisocial behavior such as crime, aggression, or competition; (3) poor health or adjustment; and (4) poor performance.

Withdrawal or Avoidance of Interaction

A few studies based on individual data found evidence of withdrawal among people who live under conditions of high density. For example, research on college dormitories has suggested that residents of suites report less crowding than do residents of rooms on double-loaded corridors (Valins & Baum, 1973).

This may be regarded as a response to high neighborhood density. In a questionnaire, corridor residents said they avoided others more than did suite residents (Baum et al., 1975). In a waiting room, corridor residents sat farther from a confederate and initiated fewer conversations than did suite residents (Valins & Baum, 1973, Study #2). In another study of dormitories by Aiello et al. (Note 2), students lived in groups of two or three in rooms built for two. "Tripled" women showed a greater number of dissolutions of roommates than did males or "doubled" females. Another study in the same dormitories (Aiello et al., Note 3) measured behaviors related to immediacy on three separate occasions. Women showed increasingly direct body orientation over time, especially the "tripled" females. (This is a puzzling find, in light of results on dissolution of roommates.) Males became increasingly indirect, especially if "tripled."

A survey conducted in a large city in Canada (Booth, Note 4) showed that subjective household crowding was inversely related to contacts with relatives among females. Subjective neighborhood crowding was inversely related to contacts by males with neighbors. For women, both objective neighborhood crowding and subjective household crowding were inversely related to contacts with relatives. However, joining of voluntary associations by women was positively related to subjective neighborhood crowding. Other measures of social interaction were unrelated to measures of crowding or density.

Two studies by Baldassare (1975a; 1975b) used individual data from males in conjunction with aggregate measures of density. One study (1975a) found a weak, inverse relationship between a measure of neighborhood density (the number of persons per square mile) and the extent to which subjects said they knew their neighbors. However, household density showed no relationship with "neighboring." The same study reported a *positive* relationship between household size and number of social organizations.

Baldassare's second study (1975b) found that among married males in Detroit the number of persons per acre was weakly but *positively* related to "closeness" with neighborhood friends. Another study based on individual data (Mitchell, 1971) reported that in Hong Kong, a measure of household density was inversely related to entertainment of others at home.

In summary, the relationship between density and withdrawal seems to depend on both sex and the type of density. For males, evidence of withdrawal under conditions of prolonged high household density appeared in only two of five studies; four of five studies showed similar results for neighborhood density. For females, evidence of withdrawal under conditions of prolonged high household density appeared in three of four studies; two of three studies showed similar results for neighborhood density, although one study contained contradictory results. In this case, the simple counting of findings suggests stronger results than the studies showed; the correlations were usually weak, and most studies contained several measures of withdrawal that were unrelated to any type of density.

Antisocial Behavior: Crime and Aggression

Many studies of crowding have examined antisocial behavior through use of aggregate data. The findings are fairly consistent—even when socioeconomic factors are taken into account, increases in density within dwellings are associated with modest increments in antisocial behavior.

Two studies based on individuals by Bickman et al. (1973) showed that students who lived in high density dormitories (large number of rooms per building) were less likely to help another person than students in less crowded buildings. A survey in Canada (Booth, Note 4) revealed that among males, subjective household crowding was associated with hitting their children; among females, hitting children was associated with objective household crowding. However, for males, subjective neighborhood crowding was inversely related to aggression outside the home.

In research based on aggregate data, crime or juvenile delinquency was related to *density within dwellings* in four studies that controlled for socioeconomic factors (Booth & Welch, Note 5; Booth & Welch, Note 6; Galle et al., 1972[11]; and Schmitt, 1966). Booth and Welch's study (Note 5) was based on data from 65 nations; the average number of persons per dwelling accounted for 16 percent of the variance in rates of homicide. On the other hand, Levy and Herzog (1974) found that in the Netherlands, crime and delinquency were *inversely* related to the number of persons per room. All these studies contained other measures of crime unrelated to household density. Although it is difficult to overlook the consistent, modest association between crime and household density (see Table 6), the data cannot be interpreted with much confidence because aggregate measures of density and crime provide only indirect information about individuals.

An association between *neighborhood density* and crime appeared in a study by Booth and Welch (Note 5). Similarly, Levy and Herzog (1974) found the number of persons per economic area to be related to crime rates. However, Freedman, Heshka, and Levy (1975a) found no relationship between the number of persons per acre in New York City and the rates of six crimes. Three other studies showed no relationship of crime or delinquency with neighborhood density (Booth & Welch, Note 6; Galle et al., 1972; Schmitt, 1966). In summary, research evidence does not support the hypothesis that antisocial behavior is associated with prolonged exposure to high density within neighborhoods.

[11]A recent reanalysis of the same aggregate data used in the Galle et al. (1972) study also employed census data from 10 years earlier (McPherson, 1975). An "over time" analysis based on a different statistical model from the one used by Galle et al. showed, according to McPherson (1975), that "controlling for the stability and previous effects of the independent variables reduces the magnitude of the estimate to a level just below that of statistical significance [p. 86]." The use of a 10-year "lag" in this reanalysis may have produced misleading conclusions, because the character of the census tracts could change markedly over 10 years. However, if McPherson's analysis is correct, the Galle et al. findings must be viewed as marginal.

Poor Health

In a study based on individual data, Booth (Note 4) reported that for males, *objective* household crowding was associated with four measures of ill health (communicative disease, cholesterol level, infectious disease, and stress disease). Also for males, *subjective* household crowding was associated with four measures of ill health (psychiatric impairment, decrement in love, stress disease, and trauma). For females, subjective household crowding was associated with three types of ill health (trauma, psychiatric impairment, and uterine dysfunction) and inversely related to one type (blood pressure). Other studies based on individuals are consistent with this association between crowding (or density within dwellings) and ill health. Stokols and Ohlig (Note 20) reported an association between reports of crowding in a dormitory during fall quarter and visits to the student health center during the next two quarters. Dean, Pugh, and Gunderson (Note 8) reported an association between crowding and illness among U.S. Navy men. Also on U.S. naval vessels, Dean et al. (1975) found an association between the perceived number of people aboard ship and visits to dispensaries. There was also a positive correlation between the perceived amount of space and visits to the dispensary, which goes against the idea that crowding is associated with ill health. Marsella, Escudero, and Gordon (1970) found an association between the number of persons per dwelling among Filipino men and a cluster of physiological symptoms. Baron et al. (1976) found no differences between "doubled" and "tripled" students in their use of the health center.

In brief, five studies of individuals associate high dwelling density, or crowding in response to high dwelling density, with ill health. Only two studies found contradictory results, although both negative findings were offset in the same studies by associations between crowding and other types of ill health. One study found no differences in health as a function of density.

Research based on aggregates generally agrees with the research based on individuals. Five studies found an association between some indicator of ill health and a measure of dwelling density (Booth & Welch, Note 5; Freedman et al., 1975d; Galle et al., 1972; Levy & Herzog, 1974; Schmitt, 1966). Mitchell (1971) found "strain" related to dwelling density among the poor in Hong Kong; "stress" was related to dwelling density if two couples shared one apartment. Freedman et al. (1975a) reported no correlation between household density and several indicators of ill health; Levy and Herzog (1974) found an inverse relationship between hospital admissions and household density.

In contrast to the studies of household density, studies using aggregate measures of neighborhood density have generally not found them to be associated with ill health. Three studies failed to find any relationship (Freedman et al., 1975; Galle et al., 1972; Schmitt, 1966). Two more (Levy & Herzog, 1974; Winsborough, 1965) reported inverse relationships between neighborhood density and measures of ill health.

Poor Performance of Tasks

Few studies have examined performance as a cumulative effect of crowding. Baron et al. (1976) reported no differences in school grades of "doubled" and "tripled" roommates in dormitories, although grades were negatively correlated with satisfaction. Valins and Baum (1973) compared residents of dormitory suites with residents of dormitory rooms or double-loaded corridors. When working on an anagram task, the suite residents performed better than did corridor residents in cooperative situations or in isolation. However, corridor residents did better in competitive or coactive situations. These results are not easily interpreted.

An interesting hypothesis follows from a theory on "learned helplessness" (Seligman, 1975), which posits that persons who have been unable to control their environments in the past are less likely to try to control their current environment than people who have achieved control in the past. If crowding represents a breakdown in control over interpersonal interaction (Altman, 1975), perhaps people who experience crowding show learned helplessness. Rodin (1976) tested this idea in two experiments. In the first, children who lived in identical units of a housing project learned multi-reinforcement contingencies. There were no differences in learning as a function of household density. A "switching key" was introduced which allowed the child to choose among contingencies. The use of this device for controlling contingencies was inversely related to the number of persons in the child's household. In a second experiment, children were given either a solvable or unsolvable problem. Responses to a subsequent series of solvable problems were recorded. Results revealed that after socioeconomic factors were controlled, both household density *and* the interaction of household density with the solvability of the first problem predicted significant proportions of the variance in the number of correct responses in the second series of problems. These findings suggest an association between household density and "learned helplessness."

In summary, even with all of its heterogeneity, the available evidence does suggest that prolonged exposure to high density within dwellings is associated with cumulative effects in the form of aggression, ill health, and possibly the learning of "helplessness" in solving problems (see Table 6). Unfortunately, these correlational data provide little information about what might have *produced* the cumulative effects. In most cases, it is not even possible to establish that prolonged exposure to high density within a dwelling produced stress. And *none* of the studies attempted to isolate the *specific aspects of dwelling density* that might have been associated with cumulative effects. The social pathology hypothesis has received support, but in many ways the evidence is not very illuminating.

CONCLUSIONS

Summary of Major Findings

Table 7 was constructed to identify hypotheses with the best empirical support. It lists hypotheses for which evidence was available from five or more studies, where at least half of the studies show supportive findings. (These criteria were, of course, arbitrary.) Of the 43 hypotheses identified in the review, 10 met the

TABLE 7
Hypotheses Supported by Current Research Evidence

Hypothesis	Research Findings	
	Supportive	Total
1. Small room size (high spatial density) produces crowding, discomfort, or other negative moods/states.	18	29
7. In *brief exposures* to a constant sized area, increases in group size are associated with crowding or discomfort.	6	9
8. In *prolonged exposures* to a constant sized area, increases in group size are associated with crowding or discomfort.	7	9
12. Crowding is more likely when a group works together or interacts than when members work alone.	4	6
20. In brief exposures to high room density in same-sex groups, males react more negatively to others than in low room density, but females react more positively to others in high than low room density.	9	18
24. A person with a history of intense or frequent social stimulation shows greater toleration for high density than does a person with a history of relative isolation (*adaptation-level effect*).	4	5
25. Performance of *complex tasks* is poorer during brief exposures to high room density than to low room density.	3	6
35c. Prolonged exposure to high household density is associated with poor health.	11	15
35d. Prolonged exposure to high household density is associated with crime or aggression.	4	5
36a. Prolonged exposure to high neighborhood density is associated with withdrawal from interaction among males.	4	5

Note: "Supported" means that the hypothesis was examined in at least five studies, of which at least one-half showed supportive findings.

criteria for inclusion in Table 7. Most of the remaining hypotheses had been examined in four or fewer studies, and for most the evidence was mixed. The first
four of the hypotheses with support as defined here indicate that crowding does
indeed occur under conditions of high social or spatial density within rooms,
especially if the occupants talked with one another. This conclusion hardly comes
as a surprise. In terms of the sequential model of crowding outlined earlier, the
evidence indicates that high room density represents an antecedent of crowding.
However, there is a conspicuous shortage of empirical evidence on the *specific
aspects of high density that produce stress.*

Hypothesized agents of crowding usually represent forms of *social overload*
(from excess immediacy or large groups) or *thwarting* (or goal blocking). However, neither hypothesis was studied enough to meet the criterion adopted for
support. For now, it appears that the best established antecedent of crowding
is high density. Unfortunately, the term *high density* has referred to a wide variety of conditions, determined by the type of density (household, neighborhood,
etc.), the way it was measured, and the duration of exposure, among other
things. Establishing that high density is an agent of crowding leaves many questions unanswered.

Two hypotheses regarding personality variables received support. First, nine
of 18 studies indicated that during brief exposures to crowded, same-sex groups,
females react positively to others, whereas males react negatively. Most of the
evidence for this effect comes from the laboratory; it is by no means clear that
the effect appears elsewhere. The second personality variable, a person's history
of social stimulation, may be important in determining crowding; evidence for
an adaptation level effect is limited but quite consistent.

As for consequences of crowding, one immediate, observable effect is poor
performance of complex tasks under some conditions, such as having two things
to do at once. This effect was not particularly well established. Evidence regarding coping responses to crowding was very sparse.

Three cumulative effects of crowding and/or exposure to high density emerged:
poor health, crime or agression, and withdrawal (among males). The origins of
these effects are unclear. Are they "costs" of coping with high density, or of a
failure to cope? Here is evidence consistent with the social pathology hypothesis.
The data are mainly correlational, and in some cases based on aggregates, but the
trends are reasonably consistent. Unfortunately, the dynamics of the effects
remain to be specified.

Directions for the Future

At its current pace, research on crowding will almost certainly make this review
obsolete before it goes to press. There are many obvious gaps in the research to
date. Perhaps the most critical one concerns the specific aspects of high density
that *sometimes* make it stressful. Once the antecedents of crowding are properly
specified, two things become possible. First, the concept of density can be more

clearly defined or replaced. As currently used, it is quite imprecise; the term *high density* has many meanings. Second, it may be possible to develop a taxonomy of high density situations that do consistently produce stress.[12] Such a task will no doubt be complicated by the necessity to recognize the effects of modifying variables, such as sex, adaptation level, and primary versus secondary environment.

A second, larger task also remains: to elaborate the sequence of events that follow the antecedents of crowding. For example: Social overload $\rightarrow$ stress $\rightarrow$ coping $\rightarrow$ reduced stress $\rightarrow$ aftereffects. Evidence related to coping and aftereffects does point to the utility of such a sequential model of crowding, but many questions remain, such as these:

1. Under what conditions and over what periods of time does adaptation occur in response to stress-producing social conditions?
2. What types of coping responses accompany aversive social conditions and under what conditions do they reduce stress?
3. What are the specific antecedents of the aftereffects observed to follow exposure to high density?
4. Under what conditions do cumulative effects of aversive social conditions emerge? Are these effects accompanied by shifts in adaptation level?

With empirically based answers to these questions, we will be much closer to understanding the phenomena we call *crowding*.

APPENDIX: SUMMARY TABLES OF RESEARCH FINDINGS

The review presented in this chapter was based on the following summary of the findings of 83 empirical papers. The findings were abstracted in terms of the sequential model of crowding shown in Table 1 in the body of the chapter.

Types of Research

For convenience of presentation, the studies were grouped into four categories. (1) *Laboratory experiments* include studies in which the researchers brought people into prepared settings and exposed them to one or more different sets of conditions related to crowding. Laboratory experiments lasted from five minutes to eight hours. (2) *Field research based on comparisons of groups* includes experiments and observational studies in settings more or less "natural" for the participants. These studies include long-term exposure to various conditions of density (e.g., Baron et al., 1976; Smith & Haythorn, 1972) and brief exposures (e.g., Aiello & Capriglione, Note 1). A few studies were arbitrarily classified as

---

[12]This idea was suggested by Daniel Stokols in a personal communication.

field research because the primary variable of interest was based on a person's residence and was not under direct control of the researchers (e.g., Baum et al. 1975). (3) *Correlational studies based on data from individuals* include field studies the results of which were reported mainly as correlation coefficients or regression equations. Many were based on questionnaires or surveys. (4) *Correlational studies based on aggregate data* consist primarily of analyses of census data; the units of analysis are groups of persons such as census tracts or city blocks. The studies of aggregates all controlled for socioeconomic factors (a few studies were excluded because their results were confounded by socioeconomic factors).

Classification of Results

For laboratory experiments, the findings from each study are listed as psychological responses, behavioral reactions, or aftereffects. *Psychological responses* refer to: (1) any paper-and-pencil measure (except a puzzle or task); and (2) any physiological measure used to reflect stress or arousal. *Behavioral reactions* include any overt behavior *during* exposure to the independent variable; most behavioral reactions were either: (1) verbal or nonverbal responses to other people; or (2) scores on performance of tasks. *Aftereffects* include behaviors that occurred immediately *after* exposure to the independent variable(s), usually in a separate setting.

For *field research,* the same categories of findings were used, but the distinction between behavioral reactions and aftereffects was not as clear. Aftereffects included cumulative effects as well as immediate aftereffects. When the independent variable was under the researcher's control and the behavior occurred *during* exposure to experimental conditions, the finding was listed as a behavioral reaction (e.g., Hutt & Vaizey, 1966). Otherwise, the behavior was called an aftereffect. (This rule was not applied to questionnaire data collected after exposure to varied conditions of density; questionnaire responses were always classified as psychological rsponses.)

In reports of correlational research, the data are listed in terms of variables correlated with either density or crowding; after each variable of interest follows a list of variables correlated with it, with the sign of the correlation in parentheses. (If a positive relationship held only for males or only for females, it is noted as +M or +F.) Different types of density are defined in a separate column, as are control variables.

Reporting Results

Findings are significant at $p < .05$ unless otherwise noted. (In a few cases in which the dependent measure was an overt behavior, a marginal effect is noted. Virtually all marginal effects on questionnaires were ignored.) Often the results listed for a particular study represent only *part* of the findings. These cases are indicated with a note that there are "other effects." Many studies included several different measures of stress or crowding; when several measures appeared redundant, only those judged critical were listed. If an independent variable was not a plausible antecedent of crowding, its main effects were omitted, but its interactions with density were reported (e.g., success-failure or style of leadership). Double and triple interactions were simplified by reporting only the most extreme means. The tables indicate cases in which measures were taken but no effects were found, unless the finding of no effects was accompanied by findings of effects on similar measures. [For example, Evans (1975) found effects of room size on the performance of one of two dual tasks. This finding was listed as an effect.] "No effects" means no effects on any measures in the category under examination.

Abbreviations

To conserve space, words that appear frequently in research on crowding were abbreviated, and the periods that normally follow abbreviations were omitted ("gp" means group; "rm" means room; "beh" means behavior; "sm" means small; "lg" means large; "perf" means performance; "compet" means competitive or competition). Other abbreviations were made when they seemed appropriate. In the tables on correlational research, different types of density are labeled "D_1" or "D_2" and defined; the definitions vary from study to study.

Reading the Tables

In order of their appearance, the tables list laboratory experiments (Table A), field studies based on comparisons of groups (Table B), field-correlational studies based on data from individuals (Table C), and correlational studies based on aggregates (Table D). In each table, studies are listed alphabetically.

TABLE A
Summary of Laboratory Research

Study	Subjects & Situation	Density & Other Independent Variables	Psychological Responses			Immediate Behavioral Reactions	Aftereffects
			Stress, Crowding or Mood	Liking and Other Responses			
Aiello, Epstein, & Karlin (Note 2) (Study #1)	120 male & female students in same-sex gps of six (30 min).	*Spatial density* (lg or sm rm); *sex;* *trials* (5 blocks of 3 trials); *order of exposure.*	*Skin conductance* (index of arousal) higher in sm rm; increased over time).	—		—	—
(Study #2)	20 male & female students alone (30 min).	*Spatial density* (lg or sm rm); *sex;* *trials;* *order of exp.*	*Skin conductance* lower than in gps; interaction of density, trials, and order of exp.	—		—	—
Baum & Davis (1976)	80 male & female students in lab asked to place miniature figures in "rooms."	*Visual complexity* (high or low); *color* (light or dark); *situation* (cocktail party or waiting rm).	*Crowding:* higher in dark rm, esp with hi complexity in waiting rm.	*Rm size:* larger for light color, esp with hi complexity in waiting rm (Other effects.)		*Figure placement:* more in light rm.	—

Baum & Greenberg (1975)	80 male & female students in waiting rm; 2 same-sex confeds enter.	*Spatial density* (lg or sm rm); *sex.*	*Crowding, expected crowding & discomfort:* higher when expecting gp of 10.	*Liking for confed:* lower when expecting gp of 10. (Other effects.)	*Affiliative responses to confed:* Ss sat farther away, looked less at confed when expecting gp of 10. *Seat positions:* more toward corners of rm if expecting gp of 10.	—
Baum & Koman (1976)	64 male & female students waiting in rm; 2 same-sex confeds enter.	*Spatial density* (lg or sm rm); *social density* (expected gp of 5 or 10); *expected structure* (leader or no leader); *sex.*	*Crowding:* higher with lg gp, low str; in lg gps, higher in sm rm than lg rm; in sm gps in sm rm, higher for men than women. (Other effects.)	(Effects on perception of rm.)	*Seat position:* less central for lg gp, low str; more central for lg rm than sm rm; in sm rm, sm gp, men more central than women. *Facial regard:* in sm gp, lower in sm rm; in lg gp, lower with low str.	—
Bergman (1971)	144 male students working on tasks.	*Social density* (gps of 3, 6 or 12); *distance* (4 inches or 3 ft, side-to-side); *success vs. failure* on test.	*Discomfort & palmar sweat:* higher at close dist. (Other effects.)	*Gp atmosphere:* warmer at close dist. (Other effects.)	*Perf of simple tasks:* no effects.	—

(continued)

TABLE A (continued)

| Study | Subjects & Situation | Density & Other Independent Variables | Psychological Responses | | | Immediate Behavioral Reactions | Aftereffects |
			Stress, Crowding or Mood	Liking and Other Responses			
Cohen, Sladen, & Bennett (1975)	80 male & female students asked to place figures in miniature rms.	Situation (social or nonsocial); activity (work or recreation); acquaintance (friends or str); Sex.	—	—		Figure placement: more in nonsocial activities; more in recreation; fewest in nonsocial work; more with acq; more with social, acq; more with working & acq than working & str.	—
Cozby (1973)	72 female students asked to rate miniature rms. (Measures of personal space had been taken earlier.)	No. of figures in rms; personal space (P.S.) (approach dist); activity (party or studying).	Crowding: higher in hi density "rms." Liking for rm: higher for hi density party & low density; for close PS, higher in hi density.	Personal space: positive corr with no. of persons per room in family. (Other effects.)		—	—

Desor (1972) (Study #1)	20 male & female students asked to place figures in miniature rms.	*Partitions* (3 types or none); *activity* (social or nonsocial); *standing vs sitting; sex.*	—	—	*Figure placement:* fewer with no partitions, with nonsocial (females only) and with seated figures.	—
(Study #2)	30 male & female students, same method.	*"Room" size.*	—	—	*Figure placement:* more as rm size increased. (Other effects).	—
(Study #3)	10 male & female students, same method.	*Doors* (2 or 6); *shape* of rm (square or rectangular); *activity* (social or nonsocial); *standing or seated; sex.*	—	—	*Figure placement:* more in 2-dr rect than 2-dr sq rms; more in 2-dr rect than 6-dr rect; fewer with nonsocial. (Other effects.)	—
Dooley (1974)	227 male students working on tasks in gps (40 min).	*Social density* (gps of 1, 3, or 6); *personal space* PS (approach dist close or far).	*Crowded, restricted:* higher with lg gps; higher with far PS.	*Perceived friendliness:* lower in lg gps; lower with far PS. (Other effects.)	*Perf of "marketing" task:* no effects of gp size; poorer with far PS.	*Proofreading* fewer lines in lg gps; more errors with far PS. *Volunteering for later discussions;* less with far PS.

(continued)

77

TABLE A *(continued)*

Study	Subjects & Situation	Density & Other Independent Variables	Psychological Responses			Immediate Behavioral Reactions	Aftereffects
			Stress, Crowding or Mood	Liking and Other Responses			
Emiley (Note#9) (Study#1)	48 male students working on tasks in gps of 4 (40 min).	*Spatial density* (lg or sm rm, varied with tables).	*Crowded:* higher in hi density.	*Rated adequacy of space:* lower in hi density.		*Task perf:* no effects.	– –
(Study#2)	144 male students working on tasks in gps of 4 (40 min).	*Spatial density* (lg or sm rm, varied with tables); *attraction* to gp (hi, med, or lo).	*Crowded:* higher in hi density.	*Rated adequacy of space:* lower in sm rm.		*Task perf* in sm rm (poorest for moderately attracted gps). *Verbal beh:* higher total in sm rm; more negative comments in sm rm; more neutral comments by highly or moderately attracted gps in sm rm.	– –

					Task perf
Epstein & Karlin (1975)	84 male & female students in same-sex gps of 6 (measures taken after density manipulation was finished).	Spatial density (lg or sm rm); sex.	Crowdedness, confinement, lack of privacy, competition for space: higher in sm rm. (Other effects.)	Evaluation of gps: higher for women in sm rm. Perceived similarity: higher for women in sm rm & men in lg rm. Group cohesiveness: lowest for men in sm rm. (Other effects.)	—	No effects on complex tasks; better perf of simple tasks by people from sm rm. Seating dispersion: more women from sm rm chose peripheral seating than from lg rm. Prisoner's dilemma: more competitive choices among men from sm rm, women from lg rm.
Evans (1975)	100 male & female students in mixed gps of 10 working on tasks (120 min)	Spatial density (lg or sm rm); sex.	Crowded, stress, uncomfortable: higher in sm rm Heart rate, blood pressure (indices of stress): higher after sm rm.	Hostility: greater in sm rm. Rated adequacy of facilities: lower in sm rm.	Perf of matrix task: poorer in sm rm Perf of secondary task: poorer in sm rm. Other tasks: no effect	Persistence in tracing task (partly impossible): greater after lg rm.

(continued)

TABLE A *(continued)*

| | | | Psychological Responses | | | |
Study	Subjects & Situation	Density & Other Independent Variables	Stress, Crowding or Mood	Liking and Other Responses	Immediate Behavioral Reactions	Aftereffects
Freedman, Heshka, & Levy (1975b)	Male & female students in mixed or all-female gps of 6 to 10.	*Spatial density* (lg or sm rm); *positive or negative feedback about speech to gp.*	*Crowded:* higher in sm rm.	*Liked other speeches, liked other people, would participate again:* all highest in sm rm—pos feedback; lowest in sm rm—neg feedback. *No. of people the rm could hold:* smaller in sm rm.	—	—
Freedman, Heshka, & Levy, (1975c)	133 male students in gps of 6 to 8 working on task (120 min).	*Spatial density* (lg or sm rm); *success or failure on task.*	—	*Liking for others, friendliness:* higher in sm rm. *Participate again, lively, not boring, good experience:* all highest in sm rm. —success; lowest in sm rm. —failure.	*Task perf:* better in sm rm.	—

Freedman, Klevansky, & Ehrlich (1971) (Study #1)	126 male & female students in mixed or same-sex gps, working on tasks (3 60-min sessions).	*Spatial density* (lg or sm rm); *social density* (gps of 5 or 9); *sex.*	—	*Perf of 7 different tasks:* no effects.	—
(Study #2)	306 male & female students in same-sex gps of 7 to 9 working on tasks (2 60-min sessions).	*Spatial density* (lg or sm rm); *motivation* (bonus or no bonus for good performance); *sex.*	—	*Perf of 3 simple tasks:* no effects.	—
(Study #3)	180 women aged 25-60 in gps of 9 working on tasks (2 240-min sessions).	*Spatial density* (lg or sm rm).	—	*Perf of 3 simple tasks:* no effects.	—
Freedman, Levy, Buchanan, & Price (1972) (Study #1)	136 males & females students in same-sex gps of 4 working on tasks (240 min).	*Spatial density* (lg or sm rm); *sex.*	—	*Compet in prisoner's dilemma:* higher for males in sm rm than in lg rm; lower for females in sm rm than in lg rm.	—

(continued)

TABLE A (continued)

Study	Subjects & Situation	Density & Other Independent Variables	Psychological Responses			Immediate Behavioral Reactions	Aftereffects
			Stress, Crowding or Mood	Liking and Other Responses			
Freedman, Levy, Buchanan, & Price, (1972) (Study #2)	191 males & females in same-sex gps of 12 working on tasks (240 min).	Spatial density (lg or sm rm); white noise; sex.	Pleasantness: higher for males in lg rm & females in sm rm.	Liking for others, friendliness: higher for males in lg & females in sm rm.		Sentences in simulated jury deliberation: least severe among females in sm rm.	—
(Study #3)	67 males & females in mixed-sex gps of 12 working on tasks (240 min).	Spatial density (lg or sm rm).	No effects.	No effects.		No effects.	—
Freedman & Staff (1975)	Males & females in mixed or same-sex gps of 4 or 5.	Spatial density (lg or sm rm); positive or negative feedback about speech to gp; source of feedback (inside or outside gp).	Anxiety: lower in sm rm.	Liking for gp: higher in sm rm; highest for sm rm—positive feedback, lowest for sm rm—negative feedback. (Other effects.)		—	—

Study	Sample	Independent variables				
Greenberg, Lichtman, & Firestone (Note 10)	48 male students waiting in rm with one confed, six chairs present.	*Spatial density* (lg or sm waiting rm); *cooperative or competitive task.*	*Crowded:* higher in sm rm.	*Compet of confed:* in coop condition, higher in sm rm.	*Head movements:* more away from confed in sm rm; more upward movements in sm rm. *Other nonverbal beh:* no effects.	—
Griffitt & Veitch (1971)	121 male & female students in same-sex gps in environmental chamber, working on individual tasks (45 min +).	*Social density* (gps of 3-5 or 12-16); *temperature* (hot or cool); *similarity* of stranger described in dossier.	*Mood:* more positive in sm gp and in cool temp. *Comfort:* higher in sm gp and in cool temp. (Other effects.)	*Liking for stranger:* greater in sm gp and in cool temp. (Other effects.)	—	—
Joy & Lehmann (Note 13)	92 male students in rm with experimenter, working on tasks (120 min).	*Spatial density* (lg or sm rm); *social density* (gps of 3 or 5).	*Crowding:* higher in sm rm; higher lg gps. *negative affect toward experiment:* higher in lg gps.	*Preference for complex figures:* no effects in sm rm. *Preference for structure:* no effects. *Positive affect toward others:* higher in sm gps.	—	*Recall of other's characteristics:* less in lg gps. *Cognitive flexibility:* lower in lg gps. *Personal space:* larger zones in lg rm. *Proofreading:* poorest performance in lg gp, sm rm.

(continued)

TABLE A (continued)

Study	Subjects & Situation	Density & Other Independent Variables	Psychological Responses			Immediate Behavioral Reactions	Aftereffects
			Stress, Crowding or Mood	Liking and Other Responses			
Keating & Snowball (Note 14)	210 female students in gps of 9-12 (about 40 min).	Spatial density (lg or sm rm); personalization (name tags or no tags).	--	Help from gp. Cooperative, Understang gp ideas: lower in sm rm. Friendly: higher with no tags. Frustrating: higher with tags. Ratings of art: no effects.		--	--
Marshall & Heslin (1975)	284 male & female students in discussion gps (90 min).	Spatial density (lg or sm rm); social density (gps of 4 or 16); sex composition (same-sex or mixed); sex.	Mood: Females most positive in lg mixed gp; males most positive in mixed gp.	Liking: females higher in sm rm, same-sex gp, & lg rm, mixed gp; males higher in sm rm, mixed gp. Desire to remain: for lg gps, greater in mixed than in same-sex gps. Liking for gp: females liked sm same-sex gps or lg mixed gps; males liked mixed gps.		--	--

Study	Sample	Variables	Results 1	Results 2	Results 3	Results 4
McClelland (1974)	164 males & female students in mixed-sex gps of 6, working on tasks (90 min).	*Spatial density* (lg or sm rm); *necessity for interaction; previous acquaintance* (moderate or none); *sex*	*Crowding:* higher in sm rm; higher with hi interaction. *Upset & task dissatisfaction:* no differences for unacq; for acq, highest for hi interaction. sm rm & lo interaction lg rm. (Other effects.)	*Perceived interference:* higher with hi interaction. *Dislike others:* for males, highest in low interaction, for females, lowest in sm rm, hi interaction (Other effects.)	*Perf of bibliography task:* lower for hi interaction; lower in sm rm; lowest in sm rm, hi interaction. *No. of others in diagram of rm:* lowest for females in lg rm, lo interaction.	*Proofreading:* poorest performance with hi interaction. *Stroop test;* no effects of rm size or interaction.
Poe (Note 16)	64 male students working in gps on tasks (150 min).	*Spatial density* (9 or 18 sq ft per person); *social density* (gps of 4 or 8); *trials.*	*Comfort:* higher in lg rm on 1st trial. *Anxiety, sadness:* in gps of 4 no differences; in gps of 8, higher in lg rm. *Neg. emotion:* in gps of 4, higher in sm rm; in gps of 8, higher in lg rm *Pos. emotion:* higher in gps of 4. (Other effects.)	*Liking:* increased over time; higher in sm rm. *Liking for gp:* increased over time; higher in gps of 4 on 3rd trial. *Participate again:* in gps of 4, higher in lg rm; in gps of 8, higher in lg rm. (Other effects.)	*Anagram task:* performance increased over time. *Mock jury:* for 5 cases, inconsistent effects (on 1st case, higher guilt in sm rm).	*Anagram task:* improved performance in gps of 8, poorer in gps of 4.

(continued)

TABLE A (continued)

Study	Subjects & Situation	Density & Other Independent Variables	Psychological Responses			Immediate Behavioral Reactions	Aftereffects
			Stress, Crowding or Mood	Liking and Other Responses			
Rall, Stokols, & Russo (Note 17)	81 male & female students waiting for interview with same-sex student.	*Spatial density* (lg or sm rm); *threatening or nonthreatening interview; sex.*	*Crowding:* higher in sm rm; higher for women in sm rm & men in lg rm. *Anticipated crowding:* higher with threat.	— —		*Chair placement:* farther from interviewer in sm rm and in high threat; greater pivot with threat. (Other effects.)	— —
Ross, Layton, Erickson, & Schopler (1973)	192 male & female students in same-sex gps of 8 working on tasks (5 or 20 min).	*Spatial density* (lg or sm rm); *duration; sex.*	*Crowding:* higher in sm rm. (Other effects.)	*Self-ratings:* more positive for males in lg rm & females in sm rm. *Ratings of others:* more positive for males in sm rm.		*Facial regard* (marginal trend): higher for males in lg rm & females in sm rm.	— —

86

Study	Subjects / Procedure	Independent Variables			
Saegert (1974)	126 male & female students in same-sex gps, working on tasks (75 min).	Spatial density (6 or 24 sq ft per person); social density (gps of 1, 2, 4, 12); sex.	Crowding & discomfort: higher in lgr gps & sm rm. Palmar sweat (index of anxiety): higher for lgr gps & sm rm. Anxiety: females in sm rm higher than females in lg rm; males, no differences. (Other effects.)	Perceived interference: higher for lg gps, sm rm (Other effects.)	Perf of card collection task: worse as gp size increased. Word associates: more as gp size increased.	—
Schopler & Walton (Note 18)	168 male & female students in same-sex gps of 6 in sm rm, waiting for gp task.	Expected structure of task; expected pleasantness of task; internal or external locus of control; sex.	Crowding: internals lower than externals; high str lower than low str. Affect: high str more positive than lo str; pleasant task more positive than unpleasant task.	Self-ratings: more positive in low str; more positive with pleasant task.	—	—
Sherrod (1974)	71 female students in gps of 8 working on tasks (120 min).	Spatial density (lg or sm rm); control (Ss told they could leave or told nothing).	Crowdedness: higher in sm rm.	—	Perf of simple tasks: no effects.	Persistence in problem solving: lower in sm rm; lowest in lo contr sm rm. Proofreading: no effects.

(continued)

TABLE A *(continued)*

Study	Subjects & Situation	Density & Other Independent Variables	Psychological Responses			Immediate Behavioral Reactions	Aftereffects
			Stress, Crowding or Mood	Liking and Other Responses			
Stokols, Rall, Pinner & Schopler (1973)	512 male & female students in same-sex gps of 8 working on tasks (70 min).	Spatial density (lg or sm rm); cooperative or competitive tasks; sex.	Crowding: greater in sm rm; greater with compet task. Comfort: lower in sm rm. (Other effects.)	Others' aggressiveness: higher in coop task; higher for females in lg rm & males in sm rm. Self-aggressiveness: higher for males in sm rm & females in lg rm.		Laughter: more in sm rm; more in compet gps; more in sm rm with compet task & lg rm with coop task. Hostile remarks: more from males. Task performance: higher for males; no other effects. Recall of names: higher for males in lg rm & females in sm rm. (Other effects.)	--

Stokols & Resnick (Note 21) (Study #1)	108 male & female students in mixed gps of 6 in sm rm working on tasks (18 min).	*Social climate* (evaluative or "get acquainted").	*Crowding:* no effects.	*Liking:* no effects.	—	*Chair distance* (in different rm): greater in eval gps.
(Study #2)	144 male & female students in mixed gps of 8 in sm rm working on tasks (18 min).	*Social climate* (evaluative or "get acquainted").	*Crowding:* higher in evaluative gps.	*Friendliness:* lower in eval gp.	*Self-manipulation* (index of tension, marginal effect): higher in eval gp. *Name recall:* fewer in eval gp.	*Time spent standing:* greater in eval gps. *Proofreading:* no effects. *Chair distance:* no effects.
Sundstrom (1975a)	96 male students in gps of 6, including 3 confederates, dyadic conversations (about 40 min.)	*Spatial density* (lg or sm rm); *intrusion* (touching & eye-contact by confed); *goal blocking* (inattention & interruption by confed); *trials* (3 conversations).	*Crowding:* higher in sm rm. *Comfort:* lower in sm rm; lower with intrusion, goal blocking, or both; increased over time. *Irritation:* increased over time with goal blocking; decreased over time with no goal blocking.	*Liking:* no effects. *Self-disclosure:* lowest with intrusion & goal blocking; increased over time.	*Facial regard:* lower in sm rm; lower with intrusion; lower with goal blocking. *Gesturing:* less with goal blocking. *Head nodding:* less with goal blocking. *Object manipulation* (index of stress): higher in sm rm on first trial.	—

(continued)

TABLE A *(continued)*

Study	Subjects & Situation	Density & Other Independent Variables	Psychological Responses			Immediate Behavioral Reactions	Aftereffects
			Stress, Crowding or Mood	Liking and Other Responses			
Wicker & Kirmeyer (1977) (Study #1)	192 male students working on "slot car task" in gps.	*Social density* (gps of 2 or 3); *required no. of persons* (2 or 3).	– –	*Feeling needed & involved:* lower for gps of 3 with 2 req'd. (Other effects.)		*Perf of slot-car task* (marginal); lower for gps of 3 with 2 req'd.	– –
(Study #2)	180 male students working on "slot car task" in gps of 4.	*Required no. of persons* (2, 4, or 6).	*Crowding:* highest with 2 req'd.	*Feeling needed & involved:* lowest with 6 req'd, highest with 2 req'd (Other effects.)		*Perf:* no effects of no. req'd (Other effects.)	– –

| Worchel & Teddlie (1976) | 283 male students in gps of 7 or 8 working on tasks (37 min). | *Spatial density* (lg or sm rm); *interpersonal distance* (chairs touching or 19.5 inches apart); *presence of pictures.* | *Crowded, confined, uncomfortable:* for far dist, higher in sm rm; for close dist, no differences. *Uncomfortable, confined, ill at ease:* for close dist, lower with pictures; for far dist, no differences. *Estimated elapsed time* (index of stress): higher for close dist, no pictures and for sm rm (in sm rm, pictures reduced the effect). | *Presence of leader:* more with close dist. *Recall for names:* poorer at close dist; poorer with no pictures. *Distracted:* higher at close dist; *Friendly:* higher in lg rm; higher with far dist; higher with pictures; lowest with close dist, no pictures. (Other effects.) | *Word formation task:* poorer with close dist; poorest with close dist, no pictures. *Johnny Rocco task:* more punitive with close dist, no pictures. | — |

TABLE B

Summary of Field Research Based on Comparisons of Groups

Study	Subjects & Setting	Density & other Independent Variables	Psychological Responses	Immediate Behavioral Reactions	Aftereffects
Aiello & Capriglione (Note 1)	56 males & females aged 60-90 yrs, in same-sex gps of 4 in field settings (portable chamber of wood panels).	Spatial density (sm or lg chamber).	Crowded, friendly: higher in sm rm. Aggressive, afraid: lower in sm rm. Skin conductance (index of arousal): highest for males in sm rm, increased over time (larger increases with females and with sm rm). (Other effects.)	Tajfel task: lower cohesiveness in lg rm (marginal).	— —
Aiello, Epstein & Karlin (Note 2)	75 male & female college students; college dormitory rms built for 2 students.	Social density: 2 per rm (doubled) or 3 per rm (tripled) for 1 semester; sex.	Crowdedness & dissatisfaction: higher in tripled rms; higher for tripled women than tripled men. Cortisol level (measure of stress): no effects.	Task perf: for doubled Ss increased over time; for tripled Ss, increased over time with simple tasks, decreased over time with complex tasks.	Health problems: most frequent for tripled women. Dissolution of roommates: highest for tripled women.

Aiello, Love, & Epstein (Note 3)	44 male & female students living in dormitory rms built for 2 students, brought to student lounge for 3 separate sessions.	*Social density:* ("doubled"—2 students per rm— or "tripled"—3 students per rm); *sessions* (1, 2, or 3); *sex*.	— —	*Axis:* females more direct over time; males less direct over time; effect pronounced in "doubled" females and "tripled" males. *Vocalization:* increased over time. *Figure placement:* females placed self-figures closer to roommate than did males. *Interpersonal dist:* no effects of density. (Other effects.)
Baron, Mandel, Adams, & Griffen (1976)	144 male residents of college dormitory in rms designed for 2 students.	*Social density* (double or triple occupancy).	— —	*Crowdedness, crampedness:* higher for triples. *Perceived control:* lower for triples. *Liking for roommates:* lower for triples. *Factor structure of dimensions of crowding:* more complex for doubles. (Other effects.)
Baum, Harpin, & Valins (1975)	Male & female college students; 2 college dormitories	*Corridor or Suite* residence.	— —	Use of gps to solve problems. Similar attitudes with neighbors. *Close to neighbors:* lower in corridors. *Crowded, avoid others:* higher in corridors. (Other effects.) *Group consensus in laboratory after discussion:* greater for suite mates than corridor neighbors.

(continued)

TABLE B *(continued)*

Study	Subjects & Setting	Density & other Independent Variables	Psychological Responses	Immediate Behavioral Reactions	Aftereffects
Baum & Valins (1973)	50 male & 50 female students in dorm rms, asked to place figures in "rooms."	*Suite or Corridor* design dormitory rm. *Type of* "*room*" (bedroom, reference rm, rec lounge).	*Crowding in actual dorm:* higher for corridor.	*Figure placement:* for corridor, fewer in bedroom than for suite but more in ref rm than for suite.	—
Bickman et al. (1973) (Study #1)	Male & female college students; 3 college dormitories.	*Outside density:* (dwelling units per structure).	*Rated friendliness:* lowest in hi density *Rated coop* inversely related to density.	—	*Returns of "lost letters":* highest in lo density, lowest in hi density dorms.
(Study #2)	Male & female college students; different set of dormitories.	*Outside density:* (dwellings per structure).	*Ratings of others:* less positive in hi density, more positive in lo density. *Ratings of buildings:* more positive in lo density, more negative in hi density.	—	*Returns of "lost letters":* highest in lo density, lowest in hi density. *Giving milk cartons for "project":* highest in lo density, lowest in hi density.
D'Atri (1975)	251 male inmates at 3 correctional institutions.	*Social density* (single cells or dormitory).	*Subjective crowding:* positively corr with blood pressure. *Systolic & diastolic blood pressure:* higher in dorms than singles.	—	—

Hutt & McGrew (Note 12) (Study #1)	15 children aged 3 to 8, in play-rooms at 2 nurseries.	*Group size* (changed by adding extra children; 6 or fewer, 7 to 11, 12 or more). *Playroom*: rectangular or clover-shaped.	—	*Territorial beh.* (attempts to defend space): higher in clover-shaped rm, but only for med & lg gps.	—
(Study #2)	4 male & 4 female children in 2 Oxford nursery schools (both indoors and outdoors).	*Spatial density* (space available; ranged from 496 sq ft to 33 sq ft per child).	—	*Nonagonistic social behavior*: higher in hi density. *Agonistic beh*: higher in hi density. *Interaction with adults*: higher in hi density.	—
Hutt & Vaizey (1966)	15 boys & girls aged 3 to 9; playroom at hospital.	*Social density* (gps of 5, 7 to 9, or 12, children added to vary density). *Diagnosis*: normal, brain-damaged or autistic.	—	*Aggressive beh.*: for normals, highest in lg gp. *Interaction*: for normals, progressively less with increased gp size. (Other effects.)	—
Ittelson, Proshansky, & Rivlin (1972)	108 psychiatric patients; wards in private, city & state hospitals.	*Social density* (no. of patients who slept in a bedroom).	—	*"Isolated passive" beh*: increased with size of bedroom. *"Social" beh*: decreased with size of bedroom. (Other effects.)	—

(continued)

TABLE B (continued)

Study	Subjects & Setting	Density & other Independent Variables	Psychological Responses	Immediate Behavioral Reactions	Aftereffects
Loo (1972)	60 male and female preschool children in mixed gps of 6 in a playroom.	*Spatial density* (lg or sm rm); *sex*.	—	*Aggression:* higher in lg rm; higher for boys than girls in lg rm. *Interaction:* lower in sm rm. *Interruptions:* more freq in sm rm (marginal). *Dominance:* for girls, higher in sm rm.	—
Loring (1956)	83 matched pairs of families in Boston.	*Disorganization* (problems reported to case workers or courts).	—	—	*Rms per family:* fewer in disorganized gp. *Environmental quality index:* lower for disorganized gp. (Other effects.)
MacDonald & Oden (1973)	65 Peace Corps trainees in 12-week, live-in program.	*Spatial density:* (sm or lg quarters). *Single or married:* (single only in lg quarters).	*Friends:* more in sm quarters. *Work with others:* lowest in lg qtrs, married. *Advice from others:* highest in sm qtrs.	*Perf.:* no effects.	—

McGrew (1970)	20 male & female nursery school children aged 3-5; nursery.	*Social density; spatial density.*	—	*"Peer proximity"* (Ss within 2 ft): increased with spatial density. *Solitary behavior:* lg gps, lower in sm rm. (Other effects.)
Paulus, Cox, McCain, & Chandler (1975)	142 male inmates at a prison, asked to place figures in "rooms."	*Social density* (no. of inmates in housing unit); *Spatial density* (sq ft per man); *single cell or dorm. Trial* (measurement 1, 2, or 3); *duration* of imprisonment (long or short).	*Ratings of actual housing unit:* neg correlation with social density.	*Figure placement:* for trials 2 & 3, fewer for dorms; fewer for long-term inmates.
Price (1971)	413 boys & girls in preschool & last grade classrooms in 18 schools.	*Spatial density* (classes averaged 19; rms modified by arranging furniture).	—	*Solitary beh* (play alone, automanipulate): higher in hi density. *Social beh* (contact, play with others): lower in hi density. *Aggression:* no effects. *Activity in general:* higher in lo density. (Other effects.)

(continued)

Study	Subjects & Setting	Density & other Independent Variables	Psychological Responses	Immediate Behavioral Reactions	Aftereffects
Rodin (1976) (Study #1)	32 black males aged 6 to 9 yrs living in same housing proj working on discrimination task in lab.	Social density (no. of persons per household, 2-8).	--	--	Perf in discrimination of multiple reinf contingencies: no differences. Use of "switching key": less as density increased ($r = 0.45$).
(Study #2)	172 male & female students (mostly black) from eighth grade in lab, in same-sex gps of 4, playing games & working on learning task.	Spatial density (lg or sm rm). pretreatment: solvable or unsolvable problem. sex.	--	Correct responses on 2nd series of learning trials: lower with unsolvable first series; no effects of rm size.	Regression analysis (controlling for sex, race no. of parents, educ of parents): residential density and residential density X solvability predicted no. of correct responses in 2nd learning series.
Rohe & Patterson (1974)	12 boys & girls, preschool age; in playroom at day care center.	Spatial density (playroom modified by partition); no. of toys (hi or lo).	--	Aggression: highest with hi density, lo toys. Destruction: highest with hi density, lo toys; lowest in lo density, lo toys. (Other effects.)	--

Study	Subjects	Independent variable			
Saegert, Mackintosh, & West (1975) (Study #1)	28 female students; shoe store.	*Social density* (no. of people in the shoe store).	*Crowding*: corr 0.76 with no. of people. *Descriptions of people*: more positive in hi density.	*Recall for objects in store*: better in lo density.	—
(Study #2)	40 males & females over 18; railroad station.	*Social density; sex*. information about the setting (a map).	*Anxiety, sadness, negative arousal, inadequacy*: all higher in hi density. *Agression & elation*: higher for crowded males.	*Completion of simple tasks*: poorer in hi density	*Stroop test*: hi density females and lo density males performed best.
Smith & Haythorn (1972)	56 men in U.S. Navy isolated in quarters in Naval lab (21 days).	*Spatial density* (lg or sm quarters) *Social density* (gp of 2 or 3); *compatibility* (hi or low); *leadership* (j or s); *days*.	*Anxiety*: increased over time; highest for gps of 2. *Stress*: highest for gps of 3 in sm qtrs during last 11 days. *Hostility*: lower in sm qtrs. (Other effects.)	—	—
Stokols, Smith, & Prostor (1975)	30 females & 62 males, all adults; waiting room at Calif. Dept. of Motor Vehicles.	*Partitions* (none, ropes, or wooden partitions).	*Crowding*: no effects (trend toward more crowding with partitions).	*Self-manipulation* (index of tension): highest with partitions, lowest with no divisions.	—
Tucker & Friedman (1972)	Males & female college students in cafeterias at 3 universities.	*Outside density*: no. of students at university (approx. 35,000, 8000, & 1200).	—	*Size of groups at lunch*: largest in lo density, smallest in hi density. *No. of isolated indiv's*: highest in hi density, lowest in lo density.	—

(continued)

TABLE B *(continued)*

Study	Subjects & Setting	Density & other Independent Variables	Psychological Responses	Immediate Behavioral Reactions	Aftereffects
Valins & Baum (1973) (Study#1)	64 male & female college student residents of dormitories; lab setting.	*Suite or corridor residence.*	*Crowdedness:* lower for suite residents. *Too many people on floor:* lower for suite residents.	—	*Figure placement:* fewer for corridor Ss in 4 settings; more for corridor Ss in reference rm.
(Study#2)	64 male & female college student residents of dormitories, lab setting.	*Suite or corridor residence.*	*Discomfort in lab waiting room:* higher for corridor Ss.	—	*Reactions to confed in laboratory waiting room:* corridor Ss sat farther away & spent less time looking toward confed & initiated fewer conversations.
(Study#3)	64 male & female college students of dormitories; lab setting.	*Suite or corridor residence; expectation of co-op or compet task in lab.*	*Discomfort in waiting room:* higher for corridor Ss, highest in corridor-coop condition.	—	*Seating dist from confed:* farther among corridor Ss in coop condition.
(Study #4)	64 male & female college students residents of dormitories; lab setting.	*Suite or corridor residence; task condition:* cooperative, competitive, coactive, alone.	—	—	*Perf of anagram task:* corridor Ss better in compet & coactive; suite Ss better in coop & alone.

Wohlwill & Kohn (1973) (Study #1)	17 adults & 18 adolescents who had recently moved to Harrisburg, Pa.	Rural or urban (Ss from cities of under 25,000 or over 100,000).	Crowding in shopping: higher for rural. Friendly service: lower for rural. Bigness of Harrisburg, air pollution, noise, pace of life: higher for rural. (Other effects.)	—	—
(Study #2)	74 recent migrants to New York City who viewed photos of cities & towns in a lab.	Size of previous city: large (1.1 million +), medium (152,000-753,000), or small (under 24,000).	Crowding & safety (depicted in photos): highest for lg city gp, lowest for sm city.	—	—
Wolfe (1975)	60 children aged 8-11, with "beh disorders" in psychiatric hospital.	Social density (1, 2, or 4 children per rm); bedroom size (1, 2, or 4 bed).	—	Rm use: highest for singles; for 4-bed, highest for 2-children; for 2-bed, highest for one child. Isolated passive: highest in singles, 2 children with 4 beds; lowest for 1 child, 4 beds, and 2 children, 2 beds. Talking: highest for 1 child, 4 beds, and 1 child, 2 beds. Isolated active: highest for 1 child, 4 beds, and 2 children, 2 beds.	—

TABLE C

Summary of Field-Correlational Studies Based on Data from Individuals

Study	Subjects & Setting	Density & Other Variables Related to Crowding	Control Variables	Variables Correlated with Crowding	Variables Correlated with Density	Other Relationships
Baldassare (1975a)	1013 male residents of Detroit (interview).	D_1 = persons per sq mile (from census); D_2 = % households with $\geqslant 1.01$ persons per rm (census); D_3 = household size	Age; education; income.	—	D_1 = know neighbors (−). D_3 = no. of soc organizations (+).	D_3 relationships due to age of children at home.
Baldassare (1975b)	333 married male residents of Detroit (survey).	D_1 = persons per residential acre (census).	Age; SES; children at home; Yrs in neighborhood; tract income.	D_1 = close with neighborhood friends (+; beta = .11).	—	—

| Booth (Note 4) | 560 families in Toronto census tracts (survey; medical exam). | D_1 = objective household crowding; D_2 = objective neighborhood crowding (both measured by self-report). | Age; income; ethnicity; education. | Subjective household crowding: blood pressure (−F); urinary protein (+M); disease affected by stress (+M); uterine dysfunction (+F); psychiatric impairment (+F); trauma (+); decrement in love (+); argue with spouse (+F); threat to leave (+F); hit children (+M); contact with relatives (−F); hrs sleeping TV (+F); support political protest (+); visit gov't official (+). Subjective neighborhood crowding: trauma (−F); threat to leave (+M); aggression outside household (−M); contact neighbors (−M); voluntary assn (+F); hrs TV (−F); support political activity (+); discuss. | D_1 = cholesterol (+M), stress disease (+M), infectious disease (+M), communicative disease (+M), hit children (+F), sibling quarrel (+F), hrs TV (+F). For children: behind in school, parent-school contact, disease, underweight, under-height (all +). D_2 = cease intercourse (−F), family problems (−F), contact relatives (−M), hrs TV (+F), sleeping (−F). | Males especially affected if they had no previous crowding. |

(continued)

TABLE C *(continued)*

Study	Subjects & Setting	Density & Other Variables Related to Crowding	Control Variables	Variables Correlated with Crowding	Variables Correlated with Density	Other Relationships
Dean, Pugh, & Gunderson (Note 8)	2898 men on U.S. Navy ships (questionnaire).	D_1 = Vol per man.	--	*Crowding:* habitability (–); illness (+); satisfaction (–).	D_1 = perceived crowding (+); D_1 = ship crowding (+); D_1 = habitability (–).	--
Dean, Pugh & Gunderson (1975)	938 men on U.S. ships (questionnaire).	D_1 = perceived amt of space; D_2 = perceived no. of people.	--	--	D_1 = dispensary visits (+) satisfaction (–); D_2 = dispensary visits (+), accidents (+), satisfaction (–).	--
Eoyang (1974)	58 college students living in 58 identical trailer homes (survey).	D_1 = no. of students in trailer; D_2 = shared or private bedroom; D_3 = measure that combines D_1 & D_2 (sm gp, private rm; sm gp, share rm; lg gp, share rm). *Family size.*	--	--	D_1 = ratings of space (+), satisfaction (+); privacy (+) (also other var); D_2 & D_3 = time at home (+), ratings of space (+), satisfaction with privacy (also other var).	Family size and ratings of space (+).

Herrenkohl & Egolf (Note 11)	405 adults who viewed & rated photos of buildings in lab.	Type of dwelling (hi rise, mobile home, single-family, etc.).	Age; sex; ethnicity; education.	Crowding: familiarity with dwelling type (–); desirability (–); having lived in hi-rise (–); having lived in single family (+); urbanization of community (–).	—
Marsella, Escudero, & Gordon (1970)	91 married Filipino men residing in Manila (survey).	D_1 = no. of people per dwelling.	Age; SES.	—	D_1 = 3 clusters of physiological complaints (all +, but 2 attributable to SES).
McClelland & Auslander (Note 15)	78 students viewing slides (laboratory).	D_1 = no. of people (in picture); D_2 = amt of space; interpersonal distance; complexity; escapes.	—	Crowding: pleasantness (–); D_1 (+); D_2 (–); distance orderliness (–); escapes (–).	—
Mitchell (1971)	Data from 3 survey studies of residents, (over 6000 interviews of individuals).	D_1 = sq ft per person within dwelling.	Age; income.	—	D_1 = attitudes toward housing (–); emotional dents); stress (+ for couples in "doubled-up" households); interaction among neighbors & friends (–).

(continued)

TABLE C *(continued)*

Study	Subjects & Setting	Density & Other Variables Related to Crowding	Control Variables	Variables Correlated with Crowding	Variables Correlated with Density	Other Relation- ships
Schiffenbauer, Brown, Perry, Shulack, & Zanzola (1977)	75 female college students in dormitory (survey).	*Floor* (ground, 1, 2, 3, etc.); *lightness of rm; placement of door.*	--	*Crowdedness:* floor (−); lightness (−); placement of door (less crowding with more usable space).	--	--
Sommer & Becker (1971)	422 students in 32 classes conducted in the same rm (questionnaire).	D_1 = class size.	--	--	D_1: complaints about ventilation (+) and rm size (+), satisfaction (−).	--

Stokols & Ohlig (Note 20)	27 college students in college dormitory (subset of Ss in Stokols & Resnick, Note 22).	*Soc environ* in dorm *physical environ* in dorm (ratings during fall qtr).	—	*Crowding:* visits to health center during Winter Qtr (+); visits during Spring (+); visits for whole yr (+).	—	Visits to health center for whole year; ratings of phys env (−), soc env (−).
Stokols & Resnick (Note 22)	32 college students in large classroom (questionnaire).	Perceived crowding in residence.	—	*Perceived crowding in classroom:* physical amenity in classroom (−); social atmosphere in classroom (−); security in classroom (−); crowding in residence (+); social and phys atmosphere in residence (+). (Other var.)	—	—

TABLE D

Summary of Correlational Studies Based on Aggregates

Study	Subjects & Setting	Density & Other variables Related to Crowding	Control Variables	Variables Correlated with Density	Other Relationships
Booth & Welch (Note 5)	Census data from 650 U.S. cities over 25,000.	D_1 = proportion of households with more than one person per rm; D_2 = dwellings per sq. mile; *City size* (larger—over 100,000—or smaller). $D_1 \times D_2$.	*Ethnicity*; *SES*; *population of city region*.	D_1 in large cities – murder rate (+), assault (+), rape (+), robbery (+), larceny (+); D_2 in large cities – manslaughter (+) robbery (+), burglary (+), auto theft (+), larceny (+). (Effects account for 1 to 5% of variance; smaller effects in sm cities; other effects for interaction terms.)	D_1 and D_2 (–); D_1 and income (–); D_1 and education (–).
Booth & Welch (Note 6)	Aggregate data on 65 countries (including the U.S.) from yearbooks and other sources.	D_1 = average no. of persons per rm in a single dwelling; D_2 = no. of occupied dwellings per hectare; $D_1 \times D_2$ interaction.	*Industrialization*; *Urbanization*; *Discrimination*; *Security forces* (in analyses of aggression); *health facilities* (in analyses of health effects).	D_1 = homicide (+; 16% var), civil strife (+), military action (+), war (+), life expectancy (–), infant mortality (+); D_2 = homicide (weak –), civil strife (–), military action (+), war (+), infant mortality (–).	--

Freedman, Heshka, & Levy (1975a)	Aggregate data from 97 standard metropolitan statistical areas in U.S.	D_1 = population per sq. mile.	*Ethnicity; SES; local gov't expenditures; total pop.*	D_1 = no relationship with any of 6 crimes.	—
Freedman, Heshka, & Levy (1975d)	Aggregate data from 334 health areas of New York City.	D_1 = average no. of persons per rm; D_2 = persons per acre.	*Income; ethnicity.*	D_1 and D_2 = terminations of psychiatric treatment (+).	D_1 = income (−); D_2 = income (−); $D_1 = D_2$ − (+).
Galle, Gove, & McPherson (1972)	Aggregate data on 75 community areas of Chicago.	D_1 = persons per rm; D_2 = rooms per dwelling; D_3 = dwellings per structure; D_4 = structures per acre.	*SES; ethnicity.*	D_1 = mortality (+), fertility (+), public assistance rate (+) juvenile delinquency rate (+); D_2 = admissions to mental hospitals (+).	D_1 = independent of persons per acre; D_3 & D_4 = *persons per acre* (+).
Levy & Herzog (1974)	Census data from 125 regional units in Netherlands.	D_1 = persons per rm; D_2 = population density (persons per economic geographic region).	*Migration; heterogeneity; SES.*	D_1 = hosp admissions (−), mental hosp admissions (+), delinquency (−), crime (−), suicide (+), accidental death (+), (also other var); D_2 = death (+), hosp. admissions (+), delinquency (+), crime (+), divorce (+), (other var).	—

(continued)

TABLE D *(continued)*

Study	Subjects & Setting	Density & Other Variables Related to Crowding	Control Variables	Variables Correlated with Density	Other Relationships
Schmitt (1966)	Census data from Honolulu.	D_1 = percent of dwellings with more than one person per room; D_2 = population per acre; D_3 = families over three; (two others also examined).	*Income; education.*	D_1 with D_2 constant = death rate (+), TB (+), VD (+), mental hosp (+), juvenile delin (+), prison (+); D_2 with D_1 constant = none.	——
Winsborough (1965)	Aggregate data from 75 community areas for 1950.	D_1 = persons per acre.	*SES; housing quality; migration.*	D_1 = infant deaths (+), deaths (−), TB (−), public assistance (−).	——

REFERENCE NOTES

1. Aiello, J. R., & Capriglione, L. *Effects of crowding on the elderly*. Unpublished manuscript, Rutgers University, 1975.
2. Aiello, J. R., & Epstein, Y. M., & Karlin, R. A. *Field experimental research on human crowding*. Paper presented at the meeting of the Eastern Psychological Association Convention, New York City, April, 1975.
3. Aiello, J. R., Love, K. D., & Epstein, Y. M. *Effects of crowding on the spatial behavior of dormitory residents*. Unpublished manuscript, Rutgers University, 1975.
4. Booth, A. *Final report: Urban crowding project*. Unpublished manuscript, Ministry of State for Urban Affairs, Canada, August 1975.
5. Booth, A., & Welch, S. *The effects of crowding: A cross-national study*. Unpublished manuscript, Ministry of State for Urban Affairs, Ottawa, Canada, 1973.
6. Booth, A., & Welch, S. *Crowding and urban crime rates*. Paper presented at the meeting of the Midwest Sociological Association, Omaha, Nebraska, 1974.
7. Collette, J., & Webb, S. D. *Urban density, crowding, and stress reactions*. Unpublished manuscript, University of Utah, Salt Lake City, 1975.
8. Dean, L. M., Pugh, W. M., & Gunderson, E. K. *The behavioral effects of crowding: Definitions and methods*. Paper presented at the 83rd Annual Convention of the American Psychological Association, Chicago, September 1975.
9. Emiley, S. F. *The effects of crowding and interpersonal attraction on affective responses, task performance and verbal behavior*. Paper presented at the 82nd annual conference of the American Psychological Association, New Orleans, September 1974.
10. Greenberg, C. I., Lichtman, C. M., & Firestone, I. J. *Behavioral and affective responses to crowded waiting rooms*. Unpublished manuscript, Wayne State University, 1975.
11. Herrenkohl, R. C., & Egolf, B. *Perceived crowding, familiarity and the choice of a residence*. Paper presented at the annual conference of the American Psychological Association, New Orleans, September 1974.
12. Hutt, C., & McGrew, W. C. *Effects of group density upon social behavior in humans*. Paper presented at Symposium on Changes in Behavior with Population Density, Annual Conference of the Association for the Study of Animal Behavior, Oxford, England, July 1967.
13. Joy, V. D., & Lehmann, N. *The cost of crowding: Responses and adaptations* (Rev. version). Unpublished manuscript, New York State Department of Mental Hygiene, 1976.
14. Keating, J. P., & Snowball, H. *The effects of crowding and depersonalization on the perception of group atmosphere*. Paper presented at the Annual Conference of the Western Psychological Association, San Francisco, April, 1974.
15. McClelland, L., & Auslander, N. *Determinants of perceived crowding and pleasantness in public settings*. Unpublished manuscript, University of Colorado, 1975.
16. Poe, D. B. *The effects of social and spatial density upon attraction, crowding, task performance, and mood*. Unpublished master's thesis, Virginia Polytechnic Institute and State University, 1975.
17. Rall, M., Stokols, D., & Russo, R. *Spatial adjustments in response to anticipated crowding*. Unpublished manuscript, City University of New York, 1975.
18. Schopler, J., & Walton, M. *The effects of structure, expected enjoyment, and participants' internality-externality upon feelings of being crowded*. Unpublished manuscript, University of North Carolina, 1974.
19. Slosnerick, M. *Social interaction by preschool children in conditions of crowding*. Paper presented at the Annual Conference of the Midwestern Psychological Association, Chicago, May 1974.

20. Stokols, D., & Ohlig, W. *The experience of crowding under different social climates.* Paper presented at the Annual Conference of the American Psychological Association, Chicago, 1975. (Abstract)
21. Stokols, D., & Resnick, S. *An experimental assessment of neutral and personal crowding experiences.* Paper presented at the Annual Conference of the Southeastern Psychological Association, Atlanta, Georgia, March 1975.
22. Stokols, D., & Resnick, S. M. *The generalization of residential crowding experiences to non-residential settings.* Paper presented at the Annual Conference of the Environmental Design Research Association, Lawrence, Kansas, April 1975.

REFERENCES

Aiello, J. R., Epstein, Y. M., & Karlin, R. A. Effects of crowding on electrodermal activity. *Sociological Symposium,* 1975, *14,* 43-57.

Altman, I. Territorial behavior in humans: An analysis of the concept. In L. Pastalan (Ed.), *Use of space in older people.* Ann Arbor: University of Michigan Press, 1970.

Altman, I. *The environment and social behavior: Privacy, personal space, territory, and crowding.* Monterey, Cal.: Brooks/Cole, 1975.

Argyle, M., & Dean, J. Eye-contact, distance & affiliation. *Sociometry,* 1965, *28,* 289-304.

Averill, J. R. Personal control over aversive stimuli and its relation to stress. *Psychological Bulletin,* 1973, *80*(4), 286-303.

Baldassare, M. The effect of density on social behavior and attitudes. *American Behavioral Scientist,* 1975, *18*(6), 815-825. (a)

Baldassare, M. Residential density, local ties, and neighborhood attitudes: Are the findings of micro-studies generalizable to urban areas? *Sociological Symposium,* 1975, *14,* 93-99. (b)

Barker, R. Ecology and motivation. *Nebraska Symposium on Motivation,* 1960, *8,* 1-50. (Reprinted in S. Friedman & J. B. Juhasz (Eds.), *Environments: Notes and selections on objects, spaces, and behavior.* Monterey, Cal.: Brooks/Cole, 1974)

Baron, R. M., Mandel, D. R., Adams, C. A., & Griffen, L. M. Effects of social density in university residential environments. *Journal of Personality and Social Psychology,* 1976, *34*(3), 434-446.

Baum, A., & Davis, G. E. Spatial and social aspects of crowding perception. *Environment and Behavior,* 1976, *8*(4), 527-544.

Baum, A., & Greenberg, C. I. Waiting for a crowd: The behavioral and perceptual effects of anticipated crowding. *Journal of Personality and Social Psychology,* 1975, *32*(4), 671-679.

Baum, A., Harpin, R. E., & Valins, S. The role of group phenomena in the experience of crowding. *Environment and Behavior,* 1975, *7*(2), 185-198.

Baum, A., & Koman, S. Differential response to anticipated crowding: Psychological effects of social and spatial density. *Journal of Personality and Social Psychology,* 1976, *34*(3), 526-536.

Baum, A., & Valins, S. Residential environments, group size, and crowding. *Proceedings of the 81st annual convention of the American Psychological Association,* 1973, *8,* 211-212.

Bergman, B. A. *The effects of group size, personal space, and success-failure on physiological arousal, test performance, and questionnaire response.* Unpublished doctoral dissertation, Temple University, Philadelphia, Pa., 1971. (Abstract, *Dissertation Abstracts International,* 1971, 2319-3420-A.)

Berkowitz, L. The frustration-aggression hypothesis revisited. In L. Berkowitz (Ed.), *Roots of aggression: A reexamination of the frustration-aggression hypothesis.* New York: Atherton Press, 1969.

Bickman, L., Teger, A., Gabriele, T., McLaughlin, C., Berger, M., & Sunaday, E. Dormitory density and helping behavior. *Environment and Behavior*, 1973, *5*(4), 465-490.

Calhoun, J. B. Population density and social pathology. *Scientific American*, 1962, *206*(1), 139-148.

Cohen, J. L., Sladen, B., & Bennett, B. The effects of situational variables on judgments of crowding. *Sociometry*, 1975, *38*(2), 273-281.

Cottrell, N. B. Social facilitation. In C. G. McClintock (Ed.), *Experimental social psychology*. New York: Holt, Rinehart & Winston, 1972.

Cozby, P. C. Effects of density, activity, and personality on environmental preferences. *Journal of Research in Personality*, 1973, *7*, 45-60.

D'Atri, D. A., Psychophysiological responses to crowding. *Environment and Behavior*, 1975, *7*(2), 237-252.

Dean, L. M., Pugh, W. M., & Gunderson, E. Spatial and perceptual components of crowding: Effects on health and satisfaction. *Environment and Behavior*, 1975, *7*(2), 225-236.

Desor, J. A. Toward a psychological theory of crowding. *Journal of Personality and Social Psychology*, 1972, *21*, 79-83.

Dooley, B. B. *Crowding stress: The effects of social density on men with "close" or "far" personal space*. Unpublished doctoral dissertation, University of California, 1974.

Epstein, Y., & Karlin, R. A. Effects of acute experimental crowding. *Journal of Applied Social Psychology*, 1975, *5*(1), 34-53.

Eoyang, C. K. Effects of group size and privacy in residential crowding. *Journal of Personality & Social Psychology*, 1974, *30*(3), 389-392.

Evans, G. W. *Behavioral and physiological consequences of crowding in humans*. Unpublished doctoral dissertation, University of Massachusetts, 1975.

Freedman, J. L. *Crowding and behavior*. San Francisco: Freeman, 1975.

Freedman, J. L., Klevansky, S., & Ehrlich, P. R. The effect of crowding on human task performance. *Journal of Applied Social Psychology*, 1971, *1*, 7-25.

Freedman, J. L., Heshka, S., & Levy, A. Crowding as an intensifier of pleasantness and unpleasantness. (Abstract, J. L. Freedman, *Crowding and Behavior*. San Francisco: Freeman, 1975, p. 149-151.) (a)

Freedman, J. L., Heshka, S. & Levy, A. Crowding as an intensifier of the effect of success and failure. (Abstract, J. L. Freedman, *Crowding and Behavior*. San Francisco: Freeman, 1975, p. 151-152.) (b)

Freedman, J. L., Heshka, S., & Levy, A. Population density and pathology in metropolitan areas. (Abstract, J. L. Freedman, *Crowding and behavior*. San Francisco: Freeman, 1975, p. 137-138.) (c)

Freedman, J. L., Heshka, S., & Levy, A. Population density and pathology: Is there a relationship? *Journal of Experimental Social Psychology*, 1975, *11*, 539-552. (Abstract, J. L. Freedman, *Crowding and behavior*, Freeman, 1975, under the title, "Population density and pathology in New York City," p. 138-142). (d)

Freedman, J. L., Levy, A. S., Buchanan, R. W., & Price, J. Crowding and human aggressiveness. *Journal of Experimental Social Psychology*, 1972, *8*, 528-548.

Freedman, J. L., & Staff, I. Crowding, aggressiveness, and external or internal crowding as an intensifier of internal vs. external pleasantness. (Abstract, J. L. Freedman, *Crowding and behavior*. San Franscisco: Freeman, 1975, p. 152-153.)

Galle, O. R., Gove, W. R., & McPherson, J. M. Population density and pathology: What are the relations for man? *Science*, 1972, *176*, 23-30.

Glass, D. C., & Singer, J. E. *Urban stress*. New York: Academic Press, 1972.

Glass, D. C., & Singer, J. E. Experimental studies of controllable and uncontrollable noise. *Representative Research in Social Psychology*, 1973, *4*, 165-183.

Griffitt, W., & Veitch, R. Influences of population density on interpersonal affective behavior. *Journal of Personality and Social Psychology*, 1971, *17*, 92-98.

Hall, E. *The hidden dimension*. Garden City, N.J.: Doubleday, 1966.

Helson, H. *Adaptation-level theory: An experimental and systematic approach to behavior.* New York: Harper & Row, 1964.

Hutt, C., & Vaizey, M. J. Differential effects of group density on social behavior. *Nature,* 1966, *209,* 1371-1372.

Ittelson, W. H., Proshansky, H. M., & Rivlin, L. G. Bedroom size and social interaction of the psychiatric ward. In J. Wohlwill & D. Carson (Eds.), *Environment and the social sciences.* Washington, D.C.: American Psychological Association, 1972, [Reports based on the same data appeared in Ittelson, W. H., Proshansky, H. M., & Rivlin, L. G., A study of bedroom use on two psychiatric wards. *Hosptial and Community Psychology,* 1970, *21,* 25-28. And Ittelson, W. H., Proshansky, H. M., & Rivlin, L. G., The environmental psychology of the psychiatric ward; In Proshansky, H. M., Ittelson, W. H., & Rivlin, L. G. (Eds.), *Environmental Psychology.* New York: Holt, Rinehart & Winston, 1970.]

Kahn, R. L., & Perlin, S. Dwelling-unit density and use of mental health services. *Proceedings of the 75th Annual Convention of the American Psychological Association,* 1967, *2,* 175-176.

Lazarus, R. S. *Psychological stress and the coping process.* New York: McGraw-Hill, 1966.

Levy, L., & Herzog, A. N. Effects of population density and crowding on health and social adaptation in the Netherlands. *Journal of Health and Social Behavior,* 1974, *15,* 228-240.

Loo, C. M. The effects of spatial density on the social behavior of children. *Journal of Applied Social Psychology,* 1972. *4,* 372-381.

Loring, W. C. Housing characteristics and social disorganization. *Social Problems,* 1956, *3,* 160-168.

MacDonald, W. S., & Oden, C. W. Effects of extreme crowding on the performance of five married couples during twelve weeks of intensive training. *Proceedings of the 81st Annual Convention of the American Psychological Association,* 1973, *8,* 209-210.

Marsella, A. J., Escudero, M., & Gordon, P. The effects of dwelling density on mental disorders in Filipino men. *Journal of Health and Social Behavior,* 1970, *11,* 288-294.

Marshall, J. E., & Heslin, R. Boys and girls together: Sexual composition and the effect of density and group size on cohesiveness. *Journal of Personality and Social Psychology,* 1975, *31*(5), 952-961.

McClelland, L. A. *Crowding and social stress.* Unpublished doctoral dissertation, University of Michigan, 1974.

McGrew, P. L. Social and spatial density effects on spacing behavior in preschool children. *Journal of Child Psychology and Psychiatry,* 1970, *11,* 197-205.

McPherson, J. M. Population density and social pathology: A reexamination. *Sociological Symposium,* 1975, *14,* 77-90.

Mehrabian, A. *Nonverbal communication.* Chicago: Aldine, 1972.

Milgram, S. The experience of living in cities. *Science,* 1970, *167,* 1461-1468.

Mitchell, R. E. Some social implications of high density housing. *American Sociological Review,* 1971, *36,* 18-29.

Patterson, M. L. Compensation in nonverbal immediacy behaviors: A review. *Sociometry,* 1973, *36,* 237-252.

Paulus, P., Cox, V., McCain, G., & Chandler, J. Some effects of crowding in a prison environment. *Journal of Applied Social Psychology,* 1975, *5*(1), 86-91.

Price, J. L. The effects of crowding on the social behavior of children (Doctoral dissertation, Columbia University, 1971). *Dissertation Abstracts International,* 1972, *33,* 471-B. (University Microfilms No. 72-19151)

Rapoport, A. Toward a redefinition of density. *Environment and Behavior,* 1975, *7*(2), 133-158.

Rodin, J. Crowding, perceived choice, and response to controllable and uncontrollable outcomes. *Journal of Experimental Social Psychology,* 1976, *12,* 564-578.

Rohe, W., & Patterson, A. H. The effects of varied levels of resources and density on behavior in a day care center. In D. H. Carson (Ed.), *EDRA 5: Man-environment interactions*. Milwaukee, Wis.: Environmental Design Research Association, 1974.

Ross, M., Layton, B., Erickson, B., & Schopler, J. Affect, facial regard, and reactions to crowding. *Journal of Personality and Social Psychology*, 1973, *28*, 69-76.

Saegert, S. Crowding: Cognitive overlead and behavioral constraint. In W. Prieser (Ed.), *Environmental design research* (Vol. II). Stroudsburg, Pa.: Dowden, Hutchinson & Ross, 1973.

Saegert, S. C. *Effects of spatial and social density on arousal, mood, and social orientation.* Unpublished doctoral dissertation, University of Michigan, 1974.

Saegert, S., Mackintosh, E., & West, S. Two studies of crowding in urban Public spaces. *Environment and Behavior*, 1975, *7*(2), 159-184. (The article lists the authors as Mackintosh, Saegert, & West, but the journal's table of contents and preprints list them as Saegert et al.)

Schiffenbauer, A. I., Brown, J. E., Perry, P. L., Shulack, L. K., & Zanzola, A. M. The relationship between density and crowding: Some architectural modifiers. *Environment and Behavior*, 1977, *9*, 3-14.

Schiffenbauer, A., & Schiavo, R. S. Physical distance and attraction: An intensification effect. *Journal of Experimental Social Psychology*, 1976, *12*, 274-282.

Schmitt, R. C. Implications of density in Hong Kong. *American Institute of Planners Journal*, 1963, *29*, 210-217.

Schmitt, R. C. Density, health, & social disorganization. *American Institute of Planners Journal*, 1966, *32*(1), 38-40.

Seligman, M. P. *Helplessness: On depression, development, and death.* San Francisco: Freeman, 1975.

Sherrod, D. R. Crowding, perceived control, and behavioral aftereffects. *Journal of Applied Social Psychology*. 1974, *4*(2), 171-186.

Smith, S., & Haythorn, W. W. Effects of compatability, crowding, group size, and leadership seniority on stress, anxiety, hostility, and annoyance in isolated groups. *Journal of Personality and Social Psychology*, 1972, *22*, 67-79.

Sommer, R., & Becker, F. D. Room density and user satisfaction. *Environment and Behavior*, 1971, *3*, 412-417.

Stokols, D. A social-psychological model of human crowding phenomena. *Journal of the American Institute of Planners*, 1972, *38*, 72-83. (a)

Stokols, D. On the distinction between density and crowding: Some implications for future research. *Psychological Review*, 1972, *79*, 275-277. (b)

Stokols, D. The experience of crowding in primary and secondary environments. *Environment and Behavior*, 1976, *8*(1), 49-86.

Stokols, D., Rall, M., Pinner, B., & Schopler, J. Physical, social, and personal determinants of the perception of crowding. *Environment and Behavior*, 1973, *5*, 87-115.

Stokols, D., Smith, T. E., & Prostor, J. J. Partitioning and perceived crowding in a public place. *American Behavioral Scientist*, 1975, *18*(6), 792-814.

Sundstrom, E. An experimental study of crowding: Effects of room-size, intrusion, and coal-blocking on nonverbal behaviors, self-disclosure, and self-reported stress. *Journal of Personality and Social Psychology*, 1975, *32*(4), 645-654. (a)

Sundstrom, E. Toward an interpersonal model of crowding. *Sociological Symposium*, 1975, *14*, 129-144. (b)

Sundstrom, E. Interpersonal behavior and the physical environment. In L. Wrightsman, *Social Psychology, 1977* (2nd ed.). Monterey, Calif.: Brooks/Cole, 1977.

Sundstrom, E., & Altman, I. Personal space and interpersonal relationships: Research review and theoretical model. *Human Ecology*, 1976, *4*, 47-67.

Tucker, J., & Friedman, S. T. Population density and group size. *American Journal of Sociology*, 1972, *77*, 742-749.

Valins, S., & Baum, A. Residential group size, social interaction, and crowding. *Environment and Behavior*, 1973, *5*(4), 421-439.

Wicker, A. W., & Kirmeyer, S. From church to laboratory to national park: A program of research on excess and insufficient populations in behavior settings. In D. Stokols (Ed.), *Psychological perspectives on environment and behavior: Conceptual and empirical trends*. New York: Plenum Press, 1977.

Winsborough, H. The social consequences of high population density. *Law & Contemporary Problems*, 1965, *30*, 120-126.

Wohlwill, J. Amount of stimulus exploration and preference as differential functions of stimulus complexity. *Perception & Psychophysics*, 1968, *4*(5), 307-312.

Wohlwill, J. Human adaptation to levels of environmental stimulation. *Human Ecology*, 1974, *2*(2), 127-147.

Wohlwill, J., & Kohn, I. The environment as experienced by the migrant: An adaptation-level view. *Representative Research in Social Psychology*, 1973, *4*, 135-164.

Wolfe, M. Room size, group size, and density. *Environment and Behavior*, 1975, *7*(2), 199-224.

Worchel, S., & Teddlie, C. Factors affecting the experience of crowding: A two-factor theory. *Journal of Personality and Social Psychology*, 1976, *34*(1), 30-40.

Zlutnick, S., & Altman, I. Crowding and human behavior. In J. Wohlwill & D. Carson (Eds.), *Environment and the social sciences*. Washington, D. C.: American Psychological Association, 1972.

3

Crowding and the Developmental Process

Gary W. Evans
University of California, Irvine

This chapter examines the physiological and behavioral effects of crowding on human development. In many cases, the research presented has not specifically examined this topic but rather contained some data or discussion that were pertinent. An attempt is made to formulate some hypotheses and to relate these to other areas of research in which more developmental data are available. Data are presented in support of the thesis that young organisms are more severely affected by crowding than adult organisms. Three mechanisms of crowding's effects on development are hypothesized. First, the position that crowding is precipitated by a state of stimulus overload is reviewed. Second, we examine the hypothesis that crowding acts as a stressor on developing organisms. Although some support for the above hypotheses is derived from related developmental research on overstimulation and stress, respectively, the two hypotheses are rejected in favor of a third more integrative arousal hypothesis, which is that the effects of crowding on development are mediated by means of an arousal mechanism. Under crowded conditions, greater than optimal arousal levels are produced that may be detrimental to normal development. Most of the research done directly on crowding and development has been done with nonhumans. It should be reemphasized here, however, that both the physiological mechanisms of our responses to crowding as well as our conceptualization of a crowded environment are probably very different from that of other species (Davis, 1971; Stokols, 1972; Thiessen, 1964).

PHYSIOLOGICAL FINDINGS

Nonhuman Research

Christian and his co-workers (Christian, 1961; Christian & Davis, 1964) have carried out much of the research on the physiological aspects of crowding. They have worked with both albino and wild-stock house mice that were well fed and cared for with density being the primary independent variable. They found that mice under more crowded conditions exhibited general symptoms of stress. More particularly, crowded mice had enlarged adrenal glands, decreased thymus weights, and a decrease of testicular androgens in males. Other data also indicate that rats reared under high density conditions have significantly greater ratios of adrenal gland to body weight (Goeckner, Greenough, & Mead, 1973; Morrison & Thatcher, 1969) and greater absolute adrenal gland weights than litter mates raised under less dense conditions (Goeckner et al., 1973). Furthermore, when female mice were crowded, reproduction dropped off and lactation activity was severely inhibited. The increase in adrenal weight that Christian has discussed at length was attributed to cellular hypertrophy and hyperphasia of the zona fasciculata of the adrenal cortex. The decrease in testicular androgens in crowded males was reflected by partial atrophy and consequent weight loss in the seminal vesicles and testes. In crowded females, Christian reported accelerated involutions of the X-zone of the adrenal cortex. The X-zone is a transitory zone that is involuted by androgens and maintained by a lutenizing hormone from the anterior pituitary gland. This zone usually disappears at puberty in males and during pregnancy in females. The abnormal involuted X-zone in grouped female mice suggests that there is either an increase in the secretion of adrenal androgens or a drop in lutenizing hormones from the anterior pituitary.

Working in a natural habitat, Snyder (1961) has found consistent morphological modifications in crowded woodchucks. First of all, a less dense population of woodchucks had a significantly lower mortality rate than woodchucks under denser conditions. Snyder allowed one area of woodchucks to reproduce and systematically removed 30 woodchucks per month for eight months from another area (the less dense group). In addition to mortality differences, the less dense group had higher reproduction rates, larger litters, less infant mortality, and a greater percentage of pregnant females.

Of those animals that died in the more dense group, the majority of these were young woodchucks. In the less dense group, this difference in mortality as a function of age was absent. Snyder cited other research with similar differential mortalities as a function of age in research with prairie dogs and snowshoe hares.

Snyder also reported that only 20 percent of the yearlings in the high density group became pregnant whereas 100 percent of the adults did. In the normally populated group, the pregnancy rates of yearlings was 36 percent greater than for those yearlings in the crowded group. The adults were similar in both populations with 100 percent being pregnant in the crowded group as well.

Kalela (1957), studying voles in the wild, found that during periods of high density the young did not reach maturity. Furthermore, these animals had few or no offspring as compared to animals who were already mature at the onset of peak density. Thus, the reproductive functioning of animals born and developed during more crowded times was severely curtailed, whereas those animals already at sexual maturity did not exhibit this retardation of reproduction. The possible adaptive value of this effect in controlling population numbers seems apparent.

Christian (1961) has found similar effects under laboratory conditions and has been able to correlate this differential severity of reproductive deficiency with testicular atrophy in males. He found that the testicular size of males under high densities declined significantly only in animals weighing less than 45 grams (adult weight). Further examination of the bacula (os penis) revealed that these males had never reached maturity. Christian also cited similar research findings with silka deer. Thus, several researchers have found some indication of inhibition of maturation under crowded conditions.

Work with tree shrews (*Tupaja belangeri*) has also indicated delayed development of the young under high density conditions (Autrum & Holst, 1968). In young males, for example, testicle descension is delayed. Furthermore, females' milk production decreases and sternal gland activity ceases. The latter means that they cannot mark their young olfactorily, which in turn increases the probability that the young will be killed by cage mates.

The indications of delayed maturation have also been discussed by Christian and Davis (1964), who reported that immature mice are known to secrete substantial quantities of 17-hydrocorticoids, especially hydrocortisone. When these animals are crowded, the total adrenal corticosteroid production level increases, but the ratio of hydrocortisone to corticosterone level also increases. At sexual maturity, the production of hydrocortisone usually drops off. With the delayed maturation under crowding conditions, the secretion of substantial amounts of hydrocortisone is prolonged. This is important because hydrocortisone is a more potent glucocorticoid than corticosterone, which is the principal 17-hydrocorticoid compound secreted by the adrenals of adult mice. Glucocorticoids reduce resistance to infectious diseases. Thus, similar degrees of stimulation such as crowding may affect the adrenals of the immature organism more than the mature organism. As an independent assessment of this theoretical sequence, Christian and Davis (1964) reported earlier work in which immature mice were injected with ACTH. They found increased thymic involution and growth suppression to a much greater extent in the immature mice than in the mature mice.

Christian and Davis also reported an increase in adrenal androgen secretion with injection of ACTH in young animals. This increase in adrenal androgen in turn inhibited gonadotrophic output. This conclusion was based on evidence that indicated that immature females, both normal and adrenalectomized, with adrenal androgen injection maintained a high level of hydrocortisone production which among other manifestations included the suppression of adult reproductive functioning. Southwick (1972) has argued, however, that the extent of the above reported changes in adrenals and gonads is limited to laboratory findings only and has not been found in field studies of natural populations. An alternative explanation of behavioral and physiological mechanisms in population regulation may be olfactory blocking in females. There is an 80-90 percent failure of implantation when impregnated females are exposed to the scents of strange males. Alternatively, under natural conditions, females during pregnancy and nesting are highly territorial, excluding males from the nest sites. During high density periods, this territorialism breaks down (Southwick, 1972). It seems, however, that these two alternative explanations are not necessarily mutually exclusive.

Myers, Hale, Myktowycz, and Hughs (1971) worked with rabbits in the wild and also reported some data that can be extracted for discussion here. Although increasing density affected the animals, Myers et al. found that the reduction of living space, with density held constant, had a more significant effect on the conditions of their rabbits. Among a multitude of significant differences between a group with adequate living space and one with reduced living space, Myers et al. reported that infant mortality, for example, was significantly greater in the group with reduced living space. In general, the measurable differences found at the adult levels between the two groups were clearly more significant for embryos, nestlings, and the recently weaned young. As an example, the reduction in living space did not significantly affect adult body weight. Embryos and nestlings, however, clearly had reduced body weights in the group with reduced living space. Similarly, the adrenal weight differences, although not significant for adults, were indeed significant for nestlings and the weaned young. It is also of interest that there was substantial retardation in development still in existence at post-weaning in the following organs of the animals with reduced living space: thymus, liver, kidney, and spleen. Finally, in their review of population regulation in insects, Harcourt and Leroux (1967) have presented some life table statistics that indicate that for key density-dependent mortality factors, the immature stages of several species were particularly susceptible.

Human Research

Unfortunately, there is very little research on the physiological response to crowding in developing humans. Hutt and Vaizey (1966) studied the effects of varying the numbers of school children (six to nine years) in a constant area. Less than 6, 7 to 11, and more than 11 children were observed in an area 27 ft. X 17.5 ft. during periods of free play. Of interest from a physiological point of view is that Hutt and Vaizey found different results dependent on the conditions of the children. Children who were brain damaged (generalized lesions of the brain) had more acute reactions to being crowded as measured by observed time spent in aggressive or destructive behavior than normal or autistic children. The latter had no such increase whereas the normals did but not to the degree that the brain-damaged children did. Only the normal children reflected a significant drop in social interaction with increased crowding, which has been found in other human crowding studies. Furthermore, only the autistic children exhibited increased withdrawal measured by increased time spent on the periphery of the room.

Booth and Johnson (1975) have recently examined the effects of neighborhood and household densities on several health and social indicators among children of blue collar families in a large Canadian city. Although they found that neighborhood densities did not significantly regress onto their criterion measures, the researchers did find significant although weak positive beta weights, which indicated that children from high density households tended to be shorter, weigh less, and were more apt to be sick than their less crowded age and social counterparts in the city who lived in less dense households. Socioeconomic status and mother's health were partialed out.

BEHAVIORAL FINDINGS

Nonhuman Research

Calhoun (1962) overcrowded rats and found a general breakdown in normal social behavior in his subjects. In his now classic study, Calhoun allowed rats to overpopulate in a confined area with adequate food and water. As population density increased, the rats developed acutely abnormal patterns of behavior that included a dramatic increase in aggressive activities, increased infant mortality, deviant sexual behavior, and cannibalism. Calhoun also noted the curious formation of a phenomenon called a "behavioral sink" in which the rats concentrated in disproportionate numbers around a particular food hopper. The maternal behavior and care of the young were also greatly affected by increased crowding. Litters were often abandoned, and eventually nest building ceased entirely.

In more recent work, Calhoun (1971) has completed some longitudinal studies of overpopulated rat colonies. In general, he found that these animals pass through four stages: (1) the establishment phase, which extends from time of birth of the first successful litter; (2) a period of rapid population growth; (3) a reduction in population growth; and (4) a stability or slight decline in population numbers.

Near the end of phase 3 aberrant social behavior sharply increased, and by the onset of phase 4 successful rearing of young was nearly absent. In addition, consistent with previous data reported above, conception dropped off significantly in these latter stages. It is of interest in light of our discussion of Christian's work that Calhoun also reported that the young in phases 3 and 4 seemed to be in a suspended juvenile state in terms of their behavior.

Research has also indicated that rats reared under high density reflect reduced behavioral indices of emotionality. Significantly less freezing and time spent in corners along with more rearing were found in rats raised in crowded cages. Furthermore, the effect of grouping in the testing situation significantly interacted with rearing density. The typical reduction of emotionality when animals are tested in groups versus individually was significantly reversed for the rats reared in crowded conditions (Morrison & Thatcher, 1969).

Consistent with Chitty's (1955) hypothesis that high population density conditions may adversely affect the viability of subsequent generations, and some physiological data of Christian (1961), one researcher has examined the effects of crowding on the unborn. Keeley (1962) placed groups of 15 or 5 pregnant albino rats in 6 X 12 X 5 1/2-inch cages. With birth imminent, the mothers were segregated to deliver their pups. All pups were then raised by either their own mother or another previously crowded or uncrowded mother in uncrowded cages with food and water freely supplied. The pups were then measured at 30 and 100 days for activity (latency of response to exit spontaneously from the opening of their cage) and amount of defecation when placed in a novel environment. The pups from crowded mothers were generally less active and defecated less than the control mice. Whether the pups were cared for or nursed by a previously crowded mother or an uncrowded mother was not significant. The responses at 30 days were also not significantly different than those at 100 days relative to group differences, which indicated some persistence in the responses measured.

Recent work indicates that rodents reared from weaning under high density conditions exhibit impaired acquisition of complex appetitively and aversively motivated learning tasks but not of simple tasks (Goeckner et al., 1973). Grouping or crowding of previously isolated adult rats, however, tends to facilitate acquisition of the same complex tasks (Wood & Greenough, 1974). Goeckner et al. found that rats reared in crowded conditions were impaired in learning a brightness discrimination task to avoid shock, as compared to previously uncrowded animals. Previously isolated (35 to 95 days) adult rats, however, when tested after spending 4 weeks under high density conditions, were superior to those previously isolated rats housed under less dense conditions. Simlarly, in a Lashley III alley maze, a tendency toward facilitation in the crowded adult group contrasted with the poorer performance of the crowded-reared young on the same task.

Human Research

Although there is an increasing amount of research on the effects of crowding on human behavior, very little work has examined the developmental aspects of such effects. There has been considerable research, however, on family size which has generally shown that larger families tend to have children with lower IQs (Anastasi, 1959; Hunt, 1961).

Waldrop and Bell (1966) have found that a composite measure of family size and family density significantly correlated with neonatal lethargy as measured by less sucking activity.[1] Furthermore, there was a low but significant positive

---

[1]This measure had three factorially weighted components: (1) number of children, (2) average span in months between births, and (3) months to next oldest sibling.

correlation between low sucking activity and later nursery school behavior at 2-1/2 years. Children who were more lethargic at birth tended to be more dependent on a female nursery school teacher as measured by child-initiated physical contact. In earlier research, Waldrop and Bell (1964) had found that children coming from large families in which the births were close together also exhibited greater dependency behavior in nursery school.

P. McGrew (1970) has observed the effects of different densities on young nursery school children ($\bar{x}$ = 47.9 months). She distinguished between two kinds of density manipulations: spatial and social. Spatial density changes alter the amount of physical space available while maintaining the same number of subjects. Social density manipulations alter the numbers of individuals in a given space. This variable is one of the ones that Loo (1973) has argued mediates the effects of crowding in humans. McGrew and her colleagues observed 20 children for 12, 30-minute free play sessions in the children's nursery school. Four proximity categories were established: (1) contact wherein two or more subjects were in physical contact; (2) close proximity wherein two or more subjects were within three feet of each other; (3) intermediate proximity wherein two or more subjects were farther than 3 ft. but occupying the same square (tape grid—7.2 X 7.2 ft.); and (4) solitary activity wherein one child occupied a square. She concluded that social density changes elicited no significant difference in proxemic behavior. When spatial density manipulations were performed, however, the frequency of close proximity encounters was higher with greater density. At the same time, more children indicated an increased amount of solitary behavior under the more dense condition. This latter finding is consistent with normal children's behavior in Hutt and Vaizey's earlier work discussed above with normal, brain-damaged, and autistic children. Even though the normal children were more tightly packed together, they interacted and related to one another significantly less than when more space in their nursery was available.

W. McGrew (1972) has reported on the observation of nursery school children in more detail. In one study, the available play space of nursery school children (spatial density manipulation) was varied according to climate and weather conditions. High density conditions (33 sq. ft. per child) were in effect during inclement weather when children had to remain inside. Following inclement weather, children could also play on an open concrete strip in front of their school but not on an adjoining grassy strip (52 sq. ft. per child). Finally, when the grass was dry, children could play in all three areas, which defined the low density condition (150 sq. ft. per child).

Four children (mean age = 3 1/2 years) were observed during free play periods. The following motor behaviors were recorded: hand movements, arm movements, leg movements, gross body movements, other movements (usually joints), and locomotion. Under the most dense condition, McGrew (1972) found a significant drop in gross body movements and locomotion, a significant increase in arm movements, and no change in the other observed behaviors. He speculated that as density increased it was more difficult for children to perform movements that in their action required certain spatial minimums. Perhaps to compensate, children increased movements that did not take up as much space, such as arm movements. McGrew also observed that in general the children under more dense conditions tended to exhibit more passive play behavior, for example, playing quietly with a toy.

In another study, W. McGrew (1972) blocked off part of a nursery room at times to create a smaller area of play. In addition, the number of children was varied in both conditions. As before, independent judges observed the free play activity of nursery school age children. They noted the frequency of the following behaviors: (1) object struggle—an attempt by two or more children to gain or regain possession of an object (usually a toy); (2) negative expletive—short, explosive verbalizations (e.g., stop it, don't, shut up, etc.); (3) hitting—beat or punch; (4) pushing—arms extended forward with vertical palms, force directly applied to person; (5) destruction—inappropriate object use likely to result in damage; (6) weeping; (7) immobility—cessation of gross movements for at least 3 seconds; (8) digit sucking; (9) automanipulation—use of fingers to manipulate part of own body (e.g., itching, fiddling with clothes, etc.); (10) laughing; (11) contact—unstructured physical contact with others (e.g., wrestling, holding hands, etc.); and (12) running.

In the reduced spatial condition with social density held constant, there was significantly greater hitting, fearful behavior (defined by increased digit sucking, automanipulative activity, and hand holding), and generally greater contact. Destructive behavior varied significantly in the opposite direction. In the social density manipulations, that is, physical space held constant, only hitting and laughing varied significantly, with more of both occurring in the high density condition. On the other hand, automanipulation and immobility differed in the opposite direction, with greater frequencies occurring under lower density. This complex pattern of results further emphasizes the complex nature of the manipulation of spatial variables with human subjects.

Preiser (1972) has also reported a decrease in social interaction with a decrease in available space in three- to four-year-old children observed at play in their nursery school. He found that there was significantly less use of a common table by the children under denser conditions. He also reported a decrease in the use of the children's record player. It is of interest that the only behaviors affected were ones in which close quarters and interaction would be more frequent. The use of a sink and a coat shelf, for example, were not similarly affected by different density conditions. Preiser also reported a drop in the number of social contacts between the children under more crowded conditions. This latter finding, it will be recalled, has turned up in much of the human literature reviewed so far and was also observed by Calhoun in his work with rats, especially among subordinates, but not for the more dominant members.

Finally, Loo (1972) has studied the effects of crowding on young children (4 to 5 years old) by varying spatial density. Results indicated a significant *decrease* in aggression for boys under higher density but not for girls. In addition, activities were interrupted more often, less time was spent in group involvement, and there was an increase in solitary play activity under conditions of greater density. In general, there was a sharp drop in interactive behavior under crowded conditions.

The decrease in aggressive acts may have been due to the establishment of certain psychological restraints on the children as manifested by greater social isolation. In any case, the establishment of greater isolation under crowded conditions has been found in several studies. Perhaps by isolating themselves, children were establishing some psychological distance in an attempt to adapt to the restrictions placed on their physical space. Thus, crowding may retard social development and interfere with a sense of task completion (Loo, 1973).[2]

One hypothesis is that the aggressiveness of the response of the organism is a function of the degree of frustration caused by the crowded condition. The relationship between invasion of personal space and increased frustration has been demonstrated (Evans & Howard, 1973). That frustration heightens aggression, particularly in children, has been concluded in a review of the literature by Feshbach (1970). Miller and Bugelski (1948), for example, manipulated frustration in a group of boys by depriving them of their scheduled movie at a work camp and substituting tedious tests instead. The resulting frustration was manifested in increased hostility toward people from other countries. Significantly fewer positive attributes were assigned to Japanese and Mexicans after the introduction of frustration than had been assigned in a prefrustration questionnaire measure. Perhaps individual differences in reactions of aggression to crowding actually reflect differences in frustration thresholds. Organisms more frustrated by conditions of the external environment would be expected to react more outwardly aggressively.

Turning to more field-oriented approaches, Booth & Johnson (1975) in the same study reported above, also found that children from high density households were more frequently the subject of contact between school authorities and parents regarding problems in school. Schmitt (1957), a sociologist, has

[2]Smith (Note 1) has suggested that an important confounding variable may have been operating in some of the experimental research on crowding in nursery school settings. He notes that with changes in numbers there are also changes in the ratio of children to resources available, such as number of toys. He and his coworkers have found that although manipulations of spatial density had no effect on agonistic behavior in preschoolers, the number of available toys did have a significant impact such that there was a good deal more altercation and aggression when there were fewer toys to go around. However, this possible confounding would apply only to manipulations of social density.

studied the effects of living density on juvenile delinquency in Honolulu. Employing partial correlation techniques, Schmitt found that the number of persons per room and population per acre showed a consistent positive correlation with the eventual crime behavior of adolescents. Freedman (1973), however, has criticized Schmitt's criteria for measuring education and income levels.

Galle, Gove, and McPherson (1972) more adequately assessed and controlled potentially confounding variables and also found a significantly high degree of correlation between the number of persons per room in the home and the juvenile delinquency rate. In addition, employing the rather questionable index of public assistance recipients under 18 as a measure of ineffectual child care, the researchers also established a significant degree of correlation with persons per room. It was suggested that in an overcrowded environment, parents were likely to be tense, harassed, and more tired. Therefore, the pressures on family stability as well as parent's lack of responsiveness to their children could adversely affect the child.

Some empirical observations lend partial support to these conjectures. Mitchell (1971), for example, found in his research on density levels in Hong Kong that with an increase in density, a greater proportion of parents did not know where their children were playing. This result held up, moreover, when income and educational levels were partialled out.

Other investigators (Munroe & Munroe, 1971) have observed various aspects of infant care in the Logoli tribe of western Kenya. This tribe has undergone massive population expansion in a very short period. Employing a modified time-sampling and event-sampling approach, the authors observed the proportion of time infants were held and the magnitude of response latency to infant crying as a function of household density (persons per house). The experimenters found that children in high density homes were held more often and were responded to more quickly when they cried than were children from less dense homes. Although these data appear to contradict the hypotheses of Galle et al. (1972), further work indicated that the mother in these high density households is significantly less often the baby's caretaker, is less often within 10 ft. of the baby, and is more likely to cause the infant to cry than a mother in a low density household. Thus, although there may in fact be less parental attention under higher densities, hypotheses concerning the effects of density on parental care need to take into consideration the possibility that greater extended family care may offset any decreased parental attention in a high density household.

RESEARCH SUMMARY

Crowding has been shown to affect young organisms both in terms of their behavior as well as in certain physiological responses. In general, animals that were crowded exhibited changes in physiological indexes that included increased adrenal gland activity, reduced testicular androgen production in males, and increased estrogen content in females. Evidence also suggested a profound effect on the course of maturation in these animals as reflected by reproduction deficiencies and growth retardation. The potential hormonal mechanisms for this prolonged maturation were discussed. Prolonged maturation under crowded conditions was also reflected in the extended juvenile behavior of these animals.

Furthermore, crowded animals also showed increased signs of social pathology, including increased aggressive behavior and deviant sexual behavior. Play activities of crowded human subjects was also affected. Several studies concluded that the play activity and motor activity of crowded children were substantially curtailed or pacified under denser conditions. There were reports of withdrawal of some individuals rather than an increase in socially pathological activity. Furthermore, studies consistently reported a decrease in the amount of social interaction by children subjected to crowded conditions.

Although there are basic similarities between the effects of crowding on the behavior of developing animals and humans, one should keep several points in mind when generalizing the animal data to humans. First, the principal cause of behavior in animals is largely biological, whereas learning and cultural inputs are often dominant in humans (Swanson, 1973). The reactions of humans to crowding, therefore, would be expected to be different from and more context-dependent than the reactions of animals to a comparable situation (see Stokols, 1972, for a discussion of this issue).

A second factor to consider in generalizing the developmental animal crowding data to humans is the comparability of the crowding conditions. Basically two criteria seem important: (1) the percentage of the subject's daily time spent crowded, and (2) the freedom of the subject occasionally to select a less crowded setting. In the research presented, animals reared in crowded settings were typically housed in crowded cages constantly through maturity. There are few instances in which humans have been reared in crowded conditions so consistently. Crowding in humans is more commonly temporary. Even in cases in which children's homes are overcrowded, the child frequently has the opportunity to leave (i.e., go out to play, go to school, etc.). The only setting that most animals in the crowding research experience is the crowded one.

THEORY

Overload Theories

It has been suggested that some of the effects of crowding in rodents and humans may be due in part to too much stimulation. From various cognitive and conceptual sources, as organisms are crowded together, both the quantity of stimulation as well as the quality of stimulation is increased; for example, as people are forced closer together physically, thermal cues and olfactory cues can be picked up and visual cues are accentuated (Davis, 1971; Esser, 1972; Hall, 1966). Milgram's analysis of urban dwellers' adaptations to the "information overload" conditions of the city is also consistent with the overload position (Milgram, 1970). Hutt (1970) has reviewed preference in young chilren for varying degrees of complexity in visual stimuli. She concluded that in general the findings were contradictory, due to the multidimensional nature of the concept. In particular dimensions, however, young chilren usually preferred a moderate amount of complexity over too little or too much complexity. In general, young children preferred orderly, regular, symmetrical patterns, and in particular, patterns of stimulation that could be comprehended and labeled. Thus, children might have difficulty in situations in which too much stimulation is present. Crowding could be such a situation.

White (1971) examined the effects of different rearing conditions on newborns (6 to 36 days old). One of his groups, the massive enrichment condition, is of interest with regard to the effects of stimulus overloading on children. Under this condition, 19 infants from day 6 to day 36 received 20 minutes of extra handling daily. In addition, a stabile mobile was hung overhead with numerous forms and contrasting colors. The infants also had multicolored sheets and buntings. From 37 to 124 days, these infants were also placed in a prone position for 15-minute intervals three times a day; in addition, their crib liners were removed during this time to reveal ward activities. The observed behaviors most clearly affected were a delay in the onset of hand regard by 12 days, a five-day delay in hand swiping at an object, and much less visual exploratory behavior for the first 75 days in comparison to infants of comparable age raised under normal nursery conditions. White also observed increased crying in the massively enriched group. It is of interest that the retarded development in the massive enrichment condition as compared to both a control group and a handled group was most severe in the infants of 45 to 75 days versus those same infants' measurements at days 75 to 100. In fact, for visual exploratory behavior, a reversal occurred after 75 days with more exploration reported for the massively enriched babies.

Although White's research does not pertain specifically to crowding, it does suggest that there may be such a thing as too much stimulation for a developing organism. The reader familiar with the early stimulation literature will recall that several lines of research with rodents have found that the administration of moderate, extra stimulation to infant laboratory subjects promotes growth and accelerates physiological and behavioral development, causes a reduction in emotional reactivity, improves learning performance, and alters physiological responses to stress experienced as an adult (Denenberg, 1972; Newton & Levine, 1968; Rosenzweig, 1971). In addition to interspecific differences, the contrast between White's work and early stimulation research with rodents may be due to the relative ages of subjects when tested or given stimulation. That age is important is illustrated both by the reversal in exploration that White found and animal research that indicates significant differences in preweaning versus post-weaning environmental stimulation effects. Furthermore, the work on crowding generally indicates that the delayed maturation occurred during the prepuberty period. The stimulation research, however, indicates an accelerated preweaning period of growth. It is conceivable that the amount of stimulation to which White exposed his subjects may have been considerably greater than the levels of stimulation employed by researchers in early stimulation research. Some investigators have suggested that one fact that may account for some of the adaptive consequences of early handling in animal research is that moderate early stimulation may counteract the detrimental effects of the relatively impoverished laboratory environment (cf. Levine, 1962).

Crowding and Stress

The effects of crowding on organisms in part resembles a stress syndrome. The enlargement of the adrenals and other related hormonal changes as discussed above are typical physiological indexes of stress (Selye, 1973). The effects of stress on developing organisms has been studied in some detail.

In a *Scientific American* article, Seymour Levine summarized much of his research on stress in infant rats (Levine, 1960). Levine found that early handling of rats resembled a mild shock as a moderate stressor in that their effects on young rats were equivalent. An interesting effect observed on young rats was that when handled or moderately shocked in infancy they had certain atypical adult behavior patterns and physiological reactions to stressful situations later in life. Previously stressed animals were less reactive to stress and had a qualitatively different physiological response pattern to stressors. These previously stressed rats had a higher output of steroids immediately following a stressor such as shock, whereas in the same condition their previously unstressed litter mates reached the same level of steroid output much more slowly and maintained that high level for a considerably longer amount of time.

Furthermore, stimulation by early handling or moderate shock was also found to hasten the maturation of the stress response in infant organisms. The normal onset of the various neural mechanisms that can affect the secretion of ACTH occur at 16 days in the rat, according to Levine. He has been able to elicit this stress response in 12-day-old rats that had been moderately stressed in infancy.

In general, the moderately stressed rats in comparison to previously unstressed rats had more rapid rates of development: They opened their eyes sooner, grew body hair more rapidly, were heavier and gained body weight proportionately faster, and were more resistant to pathogenic agents.

In addition, Levine has demonstrated that this early moderate stress must occur when the rats are between 2 to 5 days old for the later effects to be realized. Of a group of rats tested on the 14th day, only those stressed during days 2 to

5 were capable of an endocrine response. Rats stressed between 6 to 9 and 10 to 13 days were incapable of an endocrine response to stress at day 14. The short duration of this apparent critical period is particularly striking. Furthermore, Denenberg (1968) has reported that there appears to be an optimum range of stimulus intensities at different ages in the general critical period.

In a more recent paper, Levine and Mullins (1968) have discussed some of the possible mechanisms for their findings. Early moderate stress due to manipulation was found to accelerate the onset of plasma corticosteroids in infant rats. As discussed earlier, this is the principal 17-hydrocorticoid compound secreted by the adrenal glands of adult organisms. Furthermore, it is a less potent glucocorticoid than hydrocortisone, which is secreted in substantial amounts by immature organisms. This in turn makes the organism less susceptible to stimulation. Thiessen and his coworkers (Thiessen, 1964) reported that the handling of mice resulted in heavier adrenals and reduced timidity, and that these effects were similar to those that occurred when the same genetic strain of mice was subjected to crowding.

The alterations of the hormonal states of neonates most certainly should affect those organisms' later growth and development. Apparently, the increased variations of adrenal steroids due to early moderate stress affect the organism's hormonal system in part as evidenced by its later stress reactions.

An Alternative Hypothesis

Although the physiological data suggest a relationship between the effects of early crowding and stress, the psychological consequences of these two factors do not appear to be similar. Moderate stress generally seems to accelerate maturation; early crowding appears to result in the inhibition of maturation. There are several reasons for this apparent contradiction between the data on early stress and crowding. First, if in fact crowding is stressful, the intensity of the stress factor in crowding may far exceed the stress factor produced by handling and moderate shock. The physiological data suggest that crowding produces a more marked impact on development than does handling or shock. Few data are available on the consequences on later development of more intense handling or shock. Perhaps the relationship between intensity of stress and behavioral development is an inverted U-shaped curve rather than a linear one. In other words, if a moderate amount of stress (such as handling) produces an optimal level of development, then an extreme amount of stress (such as overcrowding) would result in retarded development. Conversely, too little stress may also inhibit development. Results from sensory deprivation research suggest that very low levels of stimulation may be at least discomforting if not stressful (Zubek, 1969). Furthermore, hospitalism studies suggest that when children are reared in low stimulation environments, they exhibit some retardation in development (Spitz, 1975).

An additional factor to consider in comparing the effects of early stress and crowding on developing organisms is the condition of the organism between the age at which the stress or crowding occurs and the age at which the consequent results are determined. In the handling research, the animals are typically stressed temporarily, for a few minutes several times a day, over a few days. They are then spared from abnormal stress until the time of test, somewhat later. In the crowding research, however, the animals are usually reared in crowded conditions from birth until at least the time of test. All their behavior develops and is manifested in the permanent conditions of crowding. Thus, crowding not only affects the early determinants of behavior but also the environment surrounding every behavior elicited.

There is an interesting thread running through the behavioral patterns observed in both the rodent and human studies. Although certain individuals in these studies reacted to crowding by becoming more aggressive, others seemed to withdraw more from the social activity of the group. It is intriguing to consider these differences in light of Hutt and Vaizey's work in which those individuals with lower levels of electrocortical activity (brain-damaged children) became more aggressive under crowded conditions whereas autistic children with abnormally high levels of electrocortical activity exhibited extreme withdrawal from social activity under the pressures of crowding and normal children exhibited a drop in social interaction.

Arousal theory might account for the varying response of different individuals in a crowded situation. Given that a medium level of arousal is optimal for a variety of behaviors (Berlyne, 1960; Broadbent, 1971; Kahneman, 1973), it may be that social withdrawal or movement to the periphery reflect attempts on the part of normal and autistic children, respectively, to reduce arousal in the heightened arousal circumstances due to crowding. The fact that the brain-damaged children increased their activity is significant in light of the arousal hypothesis because the brain-damaged children had abnormally low arousal states. Aggression and destructive behavior presumably may have helped these children increase their arousal levels to more optimal levels. It should be noted that several studies also found that normal children had sharp drops in social interaction under high density conditions. Furthermore, the data reported by Christian (1961) and others that less dominant organisms under high densities suffer more is interesting with regard to the arousal hypothesis in light of the fact that more subordinate animals characteristically function at higher arousal levels than more dominant animals (Welch, Note 2).

Arousal may also be helpful in understanding the overstimulation argument as well. Berlyne (1971) and others have argued that one reason persons prefer moderate amounts of complexity in their environments is because too much stimulation heightens arousal beyond the optimal range. In addition to White's findings on overstimulation, which indicated some mildly negative effects on infants, further work by the Hutts provides a possible link between arousal and stimulation levels. Hutt and Hutt (1965) found that as the complexity of a room increased, the amount of stereotypic behavior in autistic children increased. Exposure to novel environments also increases the rate of stereotypies in these children. Both stereotyped behaviors and gaze avoidance may reflect efforts by autistic children to reduce arousal by cutting off stimulation. The Hutts have found that bouts of stereotypies correlate initially with high desynchronized levels of EEG, which is believed to be characteristic of high arousal. After the onset of the stereotypies, the EEG begins to calm down, and eventually the stereotypies cease.

To summarize, we are suggesting that perhaps crowding operates by means of an arousal mechanism such that when persons feel crowded they experience a greater than optimal level of arousal (see Chapter 9 for a more detailed discussion). What effects overarousal might have on the developing child are as yet uncertain. Given the animal research reviewed here plus some limited human data on crowding, stress from overarousal, and overstimulation, we tentatively speculate that a suspension or general inhibition of maturation may occur if children are subjected to extremely crowded conditions for extended periods of time. There may be a critical period during which such exposure is more detrimental, but specification of such a period cannot be made at this time.

To our knowledge, the nature and extent of more severe stressors or of considerable overstimulation have not been investigated to any great extent in young animals or children. If more data exist or are forthcoming, they may shed additional light on our speculation about the effects of crowding on development.

Some Speculations and Further Research Topics

While writing this paper, some other related aspects of crowding occurred to us that might also be of interest relative to this developmental examination of crowding.

If it is correct that immediate stressor effects on behavior are more apparent only when the processing limits of the organism are approached, then it seems reasonable to suspect that because children presumably have smaller information-processing capacities, they would suffer information overload at a lower level of arousal than adults.

Glass and Singer's (1972) work on stress has indicated that one important variable in stress research is the person's perceived control over the stressor. Thus, persons who were stressed by noise and perceived that they had greater control over the noise exhibited less behavioral aftereffects than individuals who did not perceive that they had control over the same noise. The effects of stress may conceivably be exacerbated in children because they perceive less control over their environments than do adults. Booth and Johnson (1975) have speculated that children may experience greater discomfort from crowding than do adults because they have less control over the environment due in part to the fact that they have less mobility and are lower in social dominance. Of interest here is the recent finding by Sherrod (1974) that adults' perceived control can significantly reduce the negative effects of crowding as measured by postexperimental behavioral aftereffects. Less control presumably overlaps with lower dominance, which has been shown to be an important mediating variable in crowding's effect on rodents (Christian, 1961; Christian & Davis, 1964).

Another point worth considering is that although the laboratory work and field research discussed here provided adequate food and water, it seems that crowding in animals and humans would often coincide with malnutrition. Preweaned animals might be particularly affected because crowding has been shown to inhibit lactation (Autrum & Holst, 1968; Christian, 1961; Christian & Davis, 1964). Nutrition in general might be affected given increased demands for a fixed food supply or, in humans, a fixed economic level.

Furthermore, although under crowded conditions more organisms are jammed together, it appears that there is a marked drop in social interaction. Under extremely crowded conditions, maternal care was impaired or totally absent. In addition, there was less active exploration, play, and movement in crowded young. This may be the inverted U-shaped function in that moderate density leads to the most interaction.

Thus, the potential for social isolation and malnutrition seems realistic under severely crowded conditions. In addition to the documented effects of malnutrition (Altman, 1971; Cravioto & Robles, 1965) and Harlow's social isolation work on developing organisms (Harlow & Harlow, 1962), an article in *Science* by Levitsky and Barnes (1972) suggests that early malnutrition (during the first 7 weeks) and social isolation in male rats interacted to exaggerate their effects on the developing organisms. This was evidenced by reduced: growth, locomotor behavior, following behavior, fighting response, and exploration. Such interactions would seem to suggest some ideas about the relative overlap of various critical periods. Conditions such as the malnutrition and social isolation interaction suggest that at least in part the critical periods for these two environmental variables overlap.

Furthermore, some of the work with nursery school children suggested that crowding might constrict motor development. It will be recalled that when these children were placed in higher density environments, their body movements were inhibited and they chose more passive forms of play. In this regard, Shapiro (1974) has reported that young boys (mean age = 43 months) but not girls from high density homes (i.e., where 3 or more persons live per room) exhibited significantly less fine and gross motor competence than boys of the same age group who came from low density homes (one or less person per room). Furthermore, young rodents under crowded conditions did not explore as much as young rodents under normal density conditions. The data concerning altered motor development as affected by early motor experience, although complex, do suggest that certain later behaviors can be adversely affected by early motor restriction (Zelazo, Zelazo, & Kolb, 1972). As in the previous discussion, the possibility of an interaction between early motor experiences and malnutrition, social isolation, or both is intriguing.

We should also consider the natural occurrence of increased noise in more dense environments. Cohen, Glass, and Singer (Note 3) have reviewed the evidence for negative effects of noise on the development of verbal skills that occur even when hearing loss and various socioeconomic variables are controlled for. As they point out, the probability of increased noise levels in higher density living seems reasonable and warrants further research, particularly as to the potential interactive effects of both stressors on development.

Finally, one can speculate as to how crowding might affect the development of a sense of self or ego as differentiated from the physical and social environment. Under crowded conditions, one's privacy or ability to regulate interactions with others is presumably impaired. The development of identity is in part a process dependent on the recognition of one's ability to regulate interaction with the social environment. Furthermore, another facet of identity development is the achievement of a self-other differentiation that derives from an ability to control, manipulate, and explore one's physical surroundings. In *The Children of Sanchez*, Oscar Lewis has remarked that the children he saw seemed to have little or no property or space they could call their own, little freedom of choice in activities, and in general had little or no privacy and few opportunities to assert personally autonomous behaviors. Might not the potentially restrictive aspects of prevailing high density living impair the identity formation process?

OVERVIEW AND SUMMARY

In general, we think it would be accurate to conclude that young organisms are more severely affected by crowding than adult organisms. In addition, these young organisms seem to develop abnormally as evidenced by reduced body weight, sexual immaturity, and affected hormonal secretions and glandular structures. Perhaps this "abnormal" development can be considered as adaptation to an abnormal environment (Dubos, 1965). In particular, much evidence has suggested that crowding retards or suspends the maturation of the young organism. Some of the potential ramifications as well as physiological mechanisms for this retarded maturation were also discussed. Although there are some striking parallels in the developmental crowding literature between animals and humans, researchers are cautioned against drawing firm conclusions about the effects of crowding on children, given the small amount of human developmental data in this area. Clearly, there is some indication of restricted social interaction when children are crowded in a nursery school setting, but further hypotheses at this time must remain tentative.

In addition, we have attempted to relate some thought from research on stimulus overload and stress to further understand and predict the consequences of crowding on the developing organism. The stress and stimulus overload explanations of crowding were rejected in favor of an arousal mechanism. It was hypothesized that crowding produces greater than optimal arousal, which may be detrimental to health and well-being, particularly for the developing organism. Christian (1961) has stated that, "Any explanation of high density must account for the pronounced effects on immature as opposed to mature animals from the same population [p. 445]." Further research is clearly needed on crowding's effects on the developing organism. Potential questions include the specific relative effects at different ages, how the duration of crowding affects organisms, how crowding in humans can be altered by various acculturations, and the effects of different amounts of crowding on organisms. Developmental work might prove to be particularly useful in the study of the effects of acculturation on human responses to high density. As Draper's (1974) recent work has shown, it would be an error simply to conclude that high density is necessarily detrimental to normal development. The reader is reminded of Stokols' (1972) important distinction between density and crowding. Stokols has argued that we must consider the important constellation of various social, personal, and, we would add, ecological factors present in a situation to determine whether the level of density is perceived as crowding. For example, Draper (1974) found no physiological or social indicators of pathology in the !Kung bushmen who typically live at extremely high densities. The children in these communities are physically and emotionally healthy youngsters. Interestingly, these children appeared to be highly supervised, spending most of their early life in close physical contact with adult members of the community, although not necessarily the parents. Draper suggests that the ease of outgroup migration and large familial ties across villages, plus the proximate availability of open space, may all contribute as mediating factors to allow individual !Kung to cope with their high density living environments. In their society, one can easily leave the group and be alone temporarily or out-migrate without negative social sanction or fear of encountering primarily strangers in a new community.

The examination of the effects of crowding on the developing human presents several problems. Although it is certainly not possible experimentally to house children (or adults) for prolonged lengths of time under crowded conditions, naturalistic field research may be a workable strategy. Alternatively, age sampling developmental research might be useful as well, rather than longitudinal developmental research (Loo, 1973). Nevertheless, it is clear that much important information about how humans respond and interact with their environment may be gleaned from developmental analyses.

REFERENCE NOTES

1. Smith, P. K. *Aggression in a preschool playgroup: Effect of varying physical resources.* International Conference on Origins and Determinants of Aggressive Behavior, Monte Carlo, 1973.
2. Welch, B. *Psychophysiological response to the mean level of environmental stimulation.* Symposium on Medical Aspects of Stress in the Military Climate, Walter Reed Army Institute of Research, 1964.
3. Cohen, S., Glass, D., & Singer, J. *The effects of noise and crowding on the development of verbal skills.* International Symposium on Urban Housing and Transportation, Detroit, 1975.

ACKNOWLEDGMENTS

An earlier version of this paper was presented at the International Society for the Study of Behavioral Development, the University of Surrey, Guilford, England, July, 1975. I thank Dalton Jones, Chalsa Loo, Edward Nalband, Kathy Pezdek, and Daniel Stokols for their discussions of this paper.

REFERENCES

Altman, J. Nutritional deprivation and neural development. In M. B. Sterman, D. J. McGinty, & A. N. Adinolfi (Eds.), *Brain development and behavior.* New York: Academic Press, 1971.

Anastasi, A. Differentiating effect of intelligence and social status. *Eugenetics Quarterly*, 1959, *6*, 84-91.

Autrum, H., & Holst, D. V. Sozialer "Stress" bei Tupajas (*Tupaia glis*) und seine Wirkung auf Wachstum, Korpergewicht und Fortplflanzung. *Z. Vergleich. Physiol.*, 1968, *58*, 347-355. Cited by I. E. Eibesfeldt, *Ethology: The biology of behavior.* New York: Holt, Rinehart & Winston, 1970.

Berlyne, D. E. *Conflict, curiosity and arousal.* New York: McGraw-Hill, 1960.

Berlyne, D. E. *Aesthetics and psychobiology.* New York: Appleton-Century-Crofts, 1971.

Booth, A., & Johnson, D. The effect of crowding on child health and development. *American Behavioral Scientist*, 1975, *18*, 736-750.

Broadbent, D. *Decision and stress.* New York: Academic Press, 1971.

Calhoun, J. B. Population density and social pathology. *Scientific American,* 1962, *206*, 139-148.

Calhoun, J. B. Space and the strategy of life. In A. H. Esser (Ed.), *Behavior and environment.* New York: Plenum Press, 1971.

Chitty, D. Adverse effects of population density upon the viability of later generations. In J. Craig & N. Pirie (Eds.), *The numbers of man and animals.* Edinburgh: Oliver & Boyd, 1955.

Christian, J. Phenomena associated with population density. *Proceedings of the National Academy of Science*, 1961, *47*, 428-449.

Christian, J., & Davis, D. Endocrines, behavior and population. *Science*, 1964, *146*, 1550-1560.

Cravioto, J., & Robles, B. Evolution of adaptive and motor behavior during rehabilitation from Kwashiorkor. *American Journal of Orthopsychiatry*, 1965, *35*, 449-464.

Davis, D. E. Physiological effects of continued crowding. In A. H. Esser (Ed.), *Behavior and environment.* New York: Plenum Press, 1971.

Denenberg, V. H. A consideration of the usefulness of the critical period hypothesis as applied to the stimulation of rodents in infancy. In G. Newton & S. Levine (Eds.), *Early experience and behavior.* Springfield, Ill.: Thomas, 1968.

Denenberg, V. H. *The development of behavior.* Stamford, Conn.: Sinauer, 1972.

Draper, P. Crowding among hunter-gatherers: The !Kung bushmen. *Science*, 1974, *182*, 301-303.

Dubos, R. *Man adapting.* New Haven, Conn.: Yale University Press, 1965.

Esser, A. H. Biosocial perspective on crowding. In J. Wohlwill & D. Carson (Eds.), *Environment and the social sciences: Perspectives and applications.* Washington, D.C.: American Psychological Association, 1972.

Evans, G. W. & Howard, R. B. Personal space. *Psychological Bulletin*, 1973, *80*, 334-344.

Feshbach, S. Aggression. In P. H. Mussen (Ed.), *Carmichael's manual of child psychology.* New York: Wiley, 1970.

Freedman, J. The effects of population density on humans. In J. T. Fawcett (Ed.), *Psychological perspectives on population.* New York: Basic Books, 1973.

Galle, O., Gove, W., & McPherson, J. Population density and pathology: What are the relationships for man? *Science*, 1972, *176*, 23-30.

Glass, D., & Singer, J. *Urban stress.* New York: Academic Press, 1972.

Goeckner, D. J., Greenough, W. T., & Mead, W. R. Deficits in learning tasks following chronic overcrowding in rats. *Journal of Personality and Social Psychology*, 1973, *28*, 256-261.

Hall, E. T., *The hidden dimension.* New York: Doubleday, 1966.

Harlow, H. F., & Harlow, M. K. Social deprivation in monkeys. *Scientific American*, 1962, *207*, 136-146.

Harcourt, D. G., & Leroux, E. J. Population regulation in insects and man. *American Scientist*, 1967, *55*, 400-415.

Hunt, J. *Intelligence and experience.* New York: Ronald Press, 1961.

Hutt, C. Specific and diverse exploration. In H. W. Reese & L. P. Lipsett (Eds.), *Advances in child psychology (Vol. V).* New York: Academic Press, 1970.

Hutt, C., & Hutt, S. J. Effects of environmental complexity on stereotyped behaviors of children. *Animal Behavior*, 1965, *13*, 1-4.

Hutt, C., & Vaizey, M. Differential effects of group density on social behavior. *Nature*, 1966, *209*, 1371.

Kahneman, D. *Attention and effort.* Englewood Cliffs. N.J.: Prentice-Hall, 1973.

Kalela, O. Regulation of reproduction rate in subarctic populations of the Vole. *Ann. Acad. Sci Fennical.* Ser. A, IV, Biologica No. 34, 1957, 1-60. Cited by J. Christian, Phenomena associated with population density. *Proceedings of the National Academy of Science*, 1961, *47*, 428-449.

Keeley, K. Pre-natal influences on behavior of offspring of crowded mice. *Science*, 1962, *135*, 44-45.

Levine, S. Stimulation in infancy. *Scientific American*, 1960, Reprint No. 436.

Levine, S. Psychophysiological effects of infantile stimulation. In E. L. Bliss (Ed.), *Roots of behavior.* New York: Harper & Row, 1962.

Levine, S., & Mullins, R. F. Hormones in infancy. In S. G. Newton & S. Levine (Eds.), *Early experience and behavior.* Springfield, Ill.: Thomas, 1968.

Levitsky, D. A., & Barnes, R. H. Nutritional and environmental interactions in the behavioral development of the rat: Long term effects. *Science*, 1972, *176*, 68-71.

Lewis, O. *The children of Sanchez*. New York: Random House, 1961.

Loo, C. The effects of spatial density on the social behavior of children. *Journal of Applied Social Psychology*, 1972, *2*, 372-381.

Loo, C. Important issues in researching the effects of crowding on humans. *Representative Research in Social Psychology*, 1973, *4*, 219-226.

McGrew, P. Social and spatial density effects on spacing behavior in preschool children. *Journal of Child Psychology and Psychiatry*, 1970, *11*, 197-205.

McGrew, W. C. *An ethological study of children's behavior*. New York: Academic Press, 1972.

Milgram, S. The experience of living in cities. *Science*, 1970, *167*, 1461-1468.

Miller, N. E., & Bugelski, R. Minor studies in aggression: The influence of frustrations imposed by the in-group on attitudes expressed toward out-groups. *Journal of Psychology*, 1948, *25*, 437-442.

Mitchell, R. Some implications of high density housing. *American Sociological Review*, 1971, *26*, 18-29.

Morrison, B., & Thatcher, K. Overpopulation effects on social reduction of emotionality in albino rats. *Journal of Comparative and Physiological Psychology*, 1969, *64*, 658-662.

Munroe, R. H., & Munroe, R. G. Household density and infant care in an East African society. *Journal of Social Psychology*, 1971, *83*, 3-13.

Myers, K., Hale, C., Mykytowycz, R., & Hughs, R. The effects of varying density and space on sociality and health in mammals. In A. H. Esser (Ed.), *Behavior and environment*. New York: Plenum Press, 1971.

Newton, G., & Levine, S. *Early experience and behavior*. Springfield, Ill.: Thomas, 1968.

Preiser, W. Behavior of nursery school children under different spatial densities. *Man-Environment Systems*, 1972, *2*, 24.

Rosenzweig, M. Effects of environment on development of brain and behavior. In E. Tobach, L. R. Aronson, & E. Shaw (Eds.), *The biopsychology of development*. New York: Academic Press, 1971.

Schmitt, R. C. Density, delinquency and crime in Honolulu. *Sociology and Social Research*, 1957, *41*, 274-276.

Selye, H. The evolution of the stress concept. *American Scientist*, 1973, *61*, 692-699.

Shapiro, A. Effect of family density and mother's education on preschooler's motor skills. *Perceptual and Motor Skills*, 1974, *38*, 79-86.

Sherrod, D. Crowding, perceived control and behavioral aftereffects. *Journal of Applied Social Psychology*, 1974, *4*, 171-186.

Snyder, R. Evolution and integration of mechanisms that regulate population growth. *Proceedings of the National Academy of Sciences*, 1961, *47*, 449-455.

Southwick, C. *Ecology and the quality of our environment*. New York: Van Nostrand, 1972.

Spitz, R. A. Hospitalism: An inquiry into the genesis of psychiatric conditions in early childhood. In U. Bronfenbrenner & M. A. Mahoney (Eds.), *Influences on human development*. Hinsdale, Ill.: Dryden, 1975.

Stokols, D. On the distinction between density and crowding. *Psychological Review*, 1972, *79*, 275-277.

Swanson, C. P. *The natural history of man*. Englewood Cliffs, N.J.: Prentice-Hall, 1973.

Thiessen, D. Population density and behavior: A review of theoretical and psychological contributions. *Texas Reports on Biology and Medicine*, 1964, *22*, 266-314.

Waldrop, M., & Bell, R. Relation of preschool dependency behavior and family size and density. *Child Development*, 1964, *35*, 1187-1195.

Waldrop, M., & Bell, R. Effects of family size and density on newborn characteristics. *American Journal of Orthopsychiatry*, 1966, *36*, 544-550.

White, B. L. *Human infants.* Englewood Cliffs, N.J.: Prentice-Hall, 1971.

Wood, W., & Greenough, W. Effect of grouping and crowding on learning in isolation-reared adult rats. *Bulletin of the Psychonomic Society*, 1974, *3*, 65-67.

Zelazo, P. R., Zelazo, N. W., & Kolb, S. Walking in the newborn. *Science*, 1972, *176*, 314-315.

Zubek, J. P. (Ed.) *Sensory deprivation: Fifteen years of research.* New York: Appleton-Century-Crofts, 1969.

4

Crowding:
Methods of Study

Yakov M. Epstein
Rutgers - The State University
and
Andrew Baum
Trinity College

INTRODUCTION

Although experimental interest in crowding is a relatively recent phenomenon, the variety of approaches used to study crowding has outstripped theoretical and methodological refinement. Beginning with studies of high density animal populations and correlational treatments of archival data in the 1940s and 1950s, research on crowding has expanded into the laboratory, and experimental techniques have been applied to a variety of naturalistic settings. However, this methodological diversity has been associated with divergence of conceptual and operational definitions and has contributed to some inconsistency and confusion in the experimental literature. In this chapter, we discuss the range of crowding research methods, recognizing that many represent adaptations of more traditional research strategies. By doing so, we will attempt to identify some of the inconsistencies that have yielded somewhat different findings. Although it is clear that there is no *one* best way to study crowding, we feel that it is useful to review the strategies that have been used and to discuss the strengths and weaknesses of each. Although far from exhaustive, this review represents at least a beginning.

It is difficult to consider the adequacy of research methods without attending to the theories and conceptual frameworks that have generated them. Definition of crowding as an experiential variable and characterization of it as a function of person-situation interactions (e.g., Stokols, 1972) has suggested the importance of situational parameters and of individual differences in response to high density. Yet, many experimental treatments of crowding have failed to account for mediation of intervening goal orientations, seating arrangements, expectations, and the like (cf. Aiello, Epstein, Karlin, Note 1). Similarly, short-term laboratory studies must translate the impact of prolonged, perhaps inescapable, crowding into a brief encounter with crowding stress. To the degree that duration of exposure influences assessment of response (e.g., Baum & Valins, 1977), researchers should carefully consider how they generate experimental settings. Elsewhere in this volume, Karlin, Epstein, and Aiello (Chapter 5) have discussed another problem: generalization from experimental to real-life settings. They have, for example, differentiated between transportation, residential, and work environments, suggesting a number of critical events which evoke the label "crowded" in each of these settings. However, frequent attempts to generalize inappropriately from one setting to another continue to hinder meaningful interpretation of experimental findings.

One trap that must be avoided is "method boundedness", that is, allowing available technology to generate research questions rather than formulating questions to suggest procedural options and strategies. Crowding may appeal to some researchers because it appears relatively easy to manipulate. It is not difficult to restrict or augment the space available to a group of subjects, nor is it difficult to vary the number of people in each group. As one might expect, these two approaches are characteristically employed in laboratory studies of crowding. However, conceptual oversights resulting from a failure to recognize the experiential differences between numbers of people and available space led to confusing generalizations. It appears that conditions that evoke the label "crowding" are numerous and that they may have different effects on people. Large numbers of people, made salient by increasing group size, create problems that are different for us from those of limited amounts of space. Therefore, attempts to generalize from situations characterized by one or the other may be met with limited success. A better approach would be to consider the conditions under which spatial and social variables are important.

The importance of these issues and of more adequate conceptualization of crowding in different settings is reflected in Stokols' (Chapter 7) and in Karlin et al.'s analyses of the problem. Restricted space and inappropriately close proximity to others are major problems in crowded transit settings such as buses and subways but are of less consequence in crowded residential environments. Residential crowding is more likely to be characterized by unwanted interaction, congestion, and inadequate privacy. Although both problems seem to be centered around loss of control, each has different characteristics and should influence mood and behavior differently. This formulation suggests ways of structuring laboratory settings and specifying situations to which generalizations are appropriate. By using a setting-specific framework, researchers can determine whether their questions can be best answered in the laboratory or in the field. They can ask, for example, whether the real-life analogue involves long-term relationships, acute or chronic exposure, or whether other stressors (e.g., heat, noise) and social status variables are inextricably involved in the setting. The answers to questions such as these should dictate whether the problem would best be studied in the laboratory or by interviewing participants in the field, observing their naturalistic response to crowding, or re-referring to archival indexes of stress and pathology.

The remainder of this chapter is concerned with a variety of methods used to study response to crowding. Although we discuss a variety of research designs, data collection techniques, and modes of assessment, we are most concerned with experimental techniques. By identifying the types of questions to which each can be addressed, we attempt to attribute many conflicting findings to the differences between and the limitations of the various methodologies.

ECOLOGICAL CORRELATIONS

Research techniques differ from one another along several dimensions. Among these is the level of observation employed. The least detailed level of observation is the demographic level, at which attention is focused on relationships between gross indexes of density and pathology. Specific relationships and characteristics are not considered; women are interchangeable with men, adults with children, strangers with friends. It is as if the observer has climbed above a setting, observing occupants from a rather lofty perch. People are of concern primarily in terms of how many must use a given amount of space, and analysis of the effects of crowding at this level of observation is primarily concerned with the resulting index of proportion of space occupied. This approach affords a historical perspective on crowding and places it in the urban context in which it seems most prevalent. By considering statistical indicators of well-being and pathology, however, information about experience and coping behavior is lost, and analyses may therefore be incomplete. In addition, the use of gross indexes of density that may not adequately reflect the interpersonal nature of crowding can reduce the meaning of these studies. At the demographic level, control over variations of density may be unavailable, and we may not know whether people living in densely populated neighborhoods actually feel crowded.

The technique usually employed at the demographic level is an ecological correlational analysis. An example of one such study illustrates the technique. Galle, Gove, and McPherson (1972) investigated the relationship between population density and a range of pathologies in the city of Chicago. Chicago is divided by the Census Bureau into census tracts roughly analogous to the various neighborhoods of the city. For each of these tracts, information is available about the number of residents, the number of houses, the number of apartments in each apartment house, the number of acres covered by the tract, and so on. Also available from sources such as fact books, police records, and hospital records is information about births, deaths, crime, suicides, hospital admissions, and the like. Using this information, an investigator can devise indexes of population density and pathology. For example, the investigator can establish a density index for each tract by dividing the land area of the tract by the number of inhabitants of the tract. Thus, if a tract had 100 acres and was inhabited by 10,000 persons, the index value for the tract would be 10,000 persons/100 acres or 100 persons per acre. By determining index values for each tract and selecting specific indicators of pathology, such as the number of burglaries per 100 inhabitants, it is possible to compute the relationship between the number of persons per acre and the number of burglaries per 100 inhabitants. In practice, this procedure is not this simple. A variety of statistical controls is frequently used to eliminate confounding factors. However, in principle, the goal of this type of research is to determine the extent to which density is related to pathology.

As both Freedman (1975) and Stokols (1972) have suggested, crowding is determined by an interaction of psychological, social, and physical variables. Correlational analyses of urban density, however, do not generally consider these intervening variables and do not allow us to consider the crowding effects of density independently of other density-related urban phenomena. As a result, these studies do not allow us to determine whether pathology is the result of crowding stress or some other urban dynamic. Population density may be related to pathology, but it is difficult to adequately separate density from selection and classification variables that may determine who must live in high density areas (e.g., socioeconomic status, occupation, cultural background). As a result, observed relationships may be spurious. Social status not only suggests where people will live; behavioral options, such as escape, may be limited by earning power or background and can lead to different forms of pathology or dysfunction. Correlational studies do not enable us to specify the causes of urban pathologies and may not adequately reflect the relationships between crowding and pathology.

Some recently collected data reported by Baum, Davis, and Aiello (Note 2) suggest that these urban phenomena are best studied when the intervening influence of the neighborhood is considered. Rather than breaking tract density simply into ratios of people per room, unit, building, and tract, they considered blocks within these tracts, varying along dimensions thought to be related to group development and regulation of interaction with neighbors. When traditional persons per acre, building, unit, and room were considered, relationships with reported crowding stress, the quality of neighborhood interaction, and calls for police assistance were inconsistent and relatively small. However, when variables predicting the nature of social experience were added to the analysis, strong and consistent relationships with crowding, stress, control, and satisfaction variables emerged. Clearly, the use of indexes of density were not as meaningful in studying these phenomena as were theoretically derived interpersonal variables.

Additional problems are associated with ecological correlations. Robinson (1950), for example, has argued that ecological correlations spuriously inflate estimates of relationship for any given individual. Similarly, methods of devising input for these analyses may inflate or suppress relationships among variables. Although one could easily arrive at a consensual index of education history, accounting for the effects of poverty, for example, may cause difficulties. The choice of a criterion for poverty will, to a large extent, determine the results of the analysis. Using the same information, two different findings can be obtained. If we use median income as a criterion, our findings may be different from those based on the percentage earning less than $3000 per year. This problem is considered in a study conducted by Ward (1975). Using the same data as Galle et al. (1972) and using their criteria for index construction, Ward replicated their findings. However, when she used different criteria for index construction, her results varied from the original findings. Since the criteria for development of statistical indicators of status and well-being are frequently arbitrary, results of correlational analyses must be carefully scrutinized.

It appears that further efforts to determine statistical relationships among indexes of density, pathology, and well-being must proceed with caution. Although the use of more complex multiple correlation, regression, and path analyses may be more promising, potential bias in these procedures at nearly every choicepoint in the classification of data suggests that these analyses may be problematical. Because crowding seems to be an interpersonal process, demographic perspectives may not prove useful in studying it. Rather, these procedures may yield data more appropriate for general kinds of questions. Although it is important to continue refinements of these techniques, it is also necessary to develop alternatives to this research strategy.

OBSERVATIONAL RESEARCH

One alternative to correlational study of naturally occurring phenomena is the use of controlled observational techniques in the environments in which these phenomena occur. This research strategy may be viewed as a bridge between the experimental and nonexperimental influence, adding experimental control to a rather uncontrolled setting. Based on work by ethologists, anthropologists, and sociologists, rather complex coding scales have been developed (e.g., Hall, 1966) and complicated strategies of observation devised (e.g., Barker, 1968; Ittelson, Rivlin, Proshansky, 1970). Clearly, observer bias, uncontrollable subject variance, and limits on the identification of causal relationships can restrict the usefulness of this kind of study. However, when conducted with care, observational studies can be important additions to our experimental approximations of reality.

The observational methods initially applied to the study of crowding focused on the observation of children in high and low density settings (e.g., Hutt & Vaizey, 1966; Loo, 1972; McGrew, 1970). Using this approach, it was possible to study children on a playground, in a nursery school, or in other naturally occurring situations. By coding significant behaviors and the nature of interactions, valuable data were obtained, and researchers were able to record the ways in which social and spatial variations were related to isolated and antagonistic behavior.

More recent applications of observational methods are reflected in the development of behavior mapping techniques. This standardized observational method typically categorizes behavior and cross references each class of behavior with significant locations in the environment. Wolfe (1975), for example, obtained profiles of observed activities of children in hospital settings by having trained observers record activities into 19 analytic categories across an extended period of time. Similarly, by mapping behaviors in the dormitory settings, Baum and Valins (1977) obtained information regarding where residents of different dormitory complexes spent the most time, the nature of their activities in the dormitories, and the location of these activities. By studying ongoing processes in a particular environment, observational techniques provide a valuable and interesting mode of investigation.

EXPERIMENTAL APPROACHES

Experimental studies of crowding represent a more fine-grained level of observation than do studies using ecological observations. These studies are typically strong on internal validity and increase the likelihood of examining causal relationships, but they do so at great cost in terms of experiential realism (e.g., Patterson, 1977). Because these designs allow for the experimental manipulation of density, they give the experimenter greater control over antecedent and intervening conditions and allow selection of those effects that will be demonstrated by dependent variables. Furthermore, these procedures allow control over subject variance and represent, in some cases, valid analogues of real-life exposure to high density. However, high density laboratory conditions are necessarily limited in terms of duration and severity. Experimenters are faced with the problems of creating a situation in which subjects will experience crowding stress and of devising ways of supplying behavioral options that allow assessment of response.

Typical laboratory studies of crowding require groups of subjects to sit in a room and engage in some sort of task for a limited (and usually known) period of time. Density is artificially varied by manipulating either the number of people in each group or the size of the room. In most cases, the tasks subjects complete during the session are related to assessment of crowding, but they may be used simply as "filler" while increasing length of exposure. In either instance, however, these tasks may distract subjects from the manipulation of crowding and reduce experimental impact. As a result, subjects attending to experimental tasks may not have experienced crowding. In such an experiment, one should not expect subjects to behave as if they are crowded and should not base strong conclusions on such inconsistencies. Rather, unstructured settings in which behavior is not restricted nor attention removed from experimental manipulations would seem to represent more reflective laboratory situations.

Other problems most frequently related to the creation of an appropriate experimental setting must also be considered. Time constraints must be dealt with in a nonreactive manner, minimizing the effects of knowledge of duration as well as the rather brief exposure to laboratory conditions. Duration of exposure appears to be of considerable importance when predicting or identifying the impact of high density (e.g., Zlutnick & Altman, 1972). Short-term exposure to contrived laboratory densities may yield confusing and misleading information, and generalizations from these studies may be counterproductive (e.g., Baldassare & Fischer, 1976). However, the use of the laboratory to study crowding remains an important part of the attempt to understand complex socioenvironmental phenomena.

To eliminate some of the problems associated with the application of traditional experimental techniques to the study of crowding, several approximations of traditional methodologies have been developed. These approaches include the use of simulated high density environments, observation of preparatory responses to anticipated crowding, and observation of behavior when structure is not provided or movement is required. Specifically, these procedures address themselves to problems created by limited exposure to high density and situational mediation of this exposure. Additionally, they seek to provide conditions in which responses are possible and experience of antecedent conditions maximized.

Model Room Experiments

Desor (1972) described a technique she used to investigate the effects of architectural variations on the perception of crowding, and this model room procedure has received a great deal of attention from those interested in architectural, social, or psychological mediation of crowding (e.g., Baum & Davis, 1976; Cozby, 1973; Valins & Baum, 1973). By constructing scale models of different rooms and asking subjects to place miniature figures (representing people) in these rooms until they judged the room crowded, Desor obtained interesting findings regarding the effects of barriers, partitions, and other architectural features.

As an experimental technique, model room studies have several advantages, allowing experimenters to work with one subject at a time and permitting modification and manipulation of numerous social and physical properties of the situation. Additional control, achieved by varying definitions of the setting, allows for a great deal of flexibility in creating settings. The model rooms are easily transported to settings outside the laboratory and can be used with adults or children. The model room procedure may therefore be of particular interest to architects and designers interested in assessing user reactions to different environments. By varying specific design variables, subjects' reactions to different spatial arrangements can be studied. These procedures may be useful in obtaining pretest information that can be used in the design process. However, to determine the validity of the model room procedure, it is important to assess the correspondence between judgments rendered in model room situations and those rendered in actual rooms of the same type.

Simulations of real-world situations and environments have been used to study many aspects of psychology. Recently, projective or role-playing procedures have been used to study interpersonal spacing and more general forms of environmental response (e.g., Keuthe, 1962). However, simulation of environmental phenomena involves a reduction of experiential realism, and the correspondence between responses to simulated and actual conditions has frequently been low. Knowles and Johnsen (1974), for example, investigated intrapersonal consistency in interpersonal distancing and found that the correspondence across measurement was very low. Other findings of rather inconsistent ratings from projective or simulated situations to real-life settings also suggest problems with these kinds of procedures.

There is, however, a variant of the simulation technique that may hold more promise. In a recent series of studies, Mixon (1977) describes an active role-playing technique, drawing a distinction between it and its more common, passive form. In typical simulation experiments, subjects are provided with a script to which they are asked to react and render judgments from an "as if" perspective. An extreme example of this form is the exercise of describing Milgram's obedience experiment to psychology students and a panel of psychiatrists and asking them to state what they would do if they were subjects in that situation. These procedures require only that people *imagine* how they would behave in a given situation. In contrast to this passive stance, it may be possible to involve subjects *actively* in a similar episode (Mixon, 1977). Such involvement characterizes the behavior of stage actors or persons involved in psychodrama, and the recent report of Zimbardo, Haney, Banks, and Jaffe's Stanford Prison simulation (Note 9) is an example of actively involved subjects in "pretend" situations.

A somewhat similar extension is possible using the model room technique. Subjects could be given instructions that require them to assume the set of an individual in the model room situation. Rather than passively observing a room described as a "cocktail party," subjects could be asked to become actively involved in the role of a guest at such a party. Each new "doll" placed into the model room could be "fleshed out" so that it has a particular meaning. In such a setting, one could observe not only how many persons are placed in the model room before it is considered crowded but also the kinds of nonverbal reactions exhibited by subjects as each figure is placed in the room. An abbreviated form of this procedure was employed by Baum and Davis (1976) in which the effects of activity, room color, and visual complexity were studied. In addition to placing figures in the rooms, subjects were asked to "place themselves" (a specially marked figure) exactly where they would be in the room. This procedure yielded interesting data, especially when considering the effects of complexity, and revealed effects that were also found in studies using real people and real rooms (e.g., Worchel & Teddlie, 1976).

Other variants of the technique, however, have not been as useful. Knowles (Note 3), testing the hypothesis that the formation of groups within a larger setting will reduce perceptions of crowdedness, used methods adapted from those described by Desor (1972) and Cozby (1973). In one study, subjects placed figures into a model room in subgroups of 1, 3, or 6 figures and were allowed to place a total of 24 or 36 in the room. When placing figures one at a time, subjects were asked to continue adding figures until the addition of one more would make the room crowded. When using either group size, subjects placed the groups in the room until one more group would lead to crowding. Following figure placement, subjects were asked to rate the room as to how crowded it was, and, in group conditions, were allowed to add individual figures until one more would result in crowding.

Assuming that these instructions would establish comparable subjective definitions of crowding that would be applied to all conditions, Knowles attempted to measure the number of figures required to reach this uniform standard. Predicted effects of grouping suggesting that more figures were placed in the larger group size conditions were obtained, but the total number of figures (24 or 36) influenced ratings of crowding only when figures were placed individually. These findings suggest that uniform definitions of crowding were not being used by subjects. After listening to instructions asking them to fill the room until it became crowded, subjects rated the larger group size conditions as more crowded. Had subjects defined crowding consistently, one would expect that there would be no differences in ratings of crowding after placement.

Knowles' work suggests problems with model room procedures. To the extent that the reliability of this measure requires that the same definition of crowding be applied to each simulated setting, the index of that definition (numbers of figures placed) becomes difficult to interpret when definitions vary. Procedures that require subjects to deal with only one setting or in which subjects rate the crowdedness of rooms already "filled" with figures could eliminate most of this variance. However, it is difficult to base strong conclusions on evidence that is subject to such low intrarater reliability.

Other problems with this technique are evident, and they preclude the use of these procedures without replication in actual settings. Because subjects are not experiencing the setting, generalizability is limited. By asking subjects to project themselves into the setting, its visual properties assume artificially increased significance at the expense of auditory, olfactory, and tactile sensations present in actual settings. As a result, architectural features that reduce the degree to which figures can "see" each other may assume greatest importance to subjects and may be more readily responded to in model room situations. In practice, these visual barriers appear to be effective in reducing some problems, but it is unlikely that they are as powerful as is suggested by many simulation studies. It would appear that model room findings should be considered with caution until they are replicated and extended in actual settings.

Anticipation of Crowding

Baum and Greenberg (1975) have developed an approach to study what they term "anticipated crowding." In this procedure, subjects are brought to the laboratory and by means of highly visible cues (e.g., clipboards set out on tables, numbers of chairs, numbers of forms, numbers of pencils) as well as experimenter instructions, they are led to believe that they will interact with many or few others in a limited amount of space. As other participants (confederates) arrive, observations of nonverbal coping behaviors are recorded and subjective reports of discomfort and stress are also noted.

Studying preparatory coping behavior may reduce problems associated with the assessment of crowding in the laboratory. If subjects cope with short-term exposure to high density laboratory conditions, they may adapt to a situation *before* affective and behavioral assessment is conducted. This occurrence may result in a failure to observe coping processes and can lead to unwarranted conclusions about response to crowding. Presumably, subjects anticipating crowding are getting ready for it by assuming certain behavioral postures in advance. To some extent, then, coping processes may be observed.

Because this technique does not consider response to *actual* crowding, conclusions drawn from studies using it may have somewhat limited generalizability. However, the use of this technique does allow the study of people's cognitive respresentations of crowding. Response to anticipated crowding is guided primarily by what an individual already knows or feels about crowding; although expectations can be varied by changing elements of the situation, behavior and mood are determined primarily by what the subject expects to happen. Thus, interesting information about people's definitions of crowding and predetermined coping strategies can be studied.

Motion Techniques

One of the criticisms leveled at many studies of crowding is that they require persons to sit in rooms, sometimes silently, working alone at a task, trying to solve a problem as a group, or carrying on a discussion. Using this sedentary approach, the intrusive or goal blocking aspects of crowding are minimized. Is it not the case, argue critics, that persons become most annoyed by crowding when, for example, they cannot get to a counter to examine merchandise in a store, or they must push someone aside to get to a subway exit? The typical laboratory setting does not allow these events to occur and may reduce the negative impact of laboratory density. In an effort to create settings in which these consequences may be realized, several motion techniques have been used.

Dooley (1974) created a simulated grocery store consisting of a room wallpapered with "shelves" containing "goods" and varied the number of subjects using the "store." The subjects' task was to examine the goods and arrive at a list of "best buys" so as to obtain the most for their money. The quality of these judgments and the speed with which they were made was ascertained. The situation was both involving for subjects and corresponded to everyday experiences in supermarkets, and it suggested that people feel crowded when their view is blocked, when they bump into others, and when their goal-directed behavior is disrupted.

A similar approach was used by McClelland (1974), who required subjects to compile a bibliography. Access to resources was varied by the number of people in a given space who had to use the same card files. Several field experiments have utilized a similar approach. For example, Saegert, Mackintosh, and West (1975) created a situation in which people had to tour Pennsylvania Station in New York in a particular progression of steps, and others have studied subjects who were asked to move through high and low density settings other than laboratories. By allowing the settings to generate experiential and behavioral consequences and by not restricting the experimental procedures so as to minimize the impact of these consequences, valuable information can be obtained.

Field Research

Experimentation in the field, as has been done in several studies noted earlier, holds special promise for the study of crowding. Although there are problems with this approach that are usually related to uncontrolled variance in the setting and nonrandomization of subjects, field research typically studies real problems. As a result, realism and external validity are high, applications to the solution of problems more evident, and usefulness is more immediate.

Langer and Saegert (1977) studied the effects of increased cognitive control in high and low density supermarket settings by recruiting subjects at times when the store was crowded or relatively uncrowded. By giving some of their subjects information about the effects of crowding, they were able to improve subjects' task performance and reduce the discomfort they experienced while moving through the supermarket. One could challenge this study on a number of levels, because research in the field cannot control for as many things as can research in the laboratory. However, the strength of their findings, as well as recent evidence of similar phenomena while anticipating crowding in a laboratory (Baum & Fisher, Note 4), suggests that the problems associated with field research can be minimized.

Another interesting example of this kind of research strategy is a recent study of stress and urban commuting (Singer, Lundberg, & Frankenhaeuser, 1978).

Stress levels, as measured by subjective and physiological assays, were studied while commuters rode the train and immediately before and after the trip. All subjects rode a morning train, but half boarded the train at its first stop and rode all the way into town while the other half boarded approximately halfway between the start and finish of the line. Although the number of passengers in each car increased as the train approached its destination and subject ratings of discomfort showed a corresponding increase, commuters with longer rides were found to have lower rates of adrenaline excretion on the train. By studying a naturally occurring phenomenon in the field, Singer et al. found evidence for an ecological-social interpretation of commuters' experiences more directly related to control than to numbers.

Quasi-Experimental Strategies

Quasi-experimental designs have been used to study the effects of highway noise (Cohen, Glass, & Singer, 1973) and architectural design (e.g., Baum & Valins, 1977; Newman, 1972). Generally, these studies are very strong in terms of external validity, but the lack of randomization that characterizes these designs may result in uncontrolled subject variance. However, these problems can be overcome and can be used to study crowding.

An example of this kind of research is the series of studies conducted by Baum and Valins (1977). Designed to assess the impact of different architectural arrangements of dormitory space, this research also suggested that crowding and withdrawal were related to the size of local residential groupings. Residents of one dormitory design shared common living space with 33 other residents, whereas students living in the other design shared these spaces with only 5 others. Although housed under comparable densities and provided with equivalent amounts of space, residents of the former were more likely to feel crowded in their dormitory environment and tended to seek minimally involving social situations. Thus, an architectural treatment of group size and social control was studied and a relationship between architecture and crowding was found.

Many of the potential sources of variance in these studies were controlled in an attempt to account for the nonrandomization of subjects. Only freshmen newcomers to the dormitory settings were studied, and data were collected through survey and observational and laboratory procedures. Extensive background information was collected and included in data analyses, but it yielded no effects. Interviews with housing office personnel indicated that the assignment process was essentially random, and comparisons of students who were assigned or had chosen their residences suggested that this variable did not influence subjects' responses. The resident populations of the two different dormitory complexes were generally comparable. These analyses provided evidence that the groups would have been equivalent had it not been for the architectural treatment and suggested that the divergent mood and behavior observed were functions of the design variables being studied.

Research conducted by Baron, Mandel, Adams, and Griffen (1976) offers a second example of this kind of research. By studying response to dormitory life as a function of double and triple occupancy in bedroom units, they were able to observe several interesting dynamics. Furthermore, by considering background variables and method of assignment to dormitory residence, they were able to reduce problems associated with subject selection.

The findings of these and other studies (e.g., Aiello, Epstein, & Karlin, Note 5) have somewhat limited generalizability: All depend on rather unique and selected environments and populations. However, it appears that these strategies can be very useful in studying crowding if threats to internal validity can be minimized.

DEPENDENT VARIABLES AND THEIR MEASUREMENT

Most studies of crowding have sampled from five categories of dependent measures, assessing mood, stress or arousal, social behavior, task performance, and perception of the environment. In reviewing some of the different ways of assessing these categories, it may be possible to reveal additional methodological variance that may contribute to inconsistences in the experimental literature.

Mood

Generally, mood refers to individuals' feelings about themselves and others as a consequence of some manipulation of crowding. Several well-known instruments for assessment of mood have been used, including the Zuckerman Multiple Affect Adjective Checklist (Heft & Adams, Note 6) and the Nowlis Mood Adjective Checklist (Griffitt & Veitch, 1971; Saegert et al., 1975). These and other factor-analytic checklists have several subscales of use in studying crowding, including assessments of aggression, anxiety, perceived lack of control, and prosocial orientation. In addition, the design of many of these scales was directed toward measuring changes in mood over time and can assess rapid changes in mood. Used as a repeated measure in crowding studies, this kind of instrument can detect rather subtle changes in mood.

Other advantages of this kind of instrument are related to their use as one of several indicators of stress and arousal. Data indicate, for example, that mood scores are related to skin conductance measures of stress and to biochemical indexes such as corticosteroid secretion. However, the questions raised by crowding may not always be answered by one of these scales. Researchers have frequently created their own instruments using adjective checklists, direct questioning, and parts of scales used in other research. Assessment of attraction often uses questions derived from scales used in attraction research (e.g., Byrne, 1971), and measurement of self-perceptions may be based on instruments used in personality and social psychological experimentation. Although these "homemade" indexes of mood offer the researchers greater flexibility and allow for more fine-grained assessment of specific relationships, they vary from study to study and limit generalization of findings.

A related index of mood is the SCL-90, a 90-item psychiatric symptom checklist used to study dormitory crowding (Aiello et al., Note 5). Derived from a pool of items generated by epidemiological research, factor analysis of the scale reveals several mood subscales including anxiety, depression, interpersonal sensitivity, and hostility. This instrument assesses additional indexes of mood and represents another validated scale that can be used as a supplement to others. As a general rule, it is probably best to use one of these validated scales rather than constructing original sets of items whose psychometric properties are unknown. When questions exceed the capability of these scales, however, index construction is necessitated.

Stress and Arousal

A second aspect of crowding that has received a great deal of attention has been its stress or arousal-producing properties. One of the initial concerns of crowding research was to assess the degree to which crowding caused the kind of stress and dysfunction that had been observed in earlier animal studies. Interest in this issue has led to the development of numerous approaches to assessment, including the use of autonomic and biochemical trace measurements, performance on simple and complex tasks, observation of nonverbal behavior, frustration tolerance, and direct assessment of experience. McGrath (1970) has discussed the methodological problems connected with the measurement of stress, and we will not repeat them here. It is useful, however, to reiterate that the broad diversity of measures used to index stress is a limitation as well as a strength of crowding research. When only one mode of assessment is used, generalization of findings beyond that one procedure is limited. However, in administering different measures, studies often cannot be compared and interpretation is made more difficult.

As McGrath notes, deriving a comprehensive body of knowledge about a problem requires that we use several modes of assessment to permit generalization. Procedures such as those prescribed by the Campbell-Fiske multitrait-multimethod approach (1959) could accomplish this goal, but they are probably too costly to use in laboratory investigations of crowding. An alternate strategy, short of using as many different assessments as possible without being reactive, is the development of a comprehensive theory of crowding that would suggest appropriate measurement techniques and could specify relationships among these measures.

We do not intend to imply that the choice of modes of assessment is arbitrary. Rather, each technique has different advantages and disadvantages. The choice of assessment strategy depends on the goals of the research and the limitations imposed by its design. The assessment of skin conductance level, for example, is a relatively direct measurement of stress. Based on the assumption that under stressful conditions the electrodermal properties of the skin change, these assessments yield indexes of change in conductance level that can be recorded over time. However, movement and flexibility in the session are necessarily limited by the electrode-monitored measurement required, and the measurement of skin conductance is frequently reactive. Similarly, differences in degree of lability, as well as the sex of the subject, time of day, and other intervening variables, may add a great deal of variance.

A second psychophysiological assessment of stress has been the collection of biochemical assays of stress-related substances in the blood and urine (see Chapter 3). Less reactive than measurement of skin conductance, these measures may yield powerful indexes of prolonged stress and arousal (e.g., Singer, Lundberg, & Frankenhaeuser, 1978). However, because they depend on the accumulation of secreted substance they may not be suitable for short-term experiments. Furthermore, the assays are very costly, the assessments are very perishable, subjects are not fond of venipuncture, and often they do not want to bother collecting urine samples.

Several studies have attempted to assess crowding stress by observing its correlates in cognitive performance. Theoretically, it is expected that arousal leads to decrements in certain types of cognitive task performance as well as impairment of motor performance and interference with memory processes, reasoning, and problem solving (e.g., Zajonc, 1965). It is relatively easy to administer some of these cognitive tasks, and there are numerous tasks that have been used extensively and whose properties have been well documented and correlated with other measures. However, there are problems with these measures of stress. First, they cannot monitor arousal on a continuous basis. In fact, it is difficult to obtain repeated measures without confounding performance with practice effects and cognitive set. The introduction of tasks into high density settings may also distract subjects and reduce the amount of attention paid the stressful cues in the environment. For example, if one is involved in the solution of anagrams or in working on a proofreading task, attention may be diverted from the social stimulation provided by others in the crowded environment or from the impact of spatial restriction.

Cognitive tasks have also been used as measures of the stress-related aftereffects of crowding. In this context, several measures have been used, most notably the Stroop color test, indexes of tolerance for frustration, and proofreading tasks (Glass & Singer, 1972). The color test consists of a series of color names printed in different colors (e.g., the word "red" written in blue ink), and subjects are asked either to read the word or to identify the color. Attempts to cope with competing information provided by the word and its divergent ink color are presumably impaired when one is stressed. Frustration tolerance, usually assessed by having subjects work on unsolvable anagrams or puzzles is also used as an indication of poststressor costs. Persistence at these tasks is taken as an index of tolerance for frustration; as stress increases, persistence on the frustrating items should decrease (e.g., Sherrod, 1974).

These procedures have been used with interesting results, and they represent useful measures of stress and poststressor effects. However, they should not be administered to groups of subjects unless adequate precautions are taken to ensure that subjects are unaware of how others are responding. Conformity pressures to persist or to give up, as well as interference generated by oral responding on the Stroop, are quite likely in group testings.

Proofreading tasks have also been used to measure postadaptive costs. Subjects are typically given a passage into which errors have been systematically inserted. The number of errors correctly detected in a given amount of time is used as a measure of performance. It is probably advisable to use a standard passage with standard error insertions to allow maximal comparison with other studies. Also, by modifying the task so that subjects are required to use novel proofreading symbols, the task can measure quality of performance and test frustration tolerance.

Nonverbal behaviors such as self-manipulation, facial regard, axis of orientation, angle of leaning, and frequency of smiling have been used to measure stress indirectly. These behaviors can either be observed through one-way mirrors or recorded on videotape, each method having its strengths and limitations. At the outset, subjects who are being videotaped are somewhat self-conscious, but it is likely that they become less reactive to the presence of the camera. The amount of time required to adapt to the camera, however, may preclude its use in short-term study. It is possible to use concealed cameras, but this raises ethical problems. There are also technical problems related to videotaped recording; the clarity of visual resolution, for example, may be poor using standard videotape equipment. Although such resolution is probably of sufficient quality to allow for the coding of gross bodily movements, it may not be adequate for coding instances of eye contact. Additionally, videotape is expensive and recording entire sessions can become extremely costly, making time sampling necessary. Here, one must weigh the loss of cumulative information about the development of interaction patterns against the cost of continuous recording.

On the other hand, the use of videotape has some very clear advantages. The investigator who is initially interested in coding for one aspect of nonverbal behavior (e.g., head orientation) can later code for a different variable (e.g., body lean). By spreading out the task of coding so that coders can concentrate on only one variable at a time, information overload can be reduced and reliability increased. We have found that in order to establish sufficiently high coding reliability, observers must be trained extensively. We must also be certain that observers who are viewing live interactions do not influence one anothers' ratings by their own nonverbal responses, spuriously inflating reliabilities. If the behavior is live, it is impossible to obtain test-retest reliability. By using video-tapes, it is possible to show the same segment of behavior to several observers one at a time and to obtain independent ratings, and to show the same segment to the same observer at different times to assess rater reliability.

The theoretical and empirical link between measures of nonverbal behavior and stress has not been clearly established. The assumption underlying this approach is that stress is accompanied by tension and that individuals engage in nonverbal behaviors that reduce this tension. Although this assumption is plausible, it is necessary to specify the theoretical relationship between stress and nonverbal behavior. Only after this has been done will investigators have a sound basis for choosing appropriate nonverbal behaviors to use as dependent variables.

Social Behavior

Researchers and lay persons alike have shown great interest in the effects of crowding on social behavior, eclipsing concern for stress-inducing properties of high density settings. The popular literature has suggested that crowding leads to crime, drug addiction, aggression, and other urban pathologies (e.g., Zlutnick & Altman, 1972). To study these relationships, researchers have used many of the paradigms and procedures previously discussed. Some have used correlational approaches to assess the incidence of these pathologies, whereas others have depended primarily on assessment of laboratory analogues. Although these kinds of approaches may provide important information concerning crowding phenomena, the link between these analogues and their real world counterparts is often tenuous.

A primary cause of this lack of correspondence is related to practical limits placed on the operationalization of various symptoms of pathology. One example can be found in the research conducted by Freedman and his associates (cf., Freedman, 1975). Attempting to study the relationships between crowding and aggression, they dealt with ethical and laboratory-created limitations on the range of aggressive responses made available to subjects by using a simulated jury deliberation task. Subjects listening to a tape recording of several mock trials were asked to judge whether the defendents were guilty, and if guilty, were asked to determine an appropriate sentence. Length of sentence was used as a measure of aggressiveness. Although links between this task and more spontaneous aggressive responses are evident, it is doubtful that such an intellectualized analogue alone is adequate for the assessment of aggressive response to crowding. When tasks are highly removed from the ordinary behavior sequences in a setting, or when they are not sensitive to the problems created by the experimental treatments, conclusions based on them may be unwarranted.

Observations of social behavior among crowded subjects, then, must be sensitive to the treatment being studied and should reflect hypothetical coping strategies or costs. The use of structured tasks may be appropriate in some situations, and freer observation in an unstructured setting may be best in other situations. Task assessments may be useful in studying some forms of aggressiveness, group response to high density, and general affect for others (e.g., Baum, Harpin, & Valins, 1975; Freedman, 1975; Griffitt & Veitch, 1971). Similarly, observation of spontaneous responses may yield useful information about sociability, ability to deal with others, and aggressive- or withdrawal-oriented coping styles (e.g., Baum & Valins, 1977; Epstein & Karlin, 1975; Stokols et al., 1973).

UNITS OF ANALYSIS

One of the major procedural problems encountered when studying crowding is that many subjects are often required. It is usually difficult to recruit and schedule groups of subjects so that enough are present in each session to create crowded conditions. Faced with this problem, the researcher can schedule a few groups in each condition and use the individual subject as the unit of analysis, or he can consider many groups and use the group as the unit of analysis. For good reason, most researchers consider the latter; statistically, the use of the former can create error and reduce the accuracy of resulting analyses. However, it would be more efficient to consider each subject individually, and if independence of individual subjects can be established, nested analyses (e.g., Schiffenbauer, Schulman, & Poe, Note 7) considering individual subjects are appropriate. If groups are not allowed to interact and if there are no tasks that could result in interpersonal influence, a case for independence of response could be made. Whenever the possibility of group members' influencing one another is evident, this kind of assumption cannot be made and researchers should consider groups as the primary unit of analysis.

Rather than focus attention on ways of analyzing data obtained in rather costly laboratory investigation, it is useful to consider alternate modes of study that reduce the difficulties posed. The use of confederates, although imperfect, is one way of attacking the problem. By using confederates, the researcher can standardize interaction during the session by controlling the behavior of others present. Additionally, this procedure reduces the number of subjects required; if session behavior is standardized, individual subjects can be considered. However, the use of confederates limits the kinds of problems that can be studied and increases the likelihood of experimenter bias.

Alternately, researchers can use anticipatory crowding to investigate some issues. This method requires only two confederates and tends to reduce the likelihood of their influencing subject response. In this procedure, confederates are used primarily to confirm subjects' expectations, and interaction among participants is minimal. Other solutions require that the laboratory be used only for solitary observation (e.g., observation of crowded dormitory residents while they are waiting for the experimenter) or that the laboratory be abandoned in favor of field settings.

A related problem—choice of subject samples—is not unique to the study of crowding. Not surprisingly, most experimental work has been conducted with college students, and those studies that have considered different populations have typically used special populations (e.g., prisons, hospitals). These unusual subject pools place limits on generalization of findings and may result in unanticipated bias of findings. College students motivated by the need to fulfill course requirements are a case in point. Many of the experiments using these students have required them to work on tasks under conditions not unlike the work that they have done in 12 years of classroom experience. The fact that few decrements of task performance have been found should not be too surprising, as subjects are probably accustomed to working under these conditions.

Clearly, this problem can be overcome. Recruiting subjects for laboratory work from among noninstitutional populations (e.g., Freedman, 1975) should increase the meaning of findings. Although difficult and costly, such recruiting can be done. Similarly, field studies that involve more typical samples (e.g., McCarthy & Saegert, in press; Saegert et al., 1975) are helpful in extending the generalizability of research findings.

EXPERIMENTAL RIGOR: "DRUNKARD'S SEARCH?"

Most graduate students in social psychology and other areas of study receive training and indoctrination in the rigors of experimental design and control. We are told about the importance of subject randomization and the need to control all extraneous variables so that we can establish causal relationships between manipulated independent variables and dependent measures. Clearly, this is an ideal method of investigation. But is it a feasible approach for the study of environmental effects on behavior?

In his discussion of scientific methods in the behavioral sciences, Abraham Kaplan (1964) described an incident in which a policeman came upon a drunken citizen on all fours scratching around on the sidewalk under a lamppost. When asked what he was doing, the drunkard replied that he was searching for a lost housekey. The policeman asked him where he lived, and the drunkard pointed to a dwelling some 50 yards down the block. Concerned, the policeman asked whether he remembered losing the key in the vicinity of the lamppost. "Oh, no," replied the man, "I lost it in front of the house." "Why, then," asked the policeman, "are you looking for it in front of the lamppost?" Replied the drunkard, "Because that's where the light is." Perhaps there is a lesson in this tale for investigators studying the effects of the environment. On one hand, simple causal models amenable to controlled laboratory investigation may not adequately account for phenomena such as crowding. For example, Altman's (1975) model of crowding, an alternative to the simple causal model, represents a systems approach rather than a linear input-output model. No single laboratory experiment could adequately test his model. Rather, many different investigations are needed to accumulate information that can be seen as consistent or inconsistent with his ideas.

On the other hand, we must ask whether the laboratory, as we have been using it, is really the best place to study environmental effects. Singer et al. (in press) takes this position in a recent study of commutation stress:

> As psychologists turn to considerations of their environment, it is all important that studies be done of the environment itself. Theoretical or laboratory work can provide theories, hunches, and a host of detailed studies concerning the effects of selected and isolated variables; but they cannot substitute for a study of its aspects of the work outside the laboratory to which they are addressed. It thus requires acts of faith and extrapolation to move from a laboratory phenomena to recommendations of real application [p. 18].

Why do we cling so tenaciously to the laboratory experiment as the only acceptable source of information? Does it not require an act of faith to extrapolate from these data? We could continue to develop alternative models and paradigms with which to guide research and select experimental questions, experimenting with multimethod and quasi-experimental field and laboratory research. If we conduct field experiments or assess the effects of naturally occurring phenomena in the controlled atmosphere of the laboratory but cannot adequately control subject variance or extraneous environmental influence, a different act of faith is required. Without this added control, these approaches may yield spurious results that will have to await newer and improved studies for a better, although still imperfect, approximation of reality. However, with this control, it becomes possible better to approximate reality and to represent people's response to it. Although we should strive for the best technical approach to the generation of behavioral information, we should not do so by sacrificing creativity and methodological innovation. We should not feel that because experimental methods have been given the scientific seal of approval they should be used indiscriminately whereas less rigorous methods are to be avoided.

We are often presented with situations that we can study and that yield a great deal of fruitful information even though the information cannot be labeled "experimental" knowledge. A case in point is the program of research conducted by Baum and Valins (1977) in the dormitories at Stony Brook. Admittedly, subjects had not been randomly assigned to conditions, and it is possible that the results may have been accounted for by an explanation other than their social stimulation formulation. Yet the available alternative explanations are not as plausible as their explanation. The data "make sense." They are consistent with the findings of other studies. It would have been foolish for these investigators to pass up the opportunity to conduct these studies simply because they were unable to randomize the subjects. Likewise, it would seem unwise to dismiss their results because of their failure to exercise this control.

In this vein, we should like to suggest one alternate approach, a laboratory hybrid if you will, that might be appropriate for some investigations of crowding. This approach, discussed by Tomkins and Suedfeld (Note 8) as the "conjoint approach," is quite different from the typical laboratory orientation toward the study of complex social problems. Laboratory studies usually abstract one or two variables from the total complex of variables in the situation and attempt to randomize, control, or eliminate the others. In the laboratory method, the goal is to assess the contribution of a particular variable (e.g., density) to a set of effects. After obtaining results, the investigator often manipulates parameters and observes the ways in which results are affected. By a series of successive approximations, attempts are made to gain an understanding of the phenomenon. The implicit assumption being made is that one can eventually piece together the individual studies and that the results, taken together, will form a coherent picture.

Complex social phenomena such as crowding may be more amenable to conjoint research strategies directed toward the reliable production of the phenomenon of interest. Rather than beginning an investigation of crowding by examining the effects of high population density, an investigator using the conjoint approach would seek to create a situation in which, to the extent that it is possible, people feel the way they do in real-life crowding situations. To accomplish this, the investigator determines those variables that seem to be associated with crowding. Rather than distilling one or two essential variables, attempts are made to include as many variables as possible in order to produce the phenomenon reliably. Having reliably produced the phenomenon, the researcher, according to Tomkins and Suedfeld (Note 8), can then "examine the phenomenon itself in greater detail, its implications for futher behavior and for psychological processes such as attitude change, interpretations of the event, its interactions with personality variables of those people who are involved in the event, and the like [p.2]."

CONCLUSION

Research on crowding has generated a variety of investigative approaches and a relatively large body of information in a rather brief period. Current interest in the environment is likely to stimulate a great deal of additional research in this area. Research has been characterized by methodological innovativeness and by some degree of sophistication. It is clear, however, that many of the methodological deficiencies in the research stem from inadequate theoretical formulation. The development of theory is therefore necessary as an aid to methodological development as well as a stimulus to making research on crowding substantively interesting rather than an application of technology to an area that is, for the moment, of applied interest.

REFERENCE NOTES

1. Aiello, J., Epstein, Y., & Karlin, R. *Methodological and conceptual issues in crowding.* Paper presented at the meeting of the Western Psychological Association, San Francisco, April 1974.

2. Baum, A., Davis, G., & Aiello, J. *Neighborhood mediation of urban density.* Unpublished manuscript, Trinity College, 1976.
3. Knowles, E. *Social influences on the perception of crowding: Effects of setting and subgroup size.* Paper presented at the meeting of the Midwestern Psychological Association, Chicago, April 1976.
4. Baum, A., & Fisher, J. *Situation related information as a mediator of responses to crowding.* Paper presented at the meeting of the American Psychological Association, San Francisco, 1977.
5. Aiello, J., Epstein, Y., & Karlin, R. *Field experimental research on human crowding.* Paper presented at the meeting of the Eastern Psychological Association, New York, April, 1975.
6. Heft, H., & Adams, J. *Social stimulation and the crowding experience.* Paper presented at the meeting of the Eastern Psychological Association, Philadelphia, Pa., April 1974.
7. Schiffenbauer, A., Schulman, R., & Poe, D. *A nested analysis for data collected from groups; making crowding research more efficient.* Unpublished manuscript, Virginia Polytechnic Institute, 1976.
8. Tomkins, S., & Suedfeld, P. *The conjoint approach to psychological research.* Unpublished manuscript, Rutgers University, 1972.
9. Zimbardo, P., Haney, C., Banks, W., & Jaffe, D. *The psychology of imprisonment: Privation, power, and pathology.* Unpublished manuscript, Stanford University, 1972.

REFERENCES

Altman, I. *The environment and social behavior.* Monterey, Cal.: Brooks/Cole, 1975.

Baldassare, M., & Fischer, C. The relevance of crowding experiments to urban studies. In D. Stokols (Ed.), *Psychological perspectives on environment and behavior.* New York: Plenum Press, 1976.

Barker, R. *Ecological psychology.* Stanford, Cal.: Stanford University Press, 1968.

Baron, R., Mandel, D., Adams, C., & Griffen, L. Effects of social density in university residential environments. *Journal of Personality and Social Psychology*, 1976, *34*, 434-446.

Baum, A., & Davis, G. Spatial and social aspects of crowding perception. *Environment and Behavior*, 1976, *8*, 527-544.

Baum, A., & Greenberg, C. Waiting for a crowd: The behavioral and perceptual effects of anticipated crowding. *Journal of Personality and Social Psychology*, 1975, *32*, 671-679.

Baum, A., Harpin, R. E., & Valins, S. The role of group phenomena in the experience of crowding. *Environment and Behavior*, 1975, *7*, 185-198.

Baum, A., & Valins, S. *Architecture and social behavior: Psychological studies of social density.* Hillsdale, N.J.: Lawrence Erlbaum Associates, 1977.

Byrne, D. *The attraction paradigm.* New York: Academic Press, 1971.

Campbell, D., & Fiske, D. Convergent and discriminant validity by the multitrait-multimethod matrix. *Psychological Bulletin*, 1959, *56*, 81-105.

Cohen, S., Glass, D., & Singer, J. Apartment noise, auditory discrimination, and reading ability in children. *Journal of Experimental Social Psychology*, 1973, *9*, 407-422.

Cozby, P. Effects of density, activity, and personality on environmental preferences. *Journal of Research in Personality*, 1973, *7*, 45-60.

Desor, J. Toward a psychological theory of crowding. *Journal of Personality and Social Psychology*, 1972, *21*, 79-83.

Dooley, B. *Crowding stress: The effects of social density on men with "close" or "far" personal space.* Unpublished doctoral dissertation, University of California, Los Angeles, 1974.

Epstein, Y., & Karlin, R. Effects of acute experimental crowding. *Journal of Applied Social Psychology*, 1975, *5*, 34-53.

Freedman, J. *Crowding and behavior.* San Francisco: Freeman, 1975.

Galle, O., Gove, W., & McPherson, J. Population density and pathology: What are the relationships for man? *Science*, 1972, *176*, 23-30.

Glass, D., & Singer, J. *Urban stress.* New York: Academic Press, 1972.

Griffitt, W., & Veitch, R. Hot and crowded: Influences of population density and temperature on interpersonal affective behavior. *Journal of Personality and Social Psychology*, 1971, *17*, 92-98.

Hall, E. *The hidden dimension.* New York: Doubleday, 1966.

Hutt, C., & Vaizey, M. Differential effects of group density on social behavior. *Nature*, 1966, *209*, 1371-1372.

Ittelson, W., Rivlin, L., & Proshansky, H. The use of behavioral maps in environmental psychology. In H. Proshansky, W. Ittelson, & L. Rivlin (Eds.), *Environmental psychology.* New York: Holt, 1970.

Kaplan, A. *The conduct of inquiry.* San Francisco: Freeman, 1964.

Keuthe, J. Social schemes and the reconstruction of social object displays from memory. *Journal of Abnormal and Social Psychology*, 1962, *65*, 71-74.

Knowles, E., & Johnsen, P. Intrapersonal consistency in interpersonal distance. *JSAS Catalog of Selected Documents in Psychology*, 1974, *4*, 124.

Langer, E., & Saegert, S. Crowding and cognitive control. *Journal of Personality,* 1977, *35*, 175-182.

Loo, C. The effects of spatial density on the social behavior of children. *Journal of Applied Social Psychology,* 1972, *4*, 372-381.

McCarthy, D., & Saegert, S. Residential density, social overload, and social withdrawal. In J. R. Aiello & A. Baum (Eds.), *Residential crowding and design.* New York: Plenum, in press.

McClelland, L. *Crowding and social stress.* Unpublished doctoral dissertation, University of Michigan, 1974.

McGrath, J. (Ed.) *Social and psychological factors in stress.* New York: Holt, 1970.

McGrew, P. Social and spatial density effects on spacing behavior in preschool children. *Journal of Child Psychology and Psychiatry*, 1970, *11*, 197-205.

Mixon, D. Studying feignable behavior. *Representative Research in Social Psychology*, 1977, *7*, 89-104.

Newman, O. *Defensible space.* New York: Macmillan, 1972.

Patterson, A. Methodological developments in environment-behavioral research. In D. Stokols, *Perspectives on environment and behavior.* New York: Plenum Press, 1977.

Robinson, W. Ecological correlation and the behavior of individuals. *American Sociological Review*, 1950, *15*, 351-357.

Saegert, S., Mackintosh, E., & West, S. Two studies of crowding in urban public places. *Environment and Behavior*, 1975, *7*, 159-184.

Sherrod, D. Crowding, perceived control, and behavioral aftereffects. *Journal of Applied Social Psychology*, 1974, *4*, 171-186.

Singer, J., Lundberg, U., & Frankenhaeuser, M. Stress on the train: A study of urban commuting. A. Baum, J. Singer, & S. Valins (Eds.), *Advances in environmental psychology* (Vol. 1). Hillsdale, N.J.: Lawrence Erlbaum Associates, 1978.

Stokols, D. On the distinction between density and crowding: Some implications for future research. *Psychological Review*, 1972, *79*, 275-277.

Stokols, D., Rall, M., Pinner, B., & Schopler, J. Physical, social, and personal determinants of the perception of crowding. *Environment and Behavior,* 1973, *5*, 87-115.

Valins, S., & Baum, A. Residential group size, social interaction, and crowding. *Environment and Behavior*, 1973, *5*, 421-439.

Ward, S. Methodological considerations in the study of population density and social pathology. *Human Ecology*, 1975, *3*, 275-286.

Wolfe, M. Room size, group size, and density: Behavior patterns in a children's psychiatric facility. *Environment and Behavior*, 1975, *7*, 199-224.

Worchel, S., & Teddlie, C. The experience of crowding: A two-factor theory. *Journal of Personality and Social Psychology,* 1976, *34,* 30-40.

Zajonc, R. Social facilitation. *Science*, 1965, *149*, 269-274.

Zlutnick, S., & Altman, I. Crowding and human behavior. In J. Wohlwill & D. Carson (Eds.), *Environment and the social sciences*. Washington, D.C.: American Psychological Association, 1972.

5

A Setting-Specific Analysis
of Crowding

Robert A. Karlin
Yakov M. Epstein
John R. Aiello
Rutgers - The State University

Although the term *crowded* has been applied to many situations, most of the time spent by urban dwellers in crowded environments occurs in a relatively small number of settings. The everyday life of a city resident usually involves a fairly limited set of activities. Employed persons get up in the morning, travel on mass transit, walk or drive to work, remain at work all day (except for a lunch break), and then return home in the evening. During evenings and weekends, they shop and use recreational facilities such as parks, restaurants, and theaters. On occasions they may participate in a demonstration or large meeting or otherwise be part of a large public gathering. We submit that the majority of situations that people label as being crowded occur in one of these contexts.

There are several implications for applied research on crowding that follow from our suggestion that people are crowded in this limited set of situations. If we are to understand how crowding affects people and how it may be ameliorated, we must design studies focusing on each of these settings. The limited number of settings makes this feasible. If we are to understand crowding in residences, we must concentrate our research on variables relevant to residential crowding. Thus, seating strangers very close to each other for a short period of time and studying their task performance may shed very little light on the effects of living in a crowded apartment. Research manipulating the degree of privacy available and measuring ability to resolve conflict cooperatively would seem more relevant to residential settings.

The concern of this chapter, then, is the creation of appropriate laboratory analogues to real-world situations in which people become crowded. To create such analogues a careful consideration of the real-world situation is necessary.

For example, the applied researcher must consider what events in the environment precipitate the perception of crowding in that particular setting. He must know what kinds of activities are engaged in and are disrupted by crowding in that setting. Moreover, he must make a distinction between logical possibilities and applied reseach priorities. Although it might be interesting to know how the crowded subway rider feels about the person next to him, from an applied standpoint it is probably more important to assess the effects of the ride on his subsequent interactions with family members at home. Similarly, in terms of effective interventions, real-world considerations may be taken into account. One possible intervention in crowded subways is to provide much more space by building many additional subway cars, but practical considerations render this a low probability occurrence. Alternate strategies, such as exploring social manipulations related to traveling in the company of friends and thereby reducing the salience of the crowded environment, may be a more profitable investment of research efforts.

We would note that the basic researcher is much less subject to these constraints. He need not be concerned about shaping his experimental paradigm to conform to real-world contours. But the person who wishes to study the gross social effects of living in a crowded apartment or traveling daily on crowded public transportation facilities confronts a different problem. If he goes to the laboratory, he does so in order to create a controlled setting from which to generalize about real-world phenomena. To do so he must use a laboratory paradigm that is not conceptually different from the real-world setting about which he wishes to generalize. Although it is probably the case that some students of crowding have a basic research orientation, most of them hold an implicit value assumption about the importance of applied research. This assumption dictates a concern with generalizing from the laboratory to the real world. A survey of the introduction and discussion sections of journal articles concerned with crowding would support this hypothesis.

QUESTIONS TO BE ASKED BY THE APPLIED RESEARCHER

There are a large number of ways in which a laboratory paradigm may conceptually differ from the real-world situation that interests the applied researcher. Before beginning to design a study of crowding that has applied implications, the researcher must decide which setting he wishes to study. There seem to be five prototypical settings in which crowding occurs: residential settings, work settings, mass transit settings, shops and restuarants, and large public gatherings.

Once the setting has been chosen, the researcher must determine specific events that evoke the label "crowded" in that setting. This question is centrally important because it determines what paradigm he will choose to cause his subjects to feel crowded. Crowding always involves an imbalance between people and available space, but there seem to be three events that may occur as a result

TABLE 1
List of Questions to Be Asked in Designing Crowding Studies

A. Which central event will be manipulated to evoke the label "crowded"?
  1. Will persons lack the ability to control interpersonal interaction (i.e., will they lack privacy)?
  2. Will persons be in close physical proximity to others?
  3. Will persons experience congestion and a scarcity of resources?
B. How will concomitant environmental conditions be handled?
  4. How intimate is the relationship between the person and others with whom he is crowded? Are they family, associates, or strangers?
  5. What is the age composition of the crowded group?
  6. What is the sexual composition of the group?
  7. What is the distribution of ages within the group?
  8. What is the racial composition of the group? Is it homogeneous?
  9. What is the distribution of socioeconomic status in the group?
  10. Is the crowding a chronic situation or is it a one-time occurrence, or is it episodic (i.e., briefly occurring but repeated over several occasions)?
  11. What important activities occur in the setting? Are there tasks that must be accomplished, or is the maintenance of affective relationships the more important need in the setting?
  12. What physical features of the situation (such as heat, noise, or odors) that occur in addition to the inadequate people-space ratio may add to the stress of the situation?
  13. What important psychological factors (such as danger and unpredictability, norms, the opportunity for social comparison, adaptation, sensitization, etc.) may be inherent in the real-world setting?
C. What effects can be expected given the setting in which crowding occurs and the important central events in that setting? Which effects should be studied first given the large number of possible effects that can be studied?
  14. Are tasks performed in the setting and is it reasonable to expect that the performance will be affected by crowding?
  15. Is mood likely to be affected?
  16. Is the perception of the environment altered and is it a concern that should be given a high research priority?
  17. Are communication patterns likely to be affected?
  18. Is crowding in this setting liable to result in social pathology (crime, delinquency, etc.)?
  19. Are emotional and physical health likely to be affected? How?
  20. Would this form of crowding adversely affect the perceived quality of life?
D. In what time frame can the effects of crowding be expected to occur?
  21. Do the important effects occur prior to crowding when the person anticipates participating in a crowded setting?
  22. Do the important effects occur while the person is in the crowded setting?
  23. Do the important effects occur immediately after crowding?
  24. Do the important effects occur only after a sufficient accumulation of exposure to the stressor on repeated occasions?
E. What is the most useful research strategy for studying the effects of crowding in a given setting?
  25. Should the method be a laboratory analogue, survey research, archival research, interview, or field experiment?

of this imbalance. Each of these events will evoke the label "crowded." These events are congestion-resource scarcity, an inability to control and limit interactions with others, and extremely close physical proximity to others. We discuss each of these events in greater detail later and note their place in each of the prototypical settings.

Once the researcher has determined his central crowding manipulation, another set of setting/experiment similarity issues must be met. These involve such dimensions as the age and sex of the crowded interactants, the time frame in which crowding occurs, and other physical factors such as heat or noise that are salient aspects of the real-world environment. A more complete outline of these issues appears in Part B of Table 1.

To illustrate the importance of these issues for the ability to generalize about the effects of crowding, let us consider just one of them — the time frame in which crowding occurs. Crowding may be acute — that is, a one-time, short-term occurrence such as being in the midst of a public rally or demonstration. It may be chronic, as when people live together for many years in a crowded apartment. Finally, it may be episodic — that is, of short duration but occurring repeatedly, such as daily commutation on crowded mass transit facilities. In most laboratory studies of crowding, subjects are exposed to a single, short crowding incident. The effects of chronic exposure to crowded living conditions may be quite different from the effects of such short-term exposure.

Not taking such considerations into account may result in totally unjustified generalizations. For example, the common finding of studies of acute crowding involving extremely close interaction distances is that women react more positively than men (Freedman, Levy, Buchanan, & Price, 1972; Stokols, Rall, Pinner, & Schopler, 1973; Epstein & Karlin, 1975). However, our studies of crowded dormitory rooms at Rutgers show that in chronic situations involving lack of control over interpersonal interactions and resource scarcity, young women suffer more severely from crowding than do their male counterparts. The same interdependent style that leads to positive outcomes for women in the acute time frame seems to expose them to additional stress over long periods of time in this crowded environment. These results emerged only through study of chronic crowding. No acute experiment, no matter how carefully designed, could have revealed this pattern of results.

Thus, laboratory studies of crowding in residences may be best conducted on populations whose experience of crowding occurs not in the laboratory but in their real-world living conditions. The work of Baum and Valins (1973) and Baron, Mandel, Adams, & Griffen (1976) on residents of crowded dormitories are examples of how such research may be conducted.

Once the applied researcher is reasonably certain that his laboratory paradigm does not obviously differ from his real-world setting, other issues must be raised involving measurement. Here the central question is, "What effects seem both probable and important in the real-world crowded environment?" In some settings, crowding may disrupt task performance; in others communication may be important; in chronic or episodic crowding, there may be effects on health or social pathology. The choice of appropriate dependent variables is a very complex issue. It is easy to choose to measure reactions to crowding that are essentially irrelevant to applied concerns. In the early stages of our own work, for example, we carefully studied the effects of crowding involving close physical proximity on cohesion within the crowded group. However, crowding involving extremely close physical proximity occurs most frequently and importantly on mass transit facilities. It is probably of only minor interest, then, to understand how much cohesion such crowded interactants are liable to develop. The most important interpersonal effects of crowding probably have to do with how individuals react to others in their work and home environments after they leave the crowded subway. Therefore, rather than group cohesion during crowding we might have more effectively studied the aftereffects of crowding on such processes as conflict resolution. Sherrod's (1974) work on frustration tolerance after such crowding and Singer, Lundberg, and Frankenhaeuser's (1978) work on catecholamine levels after subjects rode commuter trains reflect a more appropriate choice of dependent variables. A list of questions having to do with measurement issues is included in Part C of Table 1.

Another series of questions involves a consideration of technological interventions that may ameliorate the effects of crowding. First, the researcher must ask what event in the crowded situation is most clearly related to user stress in the setting? For example, when one is standing in line outside a crowded restaurant (congestion), he is in close proximity to others (close physical proximity), and their presence might inhibit intimate conversation (lack of control over interpersonal interaction). However, for most people the crucial problem stems from having to wait before they can react (congestion). Effective interventions would have to address themselves to this problem in particular. A second question is: What intervention strategies are most practical? Are social or architectural interventions possible? Finally, the researcher should ask, "What measures can I use to assess the effectiveness of the intervention?" Rather than relying on his own judgment, the researcher or architect should gather input from the users of these facilities.

EVENTS THAT EVOKE THE LABEL "CROWDING"

We believe there are several events that occur in crowded settings that are responsible for evoking the label "crowded." The most salient events we have been able to identify are congestion and resource scarcity, an inability to control and limit interactions with others, and close physical proximity to others.

Lack of Control Over Interpersonal Interaction

Lack of control over interpersonal interaction has been discussed extensively in terms of privacy needs (Altman, 1975) and in terms of excessively frequent, unwanted interaction (Baum & Valins, 1973). This problem seems most important to crowding in work and residential settings. For example, in work settings constant interruptions by others may interfere with the performance of tasks. Such interruptions may occur intentionally, as when a colleague stops to chat at an accessible desk or inadvertently, as when conversations of nearby others are distracting. In dormitories Valins and Baum (1973) have found unwanted interactions with others to be a central element in a crowded residential environment. In the home, people may often wish to limit their interaction with others. For example, a husband and wife may wish to argue without the concurrent problem of dealing with their children. Inadequate space makes this type of interaction control impossible. Lack of control over interpersonal interaction is less important in other settings. In a crowded restaurant, the problem is not that one does not wish to be interrupted by other people waiting in line but rather that a number of people wish to use the same set of limited resources at the same time. Once inside the restaurant, however, tables spaced too closely together may inhibit intimate conversation. In this way, lack of control over interpersonal interaction may play a role in this setting.

Congestion

Congestion occurs when a number of people attempt to use a limited resource. Congestion in the context of crowding occurs when those people are physically present and their presence impedes the expected temporal flow or ease of progress toward the goal region. When this occurs, there often seems to be a tendency for people to congregate relatively closely together near the goal region. The analogy here is the proverbial "theater on fire." Even though the theater may be half empty, the need for rapid access to the doorway may produce a traffic jam. There are numerous examples of crowding related to congestion in city life. The traffic jam produced by too many cars attempting to use a given highway, the line at a popular movie, the cluster of people around an office Xerox machine, or children waiting their turn to use the slide in the park — all these cause a temporal delay in goal attainment. Congestion has an obvious role in crowding in residences and work settings and in shops and recreational facilities. It may play an important role in mass transit when inability to find a seat may influence reactions to crowded buses or subways.

Although congestion seems to be the central event in some crowded environments, it seems less important in other settings. As noted, once one is inside a crowded restaurant, congestion may be much less salient. Similarly, once one is positioned on a crowded bus or subway, other factors such as extremely close interaction distance may be central to the experience of crowding.

There is one form of congestion that gives rise to the label of "crowding" but that has no spatial component. This occurs when there is a shortage of roles or activities compared with the number of persons who wish to participate. Wicker (1972) has referred to this as "overmanning." Overmanning may be illustrated by the comment that the field of teaching is too crowded. An overabundance of participants may cause entrance requirements to become more stringent. Wicker believes that once one is in the setting overmanning can lead to decreased efficiency due to such factors as diffusion of responsibility and a lowered sense of involvement in the activities.

Close Physical Proximity

When people are forced into extremely proximate interaction with others, the situation is frequently labeled as being crowded. The close proximity to others contributes to the perceived lack of control often found in crowded environments (Sherrod, 1974; Singer et al., 1978). In the city, extremely proximate interaction with others is found most clearly in mass transportation. The "sardine can" quality of a rush-hour subway is an instance in which people are clearly exposed to this aspect of crowding. Although this is an important event in some forms of crowding, it is totally irrelevant in some other crowded settings. In crowded apartments, people may never have to approach one another very closely. Here other events such as lack of control of interpersonal interaction and congestion dictate that the situation is crowded.

SETTING-SPECIFIC FEATURES AND THEIR IMPLICATION FOR RESEARCH DESIGN

Let us now turn to a description of the settings in which crowding occurs. In each of these settings, we will attempt briefly to answer the questions we have previously posed. These answers are not meant to present an all inclusive picture but rather to raise some points that seem important in considering these settings. To aid the reader we have placed numbers in parentheses at various points in the discussion of residential crowding. These numbers refer to questions found in Table 1. The reader who is interested in considering the types of questions we have found helpful in conceptualizing each of these settings is advised to consult Table 1 at the appropriate points in the discussion.

Residential Crowding

Crowding in residences was probably the most important form of real-world crowding in stimulating research on the effects of crowding. Early studies on crowding often refer to the potentially severe effects of residential crowding on slum dwellers and point to Calhoun's (1962) work on the disastrous effects of such crowding on rodents. Crowding in residences usually involves two events: lack of control over interpersonal interaction and congestion (1, 3). The first event may be seen in light of the concept of optimum spacing. Here we are concerned with finding the best spacing pattern possible to avoid critical negative interactions, interactions not easily forgotten, forgiven, or even accepted, in family life. The husband who comes home in a bad mood may have a high probability of arguing with his wife if he is forced, by the space available, into her physical proximity. A den into which he can retreat may lower the probability that an argument will occur. Arguments of this kind can be quite disruptive; they can comprise a critical negative interaction. Optimal spacing can help to lower the probability that this will occur. Alternately, although enough space is usually available, the lack of sufficient facilities in one area may cause considerable friction in the family. For example, in a family of four or five people, all of whom have to leave the house by 8:30 A.M., the availability of only one bathroom may give rise to conflicts. Once again crowding, now in the form of congestion and resource scarcity, gives rise to an increase in the probability of a critical negative interaction.

Crowding in residences most often takes place with members of one's family (4). There are some major exceptions to this: these occur mainly among young adults in such situations as dormitories and shared apartments. Alternately, the aged and other institutionalized populations are other instances in which crowding in residences does not occur within a family unit (5). When attempting to study families in residences, however, differential roles and expectations comprise an important constellation of variables (13).

Crowding in residences is a chronic problem (10). In considering the effects of congestion-resource scarcity and lack of control over interpersonal interactions on the crowded family, one must consider the development of patterns of interaction. Conceptualizing this problem within a stress paradigm, chronic difficulties may lead either to adaptive coping mechanisms or to increased sensitization (13). Depending on the severity of the stress, we may first see one pattern and then the other. Avoidance responses and other patterns based on anticipation of a chronically crowded environment may also be important. It should be noted that these patterns may require time to develop (24). One might find a very different pattern of interaction among crowded roommates when they are studied at the beginning and at the end of the semester.

In speaking of residential crowding, the goal of the setting may be seen as very diverse (11). In most families, the home is used for both affective maintenance and the performance of a variety of tasks. Both functions are appropriate and necessary in the setting. Crowding may interfere with the ability of a husband and wife to resolve a conflict easily because of the interfering presence of children (17). Alternately, cooking in a kitchen that is simultaneously occupied by children at play may constitute an instance of congestion-related task interference. Task interference may also take place in the realm of cognitive activities (14). Children have to do homework, adults may wish to read books, magazines, or newspapers, and these may be interfered with by the congestion and lack of control over interpersonal interactions seen in the crowded home. Finally, when we talk about the functions of a home, we must note that it is supposed to function as a retreat from the outside world, a retreat that provides for rest, recreation, and relaxation. Crowded conditions that interfere with these functions may take their toll on mental and physical health (19).

As to the question of which effects are important, the effects of residential crowding on both the individuals in the home and their interactions, the family as a unit must be examined (22, 23). In the first case, the effects of residential crowding on work and school performance and the social lives and health of individual family members must be considered. A child who cannot do his homework easily or well because he is constantly interfered with by other family members, the adult who sets off for work in a bad mood (15) because of difficulties over use of the bathroom — these are examples of individual effects. Other important questions concern family interaction in general. Such issues as group cohesion, conflict resolution, and communication patterns seem to be fruitful areas for study.

Important effects of crowding in residences may occur before, during, and after actual crowding events. People may avoid spending time at home or refuse to invite friends to the home because of a lack of control over interpersonal interactions in the home (1, 21). The work of Mitchell (1971) provides evidence for the occurrence of this process. Furthermore, the research of Baum and Greenberg (1975) on the anticipation of crowding seems relevant here. The irritation that may arise among family members due to crowding is an example of how people may be affected while in the setting (22). Lowered tolerance for frustration at work after a crowded morning at home is an example of the after-effects of residential crowding (23). The problems we find most interesting here concern effects on family interaction.

Finally, we must consider intervention strategies to ameliorate the problems of crowded residences. Although we have no clear and practical ways to alleviate crowding in residences, several things may be tried. First, the use of partitions to afford greater control of interpersonal interaction might be helpful. Second, scheduling may be helpful. Cooperative scheduling rather than competitive congestion may reduce fights over who gets to use the bathroom first in the morning. Other strategies such as providing apartments with more space and better facilities would clearly be helpful, but unfortunately seem less practical.

Crowding in Work Settings

There are a number of similarities between residential crowding and crowding in work settings. As in residences, the events that precipitate crowding in work settings usually involve congestion-resource scarcity and lack of control over interpersonal interaction. For example, congestion occurs when many persons have to wait their turn to use a Xerox machine. Lack of interpersonal control over interactions occurs when conversation from adjacent work-related activity interferes with one's ability to concentrate on required tasks. A combination of the two occurs when a shortage of partitioned office space prevents needed privacy. In crowded work settings, interactions occur with associates. Norms governing these interactions differ from the norms governing kinship interactions or interactions with strangers. Furthermore, one's affective set toward co-workers may be positive, neutral, or negative, which may then ameliorate or aggravate crowding experiences in the work environment.

As in residential environments, crowding in work settings is usually a chronic problem. Although workers may sometimes move to new and more spacious quarters and otherwise find ways to reduce problems related to crowding, this is more the exception than the rule. In work settings, the interference with task performance is an obvious problem. However, questions of morale must also be considered because they play an important role in work efficiency. With respect to task interference, the type of tasks workers are engaged in must be considered. For example, crowding may affect attentional capacity (Cohen, 1978). The attentional demands placed on a flight control operator differ from the demands placed on a manual laborer. Heightened arousal stemming from crowding may facilitate the performance of simple tasks while interfering with the performance of complex ones. In issues involving morale, turnover and absenteeism can often be traced to low morale stemming from uncongenial work environments and are problems of serious concern to management. It should be noted that social comparison processes may also play an important part in lowered morale. The individual who is aware that comparable others in a different office have more abundant facilities or greater amounts of privacy may feel especially thwarted and may experience a lowering of morale.

The potential for intervention strategies seems greater in work settings than it does in residential settings. If the owners of a company can be convinced that an intervention can increase productivity and hence profits, they should be highly motivated to try it. Industrial designers have had considerable experience planning environments that seek to minimize task interference. We believe that user evaluation studies would probably be helpful in deciding between possible intervention strategies such as partitioning, the use of modular office furniture, and so on. Surveys of users that are sensitive to and focus on concerns about congestion and lack of privacy will probably suggest strategies that are different from surveys based on the assumption that the critical problem is aesthetics, traffic flow, or the like.

Finally, one must consider problems related to overmanning. Ironically, featherbedding may have consequences for morale when it results in there not being enough work to go around. Wicker has treated this subject extensively, and the interested reader is referred to his discussion (Wicker, 1972).

Crowding in Transportation

The rush-hour subway rider is cramped, jostled, pushed, and hassled by strangers who are often smelly, weird looking, and indifferent. Seats are often impossible to find, and the struggle to get to the exit before the doors crush your fingers must give nightmares to a fair number of New York City commuters. Thus, transportation crowding involves both extremely close physical proximity and congestion-resource scarcity.

Transportation crowding usually occurs with strangers. Norms governing interaction on mass transit usually dictate a minimization of involvement and a high degree of ritualization, which suggests some nonobvious factors in an appropriate experimental design. In our own program of research, we have found that whereas groups of males maintain low levels of interaction when asked to sit in a small room, groups of females and mixed sex groups in this same environment tend to engage in considerably higher levels of interaction. Thus, the use of groups of males seems to capture more closely the phenomenology of crowding in mass transit facilities. Transportation crowding is usually episodic — that is, it occurs for brief periods on a regularly recurring basis. When we consider the goal of the setting, the temporal context is especially important. Crowding in this context must be seen as an intermediate stage between two other settings — home and work. It follows that mass transit crowding should be considered in context. Crowding after a long and frustrating day's work may be quite different from crowding early in the day. Similarly, if one is involved in a conflict after being crowded, his behavior may be less constructive than if he had had a chance to relax.

Transportation crowding may also function as a conduit or medium through which styles that may be adaptive in one setting are brought into other settings in which they are less adaptive. For example, a clerk in the Division of Motor Vehicles treats waiting customers as numbers. He is usually serious, often harsh, and generally all business. A car salesman, a clerk in a delicatessen, and a Wall Street broker spend most of their working day competing, pressuring people, and acting superficially. Such behavior may increase their income, but the money earned may have to be spent on alimony payments if these behavioral styles are carried over into interactions at home. The pushing and shoving and rush to find a seat on the train may fan the competitive flames started at work and keep the embers burning until crossing the doorsill, whereas a chance to relax might have put out the fire. Hence, coping strategies used to mitigate the stress of the work setting may have severe effects on marriage and family life, if they are brought into the home as behavior residues. One other case of transit crowding should be noted — crowding on city sidewalks. Manhattan lunch seekers daily experience close physical proximity and congestion at noontime. However, in American cities, the level of crowding seldom reaches the level seen on buses and subways. If one has the time, a crowded city sidewalk may still display the diversity and verve of city life rather than its dehumanization and alienation.

Some of the limitations of laboratory paradigms should be considered here. Most of the laboratory studies of crowding seem most applicable to transportation settings. However, although it is easy to employ a crowding manipulation that creates close physical proximity, some of the other aspects of transportation crowding are not easily recreated in the laboratory. In the New York subway system, for example, the person next to you might well be dangerous. Readers of New York newspapers have become accustomed to reading of acts of violence occurring on mass transit facilities. Such information creates an atmosphere of fear that may be an important component of the stress associated with close physical proximity to strangers on buses and subways. Because laboratory environments are considered safe by subjects (Epstein, Suedfeld, & Silverstein, 1973), it is difficult to incorporate the unpredictability and danger of mass transit crowding in laboratory experiments.

A variety of intervention strategies might be effective in alleviating the effects of mass transit crowding. In our own program of research, we are presently studying the effects of traveling with a friend and the effect of relaxing for a short period immediately after being crowded but prior to arriving at home. Staggered work hours represent an ongoing attempt to reduce crowding in mass transit facilities. However, these strategies may be needless. Exorbitantly high fares combined with dangerous and dirty facilities may effectively reduce the incidence of transportation crowding in the foreseeable future.

OTHER SETTINGS

We have dealt at length with three settings in which crowding occurs. We will now discuss briefly the types of crowding that occur in shops and restaurants and at large public gatherings.

Shops and restaurant crowding most often involves congestion-resource scarcity. The waiting line at the checkout counter or outside a crowded restaurant is prototypical. Lack of control over interpersonal interaction may also be a factor, as is the case when an intimate conversation at the dinner table is inhibited by the presence of nearby others. However, it seems clear that laboratory paradigms designed to study crowding in shops and restaurants should concentrate on congestion.

In the situations mentioned above, crowding takes place in the presence of strangers, although one is frequently accompanied by friends and relatives. Crowding in this context tends to be epsiodic. There are certain predictable times when crowding is at its worst in stores and restaurants. Most city dwellers can fairly accurately predict how crowded a store will be at different times during the week. Although they may stay away from the store at peak shopping hours, the vision of crowds at the sales counters may dampen their enthusiasm for shopping and decrease the quality of city life. Probably the most negative aspect of this form of crowding is the sense that goods and services are not worth the trouble it takes to attain them. Repeated exposure to these experiences may lead individuals to avoid partaking of many of the available resources that lend richness and appeal to city life.

Finally, let us consider crowding in large public gatherings where close physical proximity may play a role. Congestion in the form of insufficient seats or people blocking one's view of events may also be important. Although most of the group may be strangers, usually at least one other person is a friend in crowds at demonstrations, parties, and sporting events. There are frequently norms that encourage interaction among strangers in such cases. These norms differ from those in mass transit settings where interaction with strangers is discouraged. Large public gatherings usually have a central focus. The task is usually to attend to that focus. Here, for the first time, some degree of crowding may add to the enjoyment of the event. The party that cannot get off the ground because too few people have attended and the play whose cast is upset because of the sparse audience are examples of the negative effects of too few people. The important sociopsychological variables here are those of mob psychology. Contagion effects, deindividuation, depersonalization, and diffusion of responsibility may occur when individuals are part of a large public gathering.

THE QUALITY OF CITY LIFE

We have noted that crowding occurs in conceptually different settings. Yet urban dwellers go from one setting to another in the course of a typical day. All the experiences they have in all these settings have a positive or negative effect on the way they feel about themselves and their world. In effect, this urban "gestalt" is greater than the sum of its component experiences. Thus, cities are both crowded and exhilarating, noisy and exciting, dirty and vibrant. Furthermore, a city also has a personality in the eyes of each of its inhabitants, a personality that differs depending on whether one experiences the positive or negative aspects of city life. The literature from another area of social psychology provides an analogy here. Solomon Asch has described how certain central traits influence person perception (1946). He has shown, for example, that a person described as intelligent, industrious, and warm is seen as a likeable sort of chap whereas his counterpart, who is described as intelligent, industrious, and cold, is seen as a ruthless Machiavellian. Thus, the warm-cold distinction organizes our reactions to the individual. So it is with a person's perception of city life. We suspect that a crucial determinant of a person's attitudes toward cities lies in his position on a "vibrancy-hassled" dimension. For those people whose perception of the city is organized around its central trait of vibrancy, the crowds, the noise, and the traffic jams all testify to the excitement of city life. For example, panhandlers are quaint, and sidewalk hawkers are interesting rather than annoying. The opposite is true if one's perception is that the city is a hassle.

We suggest that there is a threshold above which the city no longer appears vibrant but, rather, is seen as a hassling environment. Just as certain acts transform our perception of individuals from sane to crazy, so certain events may tip the balance in favor of a characterization of the city as a difficult place in which to live. Repeated and prolonged experiences of crowding may play an important part in such balance tipping.

SUMMARY

In this chapter several points have been made. Crowding has been used as a global term to describe a variety of different situations. Applied research must create conceptual analogues to real-world settings. To aid the researcher in constructing appropriate laboratory paradigms, three types of events that precipitate the label "crowding" have been delineated and five settings in which crowding occurs have been described. In conducting laboratory research on any of these settings, a number of questions need to be asked. Answers to these questions will help to guide the choice of dependent and independent variables that should be used in creating the appropriate laboratory analogue. Furthermore, we attempted to provide some tentative answers to the questions we have raised. The list of answers is meant to be suggestive rather than exhaustive. Finally, we have noted that the quality of city life is affected both positively and negatively by the multitude of crowded settings that are an integral part of the city. We acknowledge our own bias in favor of applied research. Certainly we are not suggesting that others need to conduct research that can provide answers to real-world problems. We have always had a high regard for basic research, but our own preference is due in large measure to our personal socialization as "practical theorists." For those sharing our "applied" predilection, we hope this schema is a useful guide.

REFERENCES

Altman, I. *The environment and social behavior: privacy, personal space, territory, and crowding.* Monterey, Cal.: Brooks/Cole, 1975.

Asch, S. E. Forming impressions of personality. *Journal of Abnormal and Social Psychology.* 1946, *41*, 258-290.

Baron, R., Mandel, D., Adams, C., & Griffen, L. Effects of social density in university residential environments. *Journal of Personality and Social Psychology,* 1976, *34*, 434-446.

Baum, A., & Greenberg, C. Waiting for a crowd: The behavioral and perceptual effects of anticipated crowding. *Journal of Personality and Social Psychology,* 1975, *32*, 671-679.

Baum, A. & Valins, S. Residential environments, group size, and crowding. *Proceedings, 81st Annual Convention, A. P. A.,* 1973, 211-212.

Calhoun, J. Population density and social pathology. *Scientific American,* 1962, *206*, 136-148.

Cohen, S. Environmental load and the allocation of attention. In A. Baum, J. Singer, & S. Valins (Eds.), *Advances in environmental psychology* (Vol. 1). Hillsdale, N.J.: Lawrence Erlbaum Associates, 1978.

Epstein, Y., & Karlin, R. Effects of acute experimental crowding. *Journal of Applied Social Psychology,* 1975, *5*, 34-53.

Epstein, Y., Suedfeld, P., & Silverstein, S. The experimental contract: Subjects' expectations of and reactions to some behaviors of experimenters. *American Psychologist,* 1973, *28*, 212-221.

Freedman, J., Levy, A., Buchanan, R., & Price, J. Crowding and human agressiveness. *Journal of Experimental Social Psychology,* 1972, *8*, 528-545.

Mitchell, R. E. Social implications of high density housing. *American Sociological Review,* 1971, *36,* 18-39.

Sherrod, D. Crowding, perceived control and behavioral aftereffects. *Journal of Applied Social Psychology,* 1974, *4,* 171-186.

Singer, J., Lundberg, U., & Frankenhaeuser, M. Stress on the train: A study of urban commuting. In A. Baum, J. Singer, & S. Valins (Eds.), *Advances in environmental psychology* (Vol. 1). Hillsdale, N.J.: Lawrence Erlbaum Associates, 1978.

Stokols, D., Rall, M., Pinner, B., & Schopler, J. Physical, social and personal determinants of crowding. *Environment and Behavior,* 1973, *5,* 87-115.

Valins, S., & Baum, A. Residential group size, social interaction, and crowding. *Environment and Behavior,* 1973, *5,* 421-439.

Wicker, A. Processes which mediate behavior-environment congruence. *Behavioral Science,* 1972, *17,* 265-177.

PART **II**

MODELS OF CROWDING
AND
DENSITY-RELATED STRESS

6

The Gravity of Crowding: Application of Social Physics to the Effects of Others

Eric S. Knowles
University of Wisconsin—Green Bay

Most research, at least in social psychology, receives its impetus from either of two sources: an interesting theoretical statement (e.g., attribution theory, dissonance theory, social comparison theory) or a socially relevant phenomenon (e.g., altruism, group polarization of opinion, conflict resolution). The former typically are theories in search of application, whereas the latter typically are applications in search of theory. The area of crowding is a clear instance of the second type of issue and exhibits the probelms characteristic of this kind of research, especially in its infancy. Crowding is a socially relevant phenomenon in search of a model—a model to define the "important" variables and to express the relationships among these variables. This chapter is an attempt to provide such a model by applying interesting statements from social physics to the socially relevant area of crowding. More specifically, this chapter has a threefold task: (1) to present a definition of crowding that is based on social influence rather than on territorial limitation, (2) to discuss gravitational models of influence that have been developed to deal with large-scale human interactions; and (3) to explore the applicability of these models to the area of crowding.

WHAT IS CROWDING?

The word *crowd* can be used either as a noun or as a verb. As a noun, the definition of crowd is clearest—a large number of people gathered closely together—as is its meaning in the history of social science concepts (Le Bon, 1895; Milgram & Toch, 1969). However, in the case of research on crowding, the word crowd is being used as a verb and its meaning is more clouded (and crowded).

Most extant definitions of crowding appear to reflect a theoretical perspective that links crowding to territorial behavior (Lawrence, 1974) in that they define crowding in terms of spatial limitation. For instance, two recent reviews (Aiello, Epstein, & Karlin, Note 1; Sundstrom, Note 8) present three alternative definitions of crowding: (1) a demographic condition of high population density, where crowding is a function of the number of people and the area available per person; (2) a phenomenological reaction to spatial restriction, where crowding is related to the perception of too many others or too little space; and (3) a social condition of high interpersonal stimulation, where crowding is a function of the unwanted, unnecessary, or interfering potential or actual interactions.

A great deal of attention has been paid to the first two definitions, with most authors following Stokols' (1972) dictum that the second be reserved as the definition of true crowding. He correctly pointed out that the difference between the first two definitions rests in whether the focus is on "... the physical condition, density, involving spatial limitation [or] the experiential state, crowding, in which the restrictive aspects of limited space are perceived by the individual exposed to them [p. 275]." This distinction, however, is essentially between objective and subjective assessment of limited space. Both definitions continue to share the common assumption that crowding is related to spatial restriction, interference, and territorial infringement. The measure of crowding from this perspective is the physical or perceived space available to a person and, indeed, degrees of crowding are usually reported in terms of the square feet available per person.

The concept of spatial restriction, either objective or subjective, is inadequate as an operationalization of crowding, mainly because it neglects psychologically important aspects of the situation. Take the example of person P in each of the four rooms depicted in Figure 1. If we take spatial restriction to mean the area in a room divided by the number of people in the room, as is usually reported in studies of crowding, then $B = D > A = C$ in terms of how crowded person P is. However, this definition doesn't seem to make sense, partly because in the

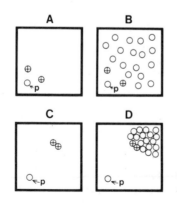

FIG. 1   Four rooms with different degrees of crowding of person P.

particular situations depicted the people aren't spaced equally. What seems to be needed here is a more particularized definition of the amount of space person P has. If we take spatial restriction to mean the amount of area person P controls, his personal territory as defined by the nearest others, then $A = B > C = D$ in terms of how crowded person P is. However, this definition doesn't make sense either, for surely room B should be considered more crowded than room A. The problem with a territorial definition of crowding is that the degree of crowding is determined only by the location of the boundary between a person's territory and the territory of others; people or events located beyond this boundary, therefore, have no direct impact on crowding.

Crowding, however, is not a territorial phenomenon but a social one, where an individual is affected by the presence of a crowd, all the crowd. Various social definitions have been suggested. Desor (1972) proposed that crowding phenomena result from the "... overall level of stimulation from social sources [p. 79]," and that feelings of being crowded were related to excessive stimulation. Consonant with this view, she demonstrated that the size and shape of a room, the presence of partitions and doors, and the type of ongoing activity all affected judgments of crowdedness. Valins and Baum (1973), also adopting a social definition. related crowding to excessive and unwanted interactions. Saegert (1973; Saegert, Mackintosh, & West, 1975; Saegert, Note 7) observed that both the number of others and their proximity are important to crowding. Increasing number of others leads to increasing informational complexity and stimulus overload, whereas the increasing proximity of others increases the salience of information and restricts freedom. Both these factors, which increase the level of social stimulation, combine in producing the experience and consequences of crowding.

These social definitions are more appropriate because they define crowding as an influence situation where the crowd influences the person. Crowding is the influence of "a large number of persons gathered closely together" on the responses of an individual. According to this definition, those characteristics that are important to the definition of a crowd, such as their number and closeness together, are the same dimensions that are important to the definition and experience of crowding. Such an approach would seem better able than a territorial definition to distinguish between the four rooms depicted in Figure 1; the amount of social stimulation presented person P would be greatest in room B (the room with both a greater number of people and greater proximity), followed by $D \cong A > C$. Although the social influence definition seems reasonable, it is not yet well defined in terms of either specifying the variables or the relationships these variables have to the experience of crowding.

Rather than developing an *in situ* model of crowding that attempts this definition, an alternative approach of applying existing models developed for other issues in the social sciences is taken. The number and distance of others as well as other variables that may be important to crowding have been topics of concern in economic and social geography, sociology, and civil engineering. Each of these disciplines has contributed to a body of theory and research that has come to be known as *social physics* (c.f., Isard, 1971; Lukermann & Porter, 1960; Stewart, 1947a, 1952). Most generally, social physics deals with the application of laws from physics to phenomena of human interaction. In the next sections, gravitational models in social physics are presented, derived for the individual, and applied to the research dealing with and related to crowding.

SOCIAL PHYSICS

Gravity As a Model for Human Interaction

The notion that an object can be affected by the presence of other objects is one of the basic assumptions of post-Galilean science and is stated perhaps most simply in the Newtonian Law of Gravity. If two masses are separated in space, a force (F) acts on each, drawing them together. The force is equal to the product of the two masses $(M_1$ and $M_2)$, divided by the square of the distance between them (D^2), and multiplied by the universal gravitational constant (G):

$$(1) \qquad F = \frac{GM_1M_2}{D^2} \quad .$$

We all learned this as a law of physical masses, and it has been applied to social masses as well. As early as 1858, Henry C. Carey observed that the gravitational model served to describe the attractive forces between populations of people, which, as with gravitational forces, were in direct ratio to the size of the masses and in inverse ratio to the distance between them. Although a number of social and physical scientists suggested social analogies to the law of gravity,[1] the formalization and wide application of social gravitational models emerged in the 1940s as the result of the work of an astronomer, John Q. Stewart (1941, 1947a, 1947b, 1948a, 1948b), and a psychologist, George K. Zipf (1941, 1942, 1946a, 1946b, 1946c, 1949). Both applied the gravitational model to macrolevel interactions, postulating that the forces for interaction between two population units (i and j) were directly proportional to the product of the population sizes $(P_i$ and $P_j)$ multiplied by a constant (k) and divided by the square of the distance between them:

$$(2) \qquad F_{ij} = \frac{kP_iP_j}{D^2_{ij}}$$

[1]For those who are interested, Carrothers (1956) and Stewart (1952) review the history of social physics and gravitational models.

and that the mutual "energy" of interaction (E_{ij}), following the analogy from the energy in a gravitational field, was equal to the product of the population sizes times a constant and divided by the first power of distance:

$$(3) \qquad\qquad E_{ij} = \frac{kP_iP_j}{D_{ij}}$$

Although the gravitational model may appear attractive because of its crispness or its association with the power of physical laws, its worth lies in its ability to describe a variety of interurban and interregion interactions accurately. Various forms of travel, communication, and economic activity have been used as indicators of the "energy" of interaction in Equation 3. The data are surprisingly consistent, showing that intercity telephone calls (Cavanaugh, 1950; Hammer & Iklé, 1957; Zipf, 1946b), newspaper circulations (Stewart, 1942; Zipf, 1946b), migrations (Folger, 1953; Zipf, 1946a), railway express shipments (Zipf, 1946c) postal money orders (Cavanaugh, 1950), automobile trips (Cavanaugh, 1950; Iklé, 1954; Wynn, 1956), airline trips (Cavanaugh, 1950; Hammer & Iklé, 1957; Iklé, 1954; Smith, 1963; Taaffe, 1956), retail trade (Converse, 1949), department store charge accounts (Zipf, 1947), as well as the origin of university undergraduates (Cavanaugh, 1950; Stewart, 1941) conform quite closely to the gravitational model. Figure 2 reproduces three graphs presented by Zipf (1949) in support of the gravitational model. These quite different kinds of interaction—circulation of the *New York Times,* railway express shipments, and telephone calls—show the quite strong relationships between the observed interactions and predicted gravitational energy.

Although the gravitational model in Equation 3 provides a prediction of interaction that is closley matched in observation, a number of investigators have suggested modifications and additions to the model in attempts to make it even more accurate. Stewart (1948b; 1952) proposed that the population size be weighted by some factor analogous to molecular weight to indicate that population's potential to participate in interaction, and argued that "the relative influence at a distance produced by primitive savages is very much less than that of people in an advanced state of material civilization [1952, p. 121]." In addition to a multiplicative weighting of the population sizes, Anderson (1956) and Carrothers (1956) have proposed that population sizes might have an exponent other than unity.

The exponents applied to distance have received a great deal of attention. Although Stewart (1958) has argued from a theoretical position that the exponent of distance should be either 1 or 2, various studies find *a posteriori* exponents that vary quite widely (Carroll, 1955; Carroll & Bevis, 1957; Garrison, 1956; Hammer & Iklé, 1957; Iklé, 1954; Isard & Peck, 1954; Smith, 1963). These variations have been linked to differences in the characteristics of the populations studied (Huff, 1961; Isard, 1960; Lukermann & Porter, 1960) and to dif-

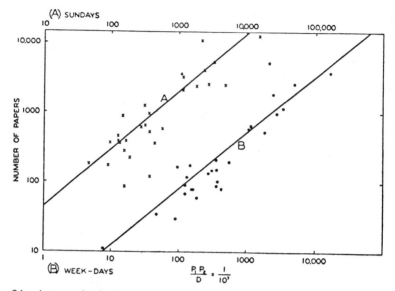

2A   Average circulation per day of the *New York Times* (*A*, Sunday circulation; *B*, weekday circulation).

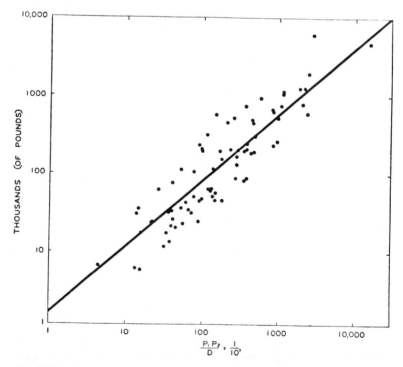

2B   Railway express. The movement by weight (less carload lots) between 13 arbitrary cities in the United States, May 1939.

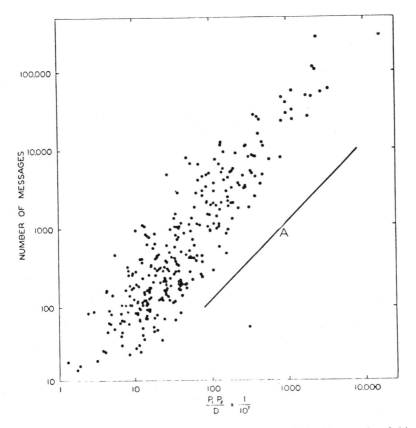

2C   Number of telephone messages interchanged between 311 arbitrary pairs of cities in 1940 (Line *A* has an ideal 1.00 slope).

FIG. 2   Examples of the relationship between gravitational energy predictions and intercity interaction. Figures 9-12, 9-14, and 9-18 from *Human behavior and the principle of least effort* by G. K. Zipf. Copyright 1949 by Addison-Wesley, Reading, Mass. Reprinted by permission.

ferences in the kind of interaction studied (Carroll & Bevis, 1957; Iklé, 1954), suggesting more generally that the exponent of distance be considered a variable parameter of gravitational energy.[2]

[2]These alterations and additions to the basic formulation are discussed in greater depth by Carrothers (1956), Isard (1960), and Olsson (1965). When these various modifications are included, the gravitational model yields the following more general equation:

$$E_{ij} = \frac{k \cdot (w_i)P_i^{e_i} \cdot (w_j)P_j^{e_j}}{D_{ij}^d},$$

Where the w's equal weights applied to the population sizes (P_i and P_j), the e's equal exponents of the population sizes, and d equals an exponent of distance.

Further modifications of the gravitational model were made by Stuart C. Dodd (1950), whose concern was not so much with the strict analogy of the Newtonian formula but with its application to the important dimensions of human groups that affect interaction. His general hypothesis (Dodd, 1950) of interactance as verbally stated was:

> Groups of people interact more as they become faster, nearer, larger, and leveled up in activity. Conversely, people will interact less in proportion as their groups (a) have fewer actions per period, (b) are further apart, (c) are smaller in population, and (d) are more unlike each other in average activity. The hypothesis thus states the factors determining the *quantity* of group interaction regardless of its quality or form, i.e., regardless of whether it is cooperating, competing, conflicting, or engaging in some other form of interaction [p. 245].[3]

Dodd's formulation is notable for including time *(T)* as a factor. Although the effects of the time span in which measures of influence are made are usually included only as one of the constituents of the situational constant *(k)*, they are important for human groups in two ways. First and most simply, as the amount of time for interaction increases, the amount of interaction will increase. But second and more important, the amount of interaction at T_1 may not be the same as the amount of interaction at T_2, especially for newly established groups. Just as a new retail store needs time to build up customers, the initial contacts between human groups may increase over time as information, resources, and persons in the other group become known. Presumably at some point in the history of interaction between two groups an equilibrium is created where the potential interactions are established and the decay of old interactions matches the initiation of new interactions so that the amount of interaction is essentially the same in any time period.

Thus far we have been considering only the energy of interaction between pairs of groups. The gravitational model, however, has been extended to describe the energy of interaction within aggregations of groups scattered at many

---

[3]Dodd's more formal statement of the interactance hypothesis was expressed in an equation:

$$I_e = \frac{k \cdot I_i P_i \cdot I_j P_j \cdot T}{D_{ij}^d},$$

where I_e equals the expected interactance between populations i and j, k equals a constant for each type of interacting in a given culture and a given period, I_i and I_j equal the weighting factors of population according to the level or amount of activity in the population, P_i and P_j equal the population sizes, T equals the total time of interacting, and D^d equals the distance between the two populations weighted by an exponent. Several of the symbols in this equation have been changed from Dodd's presentation to preserve continuity of usage.

locations. Stewart (1941; 1948b) used the concept of demographic potential $(_iV_j)$ to refer to the energy of interaction exerted at any point *(i)* by a population *(P_j)* at a distance *(D_{ij})*:

$$(4) \qquad\qquad _iV_j = k \frac{P_j}{D_{ij}}$$

Each population at a distance has some potential influence at point i, and the amount of potential influence increases with the size of the population and decreases with its distance. The sum of these influences $(_iV.)$ from all other populations defines the total potential energy of interaction acting on point i:

$$(5) \qquad\qquad _iV. = k \sum_{i=1}^{N} \frac{P_j}{D_{ij}}$$

Thus, the potential energy of interaction at point i increases as there are more *(N)*, larger *(P_j)*, and closer $(1/D_{ij})$ populations. Stewart (1948b) points out that this demographic potential "may be regarded as a measure of the *proximity of people* to that point. In computing it we consider that every person makes a contribution which is less the farther away he lives [p. 38]." Stewart (1948b) also provided evidence that the demographic potential of an area correlates strongly with an amazingly diverse array of social indicators (e.g., rents, income, deaths, rural density, railway miles, property values).

Stewart (1952) noted that the gravitational model of energy potentials provided a more satisfactory alternative to density as a conceptualization of the influence of others: "Density of populations is a physical quantity already familiar in sociology; it is the number of people divided by the area they occupy. Demographers had never introduced a term to measure the influence of people at a distance, which is what the potential does; nor had they analyzed the wealth of observed data which show that such a term has meaning and usefulness [p. 120]." As with demography, the concept of energy potentials may replace density as a means of describing crowding. Return to Figure 1 and person P standing at point p in each of the four rooms. It is possible to think of person P as standing in an energy field where the energy potential at point p is a function of the other people and their distance from that point. This is the model of crowding that will be developed more fully in the next section. Whereas the gravitational models discussed in this section have taken aggregations or populations of people as the basic unit of analysis (reflecting their origins in geography and sociology), the issue of crowding is better conceptualized with the individual as the unit of analysis.

A Gravitational Model of Interpersonal Energy

Although there have been shibboleths against applying gravitational models to the molecular level (Carrothers, 1956; Stewart, 1952), this is precisely what we propose to do in looking at the social energy fields acting on an individual. An analogy, after all, is in no way sacred or even true; its value is as a heuristic device to suggest and model relationships. Thus, the following analogy is offered as a way of organizing our understanding of interpersonal influence and as a way of suggesting relationships to be investigated.

Assume that we have a single subject of some mass (M_s) operating in a space with a number of other people, also characterized as masses $(M_{o1}, M_{o2}, M_{o3}, ... M_{oi}, ... M_{oN})$. By applying the analogy of gravitational energy to this situation, it follows that the interpersonal energy between our subject and any one other person (E_{so_i}) would be expressed as:

$$(6) \quad E_{so_i} = \frac{kM_sM_{o_i}}{D_{so_i}^d},$$

where k equals a situational constant analogous to the gravitational constant, M_s equals the mass of the subject, M_{oi} equals the mass of the other person, and D^d_{soi} equals the distance between the subject and the other person raised to a power (d). In a strict analogy to Newton's formula, d would assume a value of 1. Because Equation 6 applies to the interpersonal energy between the subject and each of the other people in the space, it follows that the sum of the energy $(\Sigma E_s.)$ involving our subject would be expressed as:

$$(7) \quad \Sigma E_s. = kM_s \sum_{i=1}^{N} \frac{M_{o_i}}{D_{so_i}^d}.$$

Equation 7 identifies three variables of importance that affect the amount of influence impinging on a subject: (1) the masses of the people, (2) the number of other people, and (3) the distances of the other people from the subject. Of these, the number and distance of others are most easily quantified. The masses, however, require comment and specification. Since this model is dealing with social rather than physical gravitation, we are dealing here with social rather than physical mass. Mass in this context refers to a person's social size, weight, potency, or importance. As such, social mass can be defined as any characteristic of the person that increases his influence or contribution of energy to the system.

In special cases, the social masses of the others may be equal $(M_o = M_{o1} = M_{o2} = M_{o3} = ... = M_{oN})$, that is, the others are undifferentiated and contribute equally to the interpersonal energy system, and the others may be situated at the same or nearly the same distance from the subject $(D^d_{so} = D^d_{so1} = D^d_{so2} = D^d_{so3} = ... = D^d_{soN})$. In this more restricted case, the sum of energy involving the subject (Equation 7) becomes:

$$(8) \qquad \sum E_s. = \frac{kM_s M_o N_o}{D^d_{so}} = \frac{KN_o}{D^d_{so}}$$

where N_o equals the number of others and $K = kM_s M_o$. In Equation 8 it is easy to see the parallel between the gravitational model and the verbal definition of crowding given earlier. Crowding was defined as the social influence created by a crowd, that is, by a number of others packed closely together. Both of these variables, the number of others (N_o) and the closeness of others $(1/D^d_{so})$, appear in Equation 8. The more general statement in Equation 7 includes these two variables but expands the definition of crowding to include the concept of social mass. Crowding then becomes the influence on the individual created by the number and potency of others packed closely together.

Equation 7 also implies that the social mass of the subject increases the interpersonal energy in the system (are kings more susceptible to crowding than paupers?). Although this inclusion may suggest at a general level that characteristics of the subject influence the experience of crowding, the gravitational analogy implies more specifically that the same characteristics would increase the experience of crowding regardless of whether they characterized the subject or the others. The social mass of the subject in this analogy is measured in the same way as the social mass of the others. However, because there are almost no data dealing with the social mass of the subject and because the focus of this chapter is on the effects of others, this issue will not be pursued further.

Although Equation 8 was derived from application of the gravitational model to the individual, it is also applicable to aggregates, leading with the same assumptions to essentially the same predictions as Equation 3. However, by applying the model initially to the individual rather than to populations, Equation 7 yields terms dealing with individual characteristics, the social masses, that were absent from the earlier gravitational models (although similar notions were introduced in the *ad hoc* population weighting factors). Note, as did Dodd (1950), that gravitational models deal with factors that determine the *quantity* of influence regardless of its quality.

The gravitational model of interpersonal influence presented in Equation 7 is offered (1) as a conceptual model for organizing the variables important to crowding; and (2) as a working hypothesis about the relationship of various variables to the experience of crowding. The first function is filled presumably in the presentation of the model. The second function, however, is an empirical one. The next sections of the chapter turn to the evidence and data that bear on this gravitational model of crowding.

EVIDENCE

The Number of Others

The notion that a number of others can influence behavior is one of the basic and oldest tenets of social psychology. As long ago as 1897, Triplett studied the effects of other competitors on performance. This and subsequent studies of social facilitation (Allport, 1920; Dashiell, 1935; Zajonc, 1965) suggest that the presence of others as an audience, as co-actors, or as competitors affects performance. Zajonc (1965) proposed that the presence of others produces a drive-like state, in a Hullian sense, enhancing the performance of a dominant response and imparing the performance of competing responses. Although there has been a perennial debate concerning whether social facilitation effects occur as a result of the "mere presence" of others (Dashiell, 1930; Zajonc, 1965) or as the result of some social motivation created by the presence of others, such as rivalry (Simms, 1928; Wittemore, 1924) or evaluation apprehension (Cottrell, 1968; Henchy & Glass, 1968), the findings consistently show that the presence of others influences behavior.

Studies of social facilitation typically have not dealt with the issue of whether different numbers of others create different amounts of influence as is implied by the gravitational model. However, a variety of other evidence suggests that this is the case. Thomas and Fink (1963) concluded that group size affected a variety of group and member behaviors; Asch (1951, 1956) and Gerard, Wilhelmy, and Conolley (1968) showed that the number of unanimous others increased conformity; Porter (1939) and Brenner (Note 3) found that a speaker's nervousness increased with the size of an audience; Milgram, Bickman, and Berkowitz (1969) demonstrated that the size of an experimental crowd stationed on a city sidewalk increased the power of the crowd to draw passing pedestrians into the crowd and into the crowd's activity; Knowles, Kreuser, Haas, Hyde, and Schuchart (1976) showed that the size of a group stationed in an alcove recessed off of a university hallway increased the distance at which pedestrians passed the group. These studies all suggest that the amount of influence on a person increases as a function of the number of other persons.

A similar conclusion comes from the several studies that have investigated the effects of the number of others on responses to crowded situations. Various laboratory experiments, field quasi experiments, and correlation studies suggest that increasing numbers of others have the following kinds of effects: (1) increased feelings of being crowded (Baum & Greenberg, 1975; Baum & Valins, 1973; Cozby, 1973; Eoyang, 1974; Griffith & Veitch, 1971; Iwata, 1974; Valins & Baum, 1973; Aiello, Epstein, & Karlin, Note 2); (2) less satisfaction with the setting (Dean, Pugh, & Gunderson, 1975; Griffith & Veitch, 1971; Aiello et al., Note 2); (3) less liking and more competitive orientation toward others (Baum & Greenberg, 1975; Griffith & Veitch, 1971; Hutt & Vaizey, 1966; Kutner,

1973; Valins & Baum, 1973); and (4) greater physiological or psychological symptoms of stress and arousal (D'Atri, 1975; Dean et al., 1975; Kutner, 1973; Paulus, McCain, & Cox, 1973; Paulus, Cox, McCain, Chandler, & Short, 1975; Aiello et al., Note 2; Saegert, Note 7).

Although these investigations of crowding studied variations in the number of others present, many of them did so while holding the total amount of space or room size constant (Baum & Greenberg, 1975; Baum & Valins, 1973; Cozby, 1973; Griffith & Veitch, 1971; Iwata, 1974; Kutner, 1973; Aiello et al., Note 2). Such a procedure confounds the manipulation of number with variations in density or interpersonal distance. A few people in a room are likely to place themselves or be placed so that the mean of the interpersonal distances is greater than when there are many people in the room. Although these studies may be considered manipulations of crowding, they are probably manipulating more than increasing numbers of others; the distances between people may be decreasing as well.

Several authors have noted this confounding and have attempted to deal with it by separately measuring (Dean et al., 1975; Eoyang, 1974; Paulus et al., 1973; Paulus et al., 1975) or manipulating (Marshall & Heslin, 1975; Saegert, Note 7) group size and room size. All find that group size has independent effects on various responses to crowding, although Marshall and Heslin found a group size effect that was qualified by higher order interactions with sex of subject and composition of the group. Although these authors have attempted to deal with the distinction between the number of others and how closely packed they are, they have been hindered by conceptions of density as territory rather than as interpersonal distance. Attention has to be paid not to the area per person but to the actual interpersonal distances involved. Thus, we cannot be sure even in these studies that the interpersonal distances were constant across group sizes.

Another way to deal with this confounding would be to add numbers of others in such a way that the average distance to the subject remains the same or, if anything, increases. Various audience and group size studies (Knowles et al., 1976; Milgram et al., 1969; Porter, 1939; Brenner, Note 3) do this by keeping the number of others closely grouped together so that increases in size do not seriously affect the average distance to the subject.

The importance of attending to both the number of others and interpersonal distance is shown in the studies by Knowles et al (1976) that provide a demonstration of the gravitational relationships expressed in Equation 8. Two studies investigated the effect of group size on the distances at which pedestrians passed the group. In a field experiment, one, two, three, or four people were sitting on a bench in an alcove recessed off of a university hallway; in a paper and pencil replication two, four, six, or eight figures were represented in an alcove either in a straight line or a closed circle formation. In both studies, the distance at which pedestrians actually passed or indicated they would pass the alcove increased with the size of the group.

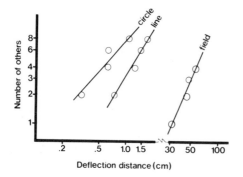

FIG. 3   Relationship between number of others and deflection distances. Adapted from "Group size and the extension of social space boundaries" by E. S. Knowles, B. Kreuser, S. Haas, M. Hyde, and G. E. Schuchart, *Journal of Personality and Social Psychology*, 1976, *33*, 647-654.

Because group members were added to the same alcove, it is safe to assume that the increasing energy of the interpersonal system was a function of their increasing numbers unconfounded by decreasing distances to the hallway. If we assume that pedestrians in these situations were responding to the numbers of others by adjusting their distance to keep the sum of the interpersonal energy at a constant minimum, then Equation 8 predicts that:

$$(9) \qquad\qquad N_o = C D^d_{so}$$

where $C = \Sigma E_s./K$ which by assumption is a constant. Figure 3 presents plots of the relationship between N_o and D_{so} on double log axes for the three conditions (representational circle, representational line, and field study).[4] The plotted regression lines of distance on number yielded least square solutions with $r^2 = 0.93$, $r^2 = 0.98$, and $r^2 = 0.95$, respectively, suggesting that they conform quite well to the prediction. In addition, the exponential values of $d = 1.17, d = 1.72$, and $d = 2.86$ show a great deal of variability and suggest the utility of including the distance exponent as a variable rather than a constant.

Social Mass of Others

Social mass variables, dealing with the importance, status, prestige, and social weight of others, have been included in a variety of social and social psychological studies, including several dealing with crowding. The general conclusion from various lines of research is that as the social mass of the others increases, so does

---

[4]Double log axes are used because of the predicted exponential relationship. With the measures transformed to log scales, exponential relationships appear as a straight line with the slope of the line equal to the value of the exponent. Equation 9, therefore, is evaluated in a simple regression of the log transformed values: $\log (N_o) = \log C + d \log (D)$. Log C and d are the estimated parameters corresponding to the intercept and slope of the best fitting regression line. In evaluating the fit of the data to the predicted equation, the value of d is reported to indicate the exponent of distance and the coefficient of determination (r^2) is reported as a rough indication of the accuracy of the regression line fit.

their influence on the subject. Studies of conformity indicate that yielding to a majority increases with the attractiveness or liking for others (Festinger, Schachter, & Back, 1950; Gerard, 1954; Lott & Lott, 1961) and the prestige or expertise of the others (Back, 1951; Fagen, 1963; Hochbaum, 1954; Samelson, 1957). In his obedience studies, Milgram (1965) found that higher status experimenters induced greater levels of compliance to the experimenter's request. Studies of attitude change also suggest that communicators of higher status and expertise produce greater acceptance of the message (Bergin, 1962; Hovland, Janis, & Kelley, 1953). More subtle manipulations of social mass have occurred in studies of social facilitation concerned with evaluation apprehension. Subjects' concern with being evaluated has been manipulated by varying the importance of others. Greater social facilitation has been shown to occur when others can watch the subject's performance rather than wearing blindfolds (Cottrell, Wack, Sekerak, & Rittle, 1968) and when subjects are led to believe that others, especially experts, will actively evaluate rather than passively observe their performance (Henchy & Glass, 1968; Paulus & Murdoch, 1971).

Spatial behavior has also been shown to be influenced by social mass variables. Knowles (1973), for instance, found that higher status groups were more able than lower status groups to prevent territorial intrusions. Subjects in dyadic situations also maintain greater distances from higher status others (Levinger & Gunner, 1967; Little, 1968; Mehrabian & Friar, 1969; Latta & Kahn, Note 4), strangers or disliked others (Keuthe, 1962; Little, 1965; Willis, 1966) and from attractive others (Dabbs & Stokes, 1975). A very different set of social mass variables was manipulated in a study by Nesbitt and Steven (1974). In a field experiment, they found that subjects stood farther away from confederates whose "stimulus intensity" was increased by wearing brightly colored clothes and a strongly scented perfume. Argyle and Dean (1965), looking at another form of stimulus intensity, found that subjects were able to approach closer to Michael Argyle when he had his eyes closed than when he had them open.

Only a few studies of crowding have dealt with what could be called social mass variables. Most investigators use subjects who are strangers to one another and assume that they are peers. Prior acquaintance, however, appears to moderate the effects of crowding (McClelland, Note 5). Quick and Crano (Note 6), interestingly, found that just saying "hello" can attenuate the negative responses to close proximity. Fisher (1974) found that dissimilarity of another increased feelings of crowding. A competitive orientation toward others also has been found to heighten responses to crowding (Stokols, Rall, Pinner, & Schopler, 1973) and the desire for interpersonal distance (Ryen & Kahn, 1975). Status differences in crowded situations have not been studied directly, although Geisen and McClaren (1976) and Geisen and Hendrick (1977) found that subjects responded to a discussion moderator rather than other discussion group members in establishing spatial norms and feelings about themselves and the group.

Distance

The gravitational model implies that the closeness of others in a situation affects the amount of energy and influence acting on a person. A number of recent crowding studies have manipulated crowding by decreasing the interpersonal distances among people. In the standard experimental paradigm, same size groups (usually four to eight members) are formed and placed in either a large room (uncrowded condition) or a small room (crowded condition) for a period of time during or after which behavioral, cognitive, or physiological measures are taken (Aiello, Epstein, & Karlin, 1975; Emiley, 1975; Freedman, Klevansky, & Ehrlich, 1971; Freedman, Levy, Buchanan, & Price, 1972; Loo, 1972; Marshall & Heslin, 1975; Ross, Layton, Erickson, & Schopler, 1973; Sherrod, 1974; Stokols et al., 1973; Saegert, Note 7). Because these studies hold the number of others constant, the variations in crowding are created only by variations in distance. Yet there have been wide differences in the amount of space per person, in the configuration of the group, in the activities required of the subjects, in the kind of dependent variables measured, and in the findings obtained.

A persistent hypothesis that crowding affects task performance has produced equivocal results. A number of studies report finding no performance differences between crowded and uncrowded subjects on a variety of tasks (Emiley, 1975; Freedman et al., 1971; Freedman et al., 1972; Ross et al., 1973; Sherrod, 1974; Stokols et al., 1973). However, two studies have found at least some effect of crowding on task performance (Epstein & Karlin, 1975; Sherrod, 1974). The search for performance differences usually has been sponsored by hypotheses concerning the drive or arousal properties of crowding, with the prediction that performance would be impared on complex tasks and improved on simple tasks. Support for the drive hypothesis has been found more consistently with physiological measures of arousal (Aiello, et al., 1975; McBride, King, & James, 1965; Middlemist, Knowles, & Matter, 1976; Saegert, Note7).

Assessments of other dependent variables have revealed generally that subjects in smaller rooms feel more uncomfortable and crowded (Epstein & Karlin, 1975; Ross et al., 1973; Stokols et al., 1973; Saegert, Note 7). However, ratings on mood, liking for others, and liking for the experiment have provided inconsistent differences that when found are often highly qualified or reversed by interactions with other variables such as sex of subject and sex composition of the group (Epstein & Karlin, 1975; Freedman et al., 1972; Marshall & Heslin, 1975; Ross et al., 1973; Stokols et al., 1973).

Although these studies have manipulated distance and suggest that this variable is related to crowding responses, they are not adequate to test the gravitational model in any but the most general way. The authors have not conceived of distance as the important variable in their manipulations nor have they reported the interpersonal distances or, one suspects, particularly controlled them. Perhaps the relationship of distance to influence is best assessed in less complex situations. When the gravitational model in Equation 8 is modified for the two-person situation (i.e., a subject and one other person), the amount of interpersonal energy influencing the subject becomes a function of an inverse power of distance from the other person:

$$(10) \qquad \sum E_{s\cdot} = K/D^d{}_{so} .$$

Equation 10, then, suggests that another person will become more influential as a function of coming closer to the subject. Two implications of this relationship can be derived: (1) Subjects will be most concerned with people and events close to them, and (2) others will become more influential as they move closer to the subject. The first implication, which relies on correlational evidence, has been studied widely in movement and friendship patterns.

Distances to friends, lovers, and accidents. The attenuating influence of distance has been shown for a variety of interpersonal contacts. The frequency of telephone calls has been found to be an inverse exponential function of distance, although the exponential value has varied from $d = 0.5$ (Zipf, 1949) to $d = 1.28$ (Hammer & Iklé, 1957). The frequency of trips also has shown the inverse relationship but again with the exponents of distance varying quite widely. Zipf (1949) reported values of $d = 0.5$ for automobile and truck trips of up to 1,000 miles; Iklé (1954) reported values of $d = 0.69$ for trips between the central business district and other areas in Dallas, Texas, and $d = 2.57$ for trips between Fort Wayne and other Indiana counties. Similarly, airline trips have been shown to decrease in frequency as a function of distance, but with wide variation in the exponential values (Hammer & Iklé, 1957; Iklé, 1954; Taaffe, 1956, 1962; Smith, 1963). Carroll and Bevis (1957) and Voorhees (1955) have suggested that the exponents of distance vary according to the purpose of the trip.

These forms of communication, however, are complexly determined, with distance probably having several different kinds of effects. Equation 10 implies that subjects will be less concerned with people living at a distance. Iklé (1954) noted, in addition, that distance increases the cost of communication, which reduces the likelihood of interaction. Thus, both these influences of distance—the intensity of concern and the relative costs—may influence the amount and frequency of interaction. The cost factors, which are extraneous to the relationships implied in Equation 10, are likely to be constant across all forms of interaction and thus relatively less important with more intense relationships, such as with friends and lovers.

The location of friendships has been studied in a variety of settings. Data from apartment houses (Deutsch & Collins, 1957; Festinger et al., 1950), homogeneous communities (Caplow & Foreman, 1950), and heterogeneous communities (Athanasiou & Yoshioka, 1973; Rosnow, 1961; Yancey, 1971) suggest a strong inverse relationship between distance and friendship formation. In residential apartment houses, Festinger et al. (1950) looked at the relationship between the proportion of neighbors on the same floor who were friends and

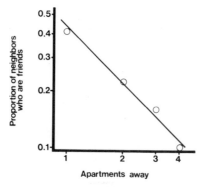

FIG. 4 Proportion of apartment house neighbors who are friends as a function of distance. Adapted from *Social pressures in informal groups: A study of human factors in housing* by L. Festinger, S. Schachter, and K. Back. Copyright 1950 by Stanford University Press. Reprinted by permission.

their distance, measured as the number of apartments away. Figure 4 presents these data plotted on double log axes where the slope of the best fitting regression line indicates the value of the exponent of distance. These data show that Equation 10, with distance raised to an exponent of $d = 1.01$, provides an accurate description of the proportion of neighbors who are friends, $r^2 = 0.99$. Similarly, in a cooperative townhouse project, Athanasiou and Yoshioka (1973) surveyed 276 households to ascertain the location of "high intensity" friends. Figure 5 presents, also on double log axes, the proportion of people living in various zones of distance who were identified as friends. The best fitting line, with $d = 1.34$, provides a fairly accurate description of these data, $r^2 = 0.96$.

The relationship between distance and friendship or communication contacts may be studied with either of two measures: (1) the frequency distribution of contacts per unit of distance; or (2) the proportion of people in each zone of distance who are contacts. If people are randomly placed over an infinite area, these two measures would be perfectly related with the distance exponent of the proportion equal to twice that of the frequency (because the area of a zone is a function of twice the distance to it). If, however, the area studied is bounded (as in the case of apartment houses and townhouse projects), so that the number of people in each zone of distance is not equal across subjects, then the propor-

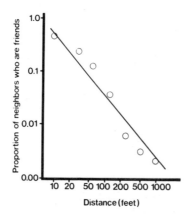

FIG. 5 Proportion of townhouse neighbors who are friends as a function of distance. Adapted from "The spatial character of friendship formation" by R. Athanasiou and G. A. Yoshioka, *Environment and Behavior*, 1973, 5, 43-65. Copyright 1973 by Sage Publications. Reprinted by permission.

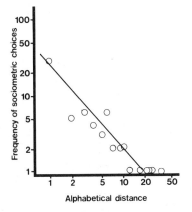

FIG. 6 Frequency of sociometric choices as a function of
alphabetical distance. Adapted
from "Alphabet and attraction:
An unobtrusive measure of the effect of propinquity in a field setting" by M. W. Segal, *Journal of
Personality and Social Psychology*,
1974, *30*, 654-657. Copyright
1974 by the American Psychological Association. Reprinted by
permission.

tion is the more accurate measure. In these cases, the relationship between the
frequency of friendship choices and distance is better estimated from the proportional data than calculated directly. Because many of the studies to follow are
based on frequency measures rather than proportions, their exponents of distance
should be compared to one-half the values observed for the Festinger et al.
(1950) (i.e., to 0.50) and Athanasiou and Yoshioka (1973) (i.e., to 0.67) studies.

Segal (1974) also looked at the relationship between propinquity and friendships, but she used a nongeographic measure of distance. She asked students at
the Maryland State Police Training Academy to name their three closest friends
on the force. Because the students were assigned to dormitory rooms and to
classroom seats on the basis of alphabetical order, their relative position in this
order provided an index of propinquity. Figure 6 presents the frequency of sociometric choices in the academy for each distance in the alphabetical order.
Friendship choices are fairly accurately described, $r^2 = 0.88$, by an inverse function of alphabetical distance where $d = 0.92$.

In addition to friends, the location of marriage partners shows the inverse
potential function of distance. Bossard's (1932) original study provided the paradigm for studying this issue: Marriage license applications are inspected, a sample
is drawn where both applicants reside in the city, the residences of the applicants
are located on a city map, and the walking distance between them is counted as
the number of city blocks. Bossard studied marriage licenses issued for Philadelphia residents in 1931; Abrams (1943) looked at marriage licenses issued in
Philadelphia in 1885, 1905, and 1915; Davie and Reeves (1939) sampled
marriage licenses for New Haven, Connecticut, in 1931; and Clarke (1952)
investigated licenses issued for Columbus, Ohio in 1949. In addition, Clarke
interviewed applicants and ascertained the location of residences at the first date.
The frequency distributions by blocks for each of these studies are presented on
double log axes in Figure 7. In all cases, the data are quite accurately described
by an inverse exponential function—the exponential values range from $d = 0.48$
to $d = 0.84$ with a median at $d = 0.54$ and the r^2s range from 0.76 and 0.98,

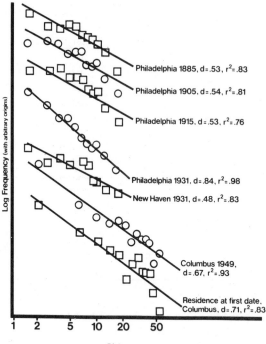

FIG. 7   Propinquity and frequency of marriage. Adapted from "Residential propinquity as a factor in marriage selection: Fifty year trends in Philadelphia" by R. H. Abrams, *American Sociological Review*, 1943, *8*, 288-294, copyright 1943 by The American Sociological Association; "Residential propinquity as a factor in marriage selection" by J. H. S. Bossard, *American Journal of Sociology*, 1932, *38*, 219-224, copyright 1932 by the University of Chicago Press; "Propinquity of residence before marriage" by M. R. Davie and R. J. Reeves, *American Journal of Sociology*, 1939, *44*, 510-517, copyright 1939 by the University of Chicago Press; and "An examination of the operation of residential propinquity as a factor in mate selection" by A. C. Clarke, *American Sociological Review*, 1952, *17*, 17-22, copyright 1952 by The American Sociological Association. Reprinted by permission.

with a median at 0.83—although the Philadelphia data from 1885, 1905, and 1915 show some systematic variation from the straight line.[5]

   In contrast to these high intensity relationships, Chandler (1948) studied the relationship between distance and chance encounters. He inspected the records of 264 pedestrian-vehicle accidents from the files of the Brookline, Massachusetts, police department, for the distance between the pedestrian's place of residence and the location of the accident. The frequency of accidents showed an inverse

[5]With the exception of Clarke's data, the plots and regression lines based on them do not include data for the first block. The first block was eliminated because of considerable ambiguity about the actual propinquity of applicants who give the same address (see Abrams, 1943, for a discussion of this issue).

relationship to distance with $d = 1.19$. These findings suggest that the likeli-hood of bumping into someone (or something) by accident, at least while on foot, decreases as a function of more than the first power of distance. Distance in these chance encounters, where the cost factors of distance are likely to be more important, showed a much steeper rate of attenuation ($d = 1.19$) than in the friendship and marriage encounters (median $d = 0.54$) where the intensity of interpersonal interest was likely to be more important.

Manipulations of interpersonal distance.   Although the distance studies dis-cussed above conform to the gravitational model and suggest that subjects are most concerned with people and events closest to them, they do not provide an accurate test of the relationships implied by Equation 10. As was noted in the discussion of these studies, the correlational evidence is not able to eliminate other effects of distance, such as the cost of communicating. Various studies of face-to-face interaction distances, however, provide experimental evidence that the effects of others increases with their closeness.

In a study of crowding, Fisher (1974) looked at the effect of four interaction distances with similar and dissimilar others on subjects' judgments of crowded-ness, appreciation of the room in which the interaction took place, and liking for the other. Judgments of the room and liking for the other were affected by the similarity of the other but not by the interaction distance. The measure of crowdedness showed a large effect for distance and smaller, although signifi-cant, effects for similarity and for the interaction between similarity and distance. These findings for judgments of crowdedness are presented in Figure 8. In this presentation, the scale of crowdedness has been reversed from Fisher's presenta-tion ($35 - X$) so that larger numbers indicate greater crowdedness, and the means for interaction distances averaged across similar and dissimilar others has been included. For the combined others, Equation 10, with $d = 0.59$, provides an accurate description of the means, $r^2 = 0.99$.

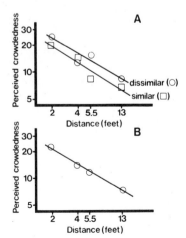

FIG. 8   Perceived crowdedness as a function of interpersonal dis-tance. *A* presents means for simi-lar and dissimilar others; *B* presents means for combined others. Adapted from "Situation-specific variables as determinants of perceived environmental aesthetic quality and perceived crowdedness" by J. D. Fisher, *Journal of Research in Personality*, 1974, *8,* 177-188. Copyright 1974 by Academic Press, Inc. Reprinted by permission.

Studies of personal space invasions also suggest that interpersonal closeness increases the effects of others, leading to increased arousal, discomfort, and flight behavior (Evans & Howard, 1973). Felipe and Sommer (1966) staged spatial invasions by having a confederate sit at one of six different distances from a subject sitting alone at a table in a university library. At the closest distance, 70 percent of the subjects left within 30 minutes as compared to 13 percent of the control subjects (a condition in which the invader sat at another table). The percentages for the four intermediate conditions were not reported separately but combined had 27 percent of the subjects leaving within 30 minutes. Barash (1973) found a similar pattern for three levels of invasion. This nonlinear but monotonic pattern of results with the closest distance having much the largest effect can be taken as evidence consistent with the relationships expressed in Equation 10. With an inverse function of distance, each successive unit of distance should have less effect than the prior one.

Patterson, Mullens, and Romano (1971) conducted a similar study in which confederates sat one, two, or three seats away from a subject sitting at a library table. Although they did not find many people leaving within the 10-minute observation period, they did find differences in the number of intruder-directed glances, leaning away from the intruder, and various blocking behaviors. In each case, the largest differences were between one and two seats away. In a study of the effects of interpersonal distance on impression formation, Patterson and Sechrest (1970) had subjects interview a confederate at two, four, six, or eight feet and then rate the friendliness, extraversion, dominance, and aggressiveness of the confederate. They found a curvilinear relationship that does not conform to Equation 10; the ratings on all scales increased between two and four feet and then decreased between four, six, and eight feet. Observations of the confederates, however, indicated that they exhibited different behavior at the two-foot distance (less eye contact, more turning and leaning away) than at the other distances. Middlemist, Knowles, and Matter (1976) looked at the effects of interpersonal distance in a men's lavatory on the micturation times (measures reflecting arousal) of urinal users. Consistent with increased arousal, they found that interpersonal closeness increased the delay of onset and decreased the duration of micturation, with the closest distances having the largest effects.

To the extent that interpersonal closeness is disquieting and arousing, it should lead to the disruption of behaviors that occur at more appropriate distances. Indeed, several studies show that interpersonal closeness decreases the occurrence of various interpersonal behaviors. Albert and Dabbs (1970) investigated the effects of interpersonal distance on attitude change by having subjects listen to persuasive messages delivered by a speaker who sat 1.5, 4.5, or 13 feet away. Significant effects of distance were found with subjects accepting the speaker's position more when he sat farther away; interpersonal closeness reduced the acceptance of the message.

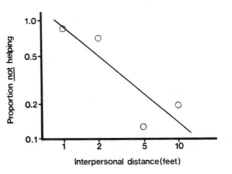

FIG. 9   Disruption of helping as a function of interpersonal distance. Adapted from "Effects of a violation of personal space on escape and helping responses" by V. J. Konečni, L. Libuser, H. Morton, and E. B. Ebbesen, *Journal of Experimental Social Psychology*, 1975, *11*, 288-299. Copyright 1975 by Academic Press, Inc. Reprinted by permission.

Konečni, Libuser, Morton, and Ebbesen (1975) showed that spatial invasions reduced the likelihood that subjects would subsequently help the invader. A confederate, the invader, approached to a distance of one, two, five, or ten feet away from a pedestrian waiting at a crosswalk for the light to turn green. In one condition, when the light turned green, the confederate maintained the distance partway through the crosswalk, then hurried ahead of the subject and apparently unknowingly dropped a pencil. The authors hypothesized and found that close interpersonal distances decreased the likelihood of helping. Figure 9 presents the data for this condition, which showed the largest effects of invasion distances. Notice that the dependent variable presented here is the disruption of helping, that is, the proportion of subjects who did not help. The best fitting regression line, with $d = 0.81$, provides an approximate description of these data, $r^2 = 0.75$.

Several studies have also shown that close interpersonal distances disrupt the amount of eye contact maintained during an interaction. Argyle and Dean (1965) hypothesized that the intimacy of a conversation can be regulated through several dimensions, including changes in interpersonal distance and changes in the amount of eye contact. One dimension can compensate for another: If interpersonal distance signals too intimate a relationship, then eye contact can be reduced to decrease the intimacy. In a study of this equilibrium hypothesis,

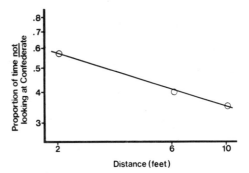

FIG. 10   Eye-contact avoidance as a function of distance from the other. Adapted from "Eye-contact, distance, and affiliation" by M. Argyle and J. Dean, *Sociometry*, 1965, *28*, 289-304. Copyright 1965 by the American Sociological Association. Reprinted by permission.

Argyle and Dean had subjects interact with a stranger, a confederate, at each of three distances—two, six, and ten feet. The confederate gazed continually at the subject while hidden observers recorded the amount of time the subject spent looking at the confederate. Interpersonal closeness significantly reduced eye contact and, although there were sex-of-subject by sex-of-confederate effects, these did not interact with the distance effect. Figure 10 presents the distance effect on double log axes with the dependent variable reflecting disruption of eye contact: the proportion of time that the subject was *not* looking at the confederate. The least squares line, with $d = 0.30$, accurately describes these means, $r^2 = 0.99$.

Using the same interpersonal distances, Aiello (1972) found comparable patterns for males but not for females. His confederates, though, were free to vary their visual behavior and also may have responded to the distance manipulations, as did the confederates in the Patterson and Sechrest (1970) study. Goldberg, Kiesler, and Collins (1969) investigated eye contact at two interview distances and found that subjects at six feet maintained more eye contact than did subjects at 2.5 feet. As with helping behavior and attitude change, eye contact behavior, which is normal at a social distance, appears to be disrupted at close interpersonal distances.

Psychophysical studies of distance.   Although the evidence reviewed above conforms to the gravitational model, the data in many cases are unable to provide an accurate description of the effects of distance. In many cases, too few levels of interpersonal distance have been sampled. In addition, various methodological and measurement problems may have reduced the accuracy of description.[6] In contrast, the work of the Swedish psychophysicist, Gösta Ekman, and his colleagues (Bratfisch, 1969; Ekman & Bratfisch, 1965; Kunnapas, 1960; Lundberg, Bratfisch, & Ekman, 1972) provides a more sophisticated treatment of data in their studies of the relationship between emotional involvement and subjective distance. In various studies, psychophysical techniques have been used to develop psychological scales of subjects' emotional involvement with events taking place in various world cities and of their subjective distance to each city. When various secondary variables, such as importance attributed to, interest in,

---

[6]Such problems have to do mainly with the quality of the scales used to measure distance and energy. Equation 10, for instance, requires that at infinite distance the value of the dependent variable approaches zero. Although this assumption may be met with frequency data, it needs to be demonstrated for scaled dependent variables. For example, Fisher's (1974) study would have benefited from an infinite distance control condition (where no one else was present) with which to determine the baseline or functional zero point on his dependent variable. Without such a control condition, a constant may be added to the dependent variable that would change the value of the exponent (multiplying by a constant, however, does not change the value). Perturbations or distortions of the exponential relationship also would occur if the measures of distance or energy are not on equal interval scales.

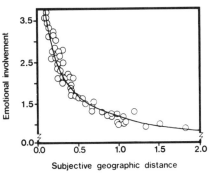

FIG. 11   Emotional involvement as a function of subjective distance to world cities. From "Emotional involvement and subjective distance: A summary of investigations" by U. Lundberg, O. Bratfisch, and G. Ekman, *Journal of Social Psychology*, 1972, *87*, 169-177. Copyright 1972 by the Journal Press. Reprinted by permission.

and knowledge of the cities, are controlled, emotional involvement decreases as a function of the square root of distance ($d = 0.5$).[7] Figure 11 presents data accumulated from eight different studies (Lundberg et al., 1972). If these data were plotted on double log axes, the curved line in this figure would be a straight line with a slope of −0.5, that is, with $d = 0.5$. The inverse square root function of distance, however, has not been found universally. Stanley (1968, 1971) also finds inverse exponential relationships, but the exponent of distance is generally closer to 0.25 and more variable than the 0.5 suggested by Ekman.

In addition to its support of Equation 10, suggesting that concern increases with closeness, Ekman's work is instructive for two reasons. First, it demonstrates that the kinds of relationships expressed in the gravitational model can be studied with a great deal of precision, both in the quality of the scales used and in the number of levels studied. Second, it shows the utility of considering psychological rather than physical distance. Ekman (1961; Ekman & Bratfisch, 1965) has argued that subjective variables should be related to other subjective variables, and various studies (Bratfisch, 1969; Lundberg et al., 1972) show that emotional involvement is more strongly related to subjective distance than to geographic distance. Subjective distance would be important for interpersonal behavior as well. Eye contact between people, the directness of head and body orientation, and a variety of other "immediacy" behaviors increase the psychological closeness between people (Argyle & Dean, 1965; Patterson, 1973). Also, the addition of objects (Patterson et al., 1971; Sommer & Becker, 1969) or other kinds of screens (Desor, 1972) between people can increase the psychological distance. More generally, these considerations suggest that distance in the gravitational model may be measured in ways other than geographic distance. Indeed, Ekman and his colleagues have studied temporal distance (Ekman & Lundberg, 1971; Lundberg, Ekman, & Frankenhaeuser, 1971), finding that the relationships to emotional involvement are similar to those found with geographic distance.

---

[7]These variables, of course, are ones that could be classified as social mass (M_O) variables, affecting the weight of each city in the energy system, and were treated as such by Ekman.

Summary. The data reviewed in this section suggest that distance affects a wide variety of interpersonal interactions. Emotional involvement, arousal, love, accidents, friendships, telephone calls, behavioral disruptions, flight, and feelings of crowdedness all seem to decrease as an exponential function of distance. Although increasing interpersonal influence, as implied by the gravitational model, may have contributed to the distance effects found with each of these dependent variables, for some it was probably not the only contributor. As was noted, the correlational studies of interpersonal communication, friendships, and marriages may have reflected the cost factors of distance as well as the decreased concern with events at a distance. The experimental studies that manipulated interpersonal distance provided more direct evidence for the relationship implied by Equation 10—that others become more influential as they move closer. The diversity of dependent variables for which this pattern was found suggests a general relationship, not tied to any particular setting or response. To this extent, the molar notion of interpersonal energy suggested by the gravitational model seems appropriate.

Although an exponential function of distance was generally found, there was some variability in the value of the exponents observed. These variations may have occurred for a variety of methodological reasons, particularly measurement problems, or because other effects of distance were not controlled. It is also possible that the exponents may vary as a function of the population studied (Huff, 1961; Isard, 1960; Lukermann & Porter, 1960), the specific dependent variable measured (Carroll & Bevis, 1957; Iklé, 1954), or the range of distances studied (Kunnapas, 1960; Teghtsoonian, 1971). Nonetheless, in the studies reviewed, particularly those dealing with more intense interpersonal relations, there was a clustering of exponential values between $d = 0.5$ and $d = 0.6$. Perhaps Ekman's (Ekman and Bratfisch, 1965; Lundberg et al., 1972) suggestion of an inverse square root law of distance is appropriate as an approximation or at least an anticipation of the relationship between distance and interpersonal energy.

SPECULATIONS CONCERNING TIME

The gravitational model in Equation 7 defines the state of energy involving the subject at any one time. However, the experience of others, the amount of influence felt, is likely to be not only a function of the state of the interpersonal system but also a function of the amount of time in that system. As was noted in the discussion of Dodd's (1950) interactance hypothesis, which included the time variable, the effects of time are probably most noticeable at the initiation of an interpersonal system. As a system becomes more established, the differences between successive time periods become less and less. These requirements suggest an exponential relationship where time *(T)* is raised to a power *(t)* that is less than one. These considerations lead to the hypothesis that the amount of effective energy or felt influence acting on a subject is the result of the amount of energy $(\Sigma E_s.)$ and the amount of time (T^t) in the interpersonal system.

The notion that time influences social behavior has not been extensively studied, although attention has been given recently to time as a dependent variable (Cohen, 1967; Doob, 1971). Similarly, in studies of crowding, the dimension of time has been neglected, although several authors have suggested its importance (Lawrence, 1974; Zlutnick & Altman, 1972) or included it as a variable to study (Ross et al., 1973; Sundstrom, 1975). Judgments of upset and irritation have been found to increase over time in conditions of high density (Ross et al., 1973) or goal interference (Sundstrom, 1975), but to decrease over time in more normal conditions. Sundstrom (1975) found that some aspects of crowding could be coped with, leading to decreasing effects over time. Although coping may be possible in the situation, two studies (Aiello et al., 1975; Sherrod, 1974) suggest that crowding may have some behavioral aftereffects (c f., Glass & Singer, 1972) that become apparent after leaving the crowded situation and which, presumably, could be affected by the duration of crowding.

These few studies suggest that time is related to the experience of crowding, but they do not allow any statements about the nature of the relationship. Thus, the hypothesis that crowding increases as an exponential function of time is presently untested. Sundstrom's findings suggest that the effects of time may be related to the ability to cope with crowding as well as to the experience of crowding. If this is the case, then the effects of time on various consequences of crowding could show very complex relationships if care is not taken to separate the influence of the crowd from the strategies used to cope with that influence.

The addition of time to Equation 8 expands the definition of crowding still further: Crowding is the influence on the individual created by the number and potency of others packed closely together over time. Clearly, the data at present are not adequate to describe the role of time or its functional relationship to the experience of crowding. However, as in physics, the notion of time seems important for understanding social phenomena. Thus, the exponential effect of time is offered as a speculative hypothesis with the more general hope that time will be given more theoretical and empirical attention in studies of crowding.

CONCLUSIONS

The gravitational model, used in this chapter as an analogy applied to social behavior, implies that the effects of others on a person's behavior increase as a function of the numbers of others, who they are, how close they are, and, it is suggested, how long they have been there. Although one may wish to quarrel with parts of this statement or with using gravity as an analogy, the more general implication of the present chapter—that others create *fields* of influence—seems to be a useful perspective.

An energy field model focuses on the multiple situational determinants of interpersonal effects. To this extent, it suggests ways of systematically studying the relation between the interpersonal situation and the experience of crowding. Although most authors seem to accept, at least as a hypothesis for study, the notion that situational density produces an experience of crowding and that these two, singly or together, produce affective, cognitive, and behavioral consequences of crowding (c.f., Stokols, 1972; Aiello et al., Note 1), they appear to be concerned primarily with explaining the consequences of crowding. In so doing, disagreement has emerged concerning which of the antecedent variables is important to study. Stokols (1972) argued that more variance in the effects of crowding is explained using the psychological state, crowding, as the predictor variable, whereas Freedman (1975) argued that more meaningful variance is explained using the situational variables as predictors. Rather than providing an explanation of the effects of crowding, an energy field model attempts to define the antecedents of crowding. It suggests fairly specific relations between the objective interpersonal situation—the numbers of others, their distance, their mass —and the subjective responses to the others in the situation. As the evidence reviewed earlier, particularly the work of Ekman, Lundberg, and their colleagues, suggests, these relationships are available to rigorous and systematic study.

The energy field perspective presented in this chapter attempts to define further the "social stimulation" or "stimulus overload" models of crowding. It separates and attempts to specify the initial conditions in the interpersonal situation that produce the stimulation or interpersonal energy. Moreover, crowding from this perspective is a quantifiable dimension, varying between high and low levels of interpersonal energy. Thus, it suggests a link between crowded and alone situations; the difference is a quantitative one, the degree of interpersonal energy, rather than a qualitative one.

The model presented in this chapter is not without its limitations. In evaluating the energy field model, three things need to be kept in mind. First, it deals quantitatively with the effects of others but not with the quality of these effects. Although supporting the quantitative predictions of the model, several studies also show that the number and closeness of others can be appreciated as well as disliked (Cozby, 1973; Desor, 1972; Epstein & Karlin, 1975; Freedman et al., 1972; Marshall & Heslin, 1975; Valins & Baum, 1973). It is clear that additional statements are needed to describe and predict the qualitative aspects of interpersonal effects.

Second, the interpersonal energy field model describes the causes of influence but not the consequences. People may respond to the feeling of being crowded or influenced in a variety of ways and may develop various strategies to deal or cope with the interpersonal situation (Epstein & Karlin, 1975; Saegert et al., 1975; Sundstrom, 1975). The energy field model makes no statements about the selection of coping strategies or their effects on the behavior of the subject or the influence in the interpersonal system.

Third, the model presented in this chapter is really quite incomplete. The variables mentioned in the various equations—number, distance, and social mass —are classes of variables whose constituents may vary widely in their interpersonal effects. Thus, the gravitational model is used in this chapter to introduce a field perspective and represents a beginning, not the end, of this theoretical approach.

Even with these limitations, an energy field model is a useful perspective. In addition to its redirection of attention to the causes of crowding, it suggests fairly specific issues for research. One direct implication is that the degree of crowding in a room can vary from person to person depending on the particular configuration of the people in the room. Because crowding, according to this model, depends on the closeness to each other person, only in a perfect circle would the sum of the interpersonal energy be equal for each person in the room, and then only if the social masses of the others were equal. When subjects are placed in ovals (e.g., Freedman et al., 1971; Stokols et al., 1973) or in straight lines (e.g., Epstein & Karlin, 1975; Griffitt & Veitch, 1971), the interpersonal energy potentials vary from person to person; subjects in the middle are closer to more other people than are subjects at the ends. Indeed, Epstein and Karlin (1975) observed in a *post hoc* analysis that subjects sitting in the middle of crowded rows exhibited greater effects of the crowding than did subjects sitting on the ends of the rows. This finding is reminiscent of Griffith's (1921) conclusion that students who are forced to sit in the middle of classrooms are more stimulated by the situation and receive better grades than students who sit at the periphery. The energy field model and these few findings suggest that one's position in the crowd affects the response to the crowd.

Although derived for and perhaps most applicable to crowding, an energy field model is not limited to only this aspect of interpersonal effects. Other, simpler, and less intense interpersonal situations are also instances where others create fields of influence. Thus, investigations of group, audience, and crowd size; status, prestige, and attraction; spatial invasions as well as geographic, alphabetical, and interpersonal distance are dealing with variables important to the understanding of crowding. As an area of study, crowding is distinguished only by the high intensity and often multiple sources of interpersonal energy created. One advantage of an energy field model is that it provides a means of organizing, relating, and studying both simple and complex interpersonal influence situations.

ACKNOWLEDGMENTS

Much of the work represented in this chapter was completed while the author was a Visiting Assistant Professor, Department of Psychology, Ohio State University. Appreciation is expressed to Ohio State University, to Robert McPeek and Rod Bassett for early discussion of these issues, to Irwin Altman, Mary Harris, Bibb Latané, Charles Matter, Miles Patterson, and Susan Saegert for reading and commenting on earlier versions of this paper, and to my interdisciplinary colleagues at the University of Wisconsin—Green Bay. Bibb Latané deserves special acknowledgment; his stimulating ideas about general models of social behavior provided part of the background out of which this review of social physics emerged.

REFERENCES NOTES

1. Aiello, J. R., Epstein, Y. M., & Karlin, R. A. *Methodological and conceptual issues in crowding*. Paper presented at the Western Psychological Association Convention, April 1974.
2. Aiello, J. R., Epstein, Y. M., & Karlin, R. A. *Field experimental research on human crowding*. Paper presented at the Eastern Psychological Association Convention, April 1975.
3. Brenner, M. *Stagefright and Stevens' Law*. Paper presented at the Eastern Psychological Association Convention, April 1974.
4. Latta, R. M., & Kahn, A. *Effects of induced status on spacing and seating position in a dyad*. Paper presented at the Midwestern Psychological Association Convention, May 1973.
5. McClelland, L. A. *Crowding and social stress*. Unpublished doctoral dissertation, University of Michigan, 1974.
6. Quick, A. D., & Crano, W. D. *Effects of sex, distance, and conversation in the invasion of personal space*. Paper presented at the Midwestern Psychological Association Convention, May 1973.
7. Saegert, S. *Effects of spatial and social density on arousal, mood, and social orientation*. Unpublished doctoral dissertation, University of Michigan, 1974.
8. Sundstrom, E. *Crowding: Some theoretical considerations*. Paper presented at the Midwestern Psychological Association Convention, May 1974.

REFERENCES

Abrams, R. H. Residential propinquity as a factor in marriage selection: Fifty year trends in Philadelphia. *American Sociological Review*, 1943, *8*, 288-294.
Aiello, J. R. A test of equilibrium theory: Visual interaction in relation to orientation, distance and sex of interactants. *Psychonomic Science*, 1972, *27*, 335-336.
Aiello, J. R., Epstein, Y. M., & Karlin, R. A. Effects of crowding on electrodermal activity. *Sociological Symposium*, 1975, *14*, 42-57.
Albert, S., & Dabbs, J. M., Jr. Physical distance and persuasion. *Journal of Personality and Social Psychology*, 1970, *15*, 265-270.
Allport, F. H. The influence of the group upon association and thought. *Journal of Experimental Psychology*, 1920, *3*, 159-182.
Anderson, T. R. Potential models and the spatial distribution of population. *Papers and Proceedings of the Regional Science Association*, 1956, *2*, 175-182.
Argyle, M., & Dean, J. Eye-contact, distance, and affiliation. *Sociometry*, 1965, *28*, 289-304.

Asch, S. E. Effects of group pressure upon the modification and distortion of judgments. In H. Guetzkow (Ed.), *Groups, leadership, and men*. Pittsburgh: Carnegie Press, 1951.

Asch, S. E. Studies of independence and conformity: I. A minority of one against a unanimous majority. *Psychological Monographs*, 1956, *70*(9, Whole No. 416).

Athanasiou, R., & Yoshioka, G. A. The spatial character of friendship formation. *Environment and Behavior*, 1973, *5*, 43-65.

Back, K. W. Influence through social communication. *Journal of Abnormal and Social Psychology*, 1951, *46*, 9-23.

Barash, D. P. Human ethology: Personal space reiterated. *Environment and Behavior*, 1973, *5*, 67-72.

Baum, A., & Greenberg, C. I. Waiting for a crowd: The behavioral and perceptual effects of anticipated crowding. *Journal of Personality and Social Psychology*, 1975, *32*, 671-679.

Baum, A., & Valins, S. Residential environments, group size, and crowding. *Proceedings of the American Psychological Association*, 1973, 211-212.

Bergin, A. E. The effect of dissonant persuasive communications upon changes in self-referring attitudes. *Journal of Personality*, 1962, *30*, 423-438.

Bossard, J. H. S. Residential propinquity as a factor in marriage selection. *American Journal of Sociology*, 1932, *38*, 219-224.

Bratfisch. O. A further study of the relation between subjective distance and emotional involvement. *Acta Psychologica*, 1969, *29*, 244-255.

Caplow, T., & Foreman, R. Neighborhood interaction in a homogeneous community. *American Sociological Review*, 1950, *15*, 357-366.

Carey, H. C. *Principles of social science*. Philadelphia: Lippincott, 1858.

Carroll, J. D. Spatial interaction and the urban-metropolitan description. *Papers and Proceedings of the Regional Science Association*, 1955, *1*, D1-D14.

Carroll, J. D., & Bevis, H. B. Predicting local travel in urban regions. *Papers and Proceedings of the Regional Science Association*, 1957, *3*, 183-197.

Carrothers, G. A. P. An historical review of the gravity and potential concepts of human interaction. *Journal of American Institute of Planners*, 1956, *22*, 94-102.

Cavanaugh, J. A. Formulation, analysis, and testing of the interactance hypothesis. *American Sociological Review*, 1950, *15*, 763-766.

Chandler, W. R. The relationship of distance to the occurrence of pedestrian accidents. *Sociometry*, 1948, *11*, 108-110.

Clarke, A. C. An examination of the operation of residential propinquity as a factor in mate selection. *American Sociological Review*, 1952, *17*, 17-22.

Cohen, J. *Psychological time in health and disease*. Springfield, Ill.: Thomas, 1967.

Converse, P. D. New laws of retail gravitation. *Journal of Marketing*, 1949, *14*, 379-384.

Cottrell, N. B. Performance in the presence of other human beings: Mere presence, audience, and affiliation effects. In E. C. Simmel, R. A. Hoppe, & G. A. Milton (Eds.), *Social facilitation and imitative behavior*. Boston: Allyn & Bacon, 1968.

Cottrell, N. B., Wack, D. L., Sekerak, G. J., & Rittle, R. H. Social facilitation of dominant responses by the presence of an audience and the mere presence of others. *Journal of Personality and Social Psychology*, 1968, *9*, 245-250.

Cozby, P. C. Effects of density, activity, and personality on environmental preferences. *Journal of Research in Personality*, 1973, *1*, 45-60.

Dabbs, J. M., Jr., & Stokes, N. A., III. Beauty is power: The use of space on the sidewalk. *Sociometry*, 1975, *38*, 551-557.

Dashiell, J. F. An experimental analysis of some group effects. *Journal of Abnormal and Social Psychology*, 1930, *25*, 190-199.

Dashiell, J. F. Experimental studies of the influence of social situations on the behavior of individual human adults. In C. Hurchison (Ed.), *A handbook of social psychology*. Worcester, Mass.: Clark University Press, 1935.

D'Atri, D. A. Psychophysiological responses to crowding. *Environment and Behavior,* 1975, *7,* 237-252.

Davie, M. R., & Reeves, R. J. Propinquity of residence before marriage. *American Journal of Sociology,* 1939, *44,* 510-517.

Dean, L. M., Pugh, W. M., & Gunderson, E. K. B. Spatial and perceptual components of crowding: Effects on health and satisfaction. *Environment and Behavior,* 1975, *7,* 225-236.

Desor, J. A. Toward a psychological theory of crowding. *Journal of Personality and Social Psychology,* 1972, *21,* 79-83.

Deutsch, M., & Collins, M. E. *Interracial housing: A psychological evaluation of a social experiment.* Minneapolis: University of Minnesota Press, 1957.

Dodd, S. C. The interactance hypothesis: A gravity model fitting physical masses and human groups. *American Sociological Review,* 1950, *15,* 245-256.

Doob, L. W. *Patterning of time.* New Haven: Yale University Press, 1971.

Ekman, G. Some aspects of psychophysical research. In W. A. Rosenblith (Ed.), *Sensory communication.* New York: Wiley, 1961.

Ekman, G., & Bratfisch, O. Subjective distance and emotional involvement: A psychological mechanism. *Acta Psychologica,* 1965, *24,* 430-437.

Ekman, G., & Lundberg, U. Emotional reaction to past and future events as a function of temporal distance. *Acta Psychologica,* 1971, *35,* 430-441.

Emiley, S. F. The effects of crowding and interpersonal attraction on affective responses, task performance and verbal behavior. *Journal of Social Psychology,* 1975, *97,* 267-278.

Eoyang, C. K. Effects of group size and privacy in residential crowding. *Journal of Personality and Social Psychology,* 1974, *30,* 289-392.

Epstein, Y. M., & Karlin, R. A. Effects of acute experimental crowding. *Journal of Applied Social Psychology,* 1975, *5,* 34-53.

Evans, G. W., & Howard, R. B. Personal space. *Psychological Bulletin,* 1973, *80,* 334-344.

Fagen, S. A. The effects of real and experimentally reported ability on confidence and conformity. *American Psychologist,* 1963, *18,* 357-358.

Felipe, N. J., & Sommer, R. Invasions of personal space. *Social Problems,* 1966, *14,* 206-214.

Festinger, L., Schachter, S., & Back, K. *Social pressures in informal groups: A study of human factors in housing.* Stanford, Cal.: Stanford University Press, 1950.

Fisher, J. D. Situation-specific variables as determinants of perceived environmental aesthetic quality and perceived crowdedness. *Journal of Research in Personality,* 1974, *8,* 177-188.

Folger, J. Some aspects of migration in the Tennessee Valley. *American Sociological Review,* 1953, *18,* 253-260.

Freedman, J. L. *Crowding and behavior.* San Francisco: Freeman, 1975.

Freedman, J. L., Klevansky, S., & Ehrlich, P. R. The effects of crowding on human task performance. *Journal of Applied Social Psychology,* 1971, *1,* 7-25.

Freedman, J. L., Levy, A. S., Buchanan, R. W., & Price, J. Crowding and human aggressiveness. *Journal of Experimental Social Psychology,* 1972, *8,* 526-548.

Garrison, W. L. Allocation of road and street costs. Part 4 of *The benefits of rural roads to rural property.* Seattle: Washington State Council for Highway Research, 1956.

Geisen, M., & Hendrick, C. Physical distance and sex in moderated groups: Neglected factors in small group interaction. *Memory and Cognition,* 1977, *5,* 79-83.

Geisen, M., & McClaren, H. A. Discussion, distance, and sex: Changes in impressions and attraction during small group interaction. *Sociometry,* 1976, *39,* 60-70.

Gerard, H. B. The anchorage of opinions in face-to-face groups. *Human Relations,* 1954, *7,* 313-325.

Gerard, H. B., Wilhelmy, R. A., & Conolley, E. S. Conformity and group size. *Journal of Personality and Social Psychology,* 1968, *8,* 79-82.

Glass, D. C., & Singer, J. E. *Urban stress*. New York: Academic Press, 1972.

Goldberg, G., Kiesler, C., & Collins, B. Visual behavior and face-to-face distance during interaction. *Sociometry*, 1969, *32*, 43-53.

Griffith, C. R. A comment upon the psychology of the audience. *Psychological Monographs*, 1921, *30* (136), 36-47.

Griffitt, W., & Veitch, R. Hot and crowded: Influences of population density and temperature on interpersonal affective behavior. *Journal of Personality and Social Psychology*, 1971, *17*, 92-98.

Hammer, C., & Iklé, F. C. Intercity telephone and airline traffic related to distance and the "propensity to interact." *Sociometry*, 1957, *20*, 306-316.

Henchy, T., & Glass, D. C. Evaluation apprehension and the social facilitation of dominant and subordinate responses. *Journal of Personality and Social Psychology*, 1968, *10*, 446-454.

Hochbaum, G. M. The relation between group members' self-confidence and their reactions to group pressure to conformity. *American Sociological Review*, 1954, *19*, 678-687.

Hovland, C. I., Janis, I. L., & Kelley, H. H. *Communication and persuasion*. New Haven, Conn.: Yale University Press, 1953.

Huff, D. L. Ecological characteristics of consumer behavior. *Papers and Proceedings of the Regional Science Association*, 1961, *7*, 19-28.

Hutt, C., & Vaizey, M. J. Differential effects of group density on social behavior. *Nature*, 1966, *209*, 1371-1372.

Iklé, F. C. Sociological relationship of traffic to population and distance. *Traffic Quarterly*, 1954, *8*, 123-136.

Isard, W. *Methods of regional analysis: An introduction to regional science*. New York: Wiley, 1960.

Isard, W. Spatial interaction analysis: Some suggestive thoughts from general relativity physics. *Papers of the regional Science Association*, 1971, *27*, 17-38.

Isard, W., & Peck, M. J. Location theory and international and interregional trade theory. *Quarterly Journal of Economics*, 1954, *68*, 97-114.

Iwata, O. Empirical examination of the perception of density and crowding. *Japanese Psychological Research*, 1974, *16*, 117-125.

Keuthe, J. Social schemas. *Journal of Abnormal and Social Psychology*, 1962, *64*, 31-36.

Knowles, E. S. Boundaries around group interaction: The effects of group size and member status on boundary permeability. *Journal of Personality and Social Psychology*, 1973, *26*, 327-331.

Knowles, E. S., Kreuser, B., Haas, S., Hyde, M., & Schuchart, G. E. Group size and the extension of social space boundaries. *Journal of Personality and Social Psychology*, 1976, *33*, 647-654.

Konecni, V. J., Libuser, L., Morton, H., & Ebbesen, E. B. Effects of a violation of personal space on escape and helping responses. *Journal of Experimental Social Psychology*, 1975, *11*, 288-299.

Kunnapas, T. Scales for subjective distance. *Scandinavian Journal of Psychology*, 1960, *1*, 187-192.

Kutner, D. H., Jr. Overcrowding: Human responses to density and visual exposure. *Human Relations*, 1973, *26*, 31-50.

Lawrence, J. E. S. Science and sentiment: Overview of research on crowding and human behavior. *Psychological Bulletin*, 1974, *81*, 712-720.

Le Bon, G. *Psychologie des foules*. 1895. Translated: *The crowd*. London: Unwin, 1903.

Levinger, G., & Gunner, J. The interpersonal grid: I. Felt and tape technique for measurement of social behavior. *Psychonomic Science*, 1967, *8*, 173-174.

Little, K. B. Personal space. *Journal of Experimental Social Psychology*, 1965, *1*, 237-247.

Little, K. B. Cultural variations in social schemata. *Journal of Personality and Social Psychology*, 1968, *10*, 1-7.

Loo, C. M. The effects of spatial density on the social behavior of children. *Journal of Applied Social Psychology*, 1972, *2*, 372-381.

Lott, A. J., & Lott, B. E. Group cohesiveness, communication level, and conformity. *Journal of Abnormal and Social Psychology*, 1961, *62*, 408-412.

Lukermann, F., & Porter, P. W. Gravity and potential models in economic geography. *Annals of the Association of American Geographers*, 1960, *50*, 493-504.

Lundberg, U., Bratfisch, O., & Ekman, G. Emotional involvement and subjective distance: A summary of investigations. *Journal of Social Psychology*, 1972, *87*, 169-177.

Lundberg, U., Ekman, G., & Frankenhaeuser, M. Anticipation of electric shock: A psychophysical study. *Acta Psychologica*, 1971, *35*, 430-441.

Marshall, J. E., & Heslin, R. Boys and girls together: Sexual composition and the effect of density and group size on cohesiveness. *Journal of Personality and Social Psychology*, 1975, *31*, 952-961.

McBride, G. C., King, M. G., & James, J. W. Social proximity effects on galvanic skin responses in adult humans. *Journal of Psychology*, 1965, *61*, 153-157.

Mehrabian, A., & Friar, J. Encoding of attitude by a seated communicator via posture and position cues. *Journal of Consulting and Clinical Psychology*, 1969, *33*, 330-336.

Middlemist, R. D., Knowles, E. S., & Matter, C. F. Personal space invasions in the lavatory: Suggestive evidence for arousal. *Journal of Personality and Social Psychology*, 1976, *33*, 541-546.

Milgram, S. Some conditions of obedience and disobedience to authority. *Human Relations*, 1965, *18*, 57-75.

Milgram, S., Bickman, L., & Berkowitz, L. Note on the drawing power of crowds of different size. *Journal of personality and Social Psychology*, 1969, *13*, 79-82.

Milgram, S., & Toch, H. Collective behavior: Crowds and social movements. In G. Lindzey & E. Aronson (Eds.), *The handbook of social psychology*, (Vol. 4). Reading, Mass.: Addison-Wesley, 1969.

Nesbitt, P. D., & Steven, G. Personal space and stimulus intensity at a Southern California amusement park. *Sociometry*, 1974, *37*, 105-115.

Olsson, G. *Distance and human interaction: A review and bibiography.* Bibliography Series Number Two. Philadelphia: Regional Science Research Institute, 1965.

Patterson, M. L. Compensation in nonverbal immediacy behaviors: A review. *Sociometry*, 1973, *36*, 237-252.

Patterson, M. L., Mullens, S., & Romano, J. Compensatory reactions to spatial intrusion. *Sociometry*, 1971, *34*, 114-121.

Patterson, M. L., & Sechrest, L. B. Interpersonal distance and impression formation. *Journal of Personality*, 1970, *38*, 161-166.

Paulus, P., Cox, V., McCain, G., Chandler, J., & Short, M. Some effects of crowding in a prison environment. *Journal of Applied Social Psychology*, 1975, *5*, 86-91.

Paulus, P., McCain, G., & Cox, V. A note on the use of prisons as environments for investigation of crowding. *Bulletin of the Psychonomic Society*, 1973, *1*, 427-428.

Paulus, P. B., & Murdoch, P. Anticipated evaluation and audience presence in the enhancement of dominant responses. *Journal of Experimental Social Psychology*, 1971, *7*, 280-291.

Porter, H. Studies in the psychology of stuttering. XIV. Stuttering phenomena in relation to size and personnel of audience. *Journal of Speech Disorders*, 1939, *4*, 323-333.

Rosnow, I. The social effects of the physical environment. *Journal of the American Institute of Planners*, 1961, *27*, 127-233.

Ross, M., Layton, B., Erickson, B., & Schopler, J. Affect, facial regard, and reactions to crowding. *Journal of Personality and Social Psychology*, 1973, *28*, 69-76.

Ryen, A. H., & Kahn, A. The effects of intergroup orientation on group attitudes and prox-emic behavior. *Journal of Personality and Social Psychology,* 1975, *31,* 302-310.

Saegert, S. Crowding: Cognitive overload and behavioral constraint. In W. F. E. Preiser (Ed.), *Environmental design research: Proceedings of EDRA IV conference.* Strouds-burg, Pa.: Dowden, Hutchinson & Ross, 1973.

Saegert, S., Mackintosh, E., & West, S. Two studies of crowding in urban public spaces. *Environment and Behavior,* 1975, *7,* 159-184.

Samelson, F. Conforming behavior under two conditions of conflict in the cognitive field. *Journal of Abnormal and Social Psychology,* 1957, *55,* 181-187.

Segal, M. W. Alphabet and attraction: An unobtrusive measure of the effect of propinquity in a field setting. *Journal of Personality and Social Psychology,* 1974, *30,* 654-657.

Sherrod, D. R. Crowding, perceived control, and behavioral aftereffects. *Journal of Applied Social Psychology,* 1974, *4,* 171-186.

Simms, V. M. The relative influences of two types of motivation on improvement. *Journal of Education Psychology,* 1928, *19,* 480-484.

Smith, D. A. Interaction within a fragmented state: The example of Hawaii. *Economic Geography,* 1963, *39,* 234-244.

Sommer, R., & Becker, F. D. Territorial defense and the good neighbor. *Journal of Person-ality and Social Psychology,* 1969, *11,* 85-92.

Stanley, G. Emotional involvement and geographic distance. *Journal of Social Psychology,* 1968, *75,* 165-167.

Stanley, G. Emotional involvement and subjective distance. *Journal of Social Psychology,* 1971, *84,* 309-310.

Stewart, J. Q. An inverse distance variation for certain social influences. *Science,* 1941, *93,* 89-90.

Stewart, J. Q. A measure of the influence of population at distance. *Sociometry,* 1942, *5,* 63-71.

Stewart, J. Q. Suggested principles of "social physics." *Science,* 1947, *106,* 179-180. (a)

Stewart, J. Q. Empirical mathematical rules concerning the distribution and equilibrium of population. *Geographical Review,* 1947, *37,* 461-485. (b)

Stewart, J. Q. Concerning social physics. *Scientific American,* 1948, *178* (5), 20-23. (a)

Stewart, J. Q. Demographic gravitation: Evidence and application. *Sociometry,* 1948, *11,* 31-58. (b)

Stewart, J. Q. A basis for social physics. *Impact of Science on Society,* 1952, *3,* 110-133.

Stewart, J. Q. Discussion: Population projection by means of income potential models. *Paper and Proceedings of the Regional Science Association,* 1958, *4,* 153-154.

Stokols, D. On the distinction between density and crowding: Some implications for future research. *Psychological Review,* 1972, *79,* 275-277.

Stokols, D., Rall, M., Pinner, B., & Schopler, J. Physical, social, and personal determinants of the perception of crowding. *Environment and Behavior,* 1973, *5,* 87-115.

Sundstrom, E. An experimental study of crowding: Effects of room size, intrusion and goal blocking on nonverbal behavior, self-disclosure and self reported stress. *Journal of Personality and Social Psychology,* 1975, *32,* 645−654.

Taaffe, E. J. Air transportation and United States urban distribution. *Geographical Review,* 1956, *46,* 219-238.

Taaffe, E. J. The urban hierarchy: An air passenger definition. *Economic Geography,* 1962, *38,* 1-14.

Teghtsoonian, R. On the exponents in Stevens' Law and the constant in Ekman's Law. *Psychological Review,* 1971, *78,* 71-80.

Thomas, E. J., & Fink, C. F. Effects of group size. *Psychological Bulletin,* 1963, *60,* 371-384.

Tripplett, N. The dynamogenic factors in pace-making and competition. *American Journal of Psychology*, 1897, *9*, 507-532.

Valins, S., & Baum, A.   Residential group size, social interaction, and crowding. *Environment and Behavior*, 1973, *5*, 421-439.

Voorhees, A. M. A general theory of traffic movement. *Proceedings of the Institute of Traffic Engineers*, 1955, 45-56.

Willis, F. N., Jr. Initial speaking distance as a function of the speaker's relationship. *Psychonomic Science*, 1966, *5*, 221-222.

Wittemore, I. C. The influence of competition on performance: An experimental study. *Journal of Abnormal and Social Psychology*, 1924, *19*, 236-253.

Wynn, F. H. Intracity traffic movements. In *Factors influencing travel Patterns*. Washington, D.C.: Highway Research Board, Bulletin 119, 1956.

Yancey, W. L. Architecture, interaction, and social control. *Environment and Behavior*, 1971, *3*, 3-21.

Zajonc, R. B. Social facilitation. *Science*, 1965, *149*, 269-274.

Zipf, G. K. *National unity and disunity*. Bloomington, Ind.: Principia Press, 1941.

Zipf, G. K. The unity of nature, least-action, and natural social science. *Sociometry*, 1942, *5*, 48-62.

Zipf, G. K. The P_1P_2/D hypothesis: On the intercity movement of persons. *American Sociological Review*, 1946, *11*, 677-686. (a)

Zipf, G. K. Some determinants of the circulation of information. *American Journal of Psychology*, 1946, *59*, 401-421. (b)

Zipf, G. K. The P_1P_2/D hypothesis: The case of Railway Express. *Journal of Psychology*, 1946, *22*, 3-8. (c)

Zipf, G. K. The hypothesis of the "minimum equation" as a unifying social principle: With attempted synthesis. *American Sociological Review*, 1947, *12*, 627-650.

Zipf, G. K. *Human behavior and the principle of least effort*. Reading, Mass.: Addison-Wesley, 1949.

Zlutnick, S., & Altman, I. Crowding and human behavior. In J. F. Wohlwill & D. H. Carson (Eds.), *Environment and the social sciences: Perspectives and applications*. Washington, D.C.: American Psychological Association, 1972.

7

A Typology of Crowding Experiences

Daniel Stokols
University of California, Irvine

OVERVIEW

This chapter examines the development of a theoretical perspective on human crowding. Specifically, a typology of crowding experiences is presented (cf., Stokols, 1976), and recent data relevant to the underlying assumptions and derivative predictions of the model are assessed. Also, linkages between the proposed typology and alternative conceptualizations of crowding are explored, and priorities for future research and theoretical development are discussed.

Before outlining the model, a brief historical sketch of the progression of crowding research over the past 15 years is presented. This sketch is intended not to provide an exhaustive review of research during this period but rather to identify a sequence of conceptual stages in the development of crowding research. (For a comprehensive historical overview of crowding research, see Chapter 1 of this volume.) Consideration of these stages should provide a context in which (1) the relationship between the proposed typology and other approaches to crowding can be specified, and (2) a more general and basic issue can be addressed —namely, the utility of the crowding construct as a means of understanding how population concentration affects human behavior.

CONCEPTUAL STAGES OF CROWDING RESEARCH

The appearance of the present volume (along with earlier books on crowding and spatial behavior—e.g., Altman, 1975; Esser, 1971; Freedman, 1975; Newman, 1973) and the swelling of psychological, sociological, and design-oriented journals with scores of articles on crowding and behavior attest to the rapid expansion of this research domain over the past five years. One can speculate on the various factors that prompted a burgeoning interest in the behavioral and psychological consequences of crowding. A recent discussion of these factors can be found elsewhere (Loo, 1975). Suffice it to say that a convergence of contemporary societal concerns (e.g., overpopulation, environmental degradation, urbanization) and parallel research developments (e.g., Calhoun's 1962 report of the devastating impact of population concentration on laboratory animals) probably account for the fact that the study of crowding in the past few years has become one of the fastest growing areas of behavioral science research.

Although crowding research has accumulated rapidly in a short period, the development of this work has been neither chaotic nor disorderly. In fact, the research literature appears to reflect at least four conceptual phases, each of which builds logically on the preceding one. These phases will be discussed as a chronological sequence although it is recognized that in some cases research reflecting the approach of a particular phase may have occurred either prior or subsequent to the apparent emergence of that phase.

Stage I (1960-1969):
Density = Crowding = Stress

The earliest systematic studies of crowding were conducted by animal researchers who reported, quite consistently and dramatically, that population concentration among members of laboratory or naturalistic communities led to severe behavioral and physiological impairments (cf. Calhoun, 1962; Christian, 1961; Christian, Flyger, & Davis, 1960; Keeley, 1962; Snyder, 1961; Thiessen & Rodgers, 1961). These findings were replicated across a variety of species and thus lent support to the notion that high density is necessarily associated with a syndrome of crowding stress.

Taking their cue from the animal data, sociologists interested in the relationship between high density and various problems in human communities began to explore the correlations between census-tract indexes of density, crime, suicide, and disease (e.g., Schmitt, 1957, 1966; Winsborough, 1965). Most of the data from these survey studies indicated a significant positive correlation between measures of population density and rates of pathology, although in the absence of certain methodological control procedures, such as matched-sampling and partial correlation, it was difficult to determine whether elevated pathology levels were actually attributable to density or to negative social conditions typically found in high-density neighborhoods (i.e., poverty, dilapidated housing). Nonetheless, despite these methodological qualifications and the pitfalls of generalizing prematurely from animal studies to human communities, the common view during the initial phase of research was that density (or crowding) operated as a stressor that necessarily promoted social and physiological anomalies among nonhumans and humans alike. The implications for community planners were clear: Avoid high-density buildings and neighborhoods if at all possible.

Stage II (1970-1971):
Density = Crowding =
The Absence of Stress at the Human Level

The second phase of crowding research was heralded by a series of experiments conducted by Jonathan Freedman and colleagues (Freedman, Klevansky, & Ehrlich, 1971; Freedman, Note 11). This group adopted a frankly empirical approach to the study of crowding. Essentially, they exposed eight-member groups to either large or small laboratory rooms and observed subjects' task performance and interactions with one another. The consistent finding from this series of studies was that task performance remained unaffected by high density and that subjects' reactions to one another and to the laboratory environment were influenced only slightly by room size, with female subjects evidencing a higher tolerance for spatial limitation than males.

Concurrently, the results from a major survey study of apartment dwellers in Hong Kong were reported by Mitchell (1971). Mitchell's findings ran parallel to those of Freedman et al. (1971) in the sense that population density appeared to exert negligible effects on the psychological and physical well-being of the crowded residents.

Another set of studies conducted during this period did produce evidence that people in large groups were more likely to act aggressively and asocially than those in smaller ones (e.g., Griffitt & Veitch, 1971; Hutt & Vaisey, 1966; Ittelson, Proshansky, & Rivlin, 1970). The behavioral effects observed in these studies, however, could have been due to any number of factors including spatial restriction, scarcity of resources, and increased noise. Thus, the message of Freedman's and Mitchell's research was simply that clear-cut evidence for the detrimental effect of high density on people was nonexistent. On the basis of this conclusion, it was surmised that the remarkable capacity of people to adapt to their environment enabled them to tolerate (and in many instances, to enjoy) their exposure to high density conditions while experiencing no negative effects of such exposure. For all practical purposes, then, population density could be viewed as a rather innocuous variable at the human level and, therefore, urban planners could turn their attention to environmental conditions more pressing than crowding (pollution, poverty, racial discrimination) in attempting to alleviate contemporary urban problems.

It should be noted that in 1970, a programmatic article by Proshansky, Ittelson, and Rivlin presented an alternative view of crowding. They suggested that density (or crowding) is not always problematic for people but becomes stressful to the extent that it precludes privacy or places other limitations on behavior. This more qualified view of the density-behavior relationship was to undergo extensive elaboration during the third phase of crowding research.

Stage III (1972-1973):
Density ≠ Crowding = Stress—
The Search for Antecedents of Crowding
Via Existing Theoretical Models

The emergence of Stage III was marked by a conceptual distinction between *density,* a physical condition of limited space, and *crowding,* an experience in which one's demand for space exceeds the available supply (cf. Stokols, 1972a, 1972b; Zlutnick and Altman, 1972). This distinction was proposed as a preliminary basis for identifying those circumstances under which people do or do not experience stress under conditions of high density. Despite the optimistic findings of Freedman and Mitchell, the fact that people often regard high-density situations as unpleasant suggested that a more extensive analysis of human crowding was required to permit an adequate assessment of its effects on people.

According to this analysis, proximity to other people was viewed as a necessary antecedent rather than a sufficient condition for the experience of crowding. Any instance of spatial limitation involves potential inconveniences, such as the restriction of movement, the preclusion of privacy, or exposure to excessive stimulation. These potential problems are not necessarily salient to the occupants of a high-density area. For the experience of crowding to occur, certain contextual variables (e.g., hostile cues from others) must be present that sensitize the individual to the inconveniences he might encounter as a result of being too proximal to others.

Analyses of human crowding during the third phase of research attempted to more fully specify critical determinants of the crowding experience. At least three theoretical perspectives were proposed as a basis for specifying the circumstances under which density exerts negative effects on behavior: (1) *stimulus overload;* (2) *behavioral constraint;* and (3) *ecological orientations.*[1]

Stimulus overload analyses portrayed high density as a stressor variable to the degree that it exposes individuals to excessive levels of stimulation (e.g., Baum & Valins, 1973; Desor, 1972; Esser, 1972; Saegert, 1973; Valins & Baum, 1973; Zlutnick & Altman, 1972). Behavioral constraint formulations viewed high density as stressful to the extent that it imposes restrictions on behavioral freedom (e.g., Proshansky, Ittelson, & Rivlin, 1970; Stokols, 1972b). And from an ecological perspective, high density was characterized as disruptive to the degree that it is accompanied by a shortage of social roles or physical resources in a particular setting (e.g., Wicker, 1973; Wicker & Kirmeyer, 1977; Hanson & Wicker, Note 14).

Each of the above analyses reflected an application of existing sociological and psychological theories of social behavior to the area of human crowding. Overload analyses were rooted in the theories of urban life developed by Simmel (1950) and Wirth (1938), and in Milgram's (1970) extension of this work from

---

[1]See Stokols (1976) for a more complete discussion of these theoretical perspectives.

the sociological realm to a psychological context. Similarly, the behavioral constraint perspective on crowding derived largely from Brehm's (1966) theory of psychological reactance and Sommer's (1969) conceptualization of personal space. And the ecological approach to crowding stemmed directly from Barker's (1968) application of ecological theory (e.g., Clements, 1905) to the study of human social behavior.

Thus the third conceptual phase of crowding research was signaled by a clearcut distinction between the terms *density* and *crowding* and an application of existing social psychological theory to an analysis of the conditions under which high density does or does not promote perceived crowding and stress in people.

Certainly, not all researchers adopted the density-crowding distinction. Freedman and others (e.g., Griffitt, Note 13) have argued consistently that "*crowding* should be understood always as referring to the physical situation of high density, not to an internal feeling," and that "it is the former that must be studied" rather than the latter (Freedman, 1975, pp. 11, 115). Enough researchers during this period, however, did incorporate a psychological (rather than a physicalistic) interpretation of crowding into their work that two contrasting research approaches were now distinctly evident: one that conceptualized crowding as an intervening construct (cf. Hull, 1943a; Spence, 1944; Tolman, 1938) to better predict specific environment-behavior relationships, and one that equated density and crowding and advocated the direct investigation of how crowding affects behavior without the hindrance of superfluous intervening variables. As is indicated more fully in the following, these approaches pose markedly different implications for social planning and urban design.

Stage IV (1974-present):
Development of New Constructs Relating to
Crowding and Spatial Behavior

Harold Proshansky (1973), in a discussion of theoretical developments within the area of environmental psychology, outlined three interrelated tasks that need to be addressed in future research: (1) the definition and elaboration of existing environment-behavioral concepts; (2) establishing their relationships to more traditional psychological concepts; and (3) actively seeking to develop new and viable environment-behavioral concepts based on the analysis of existing ones and the extant body of general psychological theory.

The first two conceptual tasks are reflected in the development of the crowding construct and the application of existing theoretical concepts (e.g., overload, reactance, overmanning) to an elaboration of this construct during the third phase of crowding research (ca. 1972-1973). Efforts to address the final task mentioned by Proshansky have begun more recently and, in effect, mark the emergence of the fourth and current stage of crowding research.

The development of new constructs dealing specifically with human spatial behavior are exemplified by earlier work in other areas of proxemic research.

Probably the best examples of innovative conceptual work in these areas are Hall's (1966) and Sommer's (1969) analyses of personal space. Further elaboration of proxemic constructs is reflected in Sundstrom and Altman's (1976) typology of personal-space intrusions, Evans and Eichelman's (1976) analysis of personal space from a functional or evolutionary perspective, and Altman's (1970) and Edney's (1974) discussions of human territoriality.

In the context of crowding, Altman (1974, 1975) and Stokols (1976) have recently developed models that build on the basic distinction between density and crowding. According to Altman's analysis, the experience of crowding results when one is unable to achieve desired levels of privacy, that is, when one is exposed to more contact with other people than he desires. Personal space and territoriality are viewed as behavioral mechanisms that enable the individual to regulate the amount of his contact with others.

Stokols' analysis provides a delineation of crowding experiences in terms of their varying antecedents, intensity, and behavioral consequences. The basic thrust of the analysis is that the intensity and persistence of felt crowding depend on (1) the individual's perception of inadequate control over the spatial and/or social environment, and (2) the type of environment in which crowding occurs. Thus, crowding experiences are categorized as being either "neutral" or "personal" in nature and are discussed in the context of either "primary" or "secondary" environments. These concepts are described more fully in a later section of the chapter.

Although the above overview of research has been more selective than complete, it serves to reveal a basic progression from a theoretical to conceptually oriented approaches in the study of human crowding. This progression is most clearly evident during the third and fourth stages of crowding research, which witnessed the initial formulation of a crowding construct, subsequent refinements and elaborations of this construct, and more recent attempts to link earlier concepts with the development of new ones in an effort to build a comprehensive theory of crowding and spatial behavior.

The present phase of research most likely will continue to reflect an increasing emphasis on conceptual consolidation and more vigorous attempts to operationalize and assess the critical assumptions of different crowding theories (cf. Baldassare & Fischer, 1977; Lawrence, 1974). At the same time, the potential utility of theoretical approaches to crowding in the context of community planning and architectural design should receive increasing scrutiny during the next few years.

A crucial assumption reflected in much of the recent research literature is that construct-oriented approaches provide a more adequate basis for understanding human crowding than do those that disavow the use of such constructs and regard them as unnecessary and confusing. Of late, this assumption has come under increasing criticism (e.g., Freedman, 1975; Griffitt, Note 13) and will be examined more fully at this point in the discussion. Therefore, in the following section, the major criticisms as well as the alleged advantages of a construct-oriented approach to crowding are discussed. Subsequently, the Stokols (1976) typology of crowding experiences will be presented as an example of this approach.

THE CROWDING CONSTRUCT: PRO AND CON

The use of hypothetical constructs, or intervening variables, in the construction of psychological theories was first discussed by Tolman (1938) and later elaborated on by Hull (1943a, 1943b) and Spence (1944, 1948). According to these theorists, the major function of intervening constructs is to aid in the discovery of empirical laws that specify enduring relationships between environmental conditions (E) on the one hand, and patterns of behavior (B) on the other.

The empirical regularities sought by behavioral scientists can be represented as follows:

$$B = f(E); \text{ or } E \rightarrow B.$$

The existence of such a law presupposes two essential conditions: (1) that all relevant environmental variables are known; and (2) that the nature of all functional relations between the environmental and behavioral variables have been ascertained. To the extent that these conditions can be met through empirical investigation alone, the introduction of intervening constructs into the E-B equation is unnecessary. For example, if a specific condition of the environment, E (e.g., high density), is observed invariably to elicit a particular response, B, (e.g., aggression), then all relevant variables in the equation are presumed to be known, and B can be represented as a direct function of E.

Human behavior, however, is known for its complexity and variability even under the most static of environmental conditions. Thus, E (high density) may be observed to elicit B_1 (aggression) and in some cases, B_2 (affiliation) in others, and B_0 (no response) in still others. It is in relation to such phenomena, where invariant E-B relationships are not readily discerned through direct observation, that intervening constructs (e.g., crowding) can be utilized to deduce the conditions under which B_0, B_1, B_2, B_3 ..., or B_n, will occur in conjunction with E_1.

As was indicated earlier, the crowding construct evolved as a logical culmination of the first two phases of research on density and behavior. During these initial stages of inquiry, repeated attempts were made to identify a direct and stable relationship between density and behavior, of the following form:

High Density $\rightarrow$ Negative Behavioral Effects

or

High Density $\rightarrow$ Neutral or Positive Behavioral Effects

The accumulation of contradictory findings from numerous studies made it clear that the relationship between density and behavior was a good deal more complex than that predicted by either of the above equations. That is, the effects of density on human behavior might be either favorable *or* unfavorable depending on other, nonspatial factors present in the situation.

Thus, an alternative formulation was proposed:

Density $\longrightarrow$ (Crowding) $\longrightarrow$ Coping   Strategies
Other Situational Conditions $\nearrow$ $\longrightarrow$ Negative Behavioral
                                                        Effects (to the extent
                                                        that coping attempts
                                                        are unsuccessful)

Crowding was defined as a motivational state directed toward the alleviation of perceived spatial restriction and infringement (Stokols, 1972a). The experience of crowding was thought to arise from conditions of high density (or interpersonal proximity) *only* in the context of certain social, personal, and cultural factors that sensitize the individual to the potential inconveniences of limited space. And on the behavioral side of the equation, three patterns of response to crowding were hypothesized: cognitive, perceptual, and overt-behavioral modes of reducing the salience of spatial restriction. To the extent that these coping strategies are unsuccessful, physiological and behavioral impairments were expected to occur.

By defining crowding as the need for more space, it was possible to deduce a variety of personal and environmental factors that might heighten or reduce this need in a particular situation. For example, a person might wish to obtain more space as a means of keeping threatening others at a distance, of performing activities that require large, open areas, or of avoiding noise and other kinds of stimuli created by the concentration of many people in a small area. As mentioned earlier, the third phase of research on density and behavior was devoted largely to the empirical assessment of these and other antecedents of crowding and its behavioral concomitants.

More recently, the utility of the crowding construct has become a topic of debate. On the one hand, advocates argue that the construct permits a more precise delineation of the density-behavior relationship and makes it possible to specify *in advance* what otherwise could be established only through a prolonged and relatively random series of empirical observations: that is, the situational factors that mediate the behavioral impact of high density. On the other hand, those who eschew use of the construct contend that it is essentially superfluous and serves only to muddle the relationship between observable conditions of the environment and overt patterns of behavior.

To date, three major criticisms of the crowding construct have been presented:

1. The crowding construct has prompted an inappropriate and premature shift in the focus of research from the effects of density on behavior to the effects of "perceived crowding" on behavior (cf. Griffitt, Note 13). This argument

is reminiscent of Brunswik's (1943) criticism of Lewin's (1936; 1943) field theory in terms of its "encapsulation," or overemphasis on intervening, subjective states without due regard for the environmental antecedents of overt behavior.

2. The perception of crowding, which is defined as stressful and is presumed to promote negative behavioral effects, is not always accompanied by stress and behavioral impairments (cf. Griffitt, Note 13).

3. To the extent that negative environmental conditions exist, correspondingly negative behavioral reactions will occur regardless of the level of density present in the situation. This position is most clearly reflected in Freedman's (1975) "density-intensity" notion, which suggests that proximity to other people merely intensifies the prevailing quality of any given situation. If a situation is pleasant to begin with (e.g., involves nice people, plenty of food and drink), density will make it better. And conversely, an inherently unpleasant situation (e.g., presence of nasty people, scarcity of resources) will be worsened by conditions of high density. From this perspective, it is unnecessary to invoke a construct of crowding to explain the effects of density on behavior.

Although these arguments touch on some important issues relating to the use of intervening constructs in the behavioral sciences, they do not, in the present writer's opinion, mitigate the value of the crowding construct as a basis for research on density and behavior. Justification for this pro-construct view is presented below in the form of replies to the aforementioned criticisms.

First, the argument that the crowding construct has led to an overemphasis on intervening states and an underemphasis of environmental and response variables is more a criticism of improper use of the construct than of the construct itself. The essential function of constructs is to suggest hypothetical connections (intervening variables) between environmental and behavioral dimensions, thereby assisting the researcher in the discovery of significant E-B regularities. The ultimate focus of the discovery process must be on the assessment and verification of the proposed E-B linkages rather than on the measurement of hypothesized intervening states of the organism. In this regard, Hull (1943a) has noted that "symbolic constructs can have nothing more than a rather dubious expository utility unless they are anchored to observable and measurable conditions on both the antecedent and consequent sides [of the E-B equation] [p. 281]." Thus, proponents of the crowding construct would agree with Griffitt's (Note 13) contention that an overemphasis on the measurement of felt crowding, in isolation from the more essential process of assessing the linkages between hypothesized antecedents and consequences of crowding, reflects a superficial and unproductive approach to the study of human crowding.

It should be emphasized, however, that direct assessments of the physiological, perceptual, and cognitive concomitants of crowding are not inappropriate so long as such measures are eventually related, in an empirical manner, to corresponding environmental antecedents and behavioral consequences or to the extent that physiological, perceptual, and cognitive states themselves can be viewed as theoretically relevant responses to environmental conditions associated with the experience of crowding.[2]

In response to the second criticism of the crowding construct, it can be argued that the frequent lack of association between subjective reports of crowding and overt manifestations of stress reflects the lack of refinement in current measures of crowding rather than the inadequacy of the crowding construct. For example, when questionnaire scales are used to assess crowding, subjects' responses may confound both the environmental (observed crowdedness or density of the setting) and experiential (felt crowding) connotations of the term.[3] Negative behavioral effects would not be expected to accompany reports of crowding to the extent that such reports reflected only the former meaning of the term. Therefore, to determine more reliably whether the experience of crowding actually promotes stress and negative behavioral consequences, it is necessary to employ multiple measures that converge on the hypothesized concomitants (e.g., physiological, cognitive, perceptual, overt-behavioral) of this experience.[4]

A related point is that crowding experiences may vary in intensity depending on relevant situational parameters. It seems reasonable to assume that the intensity of crowding, as well as the direction of the individual's response to it, would depend on his or her assessment of the potential problems of having too little space in a particular situation. In some cases, the person might decide to tolerate a certain amount of felt crowding in order to obtain other rewards in the situation. Here, reports of crowding would be associated with little evidence of stress. But in other cases, the individual might decide that certain density-related problems, if not alleviated, would lead to very serious costs. In such instances, the stressful concomitants of unrelieved crowding would tend to be more pronounced.

The parameters of crowding intensity are likely to be more readily identified as earlier versions of the crowding construct are gradually refined. The typology of crowding experiences outlined below represents a preliminary attempt to de-

---

[2]See also Spence's (1944) discussion of "neurophysiological theories" and Evans' discussion (Chapter 9) of this volume of the arousal construct as it has been applied to the study of human spatial behavior.

[3]In this discussion, the term *crowded* denotes a condition of high density and is distinguished from the term *crowding* which refers to a subjective state. Thus, the perception of being in a crowded area does not necessarily imply the experience of crowding stress, especially if the benefits derived from the situation are more salient than its potential costs.

[4]A number of other methodological issues must be considered more fully by crowding researchers, including the problem of demand characteristics. The use of extremely small rooms in many laboratory experiments often may provide subjects with cues concerning the experimenter's interest in crowding.

lineate such parameters through a distinction between two types of crowding, each of which is linked to distinctly different sets of antecedent and consequent conditions.

The third argument against the crowding construct is essentially that negative behavioral effects, when they do occur in high-density situations, are attributable to nonspatial problems in the setting (e.g., lack of resources, ongoing hostility) rather than to high density itself. Although such problems might be accentuated by high density, they will not be caused by it, and therefore the occurrence of behavioral impairments can be predicted directly from nonspatial factors and without reference to a hypothetical state of crowding.

The conclusion that density exerts negligible effects of its own on behavior is premature in view of recent experimental evidence indicating that high density or close interpersonal distance, with other factors such as group size held constant, can heighten physiological arousal (cf. Middlemist, Knowles, & Matter, 1976; Aiello, Epstein, & Karlin, Note 1; Epstein & Aiello, Note 9; Evans, Note 10) and can induce both immediate and delayed (poststressor) task-performance deficits (Evans & Howard, 1972; Sherrod, 1974; Worchel, Ch. 11, this volume; Barefoot & Kleck, Note 2; Evans, Note 10). Considering these findings in conjunction with earlier reports that high density had no effect on levels of arousal or task performance (e.g., Freedman, 1975; Note 11, Freedman et al., 1971; Ross, Layton, Erickson, & Schopler, 1973; Stokols, Rall, Pinner, & Schopler, 1973), the argument can be made that further refinement of the crowding construct, rather than abandonment, is required to permit a more precise specification of the conditions under which high density will or will not increase arousal and impair task performance.

Similarly, a refinement of the crowding construct might help to account for the currently contradictory evidence in relation to Freedman's (1975) density-intensity hypothesis. Although Freedman and Schiffenbauer and Schiavo (1976) report data that are consistent with the notion that high density merely intensifies the effects of nonspatial factors in a setting, other findings suggest that high density can exert independent behavioral effects, such as goal blocking or overload (cf. Sundstrom, 1975) to transform a previously pleasant or neutral situation into an unpleasant one (cf. Emiley, Note 8; Greenberg, Lichtman, & Firestone, Note 12; Keating & Snowball, Note 15). In light of these findings, it is conceivable that the inconveniences often associated with high density might become more problematic where people have high rather than low (or no) expectations about the favorableness of the situation, due to the disappointment arising from "comparison-level (CL) discrepancy" (Thibaut & Kelley, 1959).

The predictability of density-intensity versus CL-discrepancy effects might be aided through a conceptualization that links the intensity and quality of crowding experiences to specific situational parameters—that is those circumstances in which CL-discrepancies are most likely to arise as a result of perceived crowding. An attempt to develop such a conceptualization is outlined below.

A TYPOLOGY OF CROWDING EXPERIENCES:
ASSUMPTIONS, COMPONENTS, AND HYPOTHESES

The present analysis extends an earlier model of human crowding (Stokols, 1972b). According to that model, the experience of crowding involves a series of sequential stages: (1) exposure of the individual to certain environmental conditions; (2) the experience of psychological and physiological stress associated with the need for more space; and (3) the enactment of behavioral, cognitive, and perceptual responses aimed at alleviating the experience of stress.

The conceptualization of crowding as a subjective syndrome of stress that unfolds over a variable period of time has received substantial support from recent research (cf. Chapter 2 of this volume). Moreover, the notion that crowding can be heightened or alleviated depending on a variety of environmental and personal conditions has been borne out by research based on overload, constraint, and ecological formulations, each of which posits a somewhat different set of crowding antecedents.

The joint utility of earlier analyses is that they provide insights into the nature and determinants of crowding. Nonetheless, they share at least three major limitations: (1) they fail to provide criteria for determining the relative salience of different environmental and personal antecedents of crowding in specific situations; (2) they do not distinguish among diverse crowding experiences in terms of the intensity and persistence of each; and (3) they do not offer a basis for predicting the circumstances under which behavioral, cognitive, or perceptual adaptations to crowding stress will occur. The proposed typology of crowding experiences addresses these three basic issues.

Central Assumptions of the Model

As in earlier formulations, crowding is defined as a form of psychological stress in which one's demand for space exceeds the available supply (cf. Stokols, 1972a, 1972b). The characterization of crowding as a form of stress implies an imbalance between environmental demand and the individual's capacity to cope with it (cf. Selye, 1956). Most of the early research on stress focused on its physical dimensions, especially physiological reactions that occur as a result of abrupt environmental changes. Lazarus (1966) later extended the general notion of stress to the construct of "psychological stress," that is, a process of cognitive appraisal that reveals a disparity between *perceived* environmental demand and *perceived* ability to cope. The critical factor in psychological stress, then, is the individual's expectation that he or she will or will not be able to exert control over the situation and meet environmental demands.

In the experience of crowding, the crucial dimension of adaptive environmental control is reflected in the individual's behavioral or perceptual augmentation of space. It should be emphasized that the characterization of crowding as the need for more space does not limit this experience to feelings of restricted movement or of being cramped. It is recognized that even under conditions of low density, a person's demand for space can outstrip his supply for any number of reasons: for example, the desire to increase solitude by using open or enclosed space as a buffer against impinging stimulation, the desire to bolster security by putting more distance between oneself and hostile others, or the desire to procure more space as a means of alleviating resource scarcities in the immediate area.) Regardless of whether one desires to obtain more space as a means of increasing solitude, reducing behavioral constraints, or transcending resource scarcities in the immediate area, however, it is assumed that the person's perception of crowding and his or her attempts to cope with it presuppose a basic psychological antecedent: the desire to put more space or distance between oneself and others.

To what extent are these assumptions compatible with earlier analyses of crowding? From the foregoing discussion of overload, constraint, and ecological models, it is evident that all portray crowding as a perceived loss of control over the environment. Insufficiency of environmental control is reflected in the individual's unwilling exposure to the excessive stimulation, behavioral restrictions, or potential scarcities associated with crowding situations. Also, the assumption that crowding involves the perceived need for more space seems consistent with previous analyses in the sense that unwanted stimulation, infringements on privacy, and competition for scarce resources all represent forms of social interference that would sensitize the individual to proximity-related problems.[5] Moreover, decreased involvement with others, withdrawal from the situation, and the group's exclusion of outsiders can all be viewed as strategies designed to augment physical or "psychological" space. *(Psychological space* here refers to the individual's capacity to ignore impinging stimuli or potential interferences from the external environment; the capacity to remain unaffected by such stimuli would enable the individual to perceive the available supply of space as being larger than it actually is.)

To specify the circumstances under which overload, behavioral constraint, and resource scarcities lead to the most disruptive crowding experiences, an additional assumption is required. It is proposed that increased demand for space will be most intense, persistent, and difficult to resolve when it is associated with

[5] All these forms of social interference appear to involve the issue of self-other boundary regulation as emphasized by Altman's (1975) conceptualization of crowding. Yet, implicit in Altman's definition of crowding as a condition of desired privacy exceeding achieved privacy is the issue of desired space exceeding available space, because the process of establishing a *boundary* involves the demarcation or separation of two entities in *space,* either directly (through barriers, behavioral withdrawal) or symbolically (e.g., psychological cocooning). Certainly, greater privacy could be achieved using a variety of behavioral strategies, only one of which is the direct augmentation of physical space. But it seems reasonable to assume that the psychological antecedent of attempting to increase privacy or solitude would be the basic desire to put more space or distance between oneself and others.

perceived threats to physical or psychological security. A security threat is defined here as any stimulus, be it physical or social, that is perceived by the individual as being a potential or actual danger to his physical health or emotional well-being. Proximity to dangerous or insulting persons, for example, would lead to more intense crowding than the same degree of proximity to others who are seen as posing no threat to the individual's security.

To summarize, three major assumptions have been posited: (1) the experience of crowding involves the perception of insufficient control over the environment; (2) crowding evokes the desire to augment physical or psychological space as a means of gaining control over the environment and avoiding actual or anticipated interferences; and (3) feelings of crowding will be most intense, persistent, and difficult to resolve when the failure to augment space maximizes security threats.

Basic Components and Hypotheses of the Model

The present typology incorporates two dimensions that help to "sort out" the determinants of crowding intensity and persistence: (1) *neutral/personal thwartings;* and (2) *primary/secondary* environments. These dimensions serve to extend earlier formulations of the crowding construct by suggesting a delineation among different kinds of crowding experiences.

The thwarting dimension. The thwarting dimension pertains to the nature of interferences imposed by proximity to others. *Neutral thwartings* are essentially unintentional annoyances stemming from either the social or nonsocial environment, whereas *personal thwartings* are those interferences intentionally imposed on the individual by other persons (see Stokols, 1975, for a more complete discussion of these two types of thwartings).

On the basis of the thwarting dimension, a distinction can be drawn between *neutral crowding* and *personal crowding* experiences. Both kinds of experience presuppose an increased sensitivity to spatial limitation as a consequence of certain situational annoyances. Whereas in neutral crowding a violation of spatial expectations related primarily to the physical dimensions of the environment (e.g., architectural constraints on activities, minimal opportunities for privacy), the increased salience of space in the personal case stems largely from the security concerns made salient by proximity to hostile or unpredictable others. Thus, under conditions of personal crowding, the individual's perception of insufficient environmental control extends to both physical *and* social dimensions of the environment and, thereby, heightens the urgency of obtaining more space as a means of protecting physical and emotional security (through the avoidance of physical inconveniences as well as actual or potential social conflict).

As an example of neutral crowding, consider the residents of a dormitory suite who are sharing an area of confined space, limited bathroom facilities, and poor acoustical insulation. In this situation, the inconveniences of cramped quarters, the lack of adequate resources, and excessive noise may reduce each person's sense of control over the environment and increase the desire for more space as a means of maintaining freedom of movement, access to facilities, and privacy. Situational annoyances such as these remain neutral thwartings as long as they are attributed by the individual to features of the physical environment (e.g., inadequate architectural design) or only indirectly to well-meaning members of the social environment (e.g., even the presence of a good friend may sometimes restrict privacy).

The same inconveniences in the context of social strife, however, may promote personal crowding to the degree that spatial constraints, limited resources, and lack of privacy are directly associated with (and attributed to) the presence of others whose interests conflict with one's own and whose intentions are viewed as malevolent. When suitemates do not get along well with one another, their respective feelings of spatial restriction should be more pressing and difficult to resolve due to the perceived inadequacy and uncontrollability of both the physical and social environments. Thus, failure to reduce proximity to others in the setting should be accompanied by greater crowding stress under these circumstances than under those of neutral crowding.[6]

The distinction between neutral and personal varieties of crowding provides the basis for one of the major hypotheses of this analysis:

H1: Crowding experiences that involve a violation of spatial as well
    as social expectations will be of greater intensity and persistence
    and will be more difficult to resolve than those that derive solely
    from perceived deficiencies of the physical (spatial) environment.

Considering first the intensity of crowding experiences, those involving a personal thwarting are expected to be relatively more intense for they yield frustration associated not only with the restrictions of the physical enviornment but also with threatening social forces that accentuate these restrictions and pose additional threats as well.

---

[6]The distinction between neutral and personal varieties of crowding can be understood in terms of Deutsch's (1953, 1973) research on conflict resolution. Crowded environments can be viewed as situations in which a group of individuals is faced with a potential or actual conflict due to a scarcity of resources. Such resources may be the available supply of physical space, opportunities to engage in communication, seats on a commuter train, and so on. In any conflict situation, the likelihood of reaching a satisfactory resolution will depend on such factors as the magnitude of the issue in conflict (e.g., the severity of spatial limitation) the characteristics of group members (e.g., personality, intelligence), and the extent to which group members have had prior experience in relating to one another. In the context of a basically cooperative situation, as under conditions of neutral crowding, group members will adopt a problem-solving orientation. They will view one another as essentially benevolent and the conflict as one that has been externally imposed. They will work together to evolve cooperative strategies for transcending the conflict. In the context of a competitive situation, however, the arousal of mutual suspicion should preclude the development of cooperative problem-solving strategies, as would be predicted under conditions of personal crowding.

The persistence of crowding experiences is a function of their potential reducibility. To the extent that a person, P, is able to leave the situation, both neutral and personal varieties of crowding are potentially reversible, although it will be suggested later that the probability of cross-situational carryover effects is relatively higher in the personal case. The greater persistence of personal vis-à-vis neutral crowding experiences becomes more apparent when P is confined to the situation. Given this condition, the potential for improving the quality of the situation is lower in the personal case for at least two reasons: (1) there is a tendency on P's part to reciprocate the rejection of others, O (Berscheid & Walster, 1969); and (2) the probability of open aggression is high owing to the presence of hostile cues (e.g., insults and injury) as well as a specific target for P's counteraction (cf. Berkowitz, 1965; Buss, 1961). Therefore, cognitive and perceptual strategies of adaptation to crowding will be more obstructed in the personal pattern of experience than in the neutral one.

By contrast, a greater range of adaptive options is available in situations of neutral crowding. Since P's frustration is attributed to unintentional environmental circumstances, a basis for cooperation between P and O exists. Thus, P's response to neutral crowding will be of a problem-solving nature. In response to spatial constraints, for example, P may initially attempt to improve the coordination of his or her behavior with the activities of O, may withdraw temporarily into passive isolation, or may cooperate with O in developing interventions designed to improve the physical environment. In Calhoun's (1971) terminology, situations of neutral versus personal crowding place fewer constraints on "conceptual space," or the group's "total information pool from which rules, codes, and theories may be condensed which permit more effective coping with the physical and social environment [p. 365]."

Although the neutral/personal thwarting dimension helps to distinguish among diverse crowding experiences in terms of their intensity, persistence, and potential reducibility, it leaves a number of questions unanswered. For example, in what types of environments will neutral and personal experiences of crowding be most likely to occur? Also, are there circumstances under which neutral crowding experiences will be more intense than personal ones? In this regard, it seems reasonable to expect that the personal crowding associated with temporary proximity to an obnoxious stranger would be less troublesome than the neutral crowding experienced by members of a family unavoidably confined to an area of extremely limited space and resources. Certainly, the degree of environmental degradation, resource scarcity, and duration of exposure to the situation would have an important bearing on the intensity of crowding stress. In an effort to address these and related issues, an additional dimension is incorporated into the model.

The environmental dimension.   The primary/secondary dimension of the model concerns the continuity of social encounters in a particular setting, the psychological centrality or importance of behavioral functions performed in the setting, and the degree to which social relations occur on a personal or anonymous level. *Primary environments* are those in which an individual spends much time, relates to others on a personal basis, and engages in a wide range of personally important activities. Examples of primary settings are residential, classroom, and work environments. *Secondary environments* are those in which one's encounters with others are relatively transitory, anonymous, and inconsequential. Examples of these settings are transportation, recreation, and commercal areas.

Closely related to the distinction between primary and secondary environments is the dimension of perceived control. It is assumed that an individual's expectations for control over the environment are associated with a wider range of personal needs and goals in primary settings than in secondary ones. This assumption provides the basis for a second major hypothesis:

H2:   Social interferences arising from high density or proximity to others will be more disruptive and frustrating in primary rather than secondary environments and, consequently, crowding experiences will be more intense and persistent in the former settings than in the latter.

The importance of perceived control in mediating the behavioral effects of exposure to environmental stressors (high density, noise) has been demonstrated in a series of recent experiments (e.g., Glass & Singer, 1972; Sherrod, 1974). It should be emphasized that the stressful effects of exposure to high density are likely to occur in primary environments *only* to the extent that occupants' expectations for control over the setting (and especially over personal security) are thwarted. In many cases, the high degree of personal control exercised by persons in primary settings (especially among high-status persons; cf. Baldassare, 1977) enables them to structure the situation so as to minimize behavioral interferences and avoid feelings of crowding. Thus, the frequency of crowding experiences will not necessarily be greater in primary versus secondary settings, nor will all occupants of a given setting be equally susceptible to crowding. But to the extent that crowding experiences do occur, their impact on the individual generally will be greater in primary environments than in secondary ones.

Earlier in the discussion, it was noted that crowding experiences are distinguishable in terms of whether they involve a violation of spatial expectations alone, or of spatial as well as social needs. Similarly, Loo (1977, Note 16) has proposed a distinction between crowding situations that promote spatial stress, social stress, or both. To facilitate a further delineation of crowding experiences in terms of situationally determined thwartings, it is useful at this point to consider more fully the salient need dimensions associated with primary and secondary contexts of crowding.

Rotter, Chance, and Phares (1972) have proposed a classification of human needs that includes six basic need categories: (1) physical comfort, (2) independence; (3) protection-dependency; (4) recognition-status; (5) love and affection, and (6) dominance. Extending this framework to the present analysis, it is proposed that all six need dimensions are salient in primary environments, whereas only the first three categories of needs would typically be of importance in secondary settings. The greater variety of salient needs in primary environments is attributable to the fact that close, personal relations with others, revolving around activities of mutual importance to group members, open a wider range of potential "reinforcement paths" for the individual than arise from social encounters that are transitory, anonymous, and personally unimportant. In primary settings, then, the social dimensions of status, dominance, and affection would become just as salient as those pertaining to physical comfort, safety, and independence, whereas in secondary environments, the former set of dimensions would remain relatively less salient than the latter.

In the preceding paragraphs, two related predictions were stated: Crowding experiences will be more intense, persistent, and difficult to resolve (1) under conditions of personal versus neutral thwarting, and (2) in primary versus secondary environments. The linkage between these hypotheses now can be made. Because primary vis-à-vis secondary environments are associated with higher expectations of personal fulfillment along a greater diversity of need dimensions, interferences resulting from the proximity of others will be more likely to thwart psychologically important goals and activities and, thereby, threaten one's emotional security in the former settings. In short, the probability of exposure to personal thwarting, as a consequence of inadequate control over the regulation of space, is greater in primary environments and, thus, experiences of crowding in these settings generally will be of greater magnitude and duration than those that occur in secondary environments.

The correlation between primary environments and personal crowding, however, is by no means perfect. Transitory experiences of personal crowding can occur in secondary environments just as prolonged feelings of neutral crowding can arise in primary settings. Therefore, in the proposed typology of crowding experiences, the constructs of neutral/personal thwarting and primary/secondary environments are incorporated as separate components rather than being combined into a single dimension (see Figure 1).

Four basic types of crowding are represented in Figure 1, namely, personal and neutral experiences that occur in either primary or secondary environments. Hypothetical profiles for the four varieties of crowding are presented in terms of their respective antecedent, experiential, and behavioral dimensions. It is assumed that in each cell of the matrix spatial proximity exists among individuals in the situation. Interpersonal proximity would be positively correlated with high density but could exist under low-density conditions as well.

Given conditions of low density, intense crowding experiences could arise in both primary and secondary environments to the degree that personal thwartings occurred. The threats of a menacing stranger, for example, would heighten spatial needs in both types of environment. In general, though, it is assumed that low densities will be less promotive of intense crowding experiences in each cell

ENVIRONMENT

		Primary	Secondary
THWARTING	**Personal**	*Antecedents:* Violation of spatial and social expectations in the context of continuous, personalized interaction *Experience:* Rejection, hostility, alienation; high intensity, persistence, and generalizability *Behavior:* Behavioral withdrawal, aggression, passive isolation *Example:* Antagonistic suitemates occupying mutual living space	*Antecedents:* Violation of spatial and social expectations in the context of transitory, anonymous interaction *Experience:* Annoyance, reactance, fear; moderate intensity, low persistence and low generalizability; tendency toward "neutralization" *Behavior:* Self-defense, leave situation *Example:* Approach by threatening strangers on a crowded street
	Neutral	*Antecedents:* Violation of spatial expectations in the context of continuous, personalized interaction *Experience:* Annoyance, infringement, reactance; moderate intensity, persistence, and low generalizability; tendency toward "personalization" *Behavior:* Behavioral withdrawal, improvement coordination with others, augmentation of psychological space *Example:* Family confined to a small apartment	*Antecedents:* Violation of spatial expectations in the context of transitory, anonymous interaction *Experience:* Annoyance, reactance, low intensity, persistence, and generalizability *Behavior:* Improve coordination with others, augmentation of psychological space *Example:* Attendance at a crowded concert; laboratory experiment

FIG. 1   A typology of crowding experiences.

237

of the matrix in view of the increased potential for encountering physical and social interferences associated with high-density conditions.

For purposes of the present discussion, high density is held constant across all four cells of the matrix. Furthermore, it is assumed that preestablished social conflict is not imported into the immediate situation (e.g., as when prior enemies find themselves together in the same area). Under these circumstances and on the bases of assumptions stated earlier regarding the differential importance and variety of personal needs in diverse settings, it is expected that two modal patterns of crowding will develop over time: personal-primary and neutral-secondary experiences of crowding.

Crowding experiences occurring in the neutral-primary and personal-secondary cells of the matrix should be relatively "unstable" due to a propensity for the former experiences to become "personalized" (attributed to intentional social forces) and a similar tendency for the latter variety to become "neutralized" (attributed to unintentional sources). These perceptual shifts toward modal configurations of crowding are posited on the basis of self-attribution notions (e.g., Schachter & Singer, 1962) that emphasize the importance of cognitive cues as well as physiological arousal in the process of emotional labeling (see also Jones, Kanouse, Kelley, Nisbett, Valins, & Weiner, 1971; Kelley, 1967). In primary settings, for example, the presence of arousal as well as potentially hostile cues arising from socially mediated (albeit unintentional) thwartings of crucial personal needs should increase the likelihood of negative emotional labeling and attributions of intentionality. On the other hand, the transitory nature of secondary settings would decrease emotional investment in the situation and thereby reduce arousal in response to personal as well as neutral thwartings. Thus, feelings of crowding in personal-secondary situations, being of low intensity and duration, eventually would be assimilated to unintentional sources of environmental interference.

The present analysis suggests at least two experimental hypotheses in relation to personal-primary and neutral-secondary patterns of crowding:

> H3:   Psychological and behavioral deficits will be most pronounced subsequent to the experience of personal crowding in primary environments and least apparent following neutral crowding in secondary settings.

This prediction is consistent with earlier research on the behavioral aftereffects of exposure to environmental stressors (cf., Glass & Singer, 1972; Sherrod, 1974) and is based on the assumption that there will be fewer adaptive routes available and hence a lower level of perceived control over the situation, in the context of personal versus neutral crowding experiences. Also, the increased potential for intense emotional reactions associated with thwartings in primary versus secondary environments should contribute further to the impact and duration of postcrowding aftereffects in the former settings.

H4: Experiences of personal crowding in primary environments will generalize more readily to other situations than will neutral-secondary crowding experiences.

The major assumption underlying this prediction is that personal-primary crowding, because it typically involves negative attributions about others, would provide a cognitive base from which situation-specific anxieties regarding proximity to certain persons could generalize to other people in similar settings. This assumption is consistent with social learning theory, which postulates that one's general expectations concerning the quality of interaction with others will be determined largely by his interpersonal experiences in specific situations (cf. Duke & Nowicki, 1972; Rotter, 1966; Rotter et al., 1972). By the same reasoning, it is expected that the transitory frustrations of neutral-secondary crowding will be less closely associated with persisting attitudinal changes, more easily resolved, and thus their impact on the individual generally will be confined to the immediate situation.

EMPIRICAL EVIDENCE PERTINENT TO THE MODEL

The findings from laboratory and field-experimental research most relevant to the aforementioned hypotheses are examined in this section of the chapter. It should be noted at the outset that *conclusive* experimental evidence either supporting or disconfirming these hypotheses is not presently available. However, enough data exist that are of direct or indirect relevance to the various hypotheses to permit a preliminary empirical assessment of the proposed typology.

Intensity and Persistence of Neutral and Personal Crowding

The notion that proximity to others leads to more intense and persistent crowding when associated with perceived threats to personal security (psychological or physical) than when not has received support from several studies. In a series of laboratory experiments, Stokols and Resnick (Note 20) examined subjects' perceptions of crowding and their modulation of interpersonal distance as a function of neutral and personal thwartings. The thwarting factor was manipulated by creating either a nonevaluative or an evaluative climate in mixed-sex experimental groups. During the first phase of the experimental session, subjects were led to a small room and instructed either to "get to know each other casually" (neutral) or to "form evaluative impressions of each other" (personal) in preparation for a subsequent, group task-performance period. (In actuality, the experiment was terminated prior to the task-performance period.) In both treatment conditions, room size (49 square feet) and density (eight-or six-person groups in the two studies, respectively) were held constant.

Three basic findings emerged from these experiments. First, subjects in the evaluative groups reported feeling more crowded, rated the experimental room as "stuffier," viewed other group members as less friendly and recalled fewer of their names than did subjects in the nonevaluative groups. These treatment effects were reflected in the questionnaire data obtained from subjects after 18 minutes of pretask interaction, and before they were led from the small room into a larger one (100 square feet) for the alleged task-performance period. Second, when subjects were taken directly to the larger room after the pretask interaction phase (without filling out questionnaires) and asked to take a seat from a stack of chairs adjacent to an inside wall, subjects in the evaluative groups placed significantly greater distance between their own chair and the chairs of other group members than did subjects in the nonevaluative groups.

And third, when ratings of crowding and other subjective reactions were obtained subsequent to the group's arrangement of their chairs in the larger room, significant differences between the responses of evaluative and nonevaluative groups were not detected. Nor were significant between-group differences obtained on a postdensity measure of behavioral aftereffects (i.e., Glass & Singer's, 1972, proofreading task).

These findings suggest that the presence of potential threats to emotional security (critical evaluation by peers) under high-density conditions led to more intense feelings of crowding, as reflected in both the questionnaire and chair-placement data, than when such threats were absent.[7] Furthermore, it appears that direct behavioral adjustments of interpersonal distance in short-term, secondary situations may effectively alleviate both neutral and personal crowding as well as the aftereffects of such crowding on simple cognitive tasks.

The findings from three other laboratory studies are consistent with the prediction that personal crowding experiences will be more intensive than neutral crowding experiences. Rall, Stokols, and Russo (Note 17) found that subjects who expected to be interviewed by a threatening (critically evaluative) experimenter reported higher levels of anticipated crowding prior to the interview session than did those who expected to interact with a nonthreatening interviewer. Also, Fisher (1974) observed that subjects who were approached by an attitudinally dissimilar confederate felt more crowded than those who were

---

[7]While the results of this study indicate that perceptions of crowding can vary as a function of social factors when the level of density is held constant, they do not provide any information regarding the interactive effects of social variables and density levels on group members' reactions. To explore this issue, a subsequent experiment is being conducted which independently manipulates social climate (evaluative vs. non-evaluative) and interpersonal proximity (high vs. low).

approached by a confederate portrayed as being similar to themselves. If perceived dissimilarity serves as a stiuational cue that raises the subjective probability of social conflict and security threats, then it seems plausible that proximity to a dissimilar person would promote more intense crowding experiences than would exposure to a similar other.

In an earlier study, Stokols et al. (1973) observed eight-person, same-sex groups performing a competitive or cooperative task in either a small or large room. On measures of perceived crowding and restriction, a task-set main effect was found such that reported levels of crowding and restriction were higher in competitive groups than in cooperative ones. Thus, under varying levels of density, proximity to competitive, dissimilar, or otherwise threatening persons seems to promote more intense feelings of crowding than does proximity with nonthreatening others.

The data from three recent field studies also seem consistent with the proposed distinction between neutral and personal crowding. In an investigation of the relationship between dormitory residents perceptions of crowding and their evaluations of the physical and social dimensions of their living environment, Stokols, Ohlig, Resnick (in press) observed a significant inverse correlation between ratings of crowding and satisfaction with the social environment ($r(30) = -0.39$, $p < 0.05$), and between crowding and ratings of "other people in general" ($r(30) = -0.42$, $p < 0.01$). Also, in a field study conducted by Baum, Harpin and Valins (1975) dormitory residents who rated their social environments as "cohesive" reported lower levels of crowding than did those who viewed their dorms as noncohesive. In both these studies, the capacity of individuals to establish positive social relations with their neighbors appears to have reduced the likelihood of intense crowding experiences arising from exposure to personal thwartings.

Baron, Mandel, Adams, and Griffen (Note 3), in a subsequent dormitory study, factor-analyzed the questionnaire data of students living in two-person and three-person rooms to examine differential patterns of crowding in the two situations. As in an earlier study conducted by Aiello et al. (Note 1), it was found that tripled students reported higher levels of crowding than doubled students. But among the tripled subjects, subjective crowding was statistically associated with negative reactions on a variety of physical and social dimensions, whereas among the doubles, crowding was viewed primarily in physicalistic terms (i.e., crampedness) and was not related to assessments of interpersonal relations.

Baron et al. (Note 3) describe the crowding experiences of tripled residents as being personal in nature and those of doubled residents as being neutral. The authors hypothesize that the occurrence of personal crowding in the triples results from social overstimulation and feelings of uncertainty about interpersonal relations associated with larger group sizes (see Simmel's 1950 analysis of dyadic and triadic groups in relation to this point). Thus, it is suggested that increased numbers, by reducing the individual's control over social relations (e.g., being excluded from a coalition), raises the likelihood of personal, and consequently more intense, crowding experiences.

Investigations of personal space comprise an additional line of research that offers support for the hypothesized distinction between neutral and personal crowding. Recent reviews of the personal space literature indicate that individuals place greater distance between themselves and threatening or hostile others (cf. Evans & Howard, 1973) and exhibit higher levels of physiological arousal and compensatory responses when spatial invasions by strangers are unexpected and perceived as being intentional rather than coincidental (cf. Patterson, in press; Schiavo, Bader, Capeci, Barbi, Clyburn, Hansen, & Tomassi (Note 18); Sundstrom & Altman, 1976).

In general, the above studies provide support for the hypothesis that personal crowding will be more intense than neutral crowding. As for the relative persistence of neutral and personal crowding, the current paucity of relevant data precludes an assessment of this issue at present.

Relative Impact of Crowding Experiences in Primary and Secondary Settings

To date, the hypothesis that crowding experiences arising in primary environments are more intense and persistent than those in secondary settings, has not been tested directly. That is, there have been no systematic comparisons of crowding experiences across different types of settings. Recent data collected in primary settings alone, however, are relevant to the validity of this hypothesis.

Before examining this evidence, it is important to note that the primary-secondary distinction implies both behavioral and subjective dimensions. On the one hand, environments can be categorized on the basis of observing where individuals spend most of their time performing what types of activities with whom. It is on this basis that residential environments in general can be viewed as primary settings and commercial areas as secondary ones. On the other hand, in any given setting, individual judgments as to the importance of one's activities and the degree of anonymity and personal control in the situation are bound to vary. Therefore, although a preliminary distinction between different environments can be made in terms of their functional or behavioral dimensions, a more refined assessment of the primary or secondary nature of a particular setting can be derived through an examination of individuals' subjective reactions to it.

For example, a commercial area might serve as a secondary setting for customers but would provide a primary work environment for sales personnel. Similarly, a dormitory environment could be classified as more primary for those students who spend much time there and relate to fellow residents on a personal basis than for those individuals who are not as involved in the setting, either socially or physically.

A recent study conducted by Aiello et al. (Note 1) is quite relevant to this point. The experiences of college dormitory residents living in two-person or three-person rooms were compared in a longitudinal, field-experimental design. Among the most interesting findings of the study were that tripled females reported higher levels of crowding, dissatisfaction with the environment, and health problems than did tripled males. Moreover, tripled females were more likely to choose other roommates and living situations during the year than were tripled males. Of particular relevance to the proposed typology, it was found that female students generally spent more time in their rooms and expressed higher levels of emotional investment in the dormitory environment than did the males. Thus, to the degree that females viewed their dormitory environment as more primary than did the males, the potential social strains associated with increased group size (cf. Baron et al., Note 3) apparently provoked more intense and disruptive crowding experiences among tripled females than among tripled males.

The sex differences reported by Aiello, Epstein, and Karlin are, of course, contrary to earlier laboratory experimental evidence that females are less vulnerable to crowding stress than males (cf. Freedman, Levy, Buchanan, & Price, 1972; Ross et al., 1973; Stokols et al., 1973). The authors suggest that the greater impact of social density on females in residential settings may be related to the same interpersonal orientation that enables them to tolerate short-term crowding in secondary environments more effectively than do males: namely, their affiliative style.

The affiliative tendencies of females would promote a greater degree of psychological investment in the dormitory environment and, consequently, higher expectations of being able to exert control over a wide range of activities in the setting. In terms of the present model, it is assumed that such expectations are implicit in the reported inclination of females to view their dormitory as a primary, "home" environment. Furthermore, in the face of continuous exposure to the unavoidable hassles associated with tripled-up living arrangements, females' high expectations concerning the quality and controllability of the setting would be violated, thereby promoting more intense and persistent crowding than among tripled males whose initial expectations had been lower.

The Baron et al. (Note 3) study provides further evidence for the interactive effects of individual expectations and type of setting in determining the intensity and persistence of crowding. Laboratory experiments on the relationship between internality-externality of control (cf. Rotter, 1966) and spatial behavior suggest that "externals" require greater interpersonal distance between themselves and strangers (Duke & Nowicki, 1972) and are more likely to experience crowding in high density situations (Schopler & Walton, Note 19) than "internals." In the Baron et al. (Note 3) study, however, internals required higher levels of interpersonal distance on a projective measure of personal space than did externals, among those students who reported feeling "cramped" in their dormitory rooms. This finding suggests that in secondary environments, perceived internality of control would enhance one's tolerance of proximity to others but that in primary settings it might promote greater crowding and stress due to the continuous frustration of the person's anticipated control over the environment.

The dormitory studies discussed above suggest the importance of *anticipated* personal control in determining the intensity of crowding in primary and secondary environments. Additional research conducted at the household and neighborhood levels indicates that *actual* levels of control available to setting occupants, apart from their prior expectations of control, may be just as crucial in determining the intensity and persistence of their crowding experiences.

Earlier in the discussion, the point was made that crowding in primary environments typically interferes with a wider range of personally important goals and activities than in secondary environments. Consequently, crowding experiences in the former settings are hypothesized to be of greater impact on the individual than in the latter. Although this proposition has not been tested directly, a growing body of evidence suggests that in high-density households, those occupants who experience the greatest degree of interference in their daily activities as a result of spatial limitation exhibit the most intense and persistent stress reactions.

Numerous studies suggest, for example, that children rather than adults bear the brunt of crowding-related problems in high density residences due to their relative inability to control the allocation and usage of space (cf. Baldassare, 1977; Booth, Note 5; Ch. 3, this vol.). The curtailment of social interaction with siblings and peers (Mitchell, 1971; Suttles, 1968; Davis, Bergin, & Mazin, Note 6), blame by other family members for household problems (Chombart de Lauwe, 1961; Clausen & Clausen, 1973), increased nervousness (Gasparini, 1973), and decrements in physical and intellectual development (Booth & Johnson, 1975) are among the problems experienced more often by children than parents in crowded residences.

Although the above findings do not pertain directly to the relative intensity of perceived crowding in different settings, they do provide support for the assumptions underlying the proposed typology and serve to refine the second hypothesis of the model by linking the presumed ill effects of primary crowding experiences more directly to the differential allocation of status and control among occupants of the setting.

Aftereffects and Generalizability of Personal-Primary and Neutral-Secondary Crowding

The effects of personal-primary and neutral-secondary crowding have not been examined systematically. There exist two lines of research, however, that indicate that crowding experiences (1) in secondary environments can lead to short-term, postcrowding decrements in task performance, and (2) in primary environments can promote persisting behavioral, psychological, and physiological impairments, as well as a heightened sensitivity to crowding, all of which generalize to a variety of other settings.

Empirical evidence in support of these trends is reviewed below. Although previous studies of crowding aftereffects have not attempted to differentiate between personal and neutral crowding, their findings can be viewed as being relevant to the third and fourth hypotheses of the proposed typology if it is assumed that crowding experiences in secondary settings tend to be neutral in nature whereas those in primary environments are more likely to become personalized (see p. 238).

First, at least three experiments have demonstrated significant task performance deficits following subjects' exposure to high-density, secondary (laboratory) settings. In a study conducted by Evans (Note 10), high-density subjects reported that they felt more crowded and displayed less tolerance for frustration on a post-stressor task than did low-density subjects. Also, Sherrod (1974) reported that under conditions of high-density, those subjects who believed they could leave a crowded room at any time during the experimental session exhibited greater tolerance for frustration on a postdensity task than did those who were instructed not to leave the room. In this instance, then, perceived control over the situation served to mitigate the aftereffects of secondary crowding experiences. Finally, Dooley (Note 7) observed that under conditions of high social density, subjects with a chronically higher need for personal space performed more poorly on a post-density proofreading task than did those having a lower personal-space requirement.

The Sherrod and Dooley findings are of particular relevance to the assumptions underlying the proposed typology, *if* it can be demonstrated in future research that subjects with low perceived control and "far personal space" are especially vulnerable to personal thwartings in high density settings. Such evidence would suggest that the postdensity aftereffects observed by Sherrod and Dooley were mediated by the greater susceptibility of these subjects (as compared with high control and close personal space subjects) to personal crowding, even in secondary environments.

The aftereffects of exposure to crowded primary environments have been demonstrated in at least six recent field studies. Rodin (1976) reported that children from high-density households preferred experimenter to self-mediated rewards in a nonresidential setting. This finding was discussed in terms of a learned helplessness (Seligman, 1975) explanation of postdensity aftereffects. Moreover, Paulus, Cox, McCain, and Chandler (1975) found that prior exposure of prison inmates to high residential density decreased their tolerance for crowding in a projective, experimental situation, whereas Baron et al. (Note 3) reported that college students from high-density homes were more likely to describe their dorms as cramped than were those from lower-density backgrounds.

More direct evidence for the aftereffects and generalizability of personal-primary crowding experiences is reflected in the findings of Valins and Baum (1973), who examined the relationship between architectural design and social behavior in college dormitories. Specifically, the residents of corridor-design dorms were more likely to complain about crowding and forced interaction with persons they preferred to avoid than were residents of suite-design dorms, presumably due to the higher levels of social stimulation present in the former dorms. Furthermore, the residents of corridor-design dorms established greater interpersonal distance between themselves and strangers in laboratory settings, exhibited more discomfort in the presence of strangers, and made more trips to the student health center for psychological services than did those of suite-design dorms (cf. Baum & Valins, Note 4).

More recently, Stokols, Ohlig, and Resnick (in press) found that students' perceptions of crowding in their residential environments were positively correlated with their feelings of crowding in a classroom setting and inversely associated with their course performance (i.e., final grade in the course). Moreover, in stepwise regression analyses utilizing classroom crowding and course performance as the respective criterion variables, the levels of prediction were significantly higher when both ratings of the residential social environment and residential crowding were entered into the regression equation as predictor variables than when the crowding variable was incorporated alone.

Stokols, Ohlig, and Resnick (in press) also found that students' perception of residential crowding during the fall quarter was highly predictive of their total visits to the student health center throughout the academic year. Furthermore, the level of prediction increased significantly when ratings of the residential social environment were entered into the equation.

These results suggest that information concerning residents' satisfaction with their dormitory social environment contributes significantly to the prediction of crowding carryover effects from primary environments to other situations. Also, the finding that satisfaction with the dorm social environment was inversely correlated with residential crowding suggests that experiences of crowding in the dorm tended to be personal in nature and thereby more generalizable to other settings than had they been of a neutral nature. A similar pattern seems to be reflected in the Valins and Baum (1973) finding that subjects reporting higher levels of forced interaction with others in their dorm whom they preferred to avoid displayed a wider range of crowding aftereffects than those residents who reported less forced interaction.

The relative impact of personal-primary and neutral-secondary crowding, of course, remains a speculative issue until additional research explicitly differentiates between patterns of personal and neutral crowding and demonstrates clearly that the former leads to greater aftereffects and generalizability of crowding than does the latter, when other dimensions (e.g. personality, background variables) are statistically controlled or are utilized as independent experimental factors.

PRIORITIES FOR FUTURE RESEARCH
AND THEORETICAL DEVELOPMENT

On the whole, the existing body of research on crowding provides preliminary support for the assumptions and hypotheses of the proposed typology. There is ample evidence that proximity to other persons, in the context of security-threat or uncertainty about the others' motives, is associated with stronger feelings of crowding and behavioral attempts to augment space than when perceived threat or uncertainty are absent. And the data from recent field experiments suggest that crowding experiences in primary environments are of greater intensity and generalizability than those that occur in secondary settings, although to date no previous study has directly compared crowding experiences in the two types of environments.

Although preliminary support for the model exists, a conclusive assessment of its validity is precluded for the time being in view of certain methodological and conceptual problems that have not been resolved in previous research. First, in relation to the hypothesized differences between neutral and personal crowding, it remains to be demonstrated that the subjective feelings of restriction and increased levels of interpersonal distance associated with the latter type of crowding are, in fact, related to a heightened need for space rather than merely to the interpersonal problems existing in the situation.

An experimental test of this might be conducted by creating conditions of neutral and personal crowding and systematically varying the opportunity of groups to adjust their levels of interpersonal distance. Subsequent observations of interpersonal relations and subjective reactions would reveal whether, under conditions of personal crowding, direct augmentation of space leads to reduced levels of crowding and other forms of stress, in line with the present model, or has no effect on subjects' perceptions of crowding and interpersonal problems, due to the continued salience of negative social cues.

A second problem for future research pertains to the operationalization of the primary-secondary environment dimension. The measurement criteria for locating environments along this continuum have not been developed heretofore, yet they are crucial to any assessment of the second, third, and fourth hypotheses of the proposed typology. In this regard, it will be important to develop indices of both functional and experiential involvement in settings in order to: (1) determine whether the two types of environmental descriptions are congruent; and (2) assess whether increased levels of behavioral and subjective involvement in settings is associated with more personalized, intense crowding experiences.[8] Finally, it will be necessary to compare longitudinally the carryover effects of crowding from both primary and secondary settings.

---

[8]A different emphasis on functional and experiential levels of involvement in settings can be seen in Altman's (1975) discussion of primary, secondary, and public territories, and in the present distinction between primary and secondary environments. For example, "primary territories" are defined as geographically bounded areas associated with primary group functions. "Primary environments," on the other hand, are not confined to areas in which primary-group activities occur (e.g., homespace) and extend to settings where highly personalized and patterned secondary-group interactions occur (e.g., work environments). The definition of primary territory thus puts more emphasis on the fixed geographical features of the setting and the exclusivity of its usage, whereas the definition of a primary environment places relatively more emphasis on the experiential dimensions of the setting.

Additional directions for future research are suggested by the apparent linkages between the proposed typology and other, recently developed conceptualizations of crowding. For instance, Worchel (see Chapter 11 of this volume) portrays crowding as heightened arousal arising from personal space invasion, which is attributed by the individual to the presence of other persons in his or her immediate area. This analysis does not provide criteria for determining the quality and intensity of proximity-mediated arousal. The proposed typology, however, suggests that interpersonal proximity will lead to the most intense and negatively construed arousal under conditions of security-threat. Similarly, Sundstrom and Altman (1976) suggest that proximity to strangers will be more stressful than proximity to acquaintances or intimates. Thus, the relative contribution of spatial invasion and other potential antecedents of crowding (e.g., areal density, group size) must be examined empirically in relation to crucial situational dimensions such as perceived control and security threat.

Although recent analyses suggest that high levels of perceived control will reduce the impact of crowding and its aftereffects (cf. Rodin, 1976; Sherrod, 1974), they do not delineate the circumstances under which this relationship will or will not hold. Averill (1973) has distinguished among various kinds of personal control, each of which may have different implications with regard to the intensity and persistence of crowding (see also Baron et al., Note 3, on this point). The proposed typology suggests that perceived control over personal security will be considerably more effective in alleviating crowding than perceived control over less relevant aspects of the situation. Along these lines, Baldassare (1977) proposes that loss of control over the allocation of interpersonal power and status (dimensions closely related to security maintenance) will be particularly promotive of crowding stress in primary environments. Experimental assessments of these and related propositions remain to be carried out.

Finally, Knowles (Chapter 6 of this volume) has developed an analysis that views crowding as a form of social influence created by the number and potency of people who remain proximal to one another over time. Knowles' framework brings a great diversity of theoretical and empirical approaches to bear on such issues as the extent and duration of social influence resulting from interpersonal proximity, but it does not address the qualitative dimensions of proximity-mediated influence. In relation to this point, the proposed typology suggests that the impact of interpersonal proximity on the individual will depend on whether such proximity supports or threatens personal security.

Freedman's (1975) density-intensity hypothesis predicts that the type of social influence resulting from proximity to others will depend basically on the existing quality of the social situation. Thus, where resources are adequate and relations are friendly, interpersonal proximity should intensify the positivism of the social experiences. The typology presented earlier, however, posits that the potential interferences created by spatial limitation, particularly in primary environments, may transform previously pleasant situations into negative ones. These contrasting predictions suggest yet another direction for future research.

Throughout this discussion, the proposed typology of crowding experiences has been portrayed as an intervening construct, the utility of which derives from (1) its integration and interpretation of preliminary empirical evidence, and (2) its suggestion of future research directions toward the establishment of new environment-behavior regularities. Although the model provides a useful bridge between previous and future research on crowding, its overall utility eventually must be assessed in relation to broader theoretical and practical concerns.

At this point, the typology provides the basis for developing a comprehensive theory, not of density and crowding per se, but of spatial behavior in general. The ultimate focus of the model is not on how density affects human behavior but rather on how people symbolize and manipulate space as a means of regulating social interaction. Although physical density (vis-à-vis "affective density," cf. Rapoport, 1975) assumes a lesser theoretical role than in alternative analyses of crowding (cf. Freedman, 1975; Griffitt, Note 13), the subjective spatial concerns of the individual remain central to the model and pose direct implications for environmental design.

From the perspective of the model, the linkage between the physical environment, subjective spatial concerns, and behavior can be represented in terms of at least two sequences of events, each of which promotes some degree of crowding stress. On the one hand, the inappropriate arrangement of physical space can create perceived interferences through a disruption of ongoing social interaction. On the other hand, the development of social conflict in a previously satisfactory environment makes spatial concerns more salient and the insufficiency of existing space more apparent.

These environment-behavior and behavior-environment sequences suggest, for example, that in the context of architecture and planning, the maintenance of low-density standards may be most critical in the design of primary environments in which individuals are particularly vulnerable to both spatial and social thwartings. Also, the implementation of designs that permit maximal architectural flexibility in primary settings (e.g., the provision of movable walls and ceilings) would enable occupants to establish and maintain adequate personal space and thereby minimize threats to psychological security.

In primary spaces in which it is difficult to avoid high-density conditions, as in crowded classrooms, it may be necessary for planners to rely more heavily on the development of social intervention strategies to prevent the misattribution of situational annoyances (e.g., the behavioral constraints and spatial infringements associated with high density) to intentional and malevolent sources. Such strategies might include a concerted effort to reduce competitive cues in the situation and the establishment of opportunities for small-group interaction through which individuals could develop a sense of cohesion and identity in relation to other group members.

In secondary or public environments, personal space and privacy needs (cf. Altman's 1975 privacy-regulation model of crowding) may become less crucial for occupants of the area than concerns of mutual protection and physical safety. In these settings, architectural facilitation of collective surveillance and alleviation of congestion (cf. Jacobs, 1961; LeCorbusier, 1933; Newman, 1973) would represent effective strategies of reducing individuals' susceptibility to both personal and neutral crowding experiences.

REFERENCE NOTES

1. Aiello, J., Epstein, Y., & Karlin, R. *Field experimental research on human crowding.* Paper presented at the Eastern Psychological Association Convention, New York City, April 1975.
2. Barefoot, J., & Kleck, R. *The effects of race and physical proximity of a co-actor on the social facilitation of dominant responses.* Unpublished manuscript, Carelton University, 1970.
3. Baron, R., Mandel, D., Adams, C., & Griffen, L. *Effects of social density in university residential environments.* Paper presented at the Annual Convention of the American Psychological Association, Chicago, August 1975.
4. Baum, A., & Valins, S. *Architecture, social interaction, and crowding.* Unpublished manuscript, State University of New York at Stony Brook, 1973.
5. Booth, A. *Final report: Urban Crowding Project.* Paper presented to the Ministry of State for Urban Affairs, Government of Canada, Toronto, 1975.
6. Davis, D., Bergin, K., & Mazin, G. *When the neighbors get noisy we bang on the walls: A critical exploration of density and crowding.* Paper presented at the Annual Convention of the American Sociological Association, Montreal, September 1974.
7. Dooley, B. *Crowding stress: The effects of social density on men with close or far personal space.* Unpublished doctoral dissertation, University of California at Los Angeles, 1974.
8. Emiley, S. *The effects of crowding and interpersonal attraction on affective responses, task performance, and verbal behavior.* Paper presented at the Annual Convention of the American Psychological Association, New Orleans, September 1974.
9. Epstein, Y., & Aiello, J. *Effects of crowding on electrodermal activity.* Paper presented at the Annual Convention of the American Psychological Association, New Orleans, September 1974.
10. Evans, G. *Behavioral and physiological consequences of crowding in humans.* Unpublished doctoral dissertation, University of Massachusetts, Amherst, 1975.
11. Freedman, J. *The effects of crowding on human behavior.* Unpublished manuscript, Columbia University, 1970.
12. Greenberg, C., Lichtman, C., & Firestone, I. *Behavioral and affective responses to crowded waiting rooms.* Unpublished manuscript, Wayne State University, 1974.
13. Griffitt, W. *Density, "crowding", and attraction: What are the relationships?* Paper presented at the Annual Convention of the American Psychological Association, New Orleans, September 1974.
14. Hanson, L., & Wicker, A. *Effects of overmanning on group experience and task performance.* Paper presented at the Western Psychological Association Convention, Anaheim, April 1973.
15. Keating, J., & Snowball, H. *The effects of crowding and depersonalization on the perception of group atmosphere.* Unpublished manuscript, University of Washington, 1974.

16. Loo, C. *A social-spatial model of crowding stress.* Paper presented at the Western Psychological Association Convention, San Francisco, April 1974.
17. Rall, M., Stokols, D., & Russo, R. *Spatial adjustments in response to anticipated crowding.* Paper presented at the Eastern Psychological Association Convention, New York, April 1976.
18. Schiavo, S., Bader, A., Capeci, E., Barbi, E., Clyburn, A., Hansen, B., & Tomassi, L. *Factors mediating reaction to invasions of personal space.* Paper presented at the Rocky Mountain Psychological Association Convention, Salt Lake City, April 1975.
19. Schopler, J., & Walton, M. *The effects of expected structure, expected enjoyment, and participants' internality-externality upon feelings of being crowded.* Unpublished manuscript, University of North Carolina, 1974.
20. Stokols, D., & Resnick, S. *An experimental assessment of neutral and personal crowding experiences.* Paper presented at the Southeastern Psychological Association Convention, Atlanta, March 1975.

REFERENCES

Altman, I. Territorial behavior in humans: An analysis of the concept. In L. Pastalan & D. Carson (Eds.), *Spatial behavior of older people.* Ann Arbor: The University of Michigan-Wayne State University Press, 1970.

Altman, I. Privacy: A conceptual analysis. In D. Carson (Ed.), *Man-environment interactions: Evaluations and applications* (Vol. 6), *Privacy.* Washington, D.C.: Environmental Design Research Association, 1974.

Altman, I. *The environment and social behavior: Privacy, personal space, territory and crowding.* Monterey, Calif.: Brooks/Cole, 1975.

Averill, J. Personal control over aversive stimuli and its relationship to stress. *Psychological Bulletin,* 1973, *80,* 286-303.

Baldassare, M. Crowding, social networks, and existing neighborhood relationships. In C. Fischer (Ed.), *Networks and places.* New York: Free Press, 1977.

Baldassare, M., & Fischer, C. The relevance of crowding experiments to urban studies. In D. Stokols (Ed.), *Perspectives on environment and behavior: Theory, research, and applications.* New York: Plenum, 1977.

Barker, R. *Ecological psychology: Concepts and methods for studying the environment of human behavior.* Stanford, Calif.: Stanford University Press, 1968,

Baum, A., Harpin, R. E., & Valins, S. The role of group phenomena in the experience of crowding. *Environment and Behavior,* 1975, *7,* 185-198.

Baum, A., & Valins, S. Residential environments, group size, and crowding. *Proceedings of the American Psychological Association,* 81st Annual Convention, 1973, 211-212.

Berscheid, E., & Walster, E. *Interpersonal attraction.* Reading, Mass.: Addison-Wesley, 1969.

Berkowitz, L. The concept of aggressive drive: Some additional considerations. In L. Berkowitz (Ed.), *Advances in experimental social psychology* (Vol. 2). New York: Academic Press, 1965.

Booth, A., & Johnson, D. The effect of crowding on child health and development. *American Behavioral Scientist,* 1975, *18,* 736-749.

Brehm, J. *A theory of psychological reactance.* New York: Academic Press, 1966.

Brunswik, E. Organismic achievement and environmental probability. *Psychological Review,* 1943, *50,* 255-272.

Buss, A. *The psychology of aggression.* New York: Wiley, 1961.

Calhoun, J. Population density and social pathology. *Scientific American.* 1962, *206,* 139-148.

Calhoun, J. Space and the strategy of life. In A. H. Esser (Ed.), *Behavior and environment.* New York: Plenum Press, 1971.

Chombart de Lauwe, R. The sociology of housing methods and prospects of research. *International Journal of Comparative Sociology,* 1961, *2,* 23-41.

Christian, J. Phenomena associated with population density. *Proceedings of the National Academy of Science,* 1961, *47,* 428-449.

Christian, J., Flyger, V., & Davis, P. Factors in the mass mortality of herd of sika deer cervus nippon. *Chesapeake Science,* 1960, *1,* 79-95.

Clausen, J., & Clausen, S. The effects of family size on parents and children. In J. Fawcett (Ed.), *Psychological perspectives on population.* New York: Basic Books, 1973.

Clements, F. *Research methods in ecology.* Lincoln, Neb.: The University of Nebraska Press, 1905.

Desor, J. Toward a psychological theory of crowding. *Journal of Personality* and *Social Psychology,* 1972, *21,* 79-83.

Deutsch, M. The effects of cooperation and competition upon group process. In D. Cartwright & A. Zander (Eds.), *Group dynamics,* New York: Harper & Row, 1953.

Deutsch, M. *The resolution of conflict.* New Haven, Conn.: Yale University Press, 1973.

Duke, M., & Nowicki, S. A new measure and social-learning model for interpersonal distance. *Journal of Experimental Research in Personality,* 1972, *6,* 119-132.

Edney, J. Human territoriality, *Psychological Bulletin,* 1974, *81,* 959-975.

Esser, A. *Behavior and environment.* New York: Plenum Press, 1971.

Esser, A. A biosocial perspective on crowding. In J. Wohlwill & D. Carson (Eds.), *Environment and the social sciences: Perspectives and applications.* Washington, D.C.: American Psychological Association, 1972.

Evans, G., & Eichelman, W. Preliminary models of conceptual linkages among some proxemic variables. *Environment and Behavior,* 1976, *8,* 87-116.

Evans, G., & Howard, R. A methodological investigation of personal space. In W. J. Mitchell (Ed.), *Environmental design: Research and practice.* Los Angeles: The University of California Press, 1972.

Evans, G., & Howard, R. Personal space. *Psychological Bulletin,* 1973, *80,* 334-344.

Fisher, J. Situation-specific variables as determinants of perceived environmental aesthetic quality and perceived crowdedness. *Journal of Research in Personality,* 1974, *8,* 177-188.

Freedman, J. *Crowding and behavior.* San Francisco: Freeman, 1975.

Freedman, J., Klevansky, S., & Ehrlich, P. The effect of crowding on human task performance. *Journal of Applied Social Psychology,* 1971, *1,* 7-25.

Freedman, J., Levy, A., Buchanan, R., & Price, J. Crowding and human aggressiveness. *Journal of Experimental Social Psychology,* 1972, *8,* 526-548.

Gasparini, A. Influence of the dwelling on family. *Ekistics,* 1973, *216,* 344-348.

Glass, D., & Singer, J. *Urban stress.* New York: Academic Press, 1972.

Griffitt, W., & Veitch, R. Influences of population density on interpersonal affective behavior. *Journal of Personality and Social Psychology,* 1971, *17,* 92-98.

Hall, E. *The hidden dimension.* New York: Doubleday, 1966.

Hull, C. The problem of intervening variables in molar behavior theory. *Psychological Review,* 1943, *50,* 273-291.   (a)

Hull, C. *Principles of behavior.* New York: Appleton-Century-Crofts, 1943.   (b)

Hutt, C., & Vaizey, M. Differential effects of group density on social behavior. *Nature,* 1966, *209,* 1371-1372.

Ittelson, W., Proshansky, H., & Rivlin, L. A study of bedroom use on two psychiatric wards. *Hospital and Community Psychiatry*, 1970, *21*, 177-180.

Jacobs, J. *The death and life of great American cities*. New York: Random House, 1961.

Jones, E., Kanouse, D., Kelley, H., Nisbett, R., Valins, S., & Weiner, B. *Attribution: Perceiving the causes of behavior*. Morristown, N.J.: General Learning Press, 1971.

Keeley, K. Pre-natal influences on behavior of offspring of crowded mice. *Science*, 1962, *135*, 44-45.

Kelley, H. Attribution theory in social psychology. In D. Levine (Ed.), *Nebraska Symposium on Motivation*. Lincoln, Neb.: University of Nebraska Press, 1967.

Lawrence, J. Science and sentiment: Overview of research on crowding and human behavior. *Psychological Bulletin*, 1974, *81*, 712-720.

Lazarus, R. *Psychological stress and the coping process*. New York: McGraw-Hill, 1966.

LeCorbusier. *The radiant city*. New York: Orion Press, 1933.

Lewin, K. [*Principles of topological psychology*] (F. and G. Heider, trans.). New York: McGraw-Hill, 1936.

Lewin, K. Defining the "field at a given time." *Psychological Review*, 1943, *50*, 292-310.

Loo, C. The psychological study of crowding. *American Behavioral Scientist*, 1975, *18*, 826-842.

Loo, C. Beyond the effects of crowding: Situational and individual differences. In D. Stokols (Ed.), *Perspectives on environment and behavior: Theory, research, and applications*. New York: Plenum Press, 1977.

Middlemist, R., Knowles, E., & Matter, C. Personal space invasions in the lavatory: Suggestive evidence for arousal. *Journal of Personality and Social Psychology*, 1976, *33*, 541-546.

Milgram, S. The experience of living in cities. *Science*, 1970, *167*, 1461-1468.

Mitchell, R. Some social implications of high density housing. *American Sociological Review*, 1971, *36*, 18-29.

Newman, O. *Defensible space*. New York: Macmillan, 1973.

Patterson, M. The role of space in social interaction. In A. Siegman & S. Feldstein (Eds.), *Nonverbal behavior and communication*. Hillsdale, N.J.: Lawrence Erlbaum Associates, 1978.

Paulus, P., Cox, V., McCain, G., & Chandler, J. Some effects of crowding in a prison environment. *Journal of Applied Social Psychology*, 1975, *5*, 86-91.

Proshansky, H. Theoretical issues in environmental psychology. *Representative Research in Social Psychology*, 1973, *4*, 93-107.

Proshansky, H., Ittelson, W., & Rivlin, L. Freedom of choice and behavior in a physical setting. In H. Proshansky, W. Ittelson, & L. Rivlin (Eds.), *Environmental psychology: Man and his physical setting*. New York: Holt, Rinehart and Winston, 1970.

Rapoport, A. Toward a redefinition of density. *Environment and Behavior*, 1975, *7*, 133.

Rodin, J. Density, perceived choice, and response to controllable and uncontrollable outcomes. *Journal of Experimental Social Psychology*, 1976, *12*, 564-578.

Ross, M., Layton, B., Erickson, B., & Schopler, J. Affect, facial regard, and reactions to crowding. *Journal of Personality and Social Psychology*, 1973, *28*, 69-76.

Rotter, J. Generalized expectancies for internal vs. external control of reinforcement. *Psychological Monographs*, 1966, *80* (Whole no. 609).

Rotter, J., Chance, J., & Phares, E. *Applications of a social learning theory of personality*. New York: Holt, Rinehart & Winston, 1972.

Saegert, S. Crowding: Cognitive overload and behavioral constraint. In W. Preiser (Ed.), *Environmental design research* (Vol. II). Stroudsburg, Pa.: Dowden, Hutchinson, and Ross, 1973.

Schachter, S., & Singer, J. Cognitive, social and psychological determinants of emotional states. *Psychological Review,* 1962, *69,* 379-399.

Schiffenbauer, A., & Schiavo, S. Physical distance and attraction: An intensification effect. *Journal of Experimental Social Psychology,* 1976, *12,* 274-282.

Schmitt, R. Density, delinquency and crime in Honolulu. *Sociology and Social Research,* 1957, *41,* 274-276.

Schmitt, R. Density, health and social disorganization. *Journal of American Institute of Planners,* 1966, *32,* 38-40.

Seligman, M.E.P. *Helplessness: On depression, development and death.* San Francisco: Freeman, 1975.

Selye, H. *The stress of life.* New York: McGraw-Hill, 1956.

Sherrod, D. Crowding, perceived control and behavioral aftereffects. *Journal of Applied Social Psychology,* 1974, *4,* 171-186.

Simmel, G. The expansion of the dyad. In [*The sociology of Georg Simmel*] (K. Wolff, Ed. and trans.). New York: Free Press, 1950.

Simmel, G. The metropolis and mental life. In [*The sociology of Georg Simmel*] (K. Wolff, Ed. and trans.). New York: Free Press, 1950.

Snyder, R. L. Evolution and integration of mechanisms that regulate population growth. *Proceedings of the National Academy of Sciences,* 1961, *47,* 449-455.

Sommer, R. *Personal space: The behavioral basis of design.* Englewood Cliff, N.J.: Prentice-Hall, 1969.

Spence, K. W. The nature of theory construction in contemporary psychology. *Psychological Review,* 1944, *51,* 47-68.

Spence, K. W. The postulates and methods of "behaviorism." *Psychological Review,* 1948, *55,* 67-78.

Stokols, D. On the distinction between density and crowding: Some implications for future research. *Psychological Review,* 1972, *79,* 275-277. (a)

Stokols, D. A social-psychological model of human crowding phenomena. *Journal of the American Institute of Planners,* 1972, *38,* 72-94. (b)

Stokols, D. Toward a psychological theory of alienation. *Psychological Review,* 1975, *82,* 26-44.

Stokols, D. The experience of crowding in primary and secondary environments. *Environment and Behavior,* 1976, *8,* 49-86.

Stokols, D., Ohlig, W., & Resnick, S. Perception of residential crowding, classroom experiences, and student health. *Human Ecology,* in press.

Stokols, D., Rall, M., Pinner, B., & Schopler, J. Physical, social and personal determinants of the perception of crowding. *Environment and Behavior,* 1973, *5,* 87-115.

Sundstrom, E. An experimental study of crowding: Effects of room size, intrusion, and goal-blocking on nonverbal behavior, self-disclosure and self-reported stress. *J. of Personality and Social Psychology,* 1975, *32,* 645-654.

Sundstrom, E., & Altman, I. Interpersonal relationships and personal space: Research review and theoretical model. *Human Ecology,* 1976, *4,* 47-67.

Suttles, G. D. *The social order of the slum.* Chicago: Univeristy of Chicago Press, 1968.

Thiessen, D., & Rodgers, D. Population density and endocrine function. *Psychological Bulletin,* 1961, *58,* 441-451.

Thibaut, J., & Kelley, H. *The social psychology of groups.* New York: Wiley, 1959.

Tolman, E. The determiners of behavior at a choice point. *Psychological Review,* 1938, *45,* 1-41.

Valins, S., & Baum, A. Residential group size, social interaction, and crowding. *Environment and Behavior,* 1973, *5,* 421-439.

Wicker, A. Undermanning theory and research: Implications for the study of psychological and behavioral effects of excess populations. *Representative Research in Social Psychology,* 1973, *4,* 185-206.

Wicker, A., & Kirmeyer, S. From church to laboratory to national park: A program of research on excess and insufficient populations in behavior settings. In D. Stokols (Ed.), *Perspectives on environment and behavior: Theory, research and applications.* New York: Plenum Press, 1977.

Winsborough, H. The social consequences of high population density. *Law and Contemporary Problems,* 1965, *30,* 120-126.

Wirth, L. Urbanism as a way of life. *American Journal of Sociology,* 1938, *44,* 1-24.

Zlutnick, S., & Altman, I. Crowding and human behavior. In J. Wohlwill & D. Carson (Eds.), *Environment and the social sciences: Perspectives and applications.* Washington, D.C.: American Psychological Association, 1972.

8
High-Density Environments:
Their Personal and Social Consequences

Susan Saegert
Graduate Center of the City University of New York

A sufficient amount of research has accumulated in recent years to make it clear that high-density experiences and living conditions can provoke stress and anti-social behaviors and attitudes. Investigations of individual physiological reactions to high-density situations indicate that density is positively related to increased physiological arousal including high blood pressure (D'Atri, 1975; Aiello, Epstein, & Karlin, 1975; Saegert, 1975). Valins and Baum (1973) and Bickman and his colleagues (1973) have found that dormitory residents exposed to excessive interactions with others or living in higher-density dorms felt more withdrawn, less friendly, and more crowded; furthermore, they behaved less cooperatively and in a less socially responsible manner. Children in higher-density play groups have been observed to become more aggressive and withdrawing (Hutt & Vaizey, 1966); children living in crowded conditions have been shown to have more aggressive personalities (Murray, 1974). In both laboratory and field studies, adults have expressed more feelings of anxiety, aggressiveness, and discomfort in high-density settings than others in lower-density conditions (Griffitt & Veitch, 1971; Saegert, Mackintosh, & West, 1975). Some types of task performance have also been shown to be negatively affected by high densities (Saegert, 1975; Saegert et al., 1975). Analyses of aggregate data as well have revealed strong relationships between area density and mortality, delinquency, illegitimate births, and divorce (Levy & Herzog, 1974; Schmitt, 1966). Other investigators have found similar but weaker relationships between dwelling unit density and signs of pathology (Galle, Gove, & McPherson, 1972). It has been reported (Dean, Pugh, & Gunderson, 1975) that sailors on more crowded ships had more illnesses and that the same relationship exists even more strongly between illness complaints and density for prisoners (McCain, Cox, & Paulus, 1976).

These studies and others like them are numerous enough and careful enough to prevent their dismissal as chance findings or methodological artifacts. Yet there are many contradictory findings that cannot be ignored. Other researchers have found no task effects (Freedman, Klevansky, & Ehrlich, 1971), no mood effects (Stokols, Rall, Pinner, & Schopler, 1973), and few or no important independent correlates of area of dwelling unit density (e.g., Mitchell, 1971; Schmitt, 1963; Winsborough, 1965).

These divergent findings provide the basis for questioning what is meant by density and why it should in some instances have important psychosocial effects but not in others. One of the major points of this chapter will be to dispell the notion that there is such a thing as *density per se*. At the same time, this position does not imply that density has no effects. Rather, I want to focus on the meaning of the term *density;* people living in and moving through certain amounts of space that varies in configuration, definition, and types of inter-personal interaction. Once this approach is taken, many of the contradictions between those studies that find serious effects of high densities and those that find none can be understood. In this light, the differences in measurement of density and of its effects can be seen to create difficulties of interpretation.

As an example of the vast differences that are involved in various studies, we can compare the Welch and Booth study (1975) of aggression and den-sity in Canada, the Mitchell (1971) study of Hong Kong, the Winsborough (1965) analysis of aggregate data in Chicago, and Levy and Herzog's (1974) analysis of aggregate data in the Netherlands. These studies all draw different conclusions about the effects of high-density residential environments and attempt to general-ize them. Yet the conditions of living, the range of density studied, and the kinds of measures used are drastically dissimilar. The first study was done in relatively low-density Toronto, employing self-reports of fights and arguments as the major dependent measure and concluding that density had no effect on "aggres-sion." Both household and area density served as independent variables, but the range, means, and variance of the density variables were not presented nor was information given on the extent to which the control variables (education, ethnicity, age, and occupation) covaried with density. In addition, no evidence was presented that self-report of family aggression was a good reflection of actual aggressive behavior. Thus, questions about the conclusions can be raised on the following grounds:

1. Does the finding of a relationship between subjective crowding and self-reported aggressive behavior simply reflect a propensity of the respondent to give negative reports?

2. Does the absence of a relationship between self-reported aggression and objective crowding reflect true absence of such a relationship or the ineffective-ness of this method of measuring aggression?

3. Is there enough variance on "aggression" left that it not associated with the control variables to really allow for the discovery of a density-aggression relationship?

4. Are the ranges and values of household and neighborhood density large enough to really test the hypothesis?

Many other studies can be similarly questioned. Almost no investigators provide much distributional data about their density variables, yet conclusions are drawn as if the findings or absence of them apply generally to all situations of "high" and "low" density. None of the three other studies being compared really provide enough descriptive data related to density to know how to compare them on this continuum (although it is known that generally density in Chicago is greater than in Toronto, and still greater in Hong Kong and the Netherlands). Winsborough (1965) and Levy and Herzog (1974) looked at both household and area density, whereas Mitchell investigated only household density. The relationship between density and income is inverse and quite large in Chicago whereas it is more complex in the Netherlands: There, those with higher incomes are *more likely* to live in denser areas but *less likely* to live in *crowded homes*. One can ask whether these differences may not affect the possibility of finding density effects after controlling for income. Indeed, Winsborough found that very little variance could be accounted for by area density after controlling for income, whereas Levy and Herzog accounted for 46 percent of the variance in crimes against property, 30 percent of the variance in delinquency, 33 percent of the variance in illegitimate births and 16.8 percent of the variance in male deaths by heart attack (to list but a few of their results). However, the Netherlands data revealed negative though weaker relationships between household crowding and measures of pathology, thus indicating that in this sample crowded homes might be related to *better* health and well-being, although the tendency for people with psychological problems to live alone might also account for the finding (Maris, 1969). Mitchell's data raise issues for interpretation also. Although household density per se related only to superficial strain and difficulty in supervising children, high levels of contact with nonkin and living in upper floors of high-rises did seem to create more serious psychological difficulty and hostility.

Certainly all the differences in independent and dependent variables as well as in results create some confusion. The purpose of this chapter is to outline a systemic approach to understanding the effects of density in the context of the social-psychological limitations and abilities of those involved.

DEFINITIONS OF DENSITY

Density is a complex variable both in its definition and in its effects. As has been pointed out elsewhere (e.g., Saegert, 1973) *physical density* involves two separate components—*number of people* in a given space and *amount of space per person.* For example, the density in two studies might have been 12 square feet per person, but in one case there were 200 people in an assembly hall and in the other there were four people in half of a small laboratory room. Perceptually and socially, these situations are very different, even though each may be designated as being the "high-density" condition. Beyond these physical differences, environments may perceptually and symbolically convey different levels of density (Rapoport, 1975). In a study conducted in a Manhattan train station (Saegert et al., 1975), even subjects in the low-density condition characterized the environment as crowded when they were asked to use their own words to describe the place—despite their low numerical estimates and responses to a scale measure of crowdedness. Indeed, objectively the train station was near-empty at the low-density time, yet to these subjects it still seemed to be a crowded place. Here we may speculate that despite the actual physical conditions of the environment, the *symbolic density* associated with the place arose from such cultural sterotypes as "busy as Grand Central Station."

It has been pointed out that perceptions of *crowding* indicate a negative feeling state rather than merely a report of density (e.g., Stokols, 1972). Nondensity factors such as friendship groups and architectural features have been shown to affect feelings of crowding (Baum, Harpin, & Valins, 1975). However, in studies varying physical density, people's reports of crowding strongly reflect differences in actual density (e.g., Desor, 1972; Mitchell, 1971; Saegert et al., 1975; Stokols et al., 1973).

In this chapter, the effects of high densities are considered both as functions of increased numbers of people, limitations on available space, and the combination of high numbers of people in small spaces. The separation of these factors is important in understanding the attentional and coordination demands that characterize any particular high-density situation and that provide a starting point for analyzing perceived crowding and the potential stress-provoking aspects of such conditions.

ATTENTIONAL OVERLOAD

Cohen's (1978) model of environmental stress provides a useful starting point. His basic hypotheses state that in stress-provoking environments, demands on attentional capacity are created by the intensity, unpredictability, and uncontrollability of the stressor. These conditions reduce the amount of attention available for other tasks. Thus, when simultaneous tasks are performed under stressful conditions, attention is focused on relevant cues to the neglect of less relevant ones. Cohen draws on research concerning the effects of noise and of high densities to support his argument and attempts to suggest some of the various types of effects such a situation might have on task and social behavior.

This model seems quite helpful and accurate as far as it goes. However, high-density experiences are qualitatively different from experiences of other stressors such as noise. The presence or expected presence of other human beings and one's proximity to them is fraught with psychological and social meaning. Furthermore, unlike noise, the number and identity of other people present and their physical closeness have functional implications for behavior. Noise studies are typically conducted with tones set at varying decibel levels and sounded at certain intervals, not with broadcasts about the subject's likeability, success at problem solving, or information relevant to the task at hand. Density is a parameter of human social systems in which the subject is always involved. Therefore, the activities that engage the participants of that system, their feelings about themselves and one another, and the norms and environmental arrangements that regulate their interaction come to be of critical importance.

When considering density as a quality of social systems, it is necessary to distinguish between (1) the conditions created by the copresence of large numbers of individuals, (2) those conditions involving primarily spatial restriction, and (3) those conditions in which both occur. The differential attentional and coordination demands of each of these situations reflect the specific constraints and opportunities each offers.

SOCIAL OVERLOAD

An overload situation arises from high-density conditions when the number of potential or actual social interactions that involve or impinge on a person is so great that one's attentional capacity is taxed. Not only is this sort of social interaction unavoidable, but it creates unpredictability in the environment. Social overload may imply involuntary interaction or loss of control over encounters, but its manifestations may also be more subtle. Essentially, the term implies only that, for whatever activities being pursued, the presence of others, whether merely anticipated or actually perceived, places high levels of demands for attention and coordination on the person. Although this situation can be ignored or withdrawn from, any more active and aware transactions with the social-physical environment will be difficult to structure cognitively and to enact without experiencing uncertainty and unpredictability.

Cohen (1978) suggests that people usually will select information narrowly relevant to some primary task and ignore other cues. However, in high-density living conditions, the primary tasks can become so numerous as to render this a problematic strategy; even restricting attention only to cues relevant to everyday living and major commitments could exceed one's attentional capacity. People might therefore resort to unsystematic cue sampling or abandonment of a rational system of utilizing information. Most people deal with some situations in a rational fashion, gathering information, considering alternatives, and deciding on courses of action; in others, they act out of intuition or habit or whimsy. Thus, one way to handle overload arising from high-density living situations would be to increase the number of decisions taken in a nonrational way, perhaps confining rational decision making to situations in which reliable and representative information is attainable. Another strategy might be to reduce the number of decisions one makes. This might involve engaging in more habitual or routine activities, avoiding novel situations, withdrawing from interaction with unfamiliar people, or behaving in stereotypic ways.

On the information selection side of the problem, one might rely on certain easily available cues such as sex, race, familiarity, and so on. Another perhaps more sophisticated strategy would be to try to organize the physical and social environment into meaningful subunits so that more of the total environment could be scanned. Research has indicated that such "information chunking" schemas can increase the amount of information to which a person can attend (Miller, 1962). Alternately, a person could give up the task of selecting information to be attended to oneself and simply rely on some external source to provide information—for example, one's religious or political group or favorite publication.

Beyond deciding on one's own course of action in a socially overloaded situation, a person must coordinate behaviors with others. This is a doubly complex task because it involves selection of activities from the individual's repertoire on the basis of information about the social and physical environment, projection of the likely states of both, and selection of the most desirable probable match. In overload situations in which participants' behaviors are not coordinated by effective norms or some other social-physical structure that prevents unpredictable and perhaps unintended interference, there is a high probability that individual behavior will be interrupted and goal attainment will be frustrated. Such circumstances may provoke feelings of either competition and aggression or disengagement and withdrawal. Both are reactions to the inherent difficulty of attaining cognitive clarity and behavioral efficacy in a complex, unpredictable environment: One involves increased striving to order the situation in accordance with the individual's desires; the other indicates a giving up of attempts to relate to the environment. All these conditions create difficulty for a socially involved, problem-solving approach to decisions and courses of behavior.

The Stony Brook dormitory studies are of particular interest in evaluating these hypotheses about the effects of social overload. Valins and Baum (1973) have conducted a number of investigations of students, all living in relatively dense dormitory conditions. However, some of the students were assigned to suites of four or six people whereas others lived in double-loaded corridor facilities requiring them to share bathrooms and corridor and lounge areas with 34 others. The corridor residents felt more crowded and more sensitive to the possible disruptive effects of high density. Furthermore, in a laboratory situation, the corridor residents distanced themselves more from others and performed better under competitive than cooperative conditions, whereas the reverse is true for suite residents (Valins & Baum, 1973). In a later study of the same dormitories (Baum et al., 1975), it was found that suite respondents were more likely to solve problems in groups and to feel they shared attitudes with neighbors, knew their neighbors' opinion of them, and were willing to disclose personal information to neighbors. In addition, corridor residents reported more attempts to avoid others. However, by the second year of residency, some of the corridor-dwelling students had arranged to live near friends and to develop friendship groups; these students felt less crowded than the other corridor residents.

From these studies we see that people required to relate closely to large numbers of previously unknown others do respond in a socially withdrawing manner and feel crowded. The Stony Brook studies confirm laboratory findings that even with space per person held constant, subjects perceived more interference and a shortage of space when there were large numbers of others present (Saegert, 1975). Desor's (1972) doll-placement study, also an investigation of the relationship between social interaction and density, indicated that subjects perceived more crowding in a large undivided room than in the same room when it had been partitioned; thus, perceived crowding seemed to be related to (expected) quanitity of social interaction in addition to space per person. Similarly, Baum and Koman (1976) found that real subjects expecting larger groups to arrive later exhibited preparation for withdrawal.

An interesting question is raised by the findings concerning reduction of corridor residents' perceptions of crowding in friendship groups. We might conclude that friends already have information about one another and have coordinated habitual patterns of interaction that reduce demands on their attentional and decision-making capacities, as has been suggested by Latene and Rodin (1969) in their study of friendship effects on bystander intervention. Yet another factor may also be significant. People who interact with others whom they trust may feel less need to be in control of the situation. Therefore, individual decision making in all situations may be a less-salient consideration: They may be more willing to go along with whatever happens and feel less vulnerable to unexpected events, thus reducing their need to be constantly vigilant. These factors may indeed explain why numerous studies of dwelling-unit density fail to find any effects. First of all, fewer people are involved. Second, as Levy and Herzog (1974) conclude, cohesive, supportive family groups seem to make even very high-density situations in houses and apartments bearable. The findings of negative effects of dwelling unit density have been confined to the poor (Galle, Gove, & McPherson, 1972), families having other personal difficulties (Loring, 1956), and people living with nonkin (Mitchell, 1971). In summary, the stressful and antisocial effects of social overload seem to be exacerbated by the absence of resources, unfamiliarity among residents, frequency of turnover of inhabitants, and lack of strong social ties.

All this would lead us to expect that in societies with less individualistic and rationalistic orientations, more ritualized social interactions and less investment in personal control, people would be able to interact with more others without experiencing difficulty. Indeed, Schmitt's (1963) contentions about Hong Kong support this view. However, it is important to keep in mind that worldwide trends toward modernization, industrialization, and geographic mobility tend to erode the orientations and social groups that would ameliorate high-density conditions.

Before leaving this topic, attention should be given to the information that exists concerning the physiological concomitants of overload and their relationship to stress. The component of density most associated with social overload is number of people encountered. Several studies indicate that interactive and inescapable exposure to larger numbers of people results in increased arousal (Saegert, 1975), increased blood pressure (D'Atri, 1975), and higher rates of illness (McCain et al., 1976; Paulus, Cox, McCain, & Chandler, 1975). These findings are in keeping with studies of animal populations (e.g., Davis, 1971). However, in contrast to studies of the other major environmental stressor thought to be linked to attentional overload (Cohen, 1978), there is at present no evidence to suggest that physiological adaptation to crowding occurs. Both short-term laboratory studies (Saegert, 1975) and long-term studies of prison populations (D'Atri, 1975; McCain et al., 1976; Paulus, et al., 1975) report increasing physiological concomitants of stress over time.

These findings again point back to a systemic understanding of density effects. First, the presence of numerous others in close proximity may constantly present unresolvable conflicts and interferences, whereas even unpredictable noise can be counted on to retain more or less the same character. Unlike people, noise does not provide constantly novel forms of interruption and unpredictability.

Elsewhere (Saegert, 1976) I have suggested that three distinct kinds of overload can occur: Stimulus overload (e.g., meaningless noise), information overload (e.g., crowding or a surfeit of signs on a highway), and decisional overload (e.g., attempting to construct social relationships on a very high density environment or to respond creatively and effectively to frequent, unpredictable, complex, and changing task demands). It appears that stimulus overload is more likely to be ameliorated by adaptation, whereas the fate of a person experiencing information overload or decisional overload is likely to be more complex and dependent on specific personal and environmental factors. Whereas high-density situations can be experienced as any or all of these three kinds of overload, the pressures presented by the latter two are more likely to result in continuing arousal and to lead to stress.

In assessing the physiological consequences of density, it is important to keep in mind the time frame involved, the possibility of escaping from or controlling the situation (cf. Averill, 1973), and the meaning of the situation (cf. Averill, 1973; Kahn & French, 1970; Saegert, 1976). All these factors have been shown to influence the occurrence of physiological arousal and to be critical in determining whether such arousal, if it does occur, leads to more serious physiological changes indicative of stress.

Such physiological states will in themselves have psychological consequences. Arousal can be expected to lead to an intensification of whatever emotional state the individual is experiencing (cf. Schachter & Singer, 1962). Furthermore, it may have functional implications for cognitive and behavioral performances. It has been argued that high levels of arousal interfere with complex and/or novel information-processing tasks (cf. Broadbent, 1971; Fiske & Maddi, 1961). Thus, in high-density situations, a person may be faced with a complex and changeable environment, which would be challenging in any physical state, in a bodily condition that is not optimal for meeting the challenge. Whether information-processing decrements are caused by arousal or arousal is merely a concomitant of cognitive overload (Cohen, 1978), some feedback between these states is likely to occur in the course of transactions with the environment. Cohen (1978) has begun to describe the possible effects on social behavior of attentional overload. At the very least these effects could be expected to be accompanied by more intense emotional reactions due to higher arousal. Further decrements in information-processing may also occur. Finally, since all or most of the people composing the high-density situation could be expected to be experiencing both overload and arousal, the effects on actual and potential social behavior should be amplified.

SPATIAL CONSTRAINT

In addition to contributing to social overload, density is also usually associated with spatial constraint. The most obvious consequence of limited space is the reduction of freedom for physical movement. This means that certain types of behaviors can be selected from an individual's repertoire whereas others are impossible. Although these restrictions need not increase the cognitive demands of a particular situation, they might if a person is required consciously to modify long-standing habits, that is, if the behaviors that are excluded because of spatial constraint are ones the person automatically engages in. For example, someone who normally paces briskly around the room while thinking but has recently moved to a small studio apartment with very little floor space then must think not only about the topic of concern but also about how to act in the situation; that person's habitual behavior patterns are incompatible with the limited size of the room.

One would also expect that stimulation arising from the environment would be more salient in a smaller space. One might become more aware of the physical qualities of the environment, especially of the extent to which they facilitate or inhibit desired activities. When the social environment is concerned, the increased salience of other people would tend to magnify awareness of their characteristics and perhaps, as has been suggested (Freedman, Levy, Buchanan, & Price, 1972), to intensify existing interpersonal attitudes, emotions, and behaviors. The attentional consequences of these effects would involve greater difficulty in distancing the situation in favor of less immediate information and options. It is expected that people would need to try harder to concentrate on information that was either not physically present (e.g., a mental task) or that was difficult to discriminate (e.g., small signs in a crowded subway station). In this way, attentional load could be increased in a spatially constrained environment without the amount of information actually increasing. This effect relates to the intensity of stimulation, which Cohen (1978) has hypothesized to be a characteristic of environmental stressors generally, and which Freedman et al. (1971) have described as the major effect of spatial crowding. Yet we must keep in mind the difference between intensity of stimulation occasioned by crowding and by other environmental features. The kind of stimulation occasioned by the presence of others depends on the characteristics and behavior of those present: They may be noisy or quiet, active or immobile, visually heterogeneous or homogeneous, and so on. Once again, we are reminded that density per se is not a concept that accurately reflects either the stimulus situation or the functional qualities and psychological meanings of a situation.

The functional aspects of behaving in a spatially constrained environment have further implications for attentional overload. Clearly, when people occupy a smaller space, more interpersonal coordination is required, especially if occupants are not free to leave or if the facilities they need are available only in that space. This demand for coordination taxes the attentional and decision-making capacity of individuals if ongoing activities are disturbing (such as talking), or require movement. The weaker or less accurate people's expectations are in the situation, the greater will be the attentional demands and the possibility of frustration. Because this means that cognitive uncertainty is high and normative coordination of behavior is low, people in close proximity become more vulnerable to one another. However, on the positive side, communication and exchange may be facilitated, as well as a sense of interpersonal involvement and belonging.

Finally, as with increased group size, spatial constraint seems to be arousing, especially if others are present (Saegert, 1974; Aiello et al., 1975). The relationship between arousal and cognitive processes has already been discussed.

A number of studies have examined the effects of spatial constraint separately from those of increased number. In one study varying room size and group size orthogonally (Saegert, 1975), the results indicate that spatial constraint is independently arousing and increases perceptions of others' interference as well as desire for more space. Aiello et al. (1975) also have found people to be more aroused in smaller spaces. In other of their studies (Epstein & Karlin, 1974), they reported increases in stereotypic male and female behavior in such conditions. As in the research of Freedman et al. (1972), males manifested more negative social behaviors, whereas females were more prosocial. In both instances, females enjoyed the higher-density situation more. Karlin, McFarlan, Epstein, & Aiello (1976) then induced both male and female groups to confide their feelings to one another with the result that perceptions of crowding distress were reduced. These authors also manipulated interaction norms for groups of females. When levels of nonverbal interaction were high, women were more cohesive, whereas when interaction levels were low, female behavior resembled that of crowded males in the Epstein and Karlin (1975) experiments.

All the studies cited above, however, occurred in relatively brief laboratory sessions. There is some evidence that casts doubt on the long-term utility for crowded living conditions of the prosocial, active orientation seemingly characteristic of female groups. Aiello et al. (1975) report, as part of an ongoing study of crowded dormitories, that females were adjusting less successfully to crowded conditions than were males. Perhaps the attentiveness to social cues and social reinforcement that is often part of normative female behavior strains the attentional and coordinating capacity of women in this situation when a long time span and a multitude of behaviors are involved, as well as rendering them more vulnerable to disappointment when interactions are not smooth. The stereotypic male aptitude for distancing others, as well as lesser commitment to the dwelling unit, may ameliorate the experience of such spatial constraint. Later reports of this investigation will no doubt prove most useful in deciding these issues.

To look once more at the effects of spatial constraint, it should be noted that one part of such conditions is spatial closeness to others or propinquity. This factor has long been known to play a role in friendship formation (Athanasiou & Yoshioka, 1973; Festinger, Schachter, & Back, 1950; Lawton & Simon, 1968). Recently Nahemow and Lawton (1975) have reported evidence supporting their contention that friendships between people dissimilar in race and age occur frequently only under conditions of residential proximity. Spatial constraint is often the reverse side of ease of access. Surely many of those who have wished to deny the possible harmful effects of high-density living have in mind the opportunities afforded by physical closeness to a wide range of different facilities and kinds of people such as exists in large cities. However, the hypotheses and research discussed above suggest that spatial proximity is a blessing only when the relations among people are cordial, their activities compatible, and their resources adequate to allow them to adjust to changing contingincies.

INTERACTIVE EFFECTS OF SOCIAL OVERLOAD AND SPATIAL CONSTRAINT

Given the previous discussion, placing large numbers of people in relatively small spaces would be expected to greatly heighten the possibility that they will experience attentional overload and difficulties of coordination. The environmental complexity and potential uncertainty occasioned by large numbers of people will be made salient by their proximity. The sheer physical stimulation arising from their presence will be more intense and more arousing. Vulnerability to the intrusions and interference of others is increased on the one hand by proximity and on the other by the cognitive impossibility of monitoring and adjusting to the entire situation. The probability of overload is even higher if a person is engaged in activities requiring scanning of the environment or movement, since physical avoidance, withdrawal, or buffering is less feasible. The person loses behavioral freedom in a number of ways: (1) through lack of space to move freely; (2) through increased need to coordinate behavior; (3) through the increased number of people with whom coordination is required; and (4) through less complete and accurate knowledge of conditions in the complex, highly peopled environment, which in turn reduces awareness of behavioral options.

Studies specifically investigating the interaction effects of social overload and spatial constraint tend to confirm the hypotheses offered. Saegert et al. (1975), in two studies of urban public spaces, found that subjects exposed to social overload in restricted spaces developed a less detailed and less accurate image of the environment. Furthermore, when required to perform tasks calling for understanding of and movement through the environment, subjects during the crowded times did fewer tasks and felt more negative toward themselves and others.

It appears that the cognitive overload arising from these conditions is occasioned, on the one hand, by more potential information in the environment and, on the other, by more constraints on the selection of behaviors in high densities. If these constraints are great enough, the existence of potential information in the environment may become irrelevant because no decisions need be made. The person may be so hemmed in by others that all motoric behavior is impossible.

In such conditions, one begins to lose control over both the environment and one's own cognitive state and behaviors. Frustration at such loss of cognitive and behavioral control seems likely to be added to any other specific frustrations that may result from goal blocking in high densities.

In a study just completed (Langer & Saegert, 1977), it was found that people who were informed of the possible arousing effects of crowding before entering a supermarket were more efficient and comfortable than those not so informed. People entering a supermarket were asked to participate for pay in a study of consumer behavior that involved choosing the most economical product for each item on a 50-item shopping list. The subjects were selected equally at crowded and uncrowded times. Half of those in each condition were informed of the possible anxiety and arousal they might feel if the supermarket should become crowded. Overall, crowded subjects completed fewer choices in the 30 minutes allowed and felt less comfortable, more crowded, more interfered with by the environment, and made less economical choices of products. There was also a main effect for information: Informed subjects felt less distressed, completed more items, and made more economical choices. Thus, both crowding and information had strong effects. People who were forewarned of the effects of crowding were not only more comfortable in a crowded situation but also displayed greater cognitive facility than those not so informed.

The way in which attentional capacity is affected by information about emotional reactions requires further investigation. Schachter and Singer (1962) have suggested that emotions consist of both physiological arousal and a label designating the arousal as a particular type of emotion. In the study just described, we were providing a label for emotions that might occur. This seems likely to reduce the subject's uncertainty in the situation. This could be comforting and also serve to reduce the load on her attention by freeing her from the necessity of trying to label the arousal experienced. These findings are clearly in line with other studies indicating that subjects informed of contingencies often react less emotionally to stress-provoking situations (cf. Glass & Singer, 1972; Janis, 1962). This study does, however, seem to be the first demonstration of increased cognitive efficiency in the stressful situation by making available information about a person's own reactions. Glass and Singer found differential cognitive efficiency in response to predictable or controllable noise mainly on post-stress tasks. Janis primarily investigated the emotional adjustment and physical recovery of informed and uniformed hospital patients.

Yet the fact that information was helpful even to uncrowded subjects raises further questions. Several explanations seem plausible:

1. Even though the stores were not overly crowded, perhaps the low-density subjects did experience some increased arousal and thus were able to benefit from the availability of the label.

2. The calling of the subjects' attention to the possibility of crowding, which was not done for uninformed subjects, may have induced them to try harder and/or organize their tasks more efficiently, thus improving their performance and making them feel better.

3. The additional information may have been interpreted as a sign that the experimenter was concerned about them and thus led to better performance and more positive reactions on the part of the subjects.

4. Or perhaps something similar to (2) but less specific occurred; that is, perhaps subjects used the information about the possibility of crowding to employ some type of anticipatory coping strategy.

The last three explanations could provide alternatives for understanding the effects of the information in the crowded conditions as well. The demonstration of the effects of such information on person-environment transactions is provocative and requires further research so that it may be more clearly interpreted.

This study and the hypotheses discussed earlier clearly suggest that a crisis in personal control, both cognitive and behavioral, lies at the heart of the negative consequences of high-density experiences. Both the complexity of increased group size and the spatial restriction of crowded conditions may bring about this situation. Some of the aggressive and withdrawn behavior observed or reported in studies of high densities may reflect a reaction to this loss of freedom or control. Indeed, if one thinks of a competitive orientation as one that emphasizes personal control, the findings of Valins and Baum (1973) and trends in the data of Stokols et al. (1973) support these speculations because both indicate relationships between crowding experiences and cooperative or competitive behavior. The sex differences in response to crowding so frequently reported may also be related to a male controlling versus a female adjustive set of attitudes and behaviors in interactions with same-sex others. Yet evidence has been suggesting that children raised in high density environments show *less* propensity to control their situations when it is possible than do children from less dense homes (Rodin, 1976). Thus, perhaps some individuals may attempt to regain control in high–density environments, but those who have grown up in them may be less oriented toward controlling in general. These different findings emphasize the need for coming to understand long-term adjustments and changes brought about by high-density situations, as well as the shorter range effects that at present provide the main focus of study. The suggestive work by Rodin indicates the need for longitudinal studies spanning the life cycle of such environmental influences. In these investigations, the focus should be on both cumulative effects that have long-term manifestations in the character and behavior of individuals, and also on situationally based responses to density levels, which may be employed only in the high-density situation.

In a recent study of the relationship between social overload, perceived crowding, and various negative personal and social consequences (McCarthy & Saegert, in press), it was found that not only was overload highly related to perceived crowding but also there was a strong relationship between both of these factors and the amount of control people felt over the environment. The residents in the low-income public housing project being investigated seem to experience a loss of control over semipublic areas in their building when these are used by many other people; this experience seems to be related to feeling that the building is crowded. Furthermore, residents who more frequently experienced such situations also had less sense of control over management of the project, identified less with the project as a whole, belonged to fewer clubs and organizations, and generally withdrew from social interaction.

The data from the various studies mentioned and from others also dealing with loss of control (cf. Averill, 1973) lead one to conclude that loss of control is usually a negative experience for people, interfering with task performance and social behavior. The particular aspects of high-density situations that lead to loss of control, (i.e., cognitive overload and behavioral constraint) may induce people to give up some of their efforts to make choices and actively affect the physical and social environment. Simplification of behavior patterns, asocial behavior, and adherence to norms, rulings of authority, habits or other inflexible routines all could have value as ways of reducing the cognitive complexity of the situation. Any unambiguous external directive can serve to reduce complexity; powerful leadership, division of labor, clearly defined tasks and roles, and physical environments presenting simple, clear and sparse options are all routes to such simplification. Such adaptations to high-density situations obviously can have consequences for the social structure and norms of the social systems in which they occur as well as for the well-being of those involved.

Although most of these data and speculations lead one to expect that crowding and the loss of control it may occasion are unpleasant and undesirable, psychologists have suggested that loss of control can have its pleasurable aspects as well. Therefore, the potential positive experiences associated with crowding should also be explored.

Speculation concerning the effects of deindividuation are relevant to this concern (Festinger, Pepitone, & Newcomb, 1952; Zimbardo, 1969). Up to now in this chapter, people have been viewed as struggling to carry out plans and to control a situation; indeed, much of the itme this perspective seems valid. Yet internal motivation is seldom left on its own to maintain self-control. One's behavior is usually monitored by others. When numbers increase, the cognitive complexity of so many monitoring tasks becomes impossible at some point. Then individuals may feel freer to deviate because of the difficulty any particular other person would have in interfering. This would be especially likely in a situation in which people were moving around and where strong norms and value consensus were not operating.

Giving up at least some personal control is an element common to many adult play experiences. Here it may be that loss of control is a normative expectation. For example, alcohol, loud music, and low lighting at parties make it harder to perceive the environment clearly and to monitor what occurs, and are generally provided by party-givers. Physical proximity and large numbers may also be characteristic of parties for the same reason. When situations are constructed that limit the negative consequences of behavior, loss of control can be exciting, tension reducing, and generally pleasurable. If the effects of number and spatial closeness are of the sort hypothesized, some understanding can be gained of various group phenomena such as rallies and mobs. Group solidarity, comradely emotions, and commitment to group goals may be enhanced through loss of individual control. Conversely, the destructive forms of crowd behavior, such as lynch mobs and riots, may also be facilitated by the loss of individual behavioral and cognitive control in that situation. When a strong motive is aroused, the effect may be similar to that of a strong external definition of the situation.

In summary, it seems probable that the same mechanisms underlie both negative and positive psychological experiences of high densities. The maintenance of control over one's own behavior and that of others is opposed by attentional overload, spatial constraint, and the resultant demands of coordinating behavior. Large numbers of people have a twofold implication for the efficacy of social control: One, they may create a desire for such control as a solution to the social overload occasioned but, second, they decrease the ease with which such control can be implemented, if some people are not cooperative. The consistent finding that difficulty in child supervision and juvenile delinquency are related to high-density living (Levy & Herzog, 1974; Mitchell, 1971; Schmitt, 1966) serve to illustrate such consequences.

DENSITY AND SOCIAL SYSTEMS

Thus far, concern has been focused on the experiences, constraints, and opportunities that arise for the *individual* as a function of high density. A set of hypotheses has been presented about the social-psychological processes affected by density. However, the number of people in a social system and their proximity would seem to place certain demands on that *system* as well as on the people who comprise it.

Sociologists have claimed that the nature of society itself and the bonds among its members are pervasively affected by the density of its population concentrations. Durkheim (1933) concluded that the existence of large concentrations is the precursor of structural developments in the form of society, particularly increased specialization and division of labor. Simmel (1957/1905) emotionally described what he thought to be the deterioration of social relations among inhabitants of cities because of the cities' size, density, and heterogeneity of population. This view, also restated and expanded by Wirth (1938), has been summarized in a recent review article (Fischer, 1973) as follows:

> According to this analysis, the aggregation of great numbers of diverse people creates both the reality and the perception of individual impotence. At the same time, the protective withdrawal this environment forces the individual into and the destruction it causes to social bonds renders man isolated from, fearful of, hostile to and manipulative of his fellow man [p. 311].

Although Fischer (1973) does report evidence of a weak association between the size of a metropolitan area and felt social isolation, he concludes that the overall hypotheses are not warranted (Fischer, 1975). Other sociologists are not quite so sanguine (Guterman, 1969; Key, 1968).

It takes only a slight extension of the argument that very high density conditions exceed the capacity of individuals to attend to and process information to see the link between the cognitive uncertainty and behavioral constraint discussed earlier and the kinds of social withdrawal and alienation that have been the concern of sociologists. As the size of a system increases, each individual is less able to comprehend and control it. Therefore, various ways of limiting information and social contact are devised. For the individual, these pressures may create feelings of powerlessness and isolation. For the system, the pressures are expected to produce a compounding of problems and a need to devote more resources to communicative functions (Kasarda, 1974).

These speculations are clearly similar to the effects that would be implied by the earlier hypotheses presented in this chapter. However, until recently little attention has been given to the many different levels of adjustment possible between individuals and social systems. Sociological evidence suggests that there is some truth to these ideas; however, it also indicates that the range of social arrangements and emotional responses of people living in high-density populations is large and complexly interwoven.

Investigators of the division of labor in formal organizations have hypothesized that the larger the organization, the more complex and difficult it would become to understand and control it. Therefore, it was expected that these factors would be reflected not only in greater division of labor so that an individual's capacities would not be exceeded but also in greater organizational complexity and a larger administrative component in order to coordinate the more separated and specialized components. Although results strongly confirm the relationship between the size of the organization and the degree of division of labor, the expected relationships of size to organizational complexity and size of administrative component are weak (Anderson & Warkov, 1961; Blau, 1972; Durkheim, 1933; Hall, Haas, & Johnson, 1967; Hawley, Boland, & Boland, 1965; Raphael, 1967; Terrier & Mills, 1955). These studies seem to suggest that although large organizations require increased specialization to allow coordination of activities, this mechanism itself is often sufficient to allow the organization to function without always requiring increased size of the administrative component. However, these studies do suggest that the communications functions in larger organizations frequently do expand disproportionately.

The size of the organization also seems to affect members' psychological responses, which in turn may reinforce the need for increased specialization for diverse organizations. Many of these studies have found that size and indices of participation were inversely correlated. In a further investigation, Indik (1961) has found a link between size of an organization, amount of spontaneous communication among members, and consequent attraction to the organization that was reflected in levels of participation.

On the basis of such evidence, Barker and his colleagues (cf. Barker, 1960; Barker & Gump, 1964; Wicker, 1968, 1969) have developed a theory of undermanning predicting that when the number of social roles in a system is greater than the number of participants, people will do more things, work harder, feel more committed, and like the group more. Conversely, Wicker, McGrath, and Armstrong (1972) have suggested a theory of overmanning hypothesizing just the opposite effects when the number of participants exceeds the number of roles. Studies investigating overmanning (Hanson & Wicker, Note 1) begin to reveal the complex interactions of attentional overload at the individual level and at the system level. Participants in overmanned groups did feel less important, less needed, and less valuable to the group; however, those in undermanned groups rated themselves as feeling more crowded. These results can be interpreted in the framework of the overload model. Larger social systems require simplification and limitation of the role each member plays in order to avoid confusion in coordinating behavior. But a by-product of this for individuals seems to be less satisfaction with the system. Involved in the large system role simplification is an assumption of limited, relatively fixed attentional capacity. Those in the undermanned conditions, however, were subjected to the same task demands as the larger group. In this case, the high level of attention demanded by the task exceeded the capacity of the small groups, whereas the division of labor in the large groups made their attentional demands less than they could have handled.

The conclusions reached by Thomas and Fink (1963) concerning the effects of group size also reveal the impact of the amount and complexity of information potentially impinging on group members, group functioning, and individual feeling. Group performance generally improved in quality and productivity as size increased; under no conditions were small groups superior. This superiority is consistent with the superiority of statistically constructed groups' performances over that of individuals (Zajonc, 1962). In the few studies in which speed of performance was affected by size, small groups tended to be faster, probably reflecting greater ease in communication and coordination. Suggestions that small groups inhibit expressions of conflict and of differences emerged from several studies using interaction analysis techniques. Small groups seemed to provide more chances for each person to interact with every other person and also for each person to play the leadership role. As in studies of formal organizations, size increases were negatively related to group cohesiveness and postively related to amount of organization and division of labor. In fact, larger groups tended to break down into cliques and factions, thus redefining the unit of interaction. Both individual task performance and conformity in various situations were influenced by group size. However, these latter findings sometimes involve higher-order interactions and are often contradictory. Member satisfaction generally decreased with increasing group size.

Thomas and Fink (1963) criticize the methods employed in these studies on the grounds that sampling of group size, tasks, and subject populations was arbitrary and unsystematic. The authors offer their own conceptualization of the variables relevant to group size effects as being input quality, sample size, and potential relational complexity. Input of both resources and demands increases with size, thus providing potentially better task performance and more diverse satisfactions. However, the difficulty of each person being served increases also, especially as time, energy, and commitment become limited. Increase in sample size tends to increase hetereogeneity of demands and resources. Potential relational complexity may induce frustration beyond that arising from attentional overload because individuals may be aware of constantly forgoing certain alternatives. Furthermore, Thomas and Fink suggest that Jennings' (1960) finding that people are limited in the number of others they can like implies less overall liking in larger groups. In summary, these authors present evidence that large groups provide more opportunities, but these are accompanied by more demands, requirements for decision, and frustrations.

In the studies reviewed above, relationships among people have been by virtue of group or organizational membership. The interest of this chapter however, concerns relationships conditioned by spatial proximity, regardless of affiliation. High-density situations involve not only large group size but also spatial closeness, and thus restriction. People in high-density environments become related to those around them at some level: They lose freedom to act without affecting and being affected by others. Thus, large populations of people in high-density situations are likely to be subject to the same kind of pressures described above in relationship to large formal organizations. They will tend to be confronted with at least the potential of high levels of heterogeneous demands and resources, the possibility of relational complexity, and a greater likelihood of interacting with people with whom they have no affective bonds. Of course, the kinds of coping mechanisms described in the earlier part of this paper may serve to reduce the occurrence of these difficulties. In addition, different social-physical environments will either expose occupants to the conditions of social overload and behavioral constraint or offer them more manageable alternatives. Indeed, the relationship between these conditions and different social-physical environmental organizations remains one of the most important areas for future research.

Studies of social relationships concerned with both social overload and physical proximity have mainly been studies of urban life. Here the vast differences in physical layout, social norms, population heterogeneity, and actual size and density of population concentrations has created a welter of mutually disconfirming findings. Most of the investigators have fallen prey to the seductiveness of their own labels, not realizing that finding no effects of "high density" in Australia or Los Angeles should not lead one to predict no such effects in New York or Hong Kong. Obviously, high density in Australia would be low density in the latter places. Indeed, one study in Australia (Sutcliffe & Crabbe, 1963) found that friendship patterns were not greatly affected by density. However, another study of friendships did discover differences as a function of density (Key, 1968) when people were similar in income and type of family. In addition, hotel employees from New York City were found to have fewer friends than those from smaller places (Guterman, 1969). Kasarda and Janowitz (1974) reject the linear model relating density and population size to lower social involvement; they propose that within such ecological conditions length of residence, friendship and kinship bonds, and formal and informal associational ties play a key role. They tested their predictions on a large British sample drawn from 100 local authority areas excluding London and found that residents of urban areas tended to have more extensive social ties than rural residents and that their postulated systemic variables were indeed important. The most significant effect of larger population concentrations, in line with the linear model, was lesser commitment to residing in a particular location.

The picture of urban social life that emerges from these various studies is one of relatively high levels of social involvement, more social options, and less commitment to any one particular place. These findings, as well as reports of participant-observation studies of urban neighborhoods (e.g., Gans, 1962; Jacobs, 1961) led Fischer (1975) to propose a model of the effects of urban life that emphasizes the development of more diverse and unique affiliation groups and intensification of involvement in these. Franck, Unseld, and Wentworth (1975) present evidence that partially supports such a notion, and extend it to address the Wirth-Simmel hypothesis. They found that newcomers to New York made as many friends as those arriving in a small college town. However, New Yorkers expended more effort and thought in attaining these friendships and appeared more committed to them. The authors found that New York newcomers experienced the city as more demanding than newcomers to a small town, and the New York sample felt that they were more changed by their experiences.

The alternative models proposed by Kasarda and Janowitz (1974) and by Fischer (1975) all bear on the additional overload hypothesis. Each reminds us that large numbers of people in close proximity to one another mean more opportunities as well as more demands. Furthermore, each describes certain mediating conditions that ameliorate experiences of overload: familiarity, friendship and kinship bonds, associational ties, group identification, cognitive strategies and systematic deployment of energy, and other resources. These studies point to the need for more investigation of how people actually behave in and experience high-density situations. Particularly, attention should be paid to conditions in which high-density experiences and living situations will be distressing and provoke antisocial orientations (e.g., Baum et al., 1975; Saegert et al., 1975; Valins & Baum, 1973) and those in which they will be experienced as either neutral or positive (e.g., Kasarda & Janowitz, 1974). The variables of population size, physical proximity, and their combined presence are aspects of ecological systems: It is as unlikely that their effects are independent of other social considerations as that they are simply irrelevant. The approach taken in this chapter has been a thoroughly cybernetic one: Individuals are seen as complex systems operating within other complex systems. The goal of research in this paradigm is not to delineate the effects of so many people in so much space but rather to develop more accurate predictions about the effects of particular states of some parts of a system on other parts.

AMELIORATIONS OF HIGH-DENSITY CONSTRAINTS

Although the hypotheses set forth have been only spottily tested, the results of existing studies tend to be confirming. On this basis, it is possible to suggest certain ways of coping with those consequences of high density that are negative. Individuals have a range of possible behavioral and attitudinal modifications that could serve to limit their exposure to overload. If information on crowding conditions is available, activities can be scheduled to avoid these as much as

possible, although the necessity of such planning may be experienced as restrictive and demanding. Activities that require information about the environment or any extensive person-environment transactions can be scheduled for less
crowded times, and the opposite sort of activities can be reserved for crowded
occasions. Of course, this is not always possible; for example, a good show of
art work or a good sale may be always crowded. Milgram (1970) has described a
number of ways a person can reduce social overload when in crowded situations
by ignoring social cues and assuming an appearance and set of social behaviors
that discourage others from approaching or interfering with him. Of course, all
these adjustments can be seen as requiring a person to compromise values or
goals. However, such adjustments seem to be made by long-time city dwellers
without their being aware of any such compromises. Indeed, these qualities may
be part of an urbane character, if such exists.

Other ameliorations that might involve an additional investment of energy
and time in planning might, however, make crowding less stressful. Obtaining
information about the physical and social environment ahead of time as well as
about the effects of crowding would seem to be ways of reducing overload.
Either simple familiarization or the working out of a "chunking" system would
probably reduce stress. Chunking could involve something like studying a map
so that areas would be identifiable, learning to discriminate groups of people on
some dimension relevant to one's interaction with them, or coming to be able to
pick out patterns of behavior that typify certain situations. Preplanning one's
own behavior could have similar effects. All these strategies, however, demand
high levels of rational activity and may in themselves become stressful. Studies
of the long-range effects of such coping methods are needed to evaluate their
utility. The only individual method of coping that does not seem to place additional demands on cognitive capacities is that of being with friends. The presence
of friends seems to act as a buffer from social overload and to make environments more manageable.

Social systems and organizations also have recourse to various strategies for
controlling the effects of density. Social policies could attempt to maintain
affinity groups within such systems and to support historically developed behavioral patterns. If changes in these are required for other reasons, special efforts at limiting the amount of total adjustment required, perhaps by shielding
the people involved from social overload, would be advisable. When high-density
systems exist, there should be constant monitoring for conflicts arising from incompatible or interfering activity systems. Educational and decision-making
mechanisms should be constantly aware of the complex demands made on system
integration and maintenance. Finally, the perhaps most important and often least
feasible amelioration involves the provision of adequate resources to allow system members to cope flexibly with the numerous and complex demands made
on them. Because high-density systems seem to require more from people,
economic, health, and social disadvantages appear to take more of a toll in these

environments, although the many opportunities provided may at times offset such problems.

The implications of these hypotheses for physical design and planning of high-density environments involve each stage of design and habitation. First, investigations of standing patterns of social relations and activity systems should be conducted prior to planning. If this is not possible, efforts should be made to construct facilities and policies either to support or to develop affinity groups and patterns of behavior that have existed in other situations. The functional requirements of activity systems should be minutely considered because of the high probability of interference among systems in dense environments. A sizable proportion of money should be reserved for evaluation and building modification because the complexity of such systems makes accurate and complete foresight very unlikely. Buildings and areas should attempt to define groups of manageable size as well as provide flexible shields from interaction for groups and individuals. Areas should be planned so that inhabitants have access to lower-density environments in the course of their normal life activities. For both physical and social planners, the approach that seems required in dealing with high-density environments is an awareness of the multiple possible failures of highly complex systems and concomitant modesty and caution in their construction.

REFERENCE NOTE

1. Hanson, L., & Wicker, A. *Effects of overmanning on group experience and task performance.* Paper presented at Western Psychological Association Convention, Anaheim, California, April 1973.

REFERENCES

Aiello, J. R., Epstein, Y. M., & Karlin, R. A. The effects of crowding on electrodermal activity. *Sociological Symposium,* 1975, *4,* 43-58.

Anderson, T. R., & Warkov, S. Organizational size and functional complexity. *American Sociological Review,* 1961, *26,* 23-28.

Athanasiou, R., & Yoshioka, G. A. The spatial character of friendship formation. *Environment and behavior,* 1973, *5,* 43-65.

Averill, J. Personal control over aversive stimuli and its relation to stress. *Psychological Bulletin,* 1973, *80,* 286-303.

Barker, R. G. Ecology and motivation. In M. R. Jones (Ed.), *Nebraska Symposium on Motivation.* Lincoln, Neb.: University of Nebraska Press, 1960.

Barker, R. G., & Gump, P. *Big school, small school.* Stanford, Calif. Stanford University Press, 1964.

Baum, A. Harpin, R. E., & Valins, S. The role of group phenomena in the experience of crowding. *Environment and Behavior,* 1975, *7,* 184-198.

Baum, A., & Koman, S. Differential responses to anticipated crowding: Psychological effects of social and spatial density. *Journal of Personality and Social Psychology,* 1976, *34,* 526–536.

Bickman, L., Teger, A., Gabriele, T., McLaughlin, C., Berger, M., & Sunaday, E. Dormitory density and helping behavior. *Environment and Behavior,* 1973, *5,* 465-490.

Blau, P. M. Interdependence and hierarchy in organizations. *Social Science Research,* 1972, *1,* 1-24.

Broadbent, D. E. *Decision and stress.* New York: Academic Press, 1971.

Cohen, S. Environmental load and the allocation of attention. In A. Baum, J. Singer, & S. Valins (Eds.), *Advances in environmental psychology* (Vol. 1). Hillsdale, N.J.: Lawrence Erlbaum Associates, 1978.

D'Atri, D. Psychophysiological responses to crowding. *Environment and Behavior,* 1975, *7,* 237-252.

Davis, D. E. Physiological effects of continued crowding. In A. Esser (Ed.), *Behavior and environment.* New York: Plenum, 1971.

Dean, L. M., Pugh, W. M., & Gunderson, E. K. E. Spatial and perceptual components of crowding: Effects on health and satisfaction. *Environment and Behavior,* 1975, *7,* 225-236.

Desor, J. A. Toward a psychological theory of crowding. *Journal of Personality and Social Psychology,* 1972, *21,* 79-83.

Durkheim, E. *The division of labor in society.* New York: Macmillan, 1933.

Epstein, Y. M., & Karlin, R. A. Effects of acute experimental crowding. *Journal of Applied Social Psychology,* 1975, *5,* 34-53.

Festinger, L., Schachter, S., & Back, W. *Social pressures in informal groups.* New York: Harper & Row, 1950.

Festinger, L., Pepitone, A., & Newcomb, T. Some consequences of deindividuation in a group. *Journal of Abnormal and Social Psychology,* 1952, *47,* 382-389.

Fischer, C. On urban alienations and anomie: Powerlessness and social isolation. *American Sociological Review,* 1973, *38,* 311-326.

Fischer, C. Toward a subcultural theory of urbanism. *American Journal of Sociology,* 1975, *80,* 1319-1341.

Fiske, D., & Maddi, S. *Functions of varied experience.* Homewood, Ill.: Dorsey Press, 1961.

Franck, K. A., Unseld, C. T., & Wentworth, W. R. *Urban life: The newcomer's experience.* New York: The Center for Human Environments, Graduate Center of The City University of New York, 1975.

Freedman, J. L., Klevansky, S., & Ehrlich, P. R. The effects of crowding on human task performance. *Journal of Applied Social Psychology,* 1971, *1,* 7-25.

Freedman, J. L., Levy, A. S., Buchanan, R. W., & Price, J. Crowding and human aggressiveness. *Journal of Experimental Social Psychology,* 1972, *8,* 528-548.

Galle, O. R., Gove, W. R., & McPherson, J. M. Population density and pathology: What are the relations for man? *Science,* 1972, *176,* 23-30.

Gans, H. J. *The urban villagers: Group and class in the life of Italian-Americans.* New York: Free Press, 1962.

Glass, D. C., & Singer, J. E. *Urban stress.* New York: Academic Press, 1972.

Griffitt, W., & Veitch, R. Hot and crowded: Influences of population density and temperature on interpersonal affective behavior. *Journal of Personality and Social Psychology,* 1971, *17,* 92-98.

Guterman, S. S. In defense of Wirth's "Urbanism as a Way of Life." *American Journal of Sociology,* 1969, *74,* 492-499.

Hall, R. H., Haas, J. E., & Johnson, N. J. Organizational size, complexity and formalization. *American Sociological Review,* 1967, *32,* 903-912.

Hawley, A. H., Bolond, W., & Bolond, M. Population size and administration in institutions of higher education. *American Sociological Review,* 1965, *30,* 252-254.

Hutt, C., & Vaizey, M. J. Differential effects of group density on social behavior. *Nature,* 1966, *209,* 1371-1372.

Indik, B. P. *Organization size and member participation.* Unpublished doctoral dissertation, University of Michigan, 1961.

Jacobs, J. *Life and death of great American cities.* New York: Random House, 1961.

Janis, I. L. Psychological effects of warnings. In G. W. Baker, & D. W. Chapman (Eds.), *Man and society in disaster.* New York: Basic Books, 1962.

Jennings, H. H. Sociometric choice in personality and group formation. In J. L. Moreno (Ed.), *The sociometry reader.* Glencoe, Ill.: Free Press, 1960,

Kahn, R., & French, J. Status and conflict: Two themes in the study of stress. In S. McGrath (Ed.), *Social and psychological factors in stress.* New York: Holt, Rinehart & Winston, 1970.

Karlin, R., McFarlan, L., Epstein, Y., & Aiello, J. Normative mediation of reactions to crowding. *Environmental Psychology and Nonverbal Behavior,* 1976, *1,* 30-40.

Kasarda, J. D. The structural implications of social system size: A three-level analysis. *American Sociological Review,* 1974, *39,* 19-28.

Kasarda, J. D., & Janowitz, M. Community attachment in mass society. *American Sociological Review,* 1974, *39,* 328-339.

Key, W. H. Rural-urban social participation. In Sylvia F. Fava (Ed.), *Urbanism in world perspective.* New York: Crowell, 1968.

Langer, E., & Saegert, S. Crowding and cognitive control. *Journal of Personality and Social Psychology,* 1977, *35,* 175-182.

Lawton, M. P., & Simon, B. B. The ecology of social relationships in housing for the elderly. *Gerontologist,* 1968, *8,* 108-115.

Latene, B. & Rodin, J. A lady in distress: Inhibiting effects of friends and strangers on by-stander intervention. *Journal of Experimental Social Psychology,* 1969, *5,* 189-202.

Levy, L., & Herzog, A. N. Effects of population density and crowding on health and social adaptation in the Netherlands. *Journal of Health and Social Behavior,* 1974, *15,* 228-240.

Loring, W. C. Housing and social problems. *Social Problems,* 1956, *3,* 160-168.

McCain, G., Cox, V., & Paulus, P. The relationship between illness complaints and degree of crowding in a prison environment. *Environment and Behavior,* 1976, *8,* 289-291.

McCarthy, D., & Saegert, S. Residential density, social overload and social withdrawal. *Human Ecology,* in press.

Maris, R. W. *Social forces in urban suicide,* Homewood, Ill.: Dorsey Press, 1969.

Milgram, S. The experience of living in cities. *Science,* 1970, *167,* 1461-1468.

Miller, G. *The psychology of communication.* New York: Basic Books, 1962.

Mitchell, R. E. Some social implications of high density housing. *American Sociological Review,* 1971, *36,* 18-29.

Murray, R. The influence of crowding on children's behavior. In D. Cantor & T. Lee, (Eds.), *Psychology and the built environment.* New York: Wiley, 1974.

Nahemow, L., & Lawton, M. P. Similarity and propinquity in friendship formation. *Journal of Personality and Social Psychology,* 1975, *32,* 205-214.

Paulus, P., Cox, V., McCain, G., & Chandler, J. Some effects of crowding in a prison environment. *Journal of Applied Social Psychology,* 1975, *5,* 89-91.

Raphael, E. E. The Anderson-Warkov hypothesis in local unions: A comparative study. *American Sociological Review,* 1967, *32,* 768-776.

Rapoport, A. Toward a redefinition of density. *Environment and Behavior,* 1975, *7,* 133-156.

Rodin, J. Crowding, perceived choice and responses to controllable and uncontrollable outcomes. *Journal of Experimental Social Psychology*, 1976, *12*, 564-578.

Saegert, S. Crowding: Cognitive overload and behavioral constraint. In W. Preiser (Ed.), *Environmental design research* (Vol. II). Stroudsburg, Pa.: Dowden, Hutchinson & Ross, 1973.

Saegert, S. The effects of spatial and social density on arousal, mood and social orientation (Doctoral dissertation, University of Michigan, Ann Arbor, 1974). *Dissertation Abstracts International*, 1975, v. 35, *7*, 3649. (University Microfilms No. 75-793)

Saegert, S. Stress-inducing and stress-reducing qualities of environment. In H. M. Proshansky, W. H. Ittelson, & L. G. Rivlin (Eds.), *Environmental psychology: People and their physical settings* (2nd ed.). New York: Holt, Rinehart & Winston, 1976.

Saegert, S., Mackintosh, E., & West, S. Two studies of crowding in urban public spaces. *Environment and Behavior*, 1975, *7*, 159-184.

Schachter, S., & Singer, J. E. Cognitive, social and physiological determinants of emotional state. *Psychological Review*, 1962, *69*, 379-399.

Schmitt, R. C. Implications of density in Hong Kong. *Journal of American Institute of Planners*, 1963, *24*, 210-217.

Schmitt, R. C. Density, health and social disorganization. *Journal of American Institute of Planners*, 1966, *32*, 38-40.

Simmel, G. The metropolis and mental life (1905). In P. K. Hatt & A. J. Reiss, Jr. (Eds.), *Cities and society*. New York: Free Press, 1957.

Stokols, D. A social-psychological model of human crowding phenomena. *Journal of the American Institute of Planners*, 1972, *38*, 72-84.

Stokols, D., Rall, M., Pinner, B., & Schopler, J. Physical, social and personal determinants of the perception of crowding. *Environment and Behavior*, 1973, *5*, 87-115.

Sutcliffe, J. P., & Crabbe, B. D. Incidence and degrees of friendship in urban and rural areas. *Social Forces*, 1963, *42*, 60-67.

Terrier, F. W., & Mills, D. L. The effects of changing size upon the internal structure of organizations. *American Sociological Review*, 1955, *20*, 11-13.

Thomas, E. J. & Fink, C. F. Effects of group size. *Psychological Bulletin*, 1963, *60*, 371-384.

Valins, S., & Baum, A. Residential group size, social interaction and crowding. *Environment and Behavior*, 1973, *5*, 421-439.

Welch, S., & Booth, A. The effects of crowding on aggression. *Sociological Symposium*, 1975, *14*, 105-128.

Wicker, A. Undermanning, performances and students' subjective experience in behavior settings of large and small high schools. *Journal of Personality and Social Psychology*, 1968, *10*, 255-261.

Wicker, A. Size of church membership and members' support of church behavior settings. *Journal of Personality and Social Psychology*, 1969, *13*, 278-288.

Wicker, A., McGrath, J., & Armstrong, G. Organization size and behavior setting capacity as determinants of member participation. *Behavioral Science*, 1972, *17*, 499-513.

Winsborough, H. The social consequences of high population density. *Law and Contemporary Problems*, 1965, *30*, 120-126.

Wirth, L. Urbanism as a way of life. *American Journal of Sociology*, 1938, *44*, 1-24.

Zajonc, R. B. A note on group judgments and group size. *Human Relations*, 1962, *15*, 177-180.

Zimbardo, P. G. The human choice: Individuation, reason and order or deindividuation, impulse and chaos. In D. Levine (Ed.), *Nebraska Symposium on Motivation*. Lincoln, Neb.: University of Nebraska Press, 1969.

9
Human Spatial Behavior:
The Arousal Model

Gary W. Evans
University of California, Irvine

The study of human spatial behavior has only recently begun to adopt a theoretically based orientation (cf. Evans & Stokols, 1976). One model of human spatial behavior that some researchers have suggested is the arousal construct. The basic aim of this chapter is to examine the hypothesis that crowding and personal-space violations increase arousal beyond optimal levels and thus are stressful. The chapter is organized into four sections: (1) stress and the arousal model; (2) supporting evidence from spatial research; (3) problems with the arousal model; and (4) potential applications of the model and future research priorities.

STRESS AND THE AROUSAL MODEL

Human research on stress is an extremely complex, controversial area. Several trends that emerge from this area of research are important to this discussion. First, the complex array of different stressors' effects on human task performance has led some researchers to consider arousal as an underlying dimension of stress. Research has indicated, for example, generally opposite effects of sleep versus noise on more complex task performance. In these complex tasks, subjects have to deal with high signal input, unpredictable inputs, or more than one task at a time (usually dual-task situations with a primary and a secondary task) (Broadbent, 1971; Kahneman, 1973; Keele, 1973). Arousal can be defined as a continuum from sleep to high excitement and wakefulness (Berlyne, 1960.[1] On a

---

[1]Reductions in both stimulation (sensory deprivation) and sleep deprivation can paradoxically lead to heightened arousal under certain circumstances. Broadbent (1963) has discussed these findings and suggested that in moderately stimulating tasks the sleep-deprived subject or understimulated subject is in fact underaroused. The subject, however, is aware of this maladaptive state (vis à vis the task) and depending on his motivation may try to compensate by increasing muscle tone, exerting greater effort to pay attention, etc., and thus show increased physiological arousal.

physiological level, arousal has been viewed as a nonspecific facilitation of the cortex by the ascending reticular formation (Hebb, 1972; Malmo, 1959). Considerable data indicate that persons perform optimally on a variety of tasks at medium levels of arousal (Broadbent, 1971; Hebb, 1972; Kahneman, 1973). The fact that little or no effects of stressors are apparent on simple tasks but that decrements do occur in more-complex task situations has been explained by the Yerkes-Dodson law, which suggests that the inverted U-shaped arousal function (performance plotted over arousal level) shifts toward lower arousal under more complex tasks (see Fig. 1). Although the effects of underarousal can readily be explained, various discussions have since ensued as to why overarousal is debilitating and particularly so in more-complex task situations. The two prevailing hypotheses are that with greater arousal a narrowing of attention allocation occurs or that the complex task in itself heightens arousal. More detailed discussions of these matters can be found in Broadbent (1971), Hebb (1972), and Kahneman (1973).

A second important point about stress is that the human response to stressors is mediated by a host of psychological and situational variables (Appley & Trumbull, 1967; Glass & Singer, 1972; Lazarus, 1966; Moss, 1973). There is not a simple one-to-one relationship between the quantity of a stressor and the extent of organismic response.

Third, the theoretical analyses of Dubos (1965) and Selye (1956) plus the experimental work of Glass and Singer (1972) indicate that stress often has little or no immediate effects on simple human task performance. Rather, it is *after* the cessation of a short, acute stressor that persons exhibit performance decrements. Glass and Singer have found that these behavioral aftereffects are manifested, for example, by greater proofreading errors in subjects who had previously been stressed by uncontrollable noise in comparison to subjects who had not been stressed by the same noise conditions.

Thus, it appears that the adult human can adapt, at least for short periods to considerable stress and can perform adequately on tasks as long as those tasks are simple ones that do not push the information-processing capacities of the organism to its limits. If asked to perform more-complex tasks that demand greater capacity, then some immediate performance decrements are likely to occur under stressful conditions. Nevertheless, there appears to be some behavioral residue even in simple task situations when subjects have previously been stressed.

Finally, in addition to self-reports of discomfort or stress, persons under a state of high arousal will exhibit decreases in skin resistance (Bloch & Bonvallet, 1960; Montagu & Coles, 1966), increases in heart rate and blood pressure (Lazarus, 1966), and increased output of the adrenal cortex (Selye, 1956); if subjected to prolonged states of high arousal, subjects will eventually shift to a condition of severe exhaustion and eventual breakdown (Selye, 1956). The status of psychophysiological indicators of stress by means of heightened arousal is the most

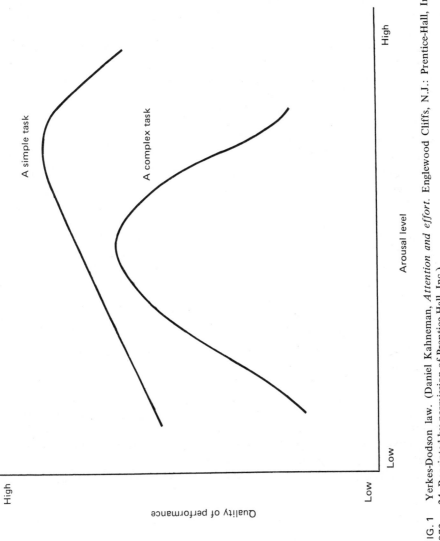

FIG. 1 Yerkes-Dodson law. (Daniel Kahneman, *Attention and effort.* Englewood Cliffs, N.J.: Prentice-Hall, Inc., 1973, p. 34. Reprinted by permission of Prentice-Hall, Inc.)

debated aspect of the arousal construct as it relates to the issue of the nonspecificity of arousal. I take up this issue—difficulties with the arousal model—in the third section of this chapter.

SPATIAL BEHAVIOR AND AROUSAL

This section presents evidence in support of the position that crowding and invasions of personal space cause states of overarousal that are experienced as stressful. Four lines of evidence include: task performance data, psychophysiological data, individual difference data, and observational data.

Task Performance Under Crowding and Spatial Invasion

Although there are several studies that reveal self-reported affective measures of stress or discomfort under conditions of personal-space invasion (Evans & Howard, 1973) and crowding (Stokols, 1976), fewer researchers have examined the effects of spatial impingement as a stressor on task performance. As one would expect in light of the Yerkes-Dodson law, most investigators have found little or no effects of crowding (Epstein & Karlin, 1975; Freedman, Klevansky, & Ehrlich, 1971; Sherrod, 1974; Aiello, Epstein, & Karlin, Note 1) or personal-space invasion (Evans & Howard, 1972; Barefoot & Kleck, Note 2) on simple-task performance. Consistent with the Yerkes-Dodson law, however, both Barefoot and Kleck (Note 2) and Evans and Howard (1972) found that invasions of personal space did cause decrements in more-complex task performance. Evans and Howard (1972), for example, found that when subjects had to process information at slow and moderate rates of input, no effects were evident from a reduction in interpersonal distance. On the other hand, at a high signal rate input, there was a marked drop in performance as interpersonal distance was reduced. Barefoot and Kleck (Note 2) found that an easy paired-associate learning task (one with strong within-pair association and weak between-pair association) was slightly facilitated by the close presence of another person. A more difficult task, in which stimulus association probability strengths were drastically reduced within pairs, was significantly affected by close interpersonal distance.

Until very recently, there has been little success in demonstrating the effects of crowding on human task performance of any kind. Two recent studies that have found complex-task decrements are discussed here. Several other studies that have attempted to examine the arousal hypothesis and found no support for complex-task decrements are addressed in the next section.

Aiello et al. (Note 1) have recently examined some of the consequences of high-density living in a field setting. Of interest, they found evidence of complex-task decrements over time in overcrowded dormitory rooms in comparison to less-crowded rooms. In a laboratory setting, Evans (1975) found that subjects in more-crowded conditions made more errors on a high signal rate task but not on a slow one. Furthermore, he found that in a dual-task situation, crowded subjects made significantly more errors than uncrowded controls on the secondary task, with no difference on the primary task. Finally, Goeckner, Greenough, and Mead (1973) have reported that laboratory rats raised under high-density conditions made more errors on complex learning tasks but that no differences were found between the experimental and control group on simple-task performance.

Several researchers have recently examined the occurrence of aftereffects following exposure to crowded conditions. Sherrod (1974), who reported no effects of crowding on immediate task performance, found that crowded subjects exhibited significant negative aftereffects. Previously crowded subjects in comparison to controls were significantly less tolerant of frustration as measured by the Glass and Singer (1972) impossible puzzle-tracing task. A poststressor measure of proofreading accuracy was not significantly affected by the crowding manipulation. Sherrod also found that the psychological construct of perceived control over a stressor significantly interacted with the stressful aftereffects of the crowding experience. Those subjects who perceived that they could remove themselves from the crowded setting experienced less severe aftereffects than those who were not given perceived control over the crowding experience. Evans (1975) has also found significant poststressor aftereffects from a crowded setting.

Psychophysiological Evidence for Heightened Arousal

There are data consistent with the hypothesis that under conditions of personal-space invasion or crowding, persons exhibit psychophysiological indexes of heightened arousal. McBride, King, and James (1965) found a decrease in skin resistance for male subjects at close interpersonal distances especially when the male subjects were interacting with a female invader. Evans and Howard (1972) have also found a decrease in skin resistance as a function of reducing interpersonal distance. Seguin (1967) reported increases in respiratory rate when subjects were closely approached by another person.

Epstein and colleagues (Aiello, Epstein, & Karlin, 1975; Epstein & Aiello, Note 3) explicitly examined the arousal hypothesis of crowding by monitoring the skin conductance (conductance is the reciprocal of resistance) of crowded and uncrowded subjects under laboratory conditions. They found that arousal significantly increased over time for crowded subjects but not for uncrowded subjects.

Heshka and Pylypuk (Note 4) and Aiello et al. (Note 1) have both examined cortisol levels in field situations of high density. Heshka and Pylypuk compared the cortisol levels of students who spent most of a day in a crowded, downtown shopping area to a control group who spent the same amount of time on a quiet, uncrowded campus. They reported significantly elevated cortisol levels in crowded males but no similar changes for crowded females or the control groups. It is important to note here that these two environments differed on several dimensions besides population density. In their study of crowded and uncrowded dormitory residents, Aiello et al. also attempted to measure cortisol levels but met with little success, although the cortisol levels of crowded subjects showed a nonsignificant increase whereas those of the uncrowded subjects indicated a decrease over time. They attributed their nonsignificant findings to large individual differences and a very small, reduced sample subset that had to be employed because of the cost of cortisol analyses.

D'Atri (1975) has recently reported some moderate, positive correlation between the density of living quarters in a prison setting and high blood pressures for prison inmates. Unfortunately, unlike the Aiello et al. (Note 1) and Epstein and Aiello (Note 3) studies, where room type was controlled, D'Atri's comparisons are confounded in that single cells (low-density condition) are contrasted with dormitory cells (high-density condition). In a more controlled study, Evans (1975) found that both blood pressure and heart rate were significantly elevated by a short-term exposure to crowded laboratory conditions.

Recently, Knowles and his associates have investigated the effects of personal-space invasion on micturation. Research has indicated that increased arousal delays the onset of micturation and decreases its duration. Subjects took significantly longer to begin urination and also had significnatly shorter periods of urination when a confederate stood immediately adjacent to a subject, as opposed to a confederate standing one urinal away or being absent from the lavatory, (Middlemist, Knowles, & Matter, 1976).

Finally, considerable research (Thiessen, 1964) suggests that under more-dense conditions, rodent populations suffer increased mortality following amphetamine ingestion. These findings are consistent with the arousal model, because amphetamine is a central nervous stimulant and thus increases arousal. The combined heightened arousal of the drug plus high density may serve to push the organism over the optimal range of arousal.

Individual Differences In Reactions To
Spatial Limitations

A third line of evidence in support of the arousal model of human spatial behavior derives from some individual difference data in the spatial literature. Personal-space investigators have found that extroverts allow an experimenter to approach them more closely than do introverts (Evans & Howard, 1973). Research also suggests that extroverts are chronically less aroused than introverts (Broadbent, 1971; Kahneman, 1973). Given that a moderate level of arousal is optimal, it seems consistent with the arousal hypothesis that the introvert could withstand less intrusion. In a somewhat analogous fashion, several lines of crowding research have found that less-dominant animals fare much worse under conditions of high density (Calhoun, 1962; Christian, 1961; Thiessen,

1961). Welch (Note 5) has demonstrated that less-dominant animals tend to be chronically more aroused than more dominant members of the same groups. These arguments are not to suggest that different arousal levels are necessarily the principal causes of these individual differences in response to crowding or personal-space invasion. Rather, I am suggesting only that these individual differences are consonant with the proposed arousal mechanism. Admittedly, there is undoubtedly a host of more complex factors operating that are also relevant to the individual's reactions to a potentially stressful situation.

Finally, the differences among autistic, brain-damaged, and normal children in their reactions to high-density exposure (Hutt & Vaizey, 1966) are consistent with the arousal model (see Chapter 3 for more detail on this study). Chronically overaroused, autistic children exhibited significnatly more extreme withdrawal behaviors under high-density conditions. Chronically underaroused, brain-damaged children, however, indicated essentially the opposite reaction. They engaged in greater social and physical contact, especially of an aggressive nature, under the same high-density conditions. Although the position that autistic children suffer from chronic overarousal is not without controversy (Hutt & Hutt, 1970), the evidence in support of this position is relevant to our examination of arousal and spatial behavior.

Observational Data

A common diagnostic indicator of autism in children is their marked avoidance of eye contact (Hutt & Hutt, 1970), which is consistent with the hyperarousal model of the autistic child, because eye contact has been shown to elevate arousal (Coss, 1970; Nichols & Champness, 1971). Hutt and Ounsted (1970) argued that autists prevent eye contact for the precise purpose of avoiding increments in their already overaroused state. A second indicator of autism is an unusually large amount of stereotypic behavior. Stereotypic behavior usually occurs in the form of repetitive object play or automanipulative activity. Research indicates that these behaviors are highly correlated with increases in arousal and seem to function as arousal-reducing mechanisms (Hutt & Hutt, 1970). Researchers in normal populations have also relied on the frequency or duration of stereotypic behaviors as indicators of behavioral tension (Altman & Taylor, 1973). The argument that gaze avoidance and increased stereotypic behavior act as arousal-reducing mechanisms is consistent with considerable ethological work reviewed by Chance (1962). Animals in agonistic encounters, for example, typically exhibit high frequencies of what Chance called "cut-off" acts that typically include the avoidance of eye contact and increases in stereotypic behaviors.

Thus, we would predict in accordance with the arousal model of spatial behavior that individuals in conditions of crowding or personal-space invasion should exhibit reduced eye contact and increased stereotypic behavior. Data generally indicate that invasions of personal space are more stressful with eye contact than when eye contact is not maintained. Argyle and Dean (1965) found that the amount of eye contact varied inversely with interpersonal distance. Although this finding and correlates of it have been replicated, the difficulty in determining when eye contact is made has led some researchers to question Argyle's conclusions (Evans & Howard, 1973). In a clever experiment, Efran and Cheyne (1974) observed the nonverbal behavior of persons who had to pass in between two people casually conversing in a hallway. They recorded the frequency and duration with which the eyes were partially closed and the head and gaze directed downward. In comparison to controls who had to pass through an empty hall or around (as opposed to between) a conversing pair, those subjects who intruded exhibited significantly greater partial eye closure and downward head and gaze behavior.

Some crowding research has examined gaze behavior as well. Kutner (1974) found moderate support for his hypothesis that visual exposure was a particularly salient dimension of the crowding experience. Groups of subjects under high-density conditions either faced one another (visual exposure condition) or sat back to back (no visual exposure condition). Subjects in the visual-exposure condition generally reacted to the crowded environment more negatively. There was greater body-protection behavior, greater feelings of exposure, more under-estimation of interpersonal distance, and generally more perceived nervousness in the face-to-face condition. On the other hand, these subjects also reported greater interpersonal attraction and no differences in perceived anxiety. Ross, Layton, Erickson, and Schopler (1973) reported a substantial drop in facial regard for males under more-crowded conditions, whereas for females the trend reversed.

Epstein and Karlin (1975) have suggested that the utilization of tasks in crowding research may provide subjects with sufficient distractions such that they can more easily ignore the close presence of others in the setting. As anyone who has ever ridden a crowded subway knows, a rather simple way to avoid eye contact and at least partially ignore those around is to stare intently at the various advertisements that line the train. The use of graphics as deliberate distractors in potentially high anxiety- or arousal-producing settings has been advocated by Coss (1973) as one means of reducing arousal. Coss suggested, for example, that art placed within a client's immediate line of vision would provide the client with an acceptable means of eye-target displacement when conversing with the office occupant. Worchel and Teddlie (Note 6) manipulated the presence of pictures in conditions of high and low density with close or far seating arrangements and found supportive evidence for the use of distractors in reducing stress. The presence of pictures reduced feelings of perceived crowding, confinement, and tension at the close interpersonal distance.

Some recent work has also begun to look at stereotypic behaviors under crowded and spatial-invasion conditions. Evans (1975), for example, has found moderate increases in the frequency of stereotypic behaviors under crowded conditions. During an unstructured free-time period, subjects who were crowded exhibited significantly greater object play and slightly more automanipulative behaviors than did uncrowded control subjects. Coss, Jacobs, and Allerton (Note 7) have also found that when a person's immediate space was invaded by a stranger, there was a moderate increase in stereotyped motor activity.

In summary, there are several lines of evidence in support of the hypothesis that crowding and invasions of personal space are stressors that are mediated by high arousal. First, research has indicated slight facilitation or no effects of spatial impingement on simple-task performance but decrements on complex tasks under the same conditions. These data are in accordance with the Yerkes-Dodson law which relates arousal level to task performance (see Fig. 1). Consistent with the general adaptation syndrome and work with other stressors, several researchers have also found negative aftereffects from crowding experiences. Second, there is considerable psychophysiological data indicating heightened arousal under conditions of crowding and personal-space intrusion. Third, some of the individual differences found in individuals' reactions to spatial limitations seems to be consistent with the proposed arousal mechanism. Finally, observations of behavioral tension and gaze behavior are in accord with this model.

PROBLEMS WITH THE AROUSAL MODEL

Criticisms of the Arousal Construct Itself

The hypothesis that crowding and personal-space invasions increase arousal suggest several immediate problems. First, the arousal construct itself has met with criticism. Arousal was originally viewed as a unitary dimension that implied that different dependent measures of arousal should correlate highly (Malmo, 1959). Lacey (1967) has focused his criticisms of arousal theory on unitary aspects of the construct, drawing on three lines of evidence:

1. There is evidence of the disassociation of somatic and behavioral arousal as indicated by examples of psychophysiological indexes of low arousal state and behavioral indexes of normal arousal level.

2. Several studies have found directional fractionation wherein one autonomic measure might indicate high arousal whereas another simultaneously indicates low arousal.

3. Instances of situational stereotypes have been reported in which different patterns of somatic response were found in different situations.

Since the early formulations, modifications of arousal theory have incorporated the directional fractionalization findings into a more limited arousal model. One such limitation that has recently received some detailed physiological support (Pribram & McGuinness, 1975) is that arousal cannot be identified overall with sympathetic dominance but contains various subtypes (Broadbent, 1971; Kahneman, 1973).

Cohen (1978) has proposed an alternative explanation of the effects of environmental stressors on human performance. He suggests that overarousal does not cause stress but rather that overarousal may be symptomatic of an information-overload state. According to Cohen's theory, stressors place some load on the information-processing system. Given the limited information-processing capacity of the individual, the load demands of a stressor plus the load demands of a task(s) will at a certain point exceed information-processing capacity and be experienced as an overload state. The differential effects of stressors on simple and complex tasks can be explained without invoking the Yerkes-Dodson law by making the reasonable argument that complex tasks place more load demands on the information-processing system than do simple tasks. The net result of this is that capacity will be exceeded more easily in the presence of the stressor plus the higher load-demand complex task.

An additional weakness in arousal theory is the lack of a straightforward explanation of aftereffects from exposure to a stressor. Cohen's overload theory can perhaps explain such aftereffects in that following overload, the system may: (1) not be able to process information accurately because it is still overloaded; or (2) the overload situation creates a state of fatigue from which it takes some time to recover.

In any case, the more traditional arousal model clearly has important limitations as a theoretical construct. The reasonable alternative proposed by Cohen (in press) needs to be tested and differentiated further from the arousal model. It is difficult at this stage of inquiry to make predictions that would distinguish the overload model from the arousal model.

Absence of Task Decrements Under Spatial Restriction

A second major objection to the arousal model of spatial behavior comes from work wherein little or no task decrements are claimed for both simple and complex tasks under crowded conditions. Freedman et al. (1971) varied spatial density and found no significant effects on simple- or complex-task performance and based on this finding suggested that crowding did not heighten arousal.

A close examination of this study reveals at least two critical flaws that may not allow Freedman et al. to draw satisfactory conclusions about the possible effects of crowding on arousal level. First, no manipulation check was performed to determine what subjects' perceived levels of crowding were. Given the important distinction between high density and crowding that Stokols (1972) has enunciated, this might have been an important omission on Freedman's part. Second, the complex tasks used by Freedman et al. consisted of two versions of the Guilford creative-uses test and forming words from a group of 10 letters. It is my contention that these two complex tasks are not complex in terms of the information-processing demands placed upon the subject. It is the latter criterion that is the critical dimension in assessing the effects of arousal level on varying levels of task difficulty. In informational terms, task complexity is typically incremented by increasing the rate of signal input, having a highly unpredictable signal, or by requiring attention to competing signals. The so-called "complex" tasks used by Freedman are not complex, because no pressure is put on total capacity either in terms of the spatial allocation of processing or in terms of time allocation (for the terms of the present definition of complexity, see the Appendix of this chapter). Considerable research in the human performance literature (Broadbent, 1971; Kahneman, 1973; Keele, 1973) suggests that human beings have a limited information-processing capacity. In order for decrements in immediate task performance to occur under stress, the organism must experience some overload such that the system's capacity to respond to the task is exceeded by the demands on attention. It is important to understand that in order to demonstrate immediate effects of an environmental stressor on human task performance, one must overload the information-processing system. Thus, as one might expect, examination of the human performance and stress literature reveals that, typically, only complex tasks such as those discussed previously or others of high information levels seem sufficiently sensitive to assess the immediate effects of moderate, nonchronic stressors on human task performance (Broadbent, 1971; Cohen, 1978; Glass & Singer, 1972; Kahneman, 1973). As Cohen (1978) has argued, this may occur because heavy requirements are placed on processing capacity through a combination of complex-task demands and the introduction of environmental stressors.

Similar criticisms apply to Epstein and Karlin's (1975) study in which the complex task employed was also a version of the Guilford creative-uses test, which is probably not a complex task in terms of information-processing demands. Unlike Freedman, however, Epstein and Karlin did employ a manipulation check on perceived crowding. Also unlike Freedman, Epstein and Karlin have reported increases in skin conductance, whereas Freedman did not employ any psychophysiological measures of arousal. Furthermore, of some importance, Epstein and Karlin's task measures were taken after the exposure to crowding. The foregoing argument suggests, however, that in order to show the differential effects of a stressor on simple- and complex-task performance, one must *concurrently* tax the system with the respective tasks. Thus, the use of simple and complex tasks *after* the cessation of the stressor may not be relevant to the Yerkes-Dodson law. Put another way, the Yerkes-Dodson law states a relationship between arousal level and simultaneous performance on tasks of varying complexity. Simple- and complex-task performance after the cessation of the stressor may not be indicators of differential arousal. It is the combination of the stressor's effects on attentional capacity plus the demands of the complex task on information processing that creates the overload situation (Cohen, 1978), resulting in immediate complex-task decrements. Exposure to a stressor alone or a stressor in combination with simple-task demands may lead to eventual states of exhaustion (Selye, 1956), which perhaps are manifested by behavioral aftereffects (Glass & Singer, 1972). But it is not clear that these stressor residues are an overload state that should interact with task complexity in the manner predicted by the Yerkes-Dodson law.

Sherrod (1974) has also reported no effects of crowding in simple- or complex-task performance. Again, however, the complex task used was problematic. Sherrod employed a written version of the Stroop task in which subjects were asked to write down the first letter of the ink color in which words were written. These words were the names of contrasting colors (for the word "blue" written in red ink, the correct response is "r"). Optimal performance on the Stroop task demands that the person focus on the relevant cue (ink color) and ignore competing cues (especially the word name). Research indicates that increases in arousal tend to facilitate Stroop performance (Houston, 1969; Houston & Jones, 1967; Tecce & Happ, 1964). These data are consistent with the suggestion (see p. 284) that task decrements during overarousal are caused by a narrowing or focusing of attention. In the complex tasks outlined previously, attention focusing is likely to be a hindrance to optimal performance (e.g., increased errors on the secondary task in the dual-task situation). One can appreciate that such focusing might facilitate Stroop performance when one is trying to ignore the competing cue of the color name. In fact, Sherrod found a slight, nonsignificant improvement in Stroop performance in crowding with the perceived-control condition.

Although there are some consistent findings of negative behavioral aftereffects of crowding (discussed previously), two exceptions should be noted. First, as mentioned earlier, although Sherrod (1974) did report a significant decrease in the number of attempted impossible figures following a crowding experience, he found no negative effects on a poststressor proofreading measure. Saegert, Mackintosh, and West (1975) employed a Stroop task as an aftereffect measure in field conditions of high and low density and found mixed results. Whereas females performed predictably poorer on the poststressor measure, males from the previous high-density experience did better on the aftereffect task. One possible explanation offered by the authors was that the better performance on the Stroop by the males was related to their increased aggressiveness. Partial support for this explanation was indicated by a moderately positive correlation between aggressiveness and Stroop performance. A measure of elation level did not correlate with task performance, however. The sex-difference finding is hard to explain, in part because it runs counter to the more typical finding that females react less negatively to crowded conditions. In any case, it remains problematic for an arousal explanation.

Absence of Psychophysiological Evidence for
Arousal Under Spatial-Invasion Conditions

Finally, at least two studies have found no significant increases in psychophysiological indexes with invasions of personal space. Dabbs (1971) reported no changes in palmar sweat indexes in close versus far encounters. In part this may have been due to the fact that no baseline measures were taken. This is important so that individual differences in sweat gland activity can be taken into account. Furthermore, a ceiling effect may have been operating, because an examination of Dabb's data indicates that extremely high levels of activity were encountered initially in all conditions. Efran and Cheyne (1974), who observed individual's reactions as they intruded between conversing people, also found that these instrusions had no effect on heart rate. Their data, however, also exhibited very high initial levels.

Summarizing, several difficulties exist with the proposed arousal explanation of crowding and personal space:

1. The construct of arousal itself has come under criticism. A more limited arousal mechanism seems to fit the data better, with an important need to examine subtypes of arousal remaining.

2. Some task-performance data were discussed that may be inconsistent with the model. In particular, findings of no effects on complex tasks were discussed. It was argued that perhaps these tasks were not complex in terms of the important dimension of information-processing capacity demand. Some aftereffect data, however, were more problematic.

3. At least two studies have not found predicted psychophysiological indexes of heightened arousal under conditions of personal-space invasion.

Nevertheless, although the arousal model is certainly not without some problems, it does seem to help organize data from several different research programs into a coherent pattern. Perhaps both its greatest strength and weakness at once lie in the precise, almost mechanistic nature of the model. The arousal construct provides rather specific predictions, many of which have been supported as discussed herein. At the same time, the specific, quasi-physiological level of analysis and prediction that the model affords lacks a certain psychological relativism. Little allowance is made for important psychological processes of individual, interpersonal, and group interaction. How attribution or reactance theory might relate to the arousal model, for example, is not readily discernible.

APPLICATIONS AND FUTURE RESEARCH

The work of Berlyne (1960, 1971) and Fiske and Maddi (1961) and recent analyses by Wohlwill (1974) suggest that persons generally seek out and prefer moderate levels of stimulation in their environments. It has been suggested that the similarly shaped, inverted U-shaped function relating preference to complexity levels is related to arousal theory. High complexity or high stimulation acts to increase organismic arousal level, whereas a lack of diversity or low-stimulus environments reduce organismic arousal level. Mehrabian and Russell (1974) have shown that persons who are high-arousal seekers prefer environments that are more arousing with the converse true as well. If the optimal arousal principle is accurate, one would expect that persons at low-arousal levels would tend to be high-arousal seekers in part out of attempts to bring their arousal levels up to the more optimal, moderate level. The converse would follow as well.

Therefore, if it is correct that crowding or personal-space invasions increase arousal level, then persons under such conditions should prefer less-arousing environments. Environments in which spatial impingements are likely to occur should be designed to minimize their arousing properties (for a more detailed discussion of arousal reduction through design, see Zimring, Evans, & Zube, Note 8). Furthermore, in light of the Yerkes-Dodson law, the importance of reducing arousal becomes critical when complex-task performance is required.

Several areas of future research warrant consideration. First, the concept of environmental stress is clearly a complex problem that involves issues of attention allocation, temporal dimensions (chronic-acute; immediate-aftereffect), and important mediating psychological variables such as perceived control. These issues need to be more thoroughly examined. For example, do invasions of personal space create aftereffects? To date, the dimension of perceived control has more or less randomly varied in crowding research. What would the already amassed data look like if perceived control were more systematically controlled?

Wohlwill (1974) has cogently argued that an important variable in a person's reaction to environmental cues is the individual's adaptation level to previous exposures to those cues. Our past experience and more long-term adaptations and adjustments to environmental stressors are important individual difference factors that beg further research.

Finally, Patterson (1976) has recently proposed an arousal model of interpersonal intimacy behaviors (e.g., interpersonal distance, eye contact, conversation topic, etc.) that bears importantly on the model proposed here. Given a dyadic, interaction context, a change in one individual's intimacy behavior is said to cause an arousal shift in the other person. This arousal shift can be labeled positively or negatively, resulting in reciprocal or compensatory responses, respectively.

Patterson's model provides an important complement to the model I am proposing in at least two ways. First, the proposed model has focused predominantly on task-oriented settings, whereas Patterson's model focuses on more interpersonal, social contexts. It is clear that the complex interactions of the social settings and salient information-processing demands on the organism have not been adequately explored either empirically or conceptually. For example, what would occur in a spatial invasion among friends during a complex-task demand as opposed to the same spatial infringement by a stranger during the same task? One can generate his or her own extensions, which are too numerous to explicate here.

Second, Patterson calls attention to an important, quasi-orthogonal dimension of the arousal construct by discussing the cognitive labeling process of arousal, which is said to occur during high arousal. Perhaps the less-holistic, more-specified arousal subtypes suggested by critics of the arousal construct can be explained as particular cognitive identifications of a more general, undifferentiated arousal state. Such labeling could be a result of the immediate environmental context and/or the individual's learning history.

In summary, this chapter has presented an arousal model of crowding and personal-space behavior that suggests that when physical space is reduced beyond certain levels, individuals experience heightened arousal, which may lead to stress.

APPENDIX

Complexity is defined here in terms of information theory. It is suggested that task complexity varies directly with the amount of information in a task. Information can be defined as a mathematical function of the average probability of occurrence of a given set of events.

Let $X = (x_1, x_2, ..., x_i, ..., x_n)$, where X is a set of possible events, x_i. Further, let $P(X)$ equal the probability that each member of the set X will occur. Thus $P(X) = [p(x_1), p(x_2), ..., p(x_i), ..., p(x_n)]$ such that for each i, $p(x_i)$ equals the probability that x_i will occur.

An important principle of information theory is that the more probable an event x_i, the less information it contains. Let $I(x_i)$ equal the amount of information contained by x_i. Note that $I(x_i)$ is theoretically a real number that may be calculated. This principle of relating an event's probability and information content can be expressed in the following form:

$$I(x_i) < I(x_k) \quad \text{if and only if} \quad p(x_i) > p(x_k). \tag{1}$$

The following equation can be shown to preserve this relationship:

$$I(x_i) = \log 1/p(x_i) \tag{2}$$
$$= -\log p(x_i).$$

which is the common expression of the amount of information contained in an event.

Another important construct in information theory is uncertainty. Uncertainty is defined as the average information associated with an event. Uncertainty is expressed as follows:

$$H(x_i) = -\Sigma_{i=1}^{n} \, p\,(x_i) \log p\,(x_i). \tag{3}$$

Thus the uncertainty or average information associated with an event, (x_i) is equal to the weighted average of the information involved in an individual alternative event.

Where $p\,(x_i)$ is equal for all values of x_i, Eq. (3) reduces to Eq. (2). It can readily be seen from this that the amount of uncertainty is reduced when the $p\,(x_i)$ are all the same.

A final tenet of information theory that is important here is that space and time are treated equivalently because events that occur are simply treated as sequences whether in space or time. This means that the information an individual receives can be incremented by having a greater number of alternative events to deal with at any one time or by having the same number of alternative events to deal with in a shorter period of time.

The foregoing discussion draws heavily from Attneave (1959) and Coombs, Dawes, and Tversky (1970). See these references for more detail on information theory.

The continuum from simple- to complex-task performance can be represented in informational terms. Examples of complex tasks cited in this chapter include ones in which the person had to deal with two or more competing signals, a highly unpredictable signal, or rapidly occurring events. Each of these complex-task examples would increase the information level. Alternatives one and three increase the number of events (x_i) that must be attended to for a given time period, whereas alternative two would decrease the probability of the occurrence of (x_i). It can easily be demonstrated that either of these changes when substituted into Eq. (3) would increase the value of $H(x_i)$.

A further issue remains. Although it can be demonstrated readily that complex tasks of the type discussed previously have greater amounts of information than less complex tasks employed by other proxemic researchers, it has not been shown that the more complex tasks are indeed "complex" whereas others are "simple" in terms of the Yerkes-Dodson law.

This inference can only be made indirectly vis a vis the arousal construct by way of a retrospective examination of the human performance and arousal literature (Broadbent, 1971; Cohen, 1978; Malmo, 1959; Kahneman, 1973). Task data used to derive and test the Yerkes-Dodson law nearly all fall neatly into this informational dichotomy. Complex tasks were almost entirely of one of the three alternatives mentioned previously, whereas nearly all simple tasks clearly were of lower information levels. Thus if one were to construct a simple-complex task dichotomy on the basis of information theory and set complex equal to or greater than the minimum information level in the three complex-task alternatives discussed previously, practically all complex-task examples used to test the Yerkes-Dodson law would fall above this amount in information quantity. Conversely, all simple tasks would fall below this amount.

An issue remains in determining what the exact value of "complex" in information level is. Because $H(x_i)$ also depends on several other situational and organismic variables, this quanitity will shift around for given persons in given task situations. An example of a situational variable is the redundancy of the events in the task. The individual's familiarity with the task context is an example of an organismic variable.

ACKNOWLEDGMENTS

I thank Shel Cohen, Steve Kaplan, Eric Knowles, Miles Patterson, Kathy Pezdek, and Dan Stokols for their help in the preparation of this chapter.

REFERENCE NOTES

1. Aiello, J., Epstein, Y., & Karlin, R. *Field experimental research on human crowding.* Paper presented at the meeting of the Western Psychological Association, Sacramento, California, April 1975.
2. Barefoot, J., & Kleck, R. *The effects of race and physical proximity of a co-actor on the social facilitation of dominant responses.* Unpublished manuscript, Carleton University, 1970.
3. Epstein, Y., & Aiello, J. *Effects of crowding on electrodermal activity.* Paper presented at the meeting of the American Psychological Association, New Orleans, August 1974.
4. Heshka, S., & Pylypuk, A. *Human crowding and adrenocortical activity.* Paper presented at the meeting of the Canadian Psychological Association, Quebec, June 1975.
5. Welch, B. Psychophysiological response to the mean level of environmental stimulation. *Symposium on medical aspects of stress in the military climate.* Walter Reed Army Institute of Research, 1964.
6. Worchel, S., & Teddlie, C. *Factors affecting the experience of crowding: A two-factor theory.* Unpublished manuscript, University of Virginia, 1975.
7. Coss, R. G., Jacobs, L. S., & Allerton, M. W. *Changes of stereotypical and non-stereotypical motor activity during intrusions of personal space by unfamiliar people.* Paper presented at the Human Ethology Meeting, University of North Carolina, Chapel Hill, May 1975.
8. Zimring, C., Evans, G. W., & Zube, E. *Space and design: The proxemic interface.* Paper presented at the meeting of the Environmental Design Research Association, Lawrence, Kansas, April 1975.

REFERENCES

Aiello, J., Epstein, Y., & Karlin, R. Effects of crowding on electrodermal activity. *Sociological Symposium*, 1975, *14*, 43-58.
Altman, I., & Taylor, D. *Social penetration.* New York: Holt, Rinehart & Winston, 1973.

Appley, M., & Trumbull, R. *Psychological stress.* NewYork: Appelton-Century-Crofts, 1967.

Argyle, M., & Dean, J. Eye contact, distance and affiliation. *Sociometry,* 1965, *38,* 289-304.

Attneave, F. *Applications of information theory to psychology.* New York: Holt, Rinehart & Winston, 1959.

Berlyne, D. E. *Conflict, curiosity and arousal.* New York: McGraw-Hill, 1960.

Berlyne, D. E. *Aesthetics and psychobiology.* New York: Appleton-Century-Crofts, 1971.

Bloch, V., & Bonvallet, M. The production of electrodermal responses from the facilitating reticular system. *Journal de Physiologie,* 1960, *52,* 25-26.

Broadbent, D. Possibilities and difficulties with the concept of arousal. In D. Buckner & J. McGrath (Eds.), *Vigilance: A symposium.* New York: McGraw-Hill, 1963.

Broadbent, D. *Decision and stress.* New York: Academic Press, 1971.

Calhoun, J. Population density and social pathology. *Scientific American,* 1962, *206,* 139-148.

Chance, M. R. A. An interpretation of some agonistic postures: The role of "cut off" acts and postures. *Symposium Zoological Society of London,* 1962, *8,* 71-89.

Christian, J. Phenonema associated with population density. *Proceedings of the National Academy of Science,* 1961, *47,* 428-449.

Cohen, S. Environmental load and the allocation of attention. In A. Baum, J. Singer, & S. Valins (Eds.), *Advances in environmental psychology* (Vol. 1). Hillsdale, N.J.: Lawrence Erlbaum Associates, 1978.

Coombs, C. H., Dawes, R. M., & Tversky, A. *Mathematical psychology.* Englewood Cliffs, N.J.: Prentice-Hall, 1970.

Coss, R. Perceptual aspects of eye-spot patterns and their relevance to gaze behavior. In S. Hutt & C. Hutt (Eds.), *Behavior studies in psychiatry.* London: Pergammon, 1970.

Coss, R. The cut off hypothesis: Its relevance to the design of public places. *Man-Environment Systems,* 1973, *3,* 417-440.

Dabbs, J. M. Physical closeness and negative feelings. *Psychonomic Science,* 1971, *23,* 141-143.

D'Atri, D. A. Psychophysiological responses to crowding. *Environment and Behavior,* 1975, *7,* 237-252.

Dubos, R. *Man adapting.* New Haven, Conn.: Yale University Press, 1965.

Efran, M. G., & Cheyne, J. A. Affective concomitants of the invasion of shared space: Behavioral, physiological, and verbal indicators. *Journal of Personality and Social Psychology,* 1974, *29,* 219-226.

Epstein, Y., & Karlin, R. Effects of acute experimental crowding. *Journal of Applied Social Psychology,* 1975, *5,* 34-53.

Evans, G. W. *Behavioral and physiological consequences of crowding in humans.* Unpublished doctoral dissertation, University of Massachusetts, Amherst, 1975.

Evans, G. W., & Howard, R. B. A methodological investigation of personal space. In W. J. Mitchell (Ed.), *Environmental design: Research and practice.* Los Angeles: The University of California Press, 1972.

Evans, G. W., & Howard, R. B. Personal space. *Psychological Bulletin,* 1973, *80,* 334-344.

Evans, G. W., & Stokols, D. (Eds.) Theoretical and empirical issues with regards to privacy, territoriality, personal space, and crowding. *Environment and Behavior,* 1976, *8,* 3-6.

Fiske, D. W., Maddi, S. R. (Eds.) *Functions of varied experience.* Homewood, Ill.: Dorsey, 1961.

Freedman, J., Klevansky, S., & Ehrlich, P. The effect of crowding on human task performance. *Journal of Applied Social Psychology,* 1971, *1,* 7-25.

Glass, D., & Singer, J. *Urban stress.* New York: Academic Press, 1972.

Goeckner, D. F., Greenough, W. T., & Mead, W. R. Deficits in learning tasks following chronic overcrowding in rats. *Journal of Personality and Social Psychology,* 1973, *28,* 256-261.

Hebb, D. O. *Textbook of psychology* (3rd ed.). Philadelphia: W. B. Saunders, 1972.

Houston, B. K. Noise, task difficulty, and Stroop color word performance. *Journal of Experimental Psychology,* 1969, *82,* 403-404.

Houston, B. K., & Jones, T. M. Distraction and Stroop color word performance. *Journal of Experimental Psychology,* 1967, *74,* 54-56.

Hutt, C., & Hutt, S. Stereotypes and their relation to arousal: A study of autistic children. In S. Hutt & C. Hutt (Eds.), *Behavior studies in psychiatry.* London: Pergammon, 1970.

Hutt, C., & Ounsted, C. Gaze aversion and its significance in childhood autism. In S. Hutt & C. Hutt (Eds.) *Behavior studies in psychiatry.* London: Pergammon, 1970.

Hutt, C. & Vaizey, M. Differential effects of group density on social behavior. *Nature,* 1966, *209,* 1371.

Kahneman, D. *Attention and effort.* Englewood Cliffs, N.J.: Prentice Hall, 1973.

Keele, S. *Attention and human performance.* Pacific Palisades, Calif.: Goodyear, 1973.

Kutner, D. H., Jr. Overcrowding: Human responses to density and visual exposure. *Human Relations,* 1973, *26,* 31-50.

Lacey, J. I. Somatic response patterning and stress: Some revisions of activation theory. In W. H. Appley & R. Trumbull (Eds.), *Psychological stress.* New York: Appleton-Century-Crofts 1967.

Lazarus, R. *Psychological stress and the coping process.* New York: McGraw-Hill, 1966.

Malmo, R. B. Activation: A neuro-psychological dimension. *Psychological Review,* 1959, *66,* 367-386.

McBride, G., King, M., & James, J. Social proximity effects on galvanic skin responses of adult humans. *Journal of Psychology,* 1965, *61,* 153-157.

Mehrabian, A., & Russell, J. *An approach to environmental psychology.* Cambridge, Mass.: M. I. T. Press, 1974.

Middlemist, R. D., Knowles, E. S., & Matter, C. F. Personal space invasions in the lavatory: Suggestive evidence for arousal. *Journal of Personality and Social Psychology,* 1976, *33,* 541-546.

Montagu, J. D., & Coles, E. M. Mechanism and measurement of the galvanic skin response. *Psychological Bulletin,* 1966, *65,* 261-279.

Moss, G. E. *Illness, immunity, and social interaction.* New York: Wiley, 1973.

Nichols, K., & Champness, B. Eye gaze and galvanic skin response. *Journal of Experimental Social Psychology,* 1971, *7,* 623-626.

Patterson, M L. An arousal model of interpersonal intimacy. *Psychological Review,* 1976, *83,* 235-245.

Pribram, K. H., & McGuiness, D. Arousal, activation, and effort in the control of attention. *Psychological Review,* 1975, *82,* 116-149.

Ross, M., Layton, B., Erickson, B., & Schopler, J. Affect, facial regard and reactions to crowding. *Journal of Personality and Social Psychology,* 1973, *28,* 69-76.

Saegert, S., Mackintosh, E., & West, S. Two studies of crowding in urban public spaces. *Environment and Behavior,* 1975, *7,* 159-184.

Seguin, C. The individual space. *International Journal of Neuropsychiatry,* 1967, *3,* 108-117.

Selye, H. *The stress of life.* New York: McGraw-Hill, 1956.

Sherrod, D. Crowding, perceived control and behavioral aftereffects. *Journal of Applied Social Psychology,* 1974, *4,* 171-186.

Stokols, D. On the distinction between density and crowding. *Psychological Review,* 1972, *79,* 275-277.

Stokols, D. The experience of crowding in primary and secondary environments. *Environment and Behavior,* 1976, *8,* 49-81.

Tecce, J. J., & Happ, S. J. Effects of shock-arousal on a card-sorting test of color-word interference. *Perceptual and Motor Skills,* 1964, *19,* 905-906.

Thiessen, D., & Rodgers, D. Population density and endocrine function. *Psychological Bulletin,* 1961, *58,* 441-451.

Thiessen, D. D. Amphetamine toxicity, population density, and behavior: A review. *Psychological Bulletin,* 1964, *62,* 401-410.

Wohlwill, J. F. Human adaptation to levels of environmental stimulation. *Human Ecology,* 1974, *2,* 1-27.

10

Toward An Ecological Model of Density Effects in Dormitory Settings

Reuben M. Baron

David R. Mandel

University of Connecticut

In this chapter we seek to demonstrate that our understanding of the impact of density on dormitory living will be significantly advanced if an ecological perspective is adopted. From this perspective, density-induced changes in everyday dormitory behaviors, such as patterns of room use for studying and socializing, are assumed to reflect the operation of ecosystems characterized by reciprocal adjustments of the physical and social environment.

At the conceptual level our ecological analysis is heavily indebted to the work of James J. Gibson (1961, 1966, 1977) for providing a functional unit of analysis that we shall attempt to demonstrate provides a common frame of reference for elucidating the ecological properties of the physical and social environment. Thus one major purpose of the present analysis is to attempt to establish a plausible relationship between certain aspects of Gibson's (1977) treatment of the process involved in regulating imminence of contact with the physical environment and aspects of social ecological theories of privacy that attempt to specify how various nonverbal mechanisms control contact with the social environment (cf. Altman, 1975; Proshansky, Ittelson, & Rivlin, 1970).

Another purpose of this chapter is to use an ecological analysis to establish the similarities and differences between dormitory studies that have focused on variations in number of persons living in equally sized dormitory rooms (Baron, Mandel, Adams, & Griffen, 1976; Aiello, Epstein, and Karlin, Note 1) and dormitory studies that have focused on architecturally created differences in the concentrations of persons encountered in secondary environments (Baum & Valins, 1977; Valins & Baum, 1973; Bickman, Teger, Gabriele, McLaughlin, Berger, & Sunday, 1973). It will also be argued that an ecological analysis of density will provide a nonarbitrary basis for architectural programming, that is, the optimal matching of physical and behavior systems (Studer & Shea, 1966). Our ecological analysis will provide strong justification for designing separate spaces for activities that do and do not require a high degree of privacy.

Before turning to a specification of the major properties of our ecological framework, it is important to clarify why we have selected dormitories as a setting in which to explore the meaning of crowding. First, a dormitory setting, although not representative of many residential settings, is a true behavior setting in that it provides a temporarily and spatially bounded context for a variety of important behaviors. Second, a major constituent of dormitory living that is representative of all residential settings is the importance of privacy for the effective performance of certain activities. Furthermore, since (1) privacy is an important component of many analyses of crowding (Altman, 1975), and (2) Gibson (1977) has recently described certain aspects of the types of optical information necessary for the perception of privacy, a natural linkage between aspects of Gibson's ecological analysis and an understanding of density effects appears clearly possible.

Moreover, dormitory studies offer a sufficiently wide but manageable range of variations in properties of persons (e.g., sex and class differences, variations in group size, etc.) and in the properties of internal and external architectural structures (e.g., number of floors, organization of rooms) that an opportunity exists to explore the complex nature of the interactions that occur between social and physical environments. At the methodological level the dormitory setting offers an excellent "halfway house," which avoids to a large degree the artificiality and transitory nature of laboratory crowding studies, as well as the naturalistic confoundings of race, poverty, and social class endemic to urban studies of residential crowding.

AFFORDANCE AS A PRIMARY UNIT OF ECOLOGICAL ANALYSIS

A central aspect of Gibson's (1961, 1966, 1977) theory of direct perception is the assumption that the functional properties of objects can be directly perceived by a mobile organism as he encounters them from many perspectives. Such multiple perspectives may occur because of changes in the position of the observer and/or the object. It is assumed that the greater the range of perspectives possible, the easier it is to become attuned to the invariant functional properties of the object (Turvey, 1976). The functional properties of objects as they are encountered in the course of an organism's active exploration of the environment are referred to by Gibson as "affordances." For Gibson (1977), "The affordances of the environment are what it *offers* an animal, what it *provides* or *furnishes* for good or evil [p. 68]." For example, if an object is rigid, level, flat, and extended, and if this surface is raised approximately at the height of the knee of the human biped, Gibson proposes it affords *sitting on*. The affordance property of *sitting on* is assumed to be directly perceived on the basis of sensory information (primarily, although not exclusively optical), if the organsim is able to observe through its own movement and/or externally induce movements of the object (e.g., the blowing of wind), the invariant structural and functional properties of the object. For example, one may learn about the sitableness of an object by observing its shape, shifting one's weight to feel the level of support it offers one's body, and so on.

These affordance properties represent a specific combination of the properties of an object's substance and its surfaces taken with reference to a particular equivalence class of organisms. Thus affordance properties are transactional in the sense that they can be specified only in the context of encounters with specific referent organisms. For example, according to Gibson (1977), "knee-high for a child is not the same as knee-high for an adult so that sit-on-ability must be taken with reference to a sub-class of the human species [p. 68]." It is this transactional nature of affordances that allows Gibson to say that they are neither objective in the sense that they exist without reference to some particular organism nor subjective in the sense that they exist only in a Lewinian type of phenomenal environment. Thus affordances are facts of the environment whose actualization in perception depends on specific encounters by specific organisms. It is this aspect of the affordance concept that for us makes it superior to other units of functional analysis that tend to be either purely subjective (e.g., assessments of goals) or purely objective (e.g., measurement of levels of radiant light present).

Another aspect of Gibson's affordance analysis that makes it particularly useful for the present purposes is his integration of affordance with broader ecological concepts such as habitat and niche. For Gibson (1977) a niche is a set of affordances that are utilized. It is a setting of environmental features suitable for a given equivalence class of animals. Moreover, Gibson distinguishes a niche from a habitat. A niche describes *how* an animal lives, its way of life in a given setting; a habitat is *where* it lives, its geographic location. This more molar use of the affordance concept allows Gibson to treat systematically such vague concepts as "life style." This aspect of an affordance analysis has proved to be particularly useful in our attempts to conceptualize the ecological significance of dormitory data such as the differential time spent in a dorm room by males and females.

Social Affordances

Another aspect of Gibson's affordance analysis that makes it especially helpful in the present context is that Gibson has proposed that an affordance analysis can be applied to both the physical and social environment. He suggests (1977) that we pay close attention to the optical information that specifies the reciprocal nature of social interaction. Gibson explicitly proposes that there are affordances for socially significant interactions such as sexual encounters, aggressive encounters, nurturant encounters, play, cooperation, and so forth. In effect, other persons afford the whole realm of socially significant interactions.

Since we propose to make extensive use of an affordance analysis of the social environment, we attempt to elaborate Gibson's proposals by citing lines of research that can be reinterpreted as supporting the concept of social affordances. First, it is proposed that at the level of individual person perception the most profitable place to look for optical information relevant to the functional properties of entities is in the area of nonverbal behavior. For example, perceptions about hostile intent are based on: (1) postural cues (Mehrabian, 1969); (2) eye contact (Ellsworth & Carlsmith, 1968; Exline, 1971); (3) facial expressions (Ekman, 1971); (4) proxemics (Sommer, 1969); and (5) paralinguistic cues (Mehrabian, 1971). Moreover, consistent with Gibson's (1966) view of the senses operating as interacting systems, Argyle and Dean (1965) have proposed that "closeness" must be defined in terms of compensating adjustments of eye contact, topics of conversion, physical distance, and the like. It is also of interest that nonverbal information has been estimated as accounting for a substantial portion of the communication variance in social interaction (Mehrabian, 1971).

Going beyond Gibson's essentially individualistic analysis of social affordances, it appears that at the level of dyadic and small group interaction, hostile intent involves establishing that territories should not be invaded. Relevant physical information involves the use of markers, barriers, and spatial buffer zones (e.g., no man's lands between the turf of gangs or warring countries). Furthermore, to anticipate our subsequent analysis, there appear to be differential implications for crowding effects of treating social entities as individuals as opposed to members of groups. For example, the work of Baum and Valins (1977) suggests that architectural arrangements that encourage aggregates (collections of strangers) as opposed to groups (individuals sharing common goals) may be an important mediator of crowding effects. Finally, a crucial component of any analysis of groups involves the specification of role relationships. In this connection it is significant that role is a concept crucial to the Barker-Wicker theory of "manning (Barker, 1968; Wicker, 1973). Specifically, in undermanned settings occupants are assumed to play more roles than in overmanned settings.

The plausibility of our affordance analysis of the social environment receives independent support from some recent cross-cultural research by Eckman and Triandis. Ekman and his associates have (Ekman, Ellsworth, & Friessen, 1972) found that a wide range of emotional states can be accurately perceived by aborigines from Australia as well as more "westernized" persons from Japan and North and South America. Similarly, in a wide ranging review of pancultural data, Triandis (1976) finds that there are a finite number of categories, for example, dominance-submission, that describe all human social interactions. Furthermore, our emphasis on the importance of distinguishing between properties of groups and aggregates is directly supported by a recent study by Jorgenson and Dukes (1976), which finds that certain presumed consequences of crowding (e.g., deindividuated antisocial behavior) may occur only when increases in number of individuals occurs for aggregates as opposed to groups. Taken together, the above data appear highly consistent with the feasibility of a differentiated affordance analysis of the social environment.

It should be noted at the outset, however, that in arguing for the utility of affordance as the basis for an ecological analysis of dormitory density effects, we do not necessarily commit ourselves one way or another as to the validity of Gibson's specific theory of direct perception as elaborated in his Ecological Optics (see Gibson, 1961; Turvey, 1976; Neisser, in press). Irrespective of its place in a general theory of perception, the affordance concept provides a meta-language potentially applicable to a number of problem areas in psychology (cf. Shaw & Wilson, 1976). Therefore, our major interest is in treating affordance as a model for sharpening our understanding of the meaning of a functional analysis of ecologically relevant human behavior. Specifically, an affordance analysis provides a way of conceptualizing how various properties of the physical and social environment may be analyzed for their adaptive significance. For example, we will demonstrate how density might modify the affordance properties of dormitory living arrangements.

In sum, we have chosen affordance as our preferred unit of ecological analysis because (1) it is transactional in nature, thereby avoiding false dichotomies between objective and subjective units of analysis; (2) it allows us to treat both molecular and molar aspects of human environmental encounters with a common frame of reference; (3) it allows us to treat functional properties of the physical and social environment with a common frame of reference.

Further appreciation for our reasons for choosing an affordance focus for our ecological analysis can be obtained by a brief comparison of the ecological perspectives of Gibson and Barker.

Barker and Gibson: A Brief Comparison

At the outset it should be observed that there are many important similarities between these two pioneers of the use of the ecological perspective for the analysis of psychological phenomena. First, Gibson's use of the concept of niche appears to be functionally equivalent to Barker's (cf. Barker, 1968) use of the concept of behavior setting. Moreover, Gibson's affordance utilization interpretation of a niche maps perfectly into Wicker's (1973) extension of Barker's theory of over- and undermanned behavior settings. We propose that Wicker's distinction between performers and nonperformers of roles in a setting may be used to concretize Gibson's affordance analysis of a niche. Specifically, it may be assumed that a given behavior setting is more likely to function as a niche for performers than for nonperformers; that is, they are more likely actually to *utilize* a wide range of affordance structures. For example, a school is more likely to be a niche for the active participants in sports, academic life, and the like.

There are, however, some basic differences in the ecological perspectives of Barker and Gibson. In our opinion Gibson offers the broader orientation because he stresses the continuities between the functional properties of the social environment and the physical environment as well as the continuities between the man-made and the natural environment. Barker, on the other hand, although offering us a more differentiated and less individualistic view of the social environment vis-à-vis the use of the role concept, has no comparable unit of analysis to offer us in understanding the physical environment or the reciprocal interactions that occur between the physical and social environment.

DORMITORY DENSITY EFFECTS IN ECOLOGICAL PERSPECTIVE

Our analysis of density effects will proceed as a series of successive approximations involving various levels of ecological analysis. Beginning with a brief review of definitions of density that focus on dormitory living, we describe ecological concepts that relate patterns of occupancy and interaction to density. By evaluating current descriptions of crowding, we argue for the efficacy of ecological analysis, concluding with an examination of the strengths and weaknesses of such a view. This discussion is based on two different kinds of adaptive problems posed by dormitory living arrangements. By applying an ecological analysis to high-density dormitory conditions, we note those factors that influence congruence or compatibility of physical and social environments as well as those determining the ways in which individuals meet their needs in these settings. It is important to establish these relationships, and we hope that our analysis will yield insight into the kinds of impacts dormitory settings have for group functioning and individual adjustment.

DENSITY AND TYPES OF SETTINGS

We begin our analysis by reviewing the kinds of problems created by high density in various settings. Bickman, et al. (1973) provides us with a logical starting point, describing density variations in residential settings. By reviewing their distinctions between within-unit and within-structure density, it is clear that current studies of dormitory density fall into one or the other, differing along several ecological dimensions.

Within-Unit Density

Within-unity density refers to problems generated by the number and kind of interactions that take place with the same individuals over time in the same spatially circumscribed area. In this context, a crucial issue concerns the effects of variations in numbers of persons per room. Two recent studies (Baron et al., 1976; Aiello et al., Note 1) address the effects of adding a third person to double occupancy dormitory rooms, holding constant architectural features such as the size of the room and building. In terms of Barker and Wicker's manning theory, one might view these studies as dealing with the problem of whether norm regulation for deviation will shift from correction to expulsion when there is a change from situations where everyone is a performer (a two-person room) to situations where coalitions might create nonperformers (a three-person room). In the broadest ecological terms these studies might be said to examine the ways in which density affects the utilization of affordances (i.e., the likelihood that the room will function as a niche for all residents).

Within-Structure Density

Here the major basis for density variations involves persons per structure (e.g., persons per dormitory and units per structure, floors per dormitory). Density in this context focuses on the number of *different* people one can encounter in a given structure—for example, the number of different individuals a resident is likely to encounter in shared facilities such as laundry rooms, hallways, elevators, lobbies, and bathrooms.

Examples of such investigations are Bickman et al.'s (1973) investigation of the impact on prosocial behavior of the number of individuals in a given structure, where number is manipulated by comparing low (e.g., four floors) and high (e.g., 25 floors) dormitory buildings. This type of density manipulation offers a highly representative and powerful treatment analogous to recent investigations of urban structures such as Newman's (1972) exploration of low- and high-rise urban projects. However, the type of density variation utilized by Bickman et al. (1973) creates a number of serious sources of potential confounding, for example, the number of persons on a given floor vary in low- and high-rise dorms as do the opportunities for ingress and egress (i.e., high-rise buildings require elevators). The work of Baum and Valins (1977) represents an example of a less confounded investigation of within-structure density effects. These investigators control on number of floors and unit space, while focusing on the manipulation of social density occasioned by variations in interior architecture involving a corridor versus a suite arrangement of rooms. In a more recent replication described in Baum and Valins (1977) dormitories with long versus short corridors are compared. We may anticipate our subsequent more detailed analysis of Baum and Valins' work by noting that in these studies architecture mediates whether persons other than one's immediate roommates will more likely be seen as having aggregate as opposed to shared group properties.

A First-Order Ecological Analysis

Altman (1975) distinguishes among primary, secondary, and public territories, whereas Stokols differentiates between primary and secondary environments. Primary territories are clearly identifiable in terms of personal control and are occupied on a permanent basis. Secondary territories are semiprivate and less clearly delimited in terms of ownership (e.g., a dormitory study lounge). Public territories are temporary and are generally open settings without identifiable personal patterns of ownership (e.g., parks, playgrounds, streets). Examples of primary environments for Stokols are homes, classrooms, and work settings. In all these there is a continuity of social encounter and a personalized level of social interaction. Secondary environments such as parks and public transportation are seen as being less consequential for social relationships in that they involve discontinuous, noninvolving, and anonymous social interactions. Comparing Altman's and Stokols' approaches, it would appear that whereas Altman's emphasis is on level of personal control, Stokols is more concerned with level and continuity of social interaction. Moreover, Altman's categories are more fine grain. For example, it would appear that Altman's primary and secondary territories can both be included under Stokols' primary environment whereas Altman's public territory corresponds to Stokols' secondary environment.

These categories are useful in distinguishing between within-structure and within-dwelling-unit density studies. Baron et al. (1976) and Aiello et al. (Note 1) have dealt with primary territories and primary environments. Bickman et al. (1973) and Baum and Valins (1977) have looked at secondary territories but primary environments. Dormitory corridors, although transitory for residents a great deal of the time, also represent a setting in which personal identification and semiprivate social interaction take place. It can also be argued that Bickman et al.'s high-rise dorms contain areas that begin to approximate public territories (e.g., elevators), whereas all the density variations in Baum and Valins occur in the context of low-rise structures. Indeed, the blatant lack of prosocial behavior in Bickman et al. (1973) can be seen as reflecting the fact that areas of a high rise dorm take on characteristics of public territories or in Newman's (1972) terms, nondefensible space. Finally, it is proposed that in public settings other persons have properties of aggregates, and encounters are depersonalized and unpredictable.

Altman's categories are particularly useful for distinguishing between corridor and suite dorms. Corridor dorms have both specific primary territories (the room) and a less clearly defined secondary territory, the corridor. Because the corridor is ill-defined as to ownership and use, the nature of social interaction is unpredictable in terms of both timing and hedonic value. In contrast, the lounge area of a suite, although at times occupied by five to six people, is usually more personalized and perceived as a personalized group territory. It is thus of interest that whereas corridor residents in Baum and Valins (1977) indicate they would prefer to interact with both friends and neighbors on their floor in their bedroom as opposed to the common hallway area, suite residents are closely split when considering interaction with a friend but manifest a strong tendency to prefer the suite lounge for neighbor interactions. It may be supposed that the bedroom is preferred for social interaction for corridor residents because it offers more possibility for social control than the hallway. In support of this interpretation, Baum and Valins (1977) find that corridor residents spend more time in the bedroom than do suite residents.

One way to summarize this analysis in terms of its relevance for understanding density effects is to speculate that whereas in Baum and Valins (1977) density variations transform secondary territories such as dorm lounges and bathrooms in the direction of public territories, in Aiello et al. (Note 1) and Baron et al. (1976), density increases move a primary territory toward a secondary territory. *In both situations, density interferes with the activities and opportunities for control over social contact normally afforded by a given set of living arrangements.* Baum and Valins (1977) discuss this type of problem in terms of a general lack of congruence between behavior and environments, or a lack of fit between intended and actual functions of environmental arrangements. For example, they suggest that dormitory hallways were intended for use as passageways to provide access to other floors, units, and so on. Under certain conditions of architecturally generated crowding, however, such hallways are forced to serve as lounge areas, that is, spaces for social interaction. In suites, on the other hand, because a separate lounge exists, the hallway is used for its intended purpose—transit between suites and other buildings.

AN AFFORDANCE ANALYSIS OF
THE DORMITORY SETTING

Although correct as far as it goes, this level of ecological analysis does not provide a basic understanding of what determines the "intended" properties of the behavior settings of a dorm. Moreover, it fails to provide an ecologically oriented analysis of the disruptive impact of density on the functional properties of the social environment. The issues of adaptive compatibility described above can be reformulated in ecological terms as involving two basic sets of problems: (1) the ability perceptually to recognize or extract appropriate affordance structures and; (2) the ability to utilize affordance structures. It is proposed that density effects can be understood in terms of the impact of density on the recognition and utilization of affordances. First, we turn to the problem of specifying the most important types of affordances that are likely to be implicated in dormitory living.

Gibson (1977) discusses the affordances of concealment by proposing that "concealment is afforded by a cluttered environment of opaque surfaces [p. 74]." What we call privacy in the design of housing is the providing of opaque enclosures. Although Gibson is referring to privacy in terms of visual perception, such an analysis has meaning for our present purposes. Internal architecture must be programmed to afford concealment from auditory, visual, and social intrusions (Studer & Stea, 1966). Similarly, from a process perspective there are important links between Gibson's (1977) recent analysis of the regulation of imminence of contact with physical environment in terms of mechanisms that create "margins of safety" as a means of reducing the likelihood of uncontrollable contacts and the social ecological theories of privacy that have been proposed by Proshansky et al. (1970) and Altman (1975). Thus it is of considerable importance that Proshansky et al.'s (1970) treatment of territory as a buffer to maintain privacy is functionally equivalent to Gibson's stress on "margins of safety" (see also Altman's 1975 treatment of the role of nonverbal mechanisms in a boundary regulation model of privacy). Privacy appears to be a concept that (1) provides a bridge between physical and social ecology systems, and (2) fits readily into the explanatory systems underlying research in high-density dormitories.

The Affordance of Dormitory Living

Considering the different affordance structures in corridor and suite bedrooms, we should note that dormitory bedrooms generally afford four kinds of activity: sleeping, studying, socializing, and individual relaxing. Corridor bedrooms are likely to be less specialized than suite bedrooms since they must afford more general kinds of behavior. Suite bedrooms are specialized for sleeping and studying, whereas socializing and relaxing are primarily properties of the lounge area. Because exterior space does not afford what suite lounges do, corridor bedrooms must provide for a greater range of activity. Apparently, the spatial layout of suites more readily provides the kind of limited access that opaque enclosures afford. Studying is an activity that requires privacy, and in physical terms this translates to a requirement for opaque enclosures that provide concealment. In social ecological terms the requirement is one of personal control over access to a territory, a condition that when accompanied by a high level of occupancy meets the definitional criteria for a primary territory (Altman, 1975). The affordance structures underlying studying involve specifiable characteristics of the physical and social environment that regulate the imminence of contact.

A second example concerns socializing. According to research in the area of social attraction (Byrr., 1969; Newcomb, 1961) similarity of attitude and value is an important basis for attraction. Another basic precondition is physical and functional propinquity or proximity (Festinger, Schachter, & Back, 1950). The first criterion involves the necessity for controllable interaction based on more than a superficial level of knowledge of other people. The question of physical and functional proximity is largely a matter of the architectural layout of passages and rooms. It would seem that suites have an advantage over corridor rooms on both of these dimensions. Specifically, the suite lounge is likely to provide for more predictable, long-term social encounters for a circumscribed but adequately sized and representative group of other persons (e.g., six two-man rooms constitute the social group described in Baum & Valins, 1977).

In the hallways of corridor dorms, on the other hand, we have a wide range of potential interactants, but (1) their appearance is likely to be highly unpredictable, (2) encounters are likely to be highly rushed (e.g., on the way to the bathroom), and (3) encounters will be under less comfortable physical conditions (e.g., standing). Moreover, the physical layout of rooms arranged around a central lounge is likely to provide an area that affords both physical and functional proximity. Although one could carry out a more fine grain analysis of the physical and social affordance structures necessary for good socializing, the above analysis is sufficiently detailed to suggest that the suite provides a set of physical and social affordances that are more likely to support effective socializing than are corridor arrangements.

In support of this line of reasoning, Baum and Valins (1977) report that corridor residents appear to deal with these problems by withdrawing from socializing in the hall as much as possible. For example, they spend more time in their bedrooms than do suite residents and indicate that they most prefer interacting with friends in their bedrooms. Suite residents, on the other hand, both spend less time in their bedroom and are equally willing to interact with friends in the suite lounge as in their bedrooms.

Density and Disruptions in Affordances

Now that we have established some of the basic affordances necessary for studying and socializing in suite versus corridor settings, let us examine the possible impact of high density for each of these activities. First, let us consider the problem of the impact of within-dwelling-unit density on the studying. Two findings from Baron et al.'s (1976) study of dormitory crowding are helpful. First, the larger a person's perceived territory, the less his perceived crampedness. Second, the inclusion of doors and windows in a territorial map is associated with less perceived crampedness in tripled (three-occupant) rooms. These reactions are relevant to the two key dimensions of density: (1) the reduced distance between elements; and (2) the amount of pressure exerted against the outer edge of the container of the dense elements. Specifically, territory is a buffer against invasion of privacy (Altman, 1975; Proshansky et al., 1970), whereas doors and windows can be viewed as extending the perceived boundaries of the container space. It is also interesting that persons in triples (three-occupant rooms) spent less time in their rooms and perceived themselves as having less control over room activities, including studying. In a subsequent study (Mandel

& Baron, Note 2), it was found that location of one's desk near the door as opposed to the window was related to (1) more time studying in the room relative to studying in alternative settings, (2) perceptions of fewer people dropping in uninvited, (3) perceptions of more people fitting into the room, and (4) perceptions of the room as being less cramped. In terms of our earlier discussion, placement of the desk appears able to affect affordances relevant to "imminence of contact."

Niches and Sex Differences

The above findings suggest that studying in the room depends on being able to maintain a segment of the room as a primary territory. Specifically, what affords studying in a high-density setting is the configuration of social and physical features that define a primary territory (see Altman, 1975). In more molar terms, it may be argued that territoriality converts a room from being only a habitat to functioning both as a habitat and a niche.

The view of a room as a niche is tied to another important dimension—time spent in the room. There is growing evidence that there are important sex differences in time spent in a dorm room, with females spending more time there (Aiello et al., Note 1). Moreover, our own recent work suggests that females are more concerned with personalizing their rooms through the use of interior decoration (Aiello et al., Note 1; Mandel, Baron, & Fisher, Note 3). A dorm room may be more niche-like to females than to males.

To these data one may add the following findings: (1) Females are more susceptible to crowding stress than are males (Aiello et al., Note 1); (2) females spend more time in their dorm room relative to males (Aiello et al., Note 1; Mandel et al., Note 3). In terms of the greater susceptibility of females to crowding stress, we refer to a situation where three in a room is more likely to have negative psychological consequences for females than for males (Aiello et al., Note 1).

How might one translate these data in affordance terms? The general proposition we are entertaining is that high density is more disruptive of activities normally afforded by a room the more time one spends in that environment. In support of this line of reasoning are some data Aiello et al. (Note 1) have collected in their comparison of two- versus three-person dorm rooms, based on an index of perceived room resource availability (e.g., perceived deprivation of drawer space, space available in room, etc.). Based on this index, females in three-occupant rooms expressed the greatest feelings of deprivation. Time and commitment to a room appear to act as multipliers of the likelihood that high social density will prove to be disruptive of physical affordance structures. Moreover, there are additional data from Aiello et al. (Note 1) that suggest the possibility that the social affordance structure is also more disrupted by density for females than for males. Specifically, Aiello et al. (Note 1) report that whereas in doubles females self-disclose more than do males, the reverse is true with tripling (i.e., female self-disclosure goes down whereas male self-disclosure goes up).

These data may be interpreted as indicating that high density interferes more with the affordance structure for socializing for females than for males. For example, females may be more willing to reveal intimate personal information to one than to two other people. However, this may be true only for females who are in a situation where a high level of self-disclosure is at issue (e.g., persons who spend a great deal of time together in a small space). Where superficial self-disclosure is concerned, as with males, adding another person may serve to increase the level of self-disclosure by decreasing the likelihood of solitary activities.

Perceived Room Density

Rapoport (1975) differentiates between perception of group and room size as an environmental feature and the perception of crowding as a normative evaluation of the adequacy of a given space for carrying out certain activities. Although the above discussions have focused primarily on crowding effects, it appears that perceived density is also affected by the affordance properties of the environment. Thus, Mandel et al.'s (Note 3) finding that females perceived their room as being larger than did males with increasing floor height may be seen in physical affordance terms as an example of how light affects perceived spatial density. Specifically, it is proposed that females perceive their rooms as being larger because they spend more daylight hours in the room; that is, higher rooms receive more unobstructed daylight than rooms on lower floors. Moreover, height increases the likelihood that females will appreciate a favorable, spacious view. On the other hand, it is assumed that since males spend less daytime hours in the room, they are more likely to view the room in the context of exterior darkness and artificial light. Recent findings by Schiffenbauer (Note 4) and Mandel and Baron (Note 2) suggest that the presence of bright sunlight increases perceived room size. Given the poor artificial lighting of dorm rooms, good light is most likely to be available during the day. Finally, it may be argued that for males accessibility to the outside environment is more important than for females (who it may be recalled make greater efforts at room personalization). Given that dorm elevators typically malfunction, if one is oriented toward easy accessibility to the campus environment outside the dorm, the higher one's floor the less one's accessibility to the exterior environment. Thus, height appears to affect different affordance structures for males and females—that is, ease of access and exit for males and comfortableness of dorm room for females—suggesting that the dorm provides different niches for males and females.

COMPARISONS OF WITHIN-DWELLING-UNIT
AND WITHIN-STRUCTURE DENSITY

The potential impact of within-dwelling-unit density appears to be moderated by factors such as the amount of time spent in one's room and by one's ability to manipulate the semifixed features of the room environment to construct a territorial domain that allows one control over the access of others. The potential impact of within-structure density variables, on the other hand, appears to be mainly mediated by one's relationship to a larger social group.

Baum, Harpin, and Valins (1975) found that persons who were part of a social group on their floor reported less crowding than persons not integrated into larger social units. More recently, Baum and Valins (1977) reported that the size of the face-to-face group one must encounter directly affects crowding stress; potential contact with 19 other people produced less crowding stress than having to confront 35 other people. Similarly, Worchel and Teddlie (1976) found evidence that an encounter with seven other people in close quarters increased the likelihood that group processes tied to an emergence of a leader would evolve. Moreover, Baum et al. (1975) report that corridor residents who became members of social groups outside of their room are less susceptible to crowding stress.

In sum, it is proposed that the effects of density in structural units such as a dormitory floor or wing are more likely to be mediated by group process factors than are the effects of density in a dwelling unit. Partly this effect is simply a matter of group size; social interaction contexts for within-structure density involve higher numbers of people. A second difference is in predictability of encounter. Encounters are less predictable due to both larger group size and the fact that interactions occur in the secondary territory of hallways where personal control over access is impossible. In this regard it appears that physical barriers and markers control access in a dwelling unit (forming a personal territory), whereas the social group functions as a buffer for within-structure density effects. That is, interactions take place primarily among members of a group. These groups may also take over-parts of a secondary environment and turn it into a primary group territory by virtue of group use; for example, members may congregate at one end of the hall at certain hours.

What remains unclear, however, are the implications of this type of solution for activities such as studying. Group involvement may remove the deleterious impact of unpredictable social encounters, but it may interfere with solitary activities such as studying. This possibility is suggested by the findings of Baron et al. (1976), recently replicated by Mandel and Baron (Note 2), that a high level of intense social interaction is inversely related to performance in academic activities. Although Baum and Valins (1977) do not present data on the relative amount of time spent on studying in the room for group integrated and nongroup integrated dorm residents, it is expected that persons who join groups will reduce the amount of time spent in the room for study.[1] If this line of reasoning is correct, it suggests an interesting moral: Informal solutions to the adjustive problems posed by density may induce an incompatibility in one set of activities (study) while rectifying an incompatibility in another (socializing). This outcome occurs because the physical and social environmental properties that afford effective socializing are typically incompatible with the physical and social environmental properties that afford studying.

DENSITY AND THE SPECIFICATION OF INVARIANTS

It has been proposed in general terms that density is likely to affect the affordance structures in dormitory living arrangements. We are now ready to examine this proposition in more formal terms deriving from Shaw's theory of event perception (Shaw, McIntyre, & Mace, 1974; Shaw & Wilson, 1976; Turvey, 1976). It is proposed that changes in density may be treated as an event that helps to reveal the invariant structural and functional properties of a dormitory living arrangement. Specifically, by observing what types of activities are disrupted and what types of activities remain essentially undisturbed, we can establish the essential affordance structure of entities such as a dormitory bedroom, hallway, and a suite-lounge. For example, high room density may be incompatible with studying in a bedroom but have less effect on studying in a hall study lounge where the spatial area is much greater and the necessity for reciprocal interaction is lower. It may be noted in this example that in order to understand the conditions that support studying we must consider features of both the physical and social environment. Distance between persons can compensate somewhat for group size if such distance is accompanied both by a large room size and by social conventions that support noninteraction (e.g., library rules against talking). In a dormitory room, density effects can be compensated for by placing furniture in areas to regulate contact with the social environment, for example, using a bookcase as a room divider or placing a desk in a location that controls access of visitors to the room (Mandel & Baron, Note 2).

In effect, density (1) reveals the types of activities that require privacy and (2) specifies the types of affordances of both the physical and social environment that support privacy. In terms of Gibson's (1977) concept of imminence of contact, what density does is specify which activities require relatively large margins of safety or wide gaps for encounters with the social environment. This type of formulation maps perfectly into Altman's (1975) proposal that personal space, territoriality, and various nonverbal gestures (e.g., kinesic and paralinguistic)

[1]It is, however, possible that group formation in this context may facilitate studying if a norm emerges for socializing to occur in the corridor rather than in one's room. That is, if socializing occurs in the corridor, more privacy is afforded in the bedroom for studying, sleeping, and the like.

serve as mechanisms to preserve an optimal level of contact with the social environment.

DENSITY AND THE SPECIFICATION OF INVARIANTS

Within-Dwelling Density

Taking this type of analysis one step further allows us to specify the structural and transformational invariants underlying the impact of within-dwelling-unit and within-structure density. It appears that within-dwelling-unit density threatens to penetrate aspects of the physical environment that provided a buffer or barrier to contact. As we move from a single person in a room to a dyad, territorial barriers replace the closed door as a mechanism to provide the necessary margin of safety. The privacy problem posed by within-structure density (e.g., Baum and Valins' corridor versus suite residents) may be viewed in terms of the differential implications for social interaction of encounters with groups as opposed to encounters with aggregates. In ecological terms the functional problem shifts from being able to maintain an adequate margin of safety (e.g., losing one's privacy because of groups demands) to unpredictability of encounter (as in the case of the aggregate-like social contacts of the corridor dorm resident). Adaptations to unpredictability have ranged from residents retreating behind their dorm room door to residents restricting their out-of-room encounters to members of their own group (Baum & Valins, 1977). In the case of changes in within-dwelling-unit density contact is primarily controlled by barrier behaviors, such as laying exclusive claim to aspects of the physical environment, whereas in the case of in-structure density, control is sought primarily in terms of modifying the affordance structures of the social environment by forming groups (a group affords more predictable contact than an aggregate).

In sum, whereas structures that protect spatial prerogatives are at the nexus of modes of coping at the level of within-room density, structures designed to produce control over temporal events are critical at the level of within-structure density. Specifically, the functional invariants for within-dwelling-unit density appear to involve affordances for physically avoiding closeness of contact. On the other hand, within-structure density appears to be controlled by affordances relevant to the *timing* of contact.

FUNCTIONAL AND STRUCTURAL INVARIANTS

Perceptions about functional invariants involve detecting the nature of the change that holds over a number of specific structures. For example, we might ask ourselves what the distal placement of bed and desk, a division of closet and drawer space, piling up of books, records, and so on to create a visual barrier have in common. The common element that ensures an adequate gap of encounter appears to involve restricting *intimacy of contact*. We may speak of an intimacy transformation as specifying the nature of change brought by increases in within-dwelling-unit density. A recent paper by Patterson (1976) provides compelling evidence concerning the stress reactions generated when intimacy transformations break down.

The intimacy transformation appears to involve structures that either preclude contact or allow contact only at a distance. Such structures allow the person to construct a room within a room that appears to be the functional equivalent of a closed door. These are structures that create barriers to both eye contact and haptic (i.e., touch) encounters. Sound screens in the form of earphones or playing the stereo at a level high enough to make normal verbal communication impossible, provide auditory barriers to contact. In the language of ecological optics, substances or entities which share relative impenetrability as an attribute provide the structural invariants which support a low level of intimacy of contact (Shaw & Wilson, 1976; Turvey, 1976).

In terms of our earlier analysis, these barriers to intimacy afford studying under high *within-room density*. One way to increase the likelihood that a dorm room will afford studying is to provide for a specialization of function so that alternative space will be available for activities such as socializing, which ordinarily would disrupt studying. The presence of a lounge in a suite arrangment of rooms is likely to increase the likelihood that the appropriate physical and social supporting conditions for studying will be available in one's dorm room. (There are also doors that insulate the rooms from the lounge.)

Ironically, the basic problem created by high *within-structure density* is an inability to engage in intimate contacts. Here we must remember that the target activity is not study but how to achieve high-quality socializing. The functional problems involve how to create a situation that in effect both slows down encounters and makes them more predictable. Although it appears that size per se creates problems for socializing, such problems are exacerbated when the physical setting itself is ill-suited to initimate contacts (Baum & Valins, 1977).

It has been noted that the crucial functional problem created by high in-structure density is how to regulate the timing of social contact so as to make it more predictable. It is proposed that this is largely accomplished by converting strangers into group members. Thus we seek invariants that transform aggregates into groups. Two group properties are critical in this context: (1) the conversion of individuals into role occupants and (2) the homogenization of individual interests, goals, and so on.

The above aspects of group membership appear to be critical functional invariants for groupness. In terms of structural invariants one can specify a hierarchy of factors. First, group formation in any setting becomes possible only if there is regularity of contact. Regularity of contact, in turn, is afforded by propinquity and by the presence of a finite number of people in a circumscribed setting. Given these basic structural preconditions for intimate group contact, manifest physical similarities in appearance involving salient factors such as race, mode of dress, and the like provide a further basis for the formation of groups. With increases in frequency and duration of contact, more subtle similarities in attitude, values, and so on can be detected. Finally, if the group grows beyond a certain size and seeks permanence, a differentiation of roles will emerge as a means of channeling communication and influence along predictable paths.

Once group formation reaches this stage, socializing is regulated by group norms and becomes largely restricted to group members. In this type of situation one essentially trades freedom of choice vis-à-vis anonymity for predictable, more permanent contacts. Such durable contacts, it may be noted, also allow a person to detect a range of basic invariants about the other people in the group. Such invariants as trait inferences supply further predictability to contacts with the social environment (Kelley, 1967).

OVERVIEW

It has been proposed that density be viewed as an intimacy transformation that affects imminence of contact with the social environment. In a setting with limited unit space and high regularity of contact with the same people, activities that require limited social contact (e.g., studying) are severely disrupted by increases in intimacy of contact. In this situation occupants appear to mobilize various aspects of the semifixed physical environment to create *physically demarcated islands of privacy*. Within-structure density creates an opposite set of problems; here we have irregular contacts with different people in a space that is not intimate in scale. In this situation the social environment is manipulated to compensate for architectural conditions that do not readily afford high-quality socializing. In this situation a "groupness" transformation applied to social aggregates creates conditions of moderately intimate, predictable social contact. Suite residents, on the other hand, are in a situation in which the "groupness" transformation is accomplished by architectural means. That is, a suite arrangement creates conditions of propinquity for a small number of people, thereby creating the basic conditions for moderately intimate, regular contacts.

At a conceptual level much remains to be done in elaborating the implications of an affordance analysis, both in terms of clarifying the nature of affordances and in terms of clarifying the meaning of density as an ecological phenomenon. There is, however, one aspect of the present analysis that highlights a basic problem in the affordance concept: the failure to specify what factors will determine when affordances will be utilized, assuming they are perceived. For example, two rooms might support the same activities, but rates of utilization of affordances might differ. One possible way to deal with this problem is to speculate about classes of variables or events that might generate an affordance utilization function. One such variable we have already spoken about is the ability to establish territorial control. Another direction is to introduce the concept of the ambience of the physical and social environment. At the level of the physical environment, aesthetic factors such as the perceived beauty or ugliness of the setting may affect its utilization (Maslow & Mintz, 1956; Mintz, 1956). At the level of social climate, factors such as whether there is an authoritarian or democratic social climate or whether there is high or low group cohesiveness, might be critical. Moreover, knowledge of an environment in terms of how it is cognitively structured may critically affect usage. For example, it would appear reasonable to expect persons with a differentiated cognitive map of an area to be better able to make use of its affordance properties. In this regard it may be noted that density results in impoverished cognitive maps (Saegert, 1973).

The above discussion highlights what might be a critical difference between the affordance structures of the built environment (and perhaps the social environment) as opposed to the affordances of the natural environment on which Gibson largely focuses. Specifically, the likelihood of utilization of affordances in the designed environment may be much more variable, perhaps because affordances of the designed environment are on the average lower in survival value than affordances in the natural environment [see Shaw et al.'s (1974) concept of the attensity of affordance values]. The most interesting problem for future research in an affordance framework might involve an attempt to specify the various classes of factors that moderate utilization of affordances in different settings. Such diverse factors as density, aesthetic ambience, and whether one is a performer or nonperformer in Wicker's (1973) sense, all appear to be promising.

Much also remains to be done before the present type of affordance analysis can be maximally useful at the level of architectural programming. A much more detailed elucidation of the physical and social basis of dormitory living must be made. The physical affordance structures of rooms, hallways, elevators, and so on need to be specified in relation to individual and group occupant characteristics. For example, the fact that Baron et al. (1976) obtained radically different factor structures for two- and three-person rooms may indicate that different affordance structures were detected, generated, or used as a function of variations in group size and/or unit space available. Just as shape may not be a fixed property of an object, so certain social-psychological properties such as cohesiveness, control, power, and the like may be event structures tied to various interactions of the physical and social environment. Encounters with the room under varying conditions of time, personalization, and light may create different programming requirements. Such encounters, in turn, may reflect interactions of occupant characteristics such as sex and architectural characteristics such as floor height and view from one's windows (Mandel et al., Note 3).

CONCLUDING COMMENT

A few years ago Altman (1973) commented on the qualitative differences in perspective between the environmental practitioner (e.g., architect) and the environmentally oriented behavior scientist. The practitioner, according to Altman, is typically interested in a specific setting whereas the behavioral scientist is concerned with general processes across settings. There has also been an almost total lack of communication among psychologists interested in social perception, environmental perception, and the mainstream work in the experimental perception of objects. Moreover, with the outstanding exception of Rapoport's (1975) paper on perceived density, there has been little contact between environmental psychologists interested in perception and those interested in crowding. We see Gibson's affordance concept as potentially providing a bridge that will bring these diverse orientations into active contact with one another.

REFERENCE NOTES

1. Aiello, J. R., Epstein, Y. M., & Karlin, R. A. *Field experimental research on human crowding.* Paper presented at the Eastern Psychological Association Meetings, New York, 1975.
2. Mandel, D. R., & Baron, R. M. *Environmental determinants of student study habits.* Paper presented at the Annual Convention of the American Psychological Association, Washington, D.C., September 1976.
3. Mandel, D. R., Baron, R. M., & Fisher, J. D. *Effects of visual spaciousness and complexity on environmental perception.* Paper presented at the Eastern Psychological Association, New York, April 1976.
4. Schiffenbauer, A. *The amelioration of crowding through design decisions.* Paper presented at EDRA 7, Vancouver, British Columbia, May 1976.

REFERENCES

Altman, I. Some perspectives on the study of man-environment phenomena. *Representative Research in Social Psychology,* 1973, *4,* 109-126.

Altman, I. *The environment and social behavior.* Monterey, Calif.: Brooks/Cole, 1975.

Argyle, M., & Dean, J. Eye contact, distance, and affiliation. *Sociometry,* 1965, *28,* 289-304.

Barker, R. G. *Ecological psychology.* Stanford, Calif.: Stanford University Press, 1968.

Baron, R. M., Mandel, D. R., Adams, C. A., & Griffen, L. M. Effects of social density in university residental environments. *Journal of Personality and Social Psychology,* 1976, *34,* 434-446.

Baum, A., Harpin, R. E., & Valins, S. The role of group phenomenon in the experience of crowding. *Environment and Behavior,* 1975, *7,* 183-197.

Baum, A., & Valins, S. *Architecture and social behavior: Psychological studies of social density.* Hillsdale, N.J.: Lawrence Erlbaum Associates, 1977.

Bickman, L., Teger, A., Gabriele, T., McLaughlin, C., Berger, M., & Sunaday, E. Dormitory density and helping behavior. *Environment and Behavior*, 1973, *5*, 465-490.

Byrne, D. Attitudes and attraction. In L. Berkowitz (Ed.), *Advances in experimental social psychology* (Vol. 4). New York: Academic Press, 1969.

Ekman, P. Universals and cultural differences in facial expression of emotion. In J. Cole (Ed.), *Nebraska Symposium on Motivation*. Lincoln, Neb.: University of Nebraska Press, 1971.

Ekman, P., Ellsworth, P. C., & Friesen, W. V. *The face and emotion: Guidelines for research and integration of findings*. New York: Pergamon Press, 1972.

Ellsworth, P. C., & Carlsmith, J. M. Effects of eye contact and verbal content on affective response to a dyadic interaction. *Journal of Personality and Social Psychology*, 1968, *10*, 15-20.

Exline, R. V. The glances of power and preference. In J. Cole (Ed.), *Nebraska Symposium on Motivation*. Lincoln, Neb.: University of Nebraska Press, 1971.

Festinger, L., Schachter, S., & Back, K. *Social pressures in informal groups: A study of human factors in housing*. Stanford, Calif.: Stanford University Press, 1950.

Gibson, J. J. Ecological optics. *Vision Research*, 1961, *1*, 253-262.

Gibson, J. J. *The senses considered as perceptual systems*. Boston: Houghton-Mifflin, 1966.

Gibson, J. J. Theory of affordances. In R. E. Shaw & J. Bransford (Eds.), *Perceiving, acting and knowing: Toward an ecological psychology*. Hillsdale, N.J.: Lawrence Erlbaum Associates, 1977.

Jorgenson, D. O., & Dukes, F. O. Deindividuation as a function of density and group membership. *Journal of Personality and Social Psychology*, 1976, *34*, 24-29.

Kelley, H. H. Attribution theory in social psychology. In D. Levine (Ed.), *Nebraska Symposium on Motivation*. Lincoln, Neb.: University of Nebraska Press, 1967.

Maslow, A. H., & Mintz, N. L. Effects of esthetic surroundings: Initial effects of three esthetic conditions upon perceiving "energy" and "well being" in faces. *Journal of Psychology*, 1956, *41*, 247-254.

Mehrabian, A. Significance of posture and position in the communication of attitude and status relationships. *Psychological Bulletin*, 1969, *71*, 359-272.

Mehrabian, A. *Silent messages*. Belmont, Calif.: Wadsworth, 1971.

Mintz, N. L. Effects of esthetic surroundings: II. Prolonged and repeated experience in a "beautiful" and an "ugly" room. *Journal of Psychology*, 1956, *41*, 459-466.

Neisser, U. Gibson's ecological optics: Consequences of a different stimulus description. *Journal of the Theory of Social Behavior*, in press.

Newcomb, T. M. *The acquaintance process*. New York: Holt, Rinehart & Winston, 1961.

Newman, O. *Defensible space*. New York: Macmillan, 1972.

Patterson, M. An arousal model of interpersonal intimacy. *Psychological Review*, 1976, *83*, 235-245.

Proshanksy, H. M., Ittelson, W. H., & Rivlin, L. G. Freedom of choice and behavior in a physical setting. In H. M. Proshansky, W. H. Ittelson, & L. G. Rivlin (Eds.), *Environmental psychology: Man and his physical setting*. New York: Holt, Rinehart & Winston, 1970.

Rapoport, A. Toward a redefinition of density. *Environment and Behavior*, 1975, *7*, 133-158.

Saegert, S. Crowding: Cognitive overload and behavioral constraint. In W. Prieser (Ed.), *Environmental design research* (Vol. II). Stroudsburg, Pa.: Dowden, Hutchinson, & Ross, 1973.

Shaw, R. B., & Wilson, B. Generative conceptual knowledge. In D. Klahr (Ed.), *Cognition and instruction*. Hillsdale, N.J.: Lawrence Erlbaum Associates, 1976.

Shaw, R. B., McIntyre, M., & Mace, W. The role of symmetry in event perception. In R. B. MacLeod & H. Pick, Jr. (Eds.), *Perception: Essays in honor of James J. Gibson.* Ithaca, N.Y.: Cornell University Press, 1974.

Sommer, R. *Personal space.* Englewood Cliffs, N.J.: Prentice-Hall, 1969.

Studer, R., & Stea, D. Architectural programming and human behavior. *Journal of Social Issues,* 1966, *22,* 127-136.

Triandis, H. C. *Interpersonal behavior.* Monterey, Calif.: Brooks/Cole, 1976.

Turvey, M. T. Perspectives in vision: Conception or perception. In M. Rawson & D. Duane (Eds.), *Reading, perception and language.* Baltimore, Md.: York Press, (1976).

Valins, S., & Baum, A. Residential group size, social interaction, and crowding. *Environment and Behavior,* 1973, *5,* 421-439.

Wicker, A. W. Undermanning theory and research: Implications for the study of psychological and behavioral effects of excess populations. *Representative Research in Social Psychology,* 1973, *4,* 185-206.

Worchel, S., & Teddlie, C. The experience of crowding: A two-factor theory. *Journal of Personality and Social Psychology,* 1976, *34,* 30-40.

PART III

DERIVATIONS AND APPLICATIONS
OF THEORETICAL SYSTEMS

11

The Experience of Crowding: An Attributional Analysis

Stephen Worchel
University of Virginia

Spurred by the gloomy results of early research on animals and by a skepticism about all that seems to be self-evident, social scientists have been flocking to investigate the effects of crowding on humans. However, to the surprise of some and the relief of many, much of this laboratory research has failed to find negative effects resulting from high population density. For example, Freedman, Klevansky, and Ehrlich (1971) found that high population density did not produce a decrement in the performance nor did it lead to greater intragroup hostility. Stokols, Rall, Pinner, and Schopler (1973) also found that density had no effect on group task performance. They did, however, find that males were somewhat more aggressive under high- as opposed to low-density conditions, whereas the reverse was true for females.

The inconsistencies between the crowding research on animals and that on humans and the surprising disagreement among the laboratory studies on human subjects have forced investigators to examine the concept of crowding carefully. The layman on the street knows that crowding is simply having "too many people in one place at the same time" and that the result is people feeling "uncomfortable and edgy." This definition, however, is neither as straightforward nor as simple as it appears. Questions such as how many people, how large a place, how close together must the people be, and for how long a time remain unanswered by this definition. Also unanswered is the question of why. What is it about too many people that causes feelings of discomfort and edginess? Why is it that people will feel crowded in some situations and not others even when the number of people and the space are the same in the two situations. It is to these questions that investigators have recently turned much of their attention, and it is to these questions that this chapter is devoted. The aim in this chapter is to present one view of the how and why of crowding and to offer some evidence in support of this view.

SPACE AND CROWDING

It is generally agreed that crowding involves some spatial component. There is, however, some question about the exact nature of this component. In the majority of cases, crowding has been manipulated by varying the amount of space available to subjects in the experimental setting (e.g., Freedman et al., 1971; Freedman, Levy, Buchanan, & Price, 1972; Stokols et al., 1973). The less space available to subjects, the more densely populated is the experimental setting. Investigators, however, have noticed that there are at least two ways in which space per person can be manipulated (e.g., Loo, 1972, 1973). This can be achieved either by keeping room size constant and varying the number of people in the room (social density) or by keeping the number of people constant and varying the room size (spatial density). Loo (1973) suggested that some of the discrepancies in the results of previous research could be due to different generic variations of density.

This distinction offered some solace, but it did not explain the multitude of discrepancies in the data on the effects of crowding nor did it offer an adequate explanation of why one type of density should lead to a certain behavior while the other type should lead to another. Thus, investigators searched elsewhere, and their attention focused on the relationship between the terms *density* and *crowding*. Stokols (1972) suggested that density and crowding were two distinct concepts and that they were not always related to each other. According to Stokols, density is a simple physical measure of the space available to an individual. Crowding, on the other hand, is a psychological state mediated by spatial, social, and personal factors.

The distinction between crowding and density has been generally endorsed by researchers. (e.g., Altman, 1975; Freedman, 1975; Lawrence, 1974). The growing consensus is that simple high density is not always experienced as crowding and that high density per se is not necessarily arousing nor will it lead to impaired performance.

Although this distinction is helpful, one can still ask: "What is crowding, and what causes people to experience crowding?" It is this question that has created some disagreement and divergent hypotheses. With the exception of Freedman and his colleagues (e.g., Freedman, 1975), most investigators agree that there is an arousal or stress component in crowding. Altman (1975) recently suggested that this stress is the result of a violation of the individual's privacy. The individual feels "crowded" when he or she cannot achieve the amount of privacy desired. The experience of crowding then leads to arousal and stress. One interesting point about Altman's view is that space per se is not a necessary variable for the individual to experience crowding. Altman focuses on social contact including verbal, paraverbal, nonverbal, and space variables. Stokols (Stokols, 1972; Stokols et al., 1973) suggests a similar mechanism. According to Stokols, the individual will experience stress and crowding when his or her activities or freedom are interfered with.

PERSONAL SPACE-ATTRIBUTION THEORY

These recent views of crowding offer some interesting possibilities, but two questions remain unanswered. First, what specific variable in the situation leads to the arousal and stress, and second, why is this stress experienced as crowding rather than frustration or some other emotion? Taking these two questions separately, we can begin by asking from where the arousal component of crowding comes? In agreement with Freedman (1975) and others, there is little theoretical or empirical evidence to suggest that simple high density is arousing. However, crowding, whether from the dictionary, layman, or experimental manipulation point of view, does have a spatial component, and there is a strong bias to view this spatial component as the inducer of stress.

Although manipulations of simple density or space available may not create arousal, there is a growing body of literature that suggests that the particular use of space may result in arousal in some cases. In his study of proxemics, Hall (1959, 1966) theorized that man is characterized by interaction distances or personal spaces. There are very definite distances at which an individual is comfortable when interacting with other individuals. The specific distance is determined by the type of interaction, the relationship that exists between the individuals, and other characteristics of the individuals themselves. For example, the appropriate interaction distance for friends is smaller than that for strangers, and the correct distance for discussing an intimate topic is less than that used when discussing a business matter (Hall, 1966). According to Hall, stress results when the appropriate distance is violated.

There have been numerous demonstrations that violations of personal space do create discomfort and arousal. Sommer and his colleagues (Felipe & Sommer, 1966; Sommer, 1969) found that such violations led to an avoidance of eye contact, shifting of body position, and often one individual would leave the scene in order to regain his space. McBride, King, and James (1965) and Middlemist, Knowles, and Matter (1976) have demonstrated that violations of personal space result in physiological arousal. Thus, although simple density may not be arousing, violations of personal space can result in stress.

Given this evidence, it would seem to be a fruitful strategy to wed personal space instead of density to crowding. As yet this marriage must be theoretical in nature because there are few data supporting its validity. In previous research, the two measures (density and interaction distance) have often been confounded —when room size is varied, interaction distance is also varied. There is one study that provides suggestive evidence that interaction distance and not density is the important spatial variable associated with arousal and crowding. Epstein and Karlin (1975) found that a person in the center of a group experienced more stress and crowding than a person at the fringes of the group. This occurred with density (space available) held constant. One difference between the two individuals is that the person in the center of the group is more likely to have his personal space violated than the individual at the fringe of the group.

It is therefore proposed that interaction distance rather than density is the spatial variable related to crowding and that it is the violation of personal space that creates the arousal associated with crowding. Utilizing a personal space approach, it becomes possible to predict that an individual may experience stress in a rather large room with a low density and a small number of other persons, or that an individual may feel relatively uncrowded in conditions of relatively high density. The former conditions should occur when the individuals are interacting at a rather close distance and utilizing only a small portion of the room. The latter condition could result when the individuals are spread out in a rather small room (Fig. 1).

The personal space approach also allows an alternative explanation for a persistent but somewhat puzzling finding in the crowding literature. Numerous investigations have shown that high density increases aggressiveness and inhibits performance in males but not in females (Freedman et al., 1972; Stokols et al., 1973; Epstein, Note 1). Freedman (1975) has explained this finding by suggesting that crowding simply intensifies the individual's dominant response. Supposedly the dominant response of males and females is different, and this accounts for the different effects of crowding. This position may be correct, but there is another possible explanation. Research on personal space (see Evans & Howard, 1973) has repeatedly shown that appropriate interaction distance is smaller in females than in males. That is, females are comfortable when interacting at closer distances than are males. If we take the personal space view of crowding, it suggests that females would have to be more densely packed together than males before they would experience violations of personal space and crowding. Stated in other terms, holding density constant, females will feel less crowded than males. In most previous research that has found sex differences in crowding, density was in fact held constant, and the reactions of males and females to the same density were investigated. It is, therefore, possible that the differences in responses of the two groups were due not to intensification of dominant responses but to the fact that females felt less crowded in these conditions than did males.

Even though it may be possible to identify the spatial factor that leads to stress, it does not necessarily follow that this factor will always lead to the experience of crowding. There are numerous cases when an individual's personal space is definitely violated, but he does not experience crowding or stress. Strangers are cramped together to the point of touching (intimate interpersonal distance) at football games, theaters, and demonstration rallies. However, feelings

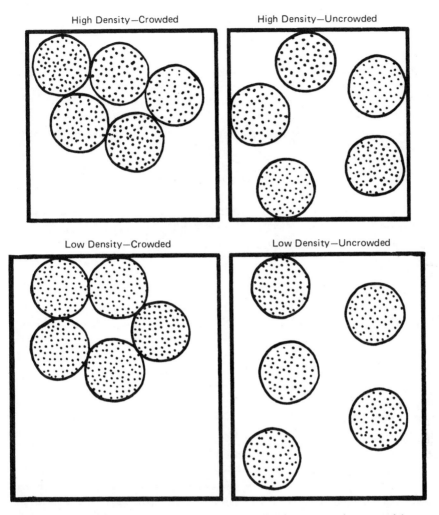

FIG. 1   Relationship between density and crowding from personal space model.

of crowding and discomfort are generally not experienced. On the other hand, people sitting in a bus or subway may become very stressed when their personal space is violated. This suggests that there must be some process by which the encroachments on personal space become interpreted as crowding. This process is flexible enough to allow the same violation to be experienced as crowding in some situations but not in others.

The recent tenor of discussions on crowding has been to view it in a light similar to an emotion (e.g., Stokols, 1972). That is, it is a psychological state with arousal qualities. Taking this viewpoint, crowding is a prime candidate for an attributional interpretation. Schachter and Singer (1962) theorized that emotions are comprised of two components—a physiological or arousal component and a cognitive or interpretative component. Once the individual becomes aroused, he searches for an explanation for the arousal. The explanation or interpretation of the arousal determines the particular emotion he will experience. Schachter and Singer (1962) demonstrated this process with the emotions of euphoria and anger, and Zanna and Cooper (1974) and Worchel and Arnold (1974) showed that cognitive dissonance might result through the same process.

This attribution process can also be applied to crowding. The individual is first aroused by violations of his personal space. He then seeks to explain why he is aroused and to place some label on his arousal. If he does, in fact, interpret his arousal as being caused by other people being too close to him, he will experience "crowding." However, if he attributes the arousal to some other source, he will not experience crowding. It is thus proposed that *the experience of crowding occurs through a two-step process: The individual first becomes aroused by a violation of personal space and then attributes the source of arousal to this violation (crowding = stress + attribution).*

This model can explain why an individual may not experience crowding even when personal space is violated. Take the situation of the spectator at a football game. He is packed in with thousands of screaming fans. He is aroused by having his personal space violated as well as by the exciting action on the gridiron. His attention, however, is not focused on the people around him but on the play on the field. He attributes the arousal he is experiencing as being caused by the exciting play and thus does not feel crowded. This view leads to the prediction that the game will be perceived as more exciting when the spectator is packed in with others than when the stands are nearly empty. In the former case, the spectator is aroused by the spatial invasions as well as the play on the field, and he attributes the cause of both arousals to the football game. In the latter case, the spectator is less aroused because the only stimulation comes from the game. In this case, too, he will attribute his arousal to the game, but because he is not as aroused as the spectator in the packed stadium, he will experience less excitement.

EFFECTS OF CROWDING

It is suggested that crowding is experienced as a negative state. Once the individual determines that he is feeling crowded, he becomes motivated to reduce or eliminate this state. His attention and his efforts become mobilized in this endeavor. The effect of this mobilization can be viewed in terms of task performance and interpersonal relations.

The quality of performance should suffer on some tasks because the individual has focused some of his efforts on reducing his crowding, and thus he is not likely to be able to give as much effort to working on other tasks at hand. The type of performance most likely to suffer is the task that involves complex or coordinated activity. This type of task is likely to require the individual's full attention and effort for an adequate job. There is some evidence that suggests that crowding does interfere with the performance of complex tasks (Evans, 1975; McClelland, 1974), whereas it has little deleterious effect on more simple tasks (Bergman, 1971; Freedman, 1975; Stokols et al., 1973).

Another manner by which tasks may be characterized is whether or not they require social interaction. The research on personal space (e.g., Evans & Howard, 1973) suggests that violations are met with a reduction in eye contact and attempts to reduce social interaction. Applying this concept to crowding, we could predict that if the individual could not physically escape the situation, he would attempt to escape it psychologically by reducing his interaction with others in his environment. If the task on which the group was required to work necessitated social interaction, crowding should have a detrimental effect on task performance. The effects of crowding should not be so drastic on tasks that do not require social interaction or on tasks where the individual can work alone. These types of task allow the individual to escape the situation psychologically.

It can also be expected from this point of view that the crowded invididual's interpersonal relations are likely to suffer. In his desire to reduce the experience of crowding, the individual might attempt to withdraw both physically and psychologically from others in his environment. If the individual cannot physically withdraw and increase his spacing to the appropriate level, research has repeatedly shown, he is likely to engage in "compensatory reactions" such as decreasing eye contact or placing a barrier such as arms or shoulder between himself and the individual violating his personal space (Argyle & Dean, 1965; Patterson, 1973). In many crowded situations, other people are likely to frustrate the individual's attempts to restore his personal space. In such cases, the simple frustration is likely to lead to an increase in hostility and aggression aimed at these other people (e.g., Dollard, Doob, Miller, Mowrer, & Sears, 1939). There is existing research suggesting that subjects do attempt to withdraw from others (Ross, Layton, Erickson, & Schopler, 1973; Sundstrom, 1975) and become more hostile (Hutt & Vaizey, 1966). There is also competing evidence that suggests that high density does not always lead to increased hostility (Loo, 1972; Price, 1971; Stokols et al., 1973).

In many cases, it is difficult to determine whether the existing results in the literature can be taken as confirmations or disconfirmations of the present approach to crowding. Most of the studies simply manipulated density which, according to the present view, may or may not have resulted in subjects' experiencing crowding. Furthermore, it is important to remember that according to the present view of crowding, detrimental effects on task performance and withdrawal should occur only after the attribution of crowding has been made. It should be possible to violate an individual's personal space but still inhibit his making the attribution of crowding. In this case, even though personal space has been violated, there should not be negative effects on task performance or interpersonal relations. This is an important point to keep in mind as we turn to how the present theory can be utilized to suggest means of reducing the experience of crowding.

REDUCTION OF CROWDING

It is obvious that crowding can be alleviated by giving people more space or by reducing the number of persons in a prescribed area. This prediction can be derived from any theory of crowding. The present theory of crowding, however, allows for numerous other predictions as to how the experience of crowding can be reduced. The theory suggests that crowding is a function of both violation of personal space and attribution. It should, therefore, be possible to reduce crowding by manipulating variables that affect the perception of personal space or affect the attribution the individual makes about the cause of his arousal.

Regarding the personal space variable, Hall (1966) hypothesized that man is characterized by a series of concentric circles or bubbles. There has, however, been some recent evidence that suggested that these "circles" may not be so circular in shape (Horowitz, Duff, & Stratton, 1964; Sommer, 1962). People generally allow others to approach them closer from the rear than from the front. This indicates that the appropriate distances may be greater for frontal approaches than for rear approaches, which leads to the prediction that placing individuals in a back-to-back arrangement would lead to less crowding than placing them in a face-to-face relationship. This relationship should occur even when density is held constant. Kutner (1973) offers direct evidence supporting this hypothesis, having found less nervousness in subjects "crowded" together in a back-to-back relationship than in subjects who faced each other. Thus, affecting the perception of personal space can be utilized to reduce the experience of crowding.

A second procedure for reducing crowding should be to inhibit the process that attributes the individual's arousal to other individuals being too close. There are at least two ways in which this could be accomplished. Zanna and Cooper (1974) found that the experience of cognitive dissonance could be reduced by giving subjects a placebo that supposedly aroused them before the subjects participated in a dissonance-producing task. This pill offered subjects a causal explanation for the arousal caused by participating in the dissonance-producing activity. Therefore, they attributed their arousal to the pill and not to the task activity, and they did not experience dissonance. According to the proposed view of crowding, the experience of crowding could be reduced in the same manner. That is, if subjects were given "cause" for arousal that was unrelated to crowding and were then placed in a densely populated environment, they should attribute any arousal to this given "cause" and not to crowding.

A second means by which crowding can be reduced is by inhibiting the attribution process through distraction. The more the individual must focus on the persons around him, the more likely it is that he will attribute any arousal he feels as being caused by these individuals. Even if the individual can periodically have his attention focused elsewhere, he should be less likely to make the continual attribution of crowding than if he is constantly focused on others around him. There are numerous ways in which attention can be distracted. Windows offer a haven where the individual can redirect his attention. Pictures or wall posters also can give the individual a place where he can focus his attention away from the people around him. The question of whether people use these attention distractors can be answered by simply observing their behavior on crowded buses. It is not uncommon to see an individual board a crowded bus, take a seat, and spend the entire ride focusing his attention on the advertising posters that rim the ceiling. According to the present theory of crowding, the addition of these attention distractors should reduce the experience of crowding, and they should do so because they inhibit the attribution process necessary for the experience of crowding.

EXPERIMENT 1

Thus far, the proposed theory has been based on conjecture and empirical data garnered from research that was not designed to test it directly. Charles Teddlie and I (Worchel & Teddlie, 1976) have recently completed a study that was aimed at directly examining some of the hypotheses derivable from the theory. Specifically, we wanted to unconfound manipulations of density and interaction distance and test the hypothesis that interaction distance and not density is the spatial variable associated with crowding. We also wanted to demonstrate that crowding (not density) would have adverse consequences for performance and intragroup cohesiveness when the group task required social interaction. Finally, we wished to examine the hypothesis that the addition of attention distractors would alleviate the experience of crowding. We felt that supporting data for this latter hypothesis would yield some evidence for the validity of the attribution process of crowding.

Groups of eight male, introductory psychology students participated in an experiment entitled "Group Performance." When subjects entered the experimental room, which was bare with the exception of a circle of chairs, they were asked to be seated and not to move the chairs. A dummy microphone hung from the ceiling, and the experimenter explained that the session was being taped and the present chair arrangement was optimal for the recording quality.

The three independent manipulations involved room characteristics:

1. *Density* was manipulated through room size. Half of the groups were in a room measuring 12 feet 6 inches by 9 feet (high density), whereas the remaining

groups were in a room measuring 20 feet 6 inches by 11 feet 6 inches (low density).

2. *Interaction distance* was manipulated by the placement of chairs in the room. In all cases, the chairs were arranged in a circle. In the close-distance condition, the front legs of each chair touched the front legs of the chairs on either side of it. In the far-distance condition, there were 19.5 inches between the front leg of one chair and the front leg of the chair next to it.

3. The *presence or absence of pictures* and posters (or distractors) was the third manipulation involved. In the pictures-present condition, the room had six prints arranged on the walls, and two wind chimes were hung from the light fixtures. In the no-picture condition, the room did not contain any pictures or wind chimes.

Except for the experimental manipulations, the rooms were identical with regard to color, ceiling tiles, number of doors (one) and windows (none), temperature, and ventilation system.

The experimenter explained that the study investigated group process. The aims of the study were to determine how well groups perform on various tasks and to examine the group processes that result as the group works. The subjects were told that the first task involved a word game. The task of the group was to form as many words as possible from the master word INDUSTRIOUSLY. After a 10-minute period, the experimenter returned to the room and collected the list of words. This task was employed because the number of words formed by the group could serve as a clear index of performance.

The experimenter then stated that the second task was a human relations problem. He gave the subjects a case history of a juvenile delinquent, Johnny Rocco. The task of the subjects was to read the case history and indicate on the accompanying Love-Punishment scale which of seven alternative courses of action should be taken. The seven alternatives varied along a punitiveness dimension. The subjects were told that they were first to make an individual decision as to what course of action to take with Rocco. After recording their individual recommendations, they were to discuss the Rocco case as a group and arrive at a group recommendation. The experimenter allowed subjects 10 minutes to arrive at the group decision. The use of the Johnny Rocco case allowed the opportunity to investigate how crowding related to the punitiveness score by looking at the separate individual and group ratings, and it was also possible to determine whether the group discussion yielded a more or less punitive recommendation than the average individual recommendation.

After subjects had completed the Johnny Rocco case, they answered a 20-item questionnaire pertaining to their reactions to the experiment and their attraction toward fellow group members. The subjects were given 17 minutes in which to complete the questionnaire.

TABLE 1
Means of Crowding Index

Density	Interaction Distance	Pictures	No Pictures
Low	Far	$4.27^{a,b}$	4.22
(large room)	Close	5.92	6.31
High	Far	5.23	5.24
(small room)	Close	5.97	6.54

[a] N = five groups per cell.

[b] Score formed by composite of how comfortable, confined, ill at ease, and crowded subjects reported being. In present table, 1 = least crowded, 10 = most crowded.

Results

The results of this experiment confirm our expectations. As predicted, subjects felt more crowded in small than in large rooms, at close rather than far interaction distances, and when no distractions were available (see Table 1). Feelings of crowding were also strongly influenced by the interactive influence of room size and interaction distance. For example, subjects in the far condition reported feeling significantly more crowded in the small room than in the large room. However, there was no significant difference in reported crowding in the high-versus low-density conditions when interaction distance was close. Although interaction distance affected the experience of crowding regardless of density conditions, variation in room size affected crowding only when interaction distance was far. In addition, under close interaction conditions, the addition of pictures to the room significantly reduced crowding. However, the addition of pictures in the far interaction condition had no effect.

Group Performance

The number of words each group was able to form from the master word (IN-DUSTRIOUSLY) was taken to be a measure of group performance. It was predicted that the experience of crowding should inhibit performance and reduce the number of words formed by the group. As can be seen from the results presented in Table 2, interaction distance significantly affected performance; groups performed better in the far than close condition. Density, however, did not significantly affect performance on this task. Although the addition of pictures to the room significantly improved performance in the close interaction condition, it did not affect performance in the far interaction condition.

TABLE 2
Performance on Word Task:
Number of Words Formed by Group

Density	Interaction Distance	Pictures	No Pictures
Low	Far	54.40	58.40
(large room)	Close	54.60	44.00
High	Far	56.80	57.00
(small room)	Close	52.80	39.00

Punitiveness

Subjects were asked to indicate which of seven alternative treatment programs (1 = most benign or all love, 7 = most punitive or all punishment) they would recommend for Johnny Rocco. Subjects first made their own individual recommendations, and then the group was asked to discuss the case and make a group recommendation. An individual average score was computed by taking the average of the individual ratings. The group consensus score is the one rating agreed on by the group as a whole. It was expected that the more stressed and crowded subjects, the more punitive would be their responses on this question. As can be seen from Table 3, subjects were significantly more punitive on both ratings in

TABLE 3
Individual and Group Punitiveness Scores

Density	Interaction Distance	Pictures		No Pictures	
Low (large room)	Far	Group	= 2.20[a]	Group	= 2.60
		Individual average	= 2.62	Individual average	= 2.80
	Close	Group	= 3.00	Group	= 3.60
		Individual average	= 3.00	Individual average	= 3.44
High (small room)	Far	Group	= 2.70	Group	= 2.60
		Individual average	= 2.78	Individual average	= 2.76
	Close	Group	= 3.20	Group	= 4.00
		Individual Average	= 3.03	Individual average	= 3.56

[a] 1 = most benign or all love, 7 = most punitive or all punishment.

the close than in the far interaction condition and in the no-picture as opposed to with-picture condition. Density had no effect on punitiveness. The addition of pictures significantly reduced punitiveness in the close interaction condition, but it did not do so in the far interaction condition. It is also interesting to note that the group decision was less punitive than the individual average scores in all the far interaction conditions. However, the reverse was true in the close interaction conditions. Thus, group discussion reduced punitiveness in the former conditions but increased punitiveness in the latter set of conditions.

Interpersonal Attraction

Finally, subjects were asked to rate the other group members on a number of dimensions. As a measure of attraction, subjects were asked, "How much did you like the people in your group?" and they were asked to rate each member on a 10-point scale (1 = not friendly, 10 = friendly). An average attraction measure was arrived at by taking the average rating given by subjects on the friendly scales and the "like" question. The results presented in Table 4 indicate that subjects were more attracted to the other group members in low as opposed to high density conditions, in far as compared with close interaction conditions, and in with-picture as opposed to no-picture conditions. Again, the strongest effect was on the interaction distance variable. The use of pictures significantly increased attraction only in the close interaction conditions.

TABLE 4
Rating of Other Group Members

Density	Interaction Distance	Picture		No Picture	
Low (large room)	Far	Attraction[a] =	8.00	Attraction =	7.69
		Nervous[b] =	2.59	Nervous =	2.60
	Close	Attraction =	7.18	Attraction =	6.17
		Nervous =	2.78	Nervous =	4.06
High (small room)	Far	Attraction =	7.60	Attraction =	7.15
		Nervous =	2.38	Nervous =	2.94
	Close	Attraction =	6.84	Attraction =	5.62
		Nervous =	2.71	Nervous =	4.51

[a]Combination of "how much did you like the people in your group?" and friendly-not-friendly ratings: = not attracted to others, 10 = very attracted to others.

[b]1 = calm, 10 = nervous.

Subjects also rated each group member as to how nervous he felt that member was. Average "nervous" scores suggested that subjects felt other group members were significantly more nervous in the close as opposed to far interaction conditions and in the no-pictures as compared with the with-pictures conditions. Density did not significantly affect the attributions of nervousness. Pictures reduced the amount of nervousness perceived in the close interaction conditions but had no effect in the far interaction conditions.

Discussion

Space and Crowding

The results of this study offer an opportunity to directly compare the relation of simple density and interaction distance to the experience of crowding. Violations of personal space led subjects to report feeling crowded and uncomfortable. In addition, the violated subjects performed more poorly on the word task and were more punitive toward Johnny Rocco and toward other members of their group. They also attributed more nervousness to other group members than did subjects in the far interaction distance condition. These effects were found regardless of room size (high or low density).

Data suggesting a relationship between density and crowding were equivocal. Although density did yield a main effect on the crowding index, this effect was small compared to the effect for interaction distance. In addition, the crowding index main effect was qualified by an interaction such that density affected crowding only under the far interaction distance condition. Furthermore, density had no effect on performance or punitiveness.

These results suggest that interaction or personal space violations are stressful and that individuals seem to be more sensitive to violations of their personal space than to the denseness of their environment. In addition, interaction distance rather than simple density is the spatial variable most closely related to the experience of crowding. Regardless of the density, individuals felt crowded when their personal space was violated and did not feel especially crowded when it was not.

Effects of Crowding

According to the present theoretical approach, crowding should result in negative psychological experiences and inhibit performance on group tasks. Greatest experience of crowding should have resulted in the close interaction, no-picture conditions. The data obtained in these conditions support the predictions for both the psychological and task performance effects.

Subjects in the close interaction, no-picture conditions reported feeling more ill-at-ease and crowded than subjects in any of the other conditions. These subjects also gave greater estimations of the time spent on the tasks than subjects in the other conditions. Thus, psychologically, crowding led to stress.

On the performance question, the most relevant data were found on the word task. Groups in the close interaction, no-picture conditions found significantly fewer words than did subjects in the other conditions. This task was a group task that required social interaction, and it was on this type of task that, according to the theory, crowding should have the greatest detrimental effect.

In light of the task distinction, it is of interest to look at the punitiveness scores on the Johnny Rocco case. Although there is no objective measure of "good" performance, we can still compare the individual performance with the group performance. In the close interaction, no picture conditions the individual average scores were less punitive than those of the group consensus in which social interaction was required. This was not the case in the conditions in which less crowding was reported. Thus, it seems that crowding does inhibit task performance, at least on tasks that require social interaction.

There is one additional effect that is of interest. There was least attraction for the group in the conditions where crowding was greatest (close interaction, no pictures), which suggests that crowding can also affect intragroup cohesiveness. It cannot be determined, however, whether this effect would also be found in groups working on individual tasks.

Reduction of Crowding

It was expected that the addition of pictures to the experimental room would reduce the experience and effect of crowding. The pictures should serve as an attribution inhibitor and distract the individual from making the attribution of crowding. Furthermore, it was expected that the pictures would have an effect only in those cases where the individual was aroused and in a position to make an attribution for the cause of this arousal. In those conditions in which there was no arousal, the pictures should have no effect since the individual would not need to make attributions. Because interaction distance and not density was predicted to be the variable that would determine arousal, the addition of pictures should have interacted with the interaction distance variable and not the density variable.

The addition of pictures to the environment had exactly the predicted effect. The picture variable interacted only with the interaction distance variable. The pictures reduced the experience of crowding and the stress associated with this experience. Performance increased and punitiveness decreased with the addition of the pictures in the crowded conditions.

The present results were congruent with the theory that relates personal-space violations and attribution to crowding. However, although the design directly tested the personal-space hypothesis, it offered only an indirect test of the attribution hypothesis. It is possible that the addition of pictures simply served to reduce arousal or that they merely distracted subjects. That is, they could have acted on processes other than the predicted attribution-crowding process.

Steve Yohai and I (Worchel & Yohai, Note 2) designed a second study to more directly examine the role of attribution in crowding. We also wanted to demonstrate that crowding would be reduced by allowing subjects to misattribute the cause of their arousal. This misattribution should occur even in situations in which the subject is not distracted. We reasoned that if subjects were given an alternative explanation for arousal, unrelated to crowding, they would be less likely to attribute the stress caused by violations of personal space as crowding. This misattribution should reduce not only the experience of crowding but also the negative effects (poor performance and deteriorated interpersonal realtions).

EXPERIMENT 2

In order to examine the relationship of attribution to crowding, we followed a procedure much like that employed by Zanna and Cooper (1974). Groups of five same-sexed subjects (both male and female groups were utilized) enlisted for a study entitled "Group Performance." When subjects arrived at the experimental room, they were met by an experimenter who ushered them into a room (8 feet 9 inches by 9 feet 10 inches). The room was bare except for a circle of five chairs and a small "transmitter" in the corner of the room. Interpersonal distance was manipulated by the distance between the chairs. In the Far condition, the front legs of the chairs were 20 inches apart from the two adjacent chairs; in the Close condition, the front legs of each chair were touching those of the neighboring chairs.

The experimenter told subjects that the aim of the study was to test the effects of subliminal stimuli on group performance. After giving a number of examples of how subliminal stimuli bombard individuals in daily life, the noise explanation was manipulated. In the Arousing condition, the experimenter pointed to the "transmitter" in the corner of the room and told subjects that while they worked a subliminal noise would be played into the room. They would not be able to hear the noise but studies had shown that it often caused individuals to experience some discomfort and stress. The same instructions were given to subjects in the Relaxing condition, but they were told that the noise should have a calming and relaxing effect on them. A No-Explanation condition was run in which subjects were told nothing about the subliminal noise.

Following these instructions, subjects worked on a word task and human relations task similar to those utilized in the Worchel and Teddlie (1976) study. After completing the work, subjects completed a questionnaire that asked them how stressed and crowded they felt during the study.

Results

Because subjects were run in groups and the data within groups could not be completely independent, group means were utilized as the unit of analysis. The data were first analyzed using sex of subject as a variable; 32 groups of male and 32 groups of female subjects were run. The analysis yielded no significant effects for the sex manipulation, and, therefore, the data were collapsed across the sex variable.

Arousal

In order to determine if the interpersonal-distance manipulation did create stress, subjects were asked to rate how "ill-at-ease" they felt during the experiment. As can be seen by Tables 5 and 6, two main effects resulted indicating that subjects were significantly more stressed in the Close than Far interpersonal-distance condition and more stressed in the Arousing-Explanation condition than in the Relaxing or No-Explanation conditions. This latter effect is particularly interesting, because it indicates that the simple expectation of arousal led subjects to report being more aroused in the Arousing-Explanation conditions.

TABLE 5
Means for Stress Index

Interpersonal Distance	Arousing	Relaxing	No Explanation
Close	6.86 (11)	5.93 (11)	5.85 (12)
Far	4.26 (10)	2.44 (10)	2.60 (10)

Note: Number in parentheses indicates number of groups per cell. Subjects were asked how relaxed or ill at ease they felt during the experiment; 1 = relaxed, 10 = ill at ease.

TABLE 6
Analysis of Variance for Stress Index

Source	df	F
A (interpersonal distance)	1	364.86[a]
B (noise explanation)	2	29.86[a]
A X B	2	2.67
Error	58	.42

[a] $p < .001$.

TABLE 7
Means for Crowding Indices

Interpersonal Distance	Arousing	Relaxing	No Explanation
Close	4.26	7.10	6.68
Far	3.36	2.67	3.11

Note: Scores are formed by a mean rating of how crowded and how confined subjects reported feeling; 1 = not at all crowded, 10 = very crowded, 1 = very unconfined, 10 = very confined.

TABLE 8
Analysis of Variance for Crowding Indices

Source	df	F
A (interpersonal distance)	1	373.25[a]
B (noise explanation)	2	26.72[a]
A X B	2	45.99[a]
Error	58	.37

[a] $p < .001$.

The marginal interaction was caused by a greater increase in reported stress in the Arousing-Far condition than in the Arousing-Close condition. Thus, these data show that the interpersonal-distance manipulation and the explanation manipulation affected self-reports of stress.

Crowding Measures

Two questions were used to measure the subjects' experiences of crowding. Subjects were asked how crowded and confined they felt during the experiment. Since subjects responded similarly to both questions, the ratings were combined to form a single "crowding" index. As can be seen by the results presented in Tables 7 and 8, two main effects indicate that subjects felt more crowded in the Far as opposed to the Close interpersonal-distance conditions and more crowded in the Relaxing or No-Explanation conditions than in the Arousing condition. These main effects were qualified by a significant interaction. The explanation had no effect on the reported crowding in the Far interpersonal-distance condition. However, in the Close interpersonal-distance condition, subjects in the Arousing condition felt significantly less crowded than subjects in either the Relaxing condition [$F(1, 58) = 115.29, p < .001$] or the No-Explanation condition [$F(1, 58) = 97.67, p < .001$].

TABLE 9
Performance on Word Task

Interpersonal Distance	Arousing	Relaxing	No Explanation
Close	85.91	74.00	77.92
Far	89.40	93.50	91.80

Note: Number represents number of word groups made from master word "observationally."

TABLE 10
Analysis of Variance for Word-Task Performance

Source	df	F
A (interpersonal distance)	1	25.10[a]
B (noise explanation)	2	1.06
A X B	2	3.58[b]
Error	58	96.55

[b] $p < .05$.

[a] $p < .001$.

Task Performance

The measure of task performance was the number of word groups formed from the master word. As can be seen from Tables 9 and 10, subjects performed better in the Far than Close condition. There was also a significant interaction [$F(2, 58) = 3.58$, $p < .05$] similar to that found with the crowding measure. The explanation manipulation created no significant ($F < 1$) differences within the Far condition. However, subjects in the Close-Arousing condition performed significantly better than subjects in the other two Close conditions [$F(1, 58) = 7.74$, $p < .01$]. In fact, there was not a significant difference in the performance of subjects in the Arousing-Close and Arousing-Far conditions [$F(1, 58) = .57$, $p = $ n.s.].

Interpersonal Attraction

Subjects were asked to rate how friendly and likeable their fellow group members were, and these ratings were combined to form an interpersonal-attraction index. The interpersonal-attraction scores followed closely the pattern found on the task performance. As shown by Tables 11 and 12, subjects in the Far condition were significantly more attracted (1 = lowest attraction, 10 = highest

TABLE 11
Mean Attraction Ratings for Other Group Members

Interpersonal Distance	Arousing	Relaxing	No Explanation
Close	8.10	7.34	7.47
Far	8.25	8.64	8.31

Note: Scores are formed by a mean rating of how much they liked fellow group members and how friendly they perceived them to be; 1 = not like, 10 = liked very much, 1 = not friendly, 10 = very friendly.

TABLE 12
Analysis of Variance for Attraction Ratings
of Other Group Members

Source	df	F
A (interpersonal distance)	1	43.55[a]
B (noise explanation)	2	2.31
A × B	2	8.17[a]
Error	58	.22

[a] $p < .001$.

attraction) to fellow group members than subjects in the Close condition [Far $\overline{X}$ = 8.41, Close $\overline{X}$ = 7.64; $F(1, 58) = 43.90$, $p < .001$]. There was also a significant interaction [$F(2, 58) = 8.26$, $p < .001$] that indicated that whereas the explanation manipulation did not affect attraction in the Far condition, subjects in the Arousing-Close condition were significantly more attracted to group members than subjects in the Relaxing-Close condition [$F(1, 58) = 14.50$, $p < .001$] and No-Explanation-Close condition [$F(1, 58) = 10.00$, $p < .001$].

Punitiveness

Subjects were asked to individually determine the treatment for Johnny (1 = most benevolent, 7 = most malevolent). Results of these individual ratings indicated that subjects in the Far condition were more lenient on Johnny than subjects in the Close condition [Far $\overline{X}$ = 2.07, Close $\overline{X}$ = 2.49; $F(1, 58)$ = 19.36, $p < .001$]. There was also a marginally significant interaction [$F(2, 58)$ = 2.76, $p < .08$] that indicated that the explanation had no effect on ratings in the Far condition but that subjects in the Close-Arousing condition were more lenient than subjects in the other two Close conditions [$F(1, 58) = 6.25$, $p < .05$].

The groups also arrived at group consensus ratings for Johnny. It was expected that the same pattern of results obtained in the individual ratings would be obtained with the group consensus ratings. However, there were no differences among any of the group consensus ratings, because all but one group arrived at the same rating (treatment program 2).

Discussion

The results of the present study support the hypothesis that crowding is experienced through an attributional process whereby the individual becomes aroused by violations of personal space and then searches the environment to determine the cause of this arousal. If the cause of the arousal is not attributed to the violations of appropriate space, crowding will not result. The support for this contention is based on the subject's report of crowding and the interaction between the spacing and explanation factors on crowding reports. Informing subjects that environmental factors would arouse them did not reduce their experience of crowding when their personal space was not violated by others. In fact, this information tended to make them feel somewhat more crowded. However, when their personal space was violated, this alternative explanation for arousal significantly reduced the experienced crowding. Supposedly, subjects in the aroused conditions attributed the cause of their arousal to the subliminal noise and, therefore, *felt* less crowded.

It is interesting to note that the explanation affected the experience of crowding and the reports of arousal in different ways. When subjects were told that the subliminal noise would arouse them, they reported feeling more ill-at-ease than when they were not told of the noise effects or were told that the noise would calm them. This occurred even when their personal space was being violated. However, at the same time that the "arousing noise" was making them feel more ill-at-ease, it was also reducing their experience of crowding in the Close interpersonal-distance condition. This finding is extremely important for the present theoretical position, because it demonstrates that the label of crowding can be independent from the arousal that an individual might feel. Thus, the actual experience of crowding does seem to be a cognitive process that can be affected by environmental factors other than simple arousal.

Another effect of theoretical importance involves the task-performance and interpersonal-attraction scores. Both of these behaviors were more affected by the crowding-attribution data than by the perception of arousal or stress. That is, performance and interpersonal attraction increased as subjects reported feeling less crowded. And under the conditions in which personal space was violated, there was an increase in performance and interpersonal attraction despite the increasing feelings of being ill-at-ease in the Arousing-Explanation condition. These results are congruent with the hypothesis that the attribution of crowding causes the individual to turn his or her attention to reducing the uncomfortable condition, and the redirection of attention necessary for this effort results in reduced performance.

In addition to being theoretically important, these results have implications for the applied setting. They suggest that performance and interpersonal attraction may be enhanced by altering the individual's perception of the environment without directly reducing the stress involved in such environment or altering the environment. Attributions about crowding seem to be rather plastic and can be molded by either redirecting the individual's focus (Worchel & Teddlie, 1976) or by giving the individual "explanations" for arousal. Conversely, it can be implied that performance and attraction will not necessarily be enhanced by moderate reductions in the stress associated with a rather dense environment if the individual's focus is still placed on the violations of his or her personal space. In this case, the individual will still feel "crowded," and this feeling will inhibit performance and adjustment to the environment.

Another result of interest is the failure to find sex differences in the present study. A number of previous studies reported such sex differences, and such differences are not consistent with the present theoretical framework. It was suggested that one possible reason for these sex differences was the possibility that the personal space of females in some of the previous work was not severely violated. Care was taken to ensure that such violations occurred in the present study, and the result was no differences in the responses of male and females subjects. Although caution must be exercised in extrapolating from failure to find differences, it does suggest that females do experience crowding and respond to it in a manner similar to males. It may, however, take closer interpersonal distances before females will feel stressed and experience crowding.

In sum, the present results support a two-factor theory of crowding that suggests that individuals become aroused by violations of their personal space and experience crowding only when they make the attribution that their arousal is being caused by these violations. Further, task performance and interpersonal attraction are affected by the attributions the individual makes about the experience rather than the amount of arousal he or she may feel.

Although the present results help to clarify the process by which an individual experiences crowding, there are some interesting questions left unanswered. One such question deals with the factors that determine whether or not the individual will attribute his or her arousal to violations of personal space or to an alternative source. It can easily be predicted that when no plausible outside source exists, the individual will attribute arousal to personal-space violations and will experience crowding. However, when a plausible alternative explanation exists, what is the factor that determines where the attribution for the cause of arousal will be made? Is the determining factor salience of the cue, or is it the amount of threat involved in the alternative explanation? For example, in the present study, attributing the cause of arousal to subliminal noise enabled the individual not to blame other members of the group for causing uncomfortableness. Thus, it became easier to deal with these other members, and therefore the noise explanation was less "threatening" than the "crowding" explanation. Another question involves the time factor. Does the attribution of arousal to an alternative source such as the subliminal noise serve to permanently reduce the crowding experience in the situation, or does it simply delay the experience of crowding? These and other questions must be answered by further research on the experience of crowding.

CONCLUSION

The present research supports the position that the experience of crowding is a function of violations of personal space and attributions relating stress to the violations of personal space. Although there are numerous implications of this view of crowding, the more general point to be made is that the experience of crowding is a complex process. It is impossible to determine when an individual will feel crowded by simply looking at the space that may be available in a particular situation. The importance of looking at variables other than spatial ones has been suggested by numerous other theorists. The present view sharpens the focus of previous theories by suggesting that we examine those social variables related to personal space and those situational variables that could affect attributions.

If the present view of crowding is correct, it offers a more optimistic outlook for the reduction of crowding than theories that assume that crowding is solely related to spatial variables. Previous research and theory have attested that the attribution process is extremely plastic and can be shaped and reshaped. Although it may not always be feasible to create changes in spatial factors, it should be possible to manipulate conditions to affect attributions. Thus, it may be impossible to make the world more livable by making it less crowded, but it may be possible to make it more livable by helping people to "see" it as less crowded.

ACKNOWLEDGMENTS

This research was supported in part by an NSF grant (GS-37062). I would like to thank Andrew Baum, Yakov Epstein, and Philip Worchel for helpful comments on earlier versions of the manuscript, and I would like to acknowledge the assistance of Steven Yohai and Charles Teddlie, whose persistent interest in crowding and probing comments helped me to refine many aspects of the proposed theory.

REFERENCE NOTES

1. Epstein, Y. M. *Effects of crowding on cognitive performance and social behavior.* Unpublished manuscript, 1973.
2. Worchel, S., & Yohai, S. *Role of attribution in the experience of crowding.* Paper presented at the meeting of the American Psychological Association, San Francisco, August 1977.

REFERENCES

Altman, I. *The environment and social behavior.* Monterey, Calif: Brooks/Cole, 1975.

Argyle, M., & Dean, J. Eye contact, distance, and affiliation. *Sociometry,* 1965, *28,* 289-304.

Bergman, B. A. *The effects of group size, personal space, and success-failure on physiological arousal test performance and questionnaire response.* (Doctoral dissertation, Temple University, Philadelphia, Pa., 1971). *Dissertation Abstracts International,* 1971, 2319-3420-A. (University Microfilms No. 71-31072)

Dollard, J., Doob, L., Miller, N., Mowrer, O. H., & Sears, R. *Frustration and aggression.* New Haven, Conn.: Yale University Press, 1939.

Epstein, Y. M., & Karlin, R. A. Effects of acute experimental crowding. *Journal of Applied Social Psychology,* 1975, *5,* 34-53.

Evans, G. *Behavioral and physiological consequences of crowding in humans.* Unpublished doctoral dissertation, University of Massachusetts, 1975.

Evans, G. W., & Howard, R. B. Personal space. *Psychological Bulletin,* 1973, *80,* 334-344.

Felipe, N. J., & Sommer, R. Invasions of personal space. *Social Problems,* 1966, *14,* 206-214.

Freedman, J. L. *Crowding and behavior.* San Francisco: Freeman, 1975.

Freedman, J. L., Klevansky, S., & Ehrlich, P. R. The effect of crowding on human task performance. *Journal of Applied Social Psychology,* 1971, *1,* 7-25.

Freedman, J. L., Levy, A., Buchanan, R., & Price, J. Crowding and human aggressiveness. *Journal of Experimental Social Psychology,* 1972, *8,* 528-548.

Hall, E. T. *The silent language.* Garden City, N.Y.: Doubleday, 1959.

Hall, E. T. *The hidden dimension.* Garden City, N.Y.: Doubleday, 1966.

Horowitz, M. J., Duff, D. F., & Stratton, L. O. Body-buffer zone. *Archives of General Psychiatry,* 1964, *11,* 651-656.

Hutt, C., & Vaizey, M. J. Differential effects of group density on social behavior. *Nature,* 1966, *209,* 1371-1372.

Kutner, D. H. Overcrowding: Human response to density and visual exposure. *Human Relations,* 1973, *26,* 31-50.

Lawrence, J. E. S. Science and sentiment: Overview of research on crowding and human behavior. *Psychological Bulletin,* 1974, *81,* 712-720.

Loo, C. The effects of spatial density on the social behavior of children. *Journal of Applied Social Psychology,* 1972, *2,* 372-381.

Loo, C. Important issues in researching the effects of crowding on humans. *Representative Research in Social Psychology,* 1973, *4,* 219-226.

McBride, G. C., King, M. G., & James, J. W. Social proximity effects on galvanic skin responses in adult humans. *Journal of Psychology,* 1965, *61,* 153-157.

McClelland, L. *Crowding and social stress.* Unpublished doctoral dissertation. University of Michigan, 1974.

Middlemist, R. D., Knowles, E. S., & Matter, L. F. Personal space invasions in the lavatory: Suggestive evidence for arousal. *Journal of Personality and Social Psychology,* 1976, *36,* 541-546.

Patterson, M. Compensation and nonverbal immediacy behaviors; A review. *Sociometry,* 1973, *36,* 237-253.

Price, J. *The effects of crowding on the social behavior of children.* Unpublished doctoral dissertation, Columbia University, New York, 1971.

Ross, M., Layton, B., Erickson, B., & Schopler, J. Affect, facial regard, and reactions to crowding. *Journal of Personality and Social Psychology,* 1973, *28,* 69-76.

Schachter, S., & Singer, J. E. Cognitive, social, and physiological determinants of emotional state. *Psychological Review*, 1962, *69*, 379-399.

Sommer, R. The distance for comfortable conversation: A further study. *Sociometry*, 1962, *25*, 111-116.

Sommer, R. *Personal space: The behavioral basis of design.* Englewood Cliffs, N.J.: Prentice-Hall, 1969.

Stokols, D. On the distinction between density and crowding: Some implications for future research. *Psychological Review*, 1972, *79*, 275-277.

Stokols, D., Rall, M., Pinner, B., & Schopler, J. Physical, social, and personal determinants of the perception of crowding. *Environment and Behavior*, 1973, *5*, 87-115.

Sundstrom, E. Toward an interpersonal model of crowding. *Sociological Symposium*, 1975, *14*, 129-144.

Worchel, S., & Arnold, S. E. The effect of combined arousal states on attitude change. *Journal of Experimental Social Psychology*, 1974, *10*, 549-560.

Worchel, S., & Teddlie, C. The experience of crowding: A two-factor theory. *Journal of Personality and Social Psychology*, 1976, *34*, 30-40.

Zanna, M. P., & Cooper, J. Dissonance and the pill: An attribution approach to studying the arousal properties of dissonance. *Journal of Personality and Social Psychology*, 1974, *29*, 703-709.

12

Designing for Residential Density

Glenn E. Davis[1]
State University of New York, Stony Brook

> *The time has come at last to start painting our real homeland, the big city which we all love so much. . . . Light explodes over a confused jumble of buildings. Between moving vehicles light flashes. . . . Sharp contours waver in the glare and multitudes of right angles retreat in whirling rhythms. . . . Our feverish hands should race across countless canvasses, let them be as large as frescoes, sketching the glorious and fantastic, the monstrous and dramatic. . . . Be brutal and unashamed; your subject is also brutal and without shame.*
> —Ludwig Meidner,
> *An Introduction to Painting Big Cities*

> *I'd even choose a desert isle, myself, to midtown Rome. For what a place have we seen so vile, so lonely.*
> —Juvenal,
> *The Satires of Juvenal III*

It has been estimated that by the end of this century a substantial percentage of the world's population will live in densely populated urban areas (Davis, 1965). The result of continuing urbanization is that in the United States, where overall population density is low relative to most of the rest of the industrialized world, 70 percent of the populace now lives under high-density conditions in urban centers and surrounding suburban areas (Freedman, 1975). Urban settlement patterns are not new to the human scene; they have existed for several thousand years and have played a powerful role in shaping human political and economic behavior (Jacobs, 1969). A body of early urban sociological thought, of which Louis Wirth's (1938) writings are representative, stressed that urban environments have an equally formative influence on social behavior and the development of urban personality. Wirth characterized urban social relations as superficial and anomic, and he concluded that the urban personality was schizoid in nature. In the last 15 years, the notion that high human density itself may act as a psycho-

[1]Presently at the Department of Psychology, Washington College, Chestertown, Md.

social stressor responsible for some portion of urban social malaise motivated the initiation of four basic research paradigms. Some researchers empirically investigated the effects of population density on various types of social pathology (e.g., Galle, Gove, & McPherson, 1972; Schmitt, 1963; Schmitt, 1966). Methodological problems associated with this work, notably the difficulty of controlling for confounding social and economic factors, and equivocal results led behavioral scientists to investigate experimentally the effects of varying human density on behavior under controlled laboratory conditions and in naturalistic settings (e.g., Epstein & Karlin, 1975; Freedman, Klevansky, & Ehrlich, 1971; Freedman, Levy, Buchanan, & Price, 1972; Griffitt & Veitch, 1971; Loo, 1972). Other studies have been concerned with how high density influences social behavior and have focused on crowding (e.g., Valins & Baum, 1973; Aiello, Epstein, & Karlin, Note 1). Finally, a small group of experimental studies using projective techniques and scaled-down architectural models has examined the perceptual and normative or social parameters of settings that determine the perception of crowding (e.g., Baum & Davis, 1976; Desor, 1972).

Although not meant to be an exhaustive review of studies of human density and crowding phenomena, this chapter is concerned with the application of behavioral research data to the design of high-density residential environments. Modern behavioral scientists have also suggested that high-density urban life has unavoidable consequences for human adjustment and social behavior. Zimbardo (1969) has conceptualized these implications in terms of anonymity and deindividuation. When conditions of social life do not foster individual identity and social responsibility, deindividuated behaviors such as vandalism and antisocial acts may result. Milgram (1970) has further suggested that the stimulus demands characteristic of complex urban environments result in the development of interpersonal orientations that minimize involving interactions between strangers. Although not all research has found that high density has adverse effects on social relations or individual performance (cf. Freedman, 1975), a body of research on high-density residential environments indicates that lack of congruence or "fit" between architectural and behavioral systems can result in the experience of crowding, interpersonal avoidance, social isolation, and inhibited development of local social networks (Valins & Baum, 1973; Yancey, 1972). When the architectural design of high-density housing makes the formation and evolution of residential affiliation patterns and social groups more difficult and thereby reduces the likelihood of satisfying and predictable social contacts in the local environment, the behavioral effects mentioned by Zimbardo (1969) may become more prevalent, because participation in social networks presumably helps to foster individual identity and responsiveness to group norms and enhances subjective feelings of control over the local environment. The intensity of social relations that characterize local networks may range from "mutual awareness" to friendship (Lee, 1968, p. 250). However intense, some level of interpersonal knowledge is basic to the development of mechanisms of informal social control in the residential setting. High density, in turn, may serve to intensify the negative effects of social isolation and anonymity (Freedman, 1975).

Although behavioral scientists cannot directly affect the growth of densely populated urban concentrations, their methods can lead to data that may suggest how to design residential environments to ameliorate some of the undesirable effects of high-density living. I am not proposing that architecture *determines* or imposes necessary patterns of behavior, but I agree with Osmond (1966) that "buildings engender social relationships [p. 314]." In other words, architectural spaces are conceived of as facilitators of certain perceptions and behaviors (Lang & Moleski, 1973). The design of dense residential environments can support or inhibit locally based social interaction by influencing the ease with which these behaviors can be performed by users. Another key issue is whether a building's design will support and maintain social behavior repertoires that people bring with them into a new setting (Bryce-Laporté, 1970; Yancey, 1972).

The success with which building spaces and user behavior are made congruent through adequate design ultimately depends on better knowledge of how people and environments mutually influence each other and how the spatial organization of social life influences experience and behavior. One way to conceptualize man-environment congruence is in terms of the manifest and latent functions that architectural spaces fulfill (Zeisel, 1975). Whether particular areas are used in the manner originally intended by the architect touches on the important issue of environmental flexibility and the need to design buildings that will support a wide range of behavior emitted by diverse user groups. The perspective taken in this chapter is very similar to Altman's (1973) general orientation: Human behavior and the environment in which it occurs comprise two interdependent components of an ecological system. DeLong (1974) has suggested that the point required for a man-environment approach to architectural design entails "approach[ing] social existence as a system [p. 15]." From this point of view, behavior-environment congruence can be thought of as an interlocking set of relationships in which the physical characteristics of built environments are conceptualized as mediums for social systems.

An important question that needs to be addressed during the design process is how the physical environment distributes resources of value to the continuing social lives of individual users and user groups. At the individual level, environmental resources are often conceived of in terms of the spatial complement per person within each dwelling unit, the ergonomics of specific areas such as kitchens, bathrooms, and stairways, and the adequacy of temperature control, lighting, ventilation systems, and so on. However, in terms of social relations, architects need to consider carefully how the physical system spatially distributes residents. Early studies of homogeneous residential groups suggested that spatial and functional propinquity determined friendships (e.g., Caplow & Foreman, 1950;

Festinger, Schachter, & Back, 1950). The acquaintance process was hypothesized to follow these general steps: Face-to-face contact in circulation areas connecting individual units led to casual neighboring, which in turn served as the basis for the development of more intense social relationships. Other data show, however, that various indicators of similarity are more reliable predictors of friendship than proximity factors. Similarity of life style and status (Gans, 1967), of values and interests (Gans, 1961a, 1961b), of income (Smith, Form, & Stone, 1954), and life cycle stage (Athanasiou & Yoshioka, 1973) have all been found to be significantly associated with friendship patterns. A recent study of ethnically mixed middle-income residents of New York City housing (Nahemow & Lawton, 1975) found that although similarity of age and of ethnicity were important predictors of friendship, close proximity resulted in friendship formation across age and ethnic groups. Dissimilar friends were found most frequently on the same floor, less frequently when the building was considered as a unit, and almost never in other buildings. Interestingly, similarity-dissimilarity made no difference in friendship intensity. Nahemow and Lawton (1975) attribute their findings to the "presence of environmental supports [p. 212] " as the circulation system of the buildings brought people into regular face-to-face contact with a fairly hetero-geneous group of neighbors.

In view of the inconsistent findings regarding the roles of proximity and similarity on friendship formation, architects and planners may justifiably ques-tion the value of such data as a guide to designing high-density residential settings that will promote local social networks. During the early residential history of socially homogeneous populations, functional proximity plays a powerful role, but unequivocal conclusions regarding the relative importance of proximity and similarity factors in determining local friendships among different socioeconomic groups and in heterogeneous populations do not yet seem warranted. The architect cannot design for friendship because there is no assurance that face-to-face contacts and casual interaction will escalate into more enduring and intense relationships. Such a guarantee is possible only within a deterministic system in which architecture imposes certain patterns of social behavior that inevitably lead to affective bonds between members of the user population. Nonetheless, face-to-face contact mediated by the manner in which dwelling units are grouped around shared semiprivate areas is important for the develop-ment of ecologically local social networks. Although neither propinquity nor casual neighboring alone is a sufficient cause of interpersonal attraction and *intense* social relations (Gans, 1961a; Newcomb, 1956), both will promote local "mutual awareness," which Lee (1968, p. 250) has described as the most perva-sive form of urban social relations. Simply knowing who one's neighbors are contributes to a more certain and predictable local environment and may facilitate informal social control.

In their efforts to facilitate the development of local social networks, the architects can design settings that do not impede the acquaintance process. I am proposing that the architect's goal in this connection should be to plan residential environments that optimize the probability that users will meet one another under positive environmental conditions. The result of these design interventions is provision of greater behavioral options for people vis-à-vis neighbors. If opportunities for *comfortable* face-to-face interaction and casual neighboring are enhanced by design, then interpersonal knowledge, discovery of common interests and values, and the potential for gratifying social relationships may ensue. As Weick (1969) has noted, contact and mutual acknowledgment set the stage for more involving future social relations.

To facilitate positive social interaction among residents of high-density housing, design principles that deal with the following issues need to be developed and implemented: (1) planning adequate semiprivate space between individual dwelling units that will support casual and more intense social contacts; (2) fostering interunit communication and interpersonal knowledge; and (3) balancing privacy needs against the consequences of local anonymity. From an ecological perspective, these problems are highly related. Settings that do not provide adequate semiprivate interaction loci have been found to be associated with social isolation, uncertainty, and inhibited residential social networks (Yancey, 1972). Designs that have grouped residential units without regard to the social impact their arrangement may have, have been characterized by behavioral interference, stressful local social interactions, and interpersonal avoidance outside of the residential environment (Baum & Valins, 1977). Architectural features of site plans appear to mediate the quality of individual users' local social experiences and thereby exert considerable influence on local social organization.

The remainder of this chapter is devoted to analysis and application of behavioral research data to the design of high-density residential settings. Data on which specific design recommendations can be made are largely found in the human crowding literature. For our purposes, crowding is socially defined and refers to a psychological state or experience rather than physical conditions of population density. Studies of human crowding should prove to be of value to architects and designers, because this research provides clear evidence of how the architectural features of residential environments impact interpersonal behavior and emotion. Proshansky (1973) has suggested that one of the primary goals of environmental psychology should be to relate the "setting as is" to the "setting as experienced [p. 103]." Accordingly, a prominent characteristic of human crowding research has been a multimethod approach. Based on what we now know, it is possible to *begin* constructing linkages between physical aspects of the built environment, their perceptual correlates, and their experiential and behavioral consequences.

ARCHITECTURE AND SOCIAL BEHAVIOR

In a series of studies of college dormitory environments, Baum and Valins (1977) investigated the effects of two different architectural designs on social behavior and the experience of crowding. Their basic findings are of interest for our purposes, because they detail how the physical parameters of residential settings affect local social experiences.

The designs of the two different dormitory styles that were studied differ in two basic ways. Corridor-style buildings are constructed with double-occupancy bedrooms arranged along double-loaded corridors. A large central bath and a lounge at the end of the hall are shared by residents of each floor. Suite-style dormitories differ in that two or three double-occupancy bedrooms and a small bathroom are clustered around a common lounge that opens onto a double-loaded corridor. Whereas about 34 residents share a common lounge and bathroom in corridor-style residence halls, four to six students share these facilities in suite-style housing. Residential density in terms of physical space per person is virtually identical in the two building types, and about the same number of students lived on the floors sampled from each complex during the life of the research program.

Although residential groups appear to be approximately the same size if each floor is considered as a unit, the architectural features of each dormitory type cluster students into different-size living groups because of the arrangement of dwelling units in relation to one another and common areas. The two settings have been found to be associated with the development of differential patterns of passive contact and casual neighboring. Sociometric data that I collected (see Baum & Valins, 1977) indicate that residents of corridor-style housing less frequently encounter immediately adjacent neighbors and more frequently meet physically distant neighbors than do suite residents. These behaviors facilitated by architectural factors are of considerable importance, because they mediate the perception of local crowding, the desirability of face-to-face contact, and casual socializing. Corridor residents report that their floors are significantly more crowded, that they interact with others in the hallway when such contact is inconvenient or unwanted, and that they would like to avoid others on their floor, indicating that they cannot effectively deal with their neighbors (Baum, Harpin, & Valins, 1975). In terms of more enduring social relations, a significantly higher proportion of suite residents state that the majority of their college friends live on their floor (Baum & Valins, 1977). Other sociometric data (Davis, cited in Baum & Valins, 1977) indicate that corridor residents are less likely to report satisfying social interactions with immediately adjacent neighbors than are suite residents. Therefore, in addition to being related to different patterns of passive contact, the physical systems of corridor and suite residence halls have consequences for local group interaction and friendship formation. These data are intriguing in light of previous findings regarding the role of proximity factors on interpersonal attraction and sociometric choice in homogeneous college populations (e.g., Caplow & Foreman, 1950; Festinger et al., 1950). Although there is an overall positive relationship among propinquity, face-to-face contact, and friendships in suite dormitories, data from corridor residence halls indicate a weaker degree of association among these factors.

Suite residents are more apt to participate in local social groups than their corridor counterparts and Baum et al. (1975) have noted that the formation of locally based social groups substantially reduces the perception of local crowding. The nature of local social relations among suite dormitory neighbors is qualitatively different from that which characterizes corridor environments. Suite neighbors are significantly more likely to engage in self-disclosure and collective problem solving than are corridor students, and local social conditions in suites are marked by a greater degree of certainty. For example, although both populations are socially homogeneous, students in suite-style housing perceive greater attitudinal similarity among themselves and their neighbors and are much more certain of how neighbors feel about them as people (Baum & Valins, 1977).

These effects are not limited to the local residential setting. Local social experiences of these user groups have a marked impact on behavior and interpersonal orientations manifested toward other people in other places. Baum and Valins (1977) found that corridor residents, while waiting with a confederate for an experimental game to begin, look less at and sit farther from the confederate when the nature of anticipated interaction with the confederate is cooperative in nature. Furthermore, subjects from corridor-style housing report greater discomfort in the waiting room situation when cooperative norms are operative. Additional data indicate that corridor residents perform significantly worse under cooperative conditions than do suite residents but do better under competitive orientations that tend to inhibit personal involvement with the opponent. These data strongly suggest that the conditions of social life in corridor-style dormitories can be considered a kind of social conditioning that results in the avoidance of social interactions, leading to involvement with strangers. It appears that the ways in which corridor residents characterize their social environment reflect a state of social overload in which they have difficulty regulating frequency and place of contact with others. As Milgram (1970) has suggested, when the environment overloads the individual with social stimulation, the development of interpersonal orientations that inhibit involving interactions with others may result.

The results of two other studies have significant bearing on these phenomena and further highlight the differential social behavior of corridor and suite residents. In an experimental group-discussion task (Reichner, Note 2), participants from both dormitories were systematically ignored by confederates posing as discussants. In contrast to the responses of suite subjects, those from corridor-style housing reported greater comfort in the situation when their contributions were ignored than when they were not ignored. Also, corridor residents did not feel that prior acquaintance with members of the discussion group would have facilitated solution of the group's task. These data again strongly suggest that corridor residents feel more comfortable in the presence of strangers under conditions minimizing probability of interaction. However, results from another group-discussion experiment are more revealing of the quality of local social ties developed and maintained by each user group (Baum & Valins, 1977). In this study, discussion groups comprised of corridor and suite neighbors were asked to reach consensus. Neighbors from suites reached significantly greater postdiscussion agreement than did corridor neighbors. A similar trend was found for discussion groups whose members were not neighbors and resided on different floors. Therefore, it appears that the quality of social life in residential settings has important implications for interpersonal behavior with frequently met associates as well as strangers beyond the confines of the local residential environment.

In summary, the studies reviewed in this section lead to the conclusion that architecture can mediate the quantity and quality of social relations in the local residential environment. The interaction of different architectural systems and user behavior promotes distinct social learning histories that result in generalized patterns of interpersonal affect and sociality. A more thorough analysis of the interface between architecture and behavior is necessary, however, before design recommendations can be made.

DESIGNING SEMIPRIVATE INTERACTION LOCI

Behavior-Environment Congruence

The reasons locally based social interaction in corridor-designed dormitories becomes associated with the desire to avoid neighbors and the perception of crowding are not readily apparent until one further investigates the manner in which both corridor and suite designs meet the wants and needs of residents. Earlier, I suggested that the design of semiprivate interaction spaces connecting individual dwelling units was one of the primary factors responsible for the quality of local affiliation and social networks. When the functional spatial relationships between these zones and residential units preclude their surveillance in advance of use and render them functionally isolated from units, as in the case of Pruitt-Igoe, residents will not use semiprivate areas for social purposes, and anonymity may come to characterize local social conditions (Yancey, 1972).

Social isolation does not accurately describe the social relations that corridor residents maintain with their neighbors. These people do not suffer from a lack of social stimulation. Instead, they meet what they perceive to be excessively high levels of social encounter. The inadequacy of semiprivate interaction zones provided in the corridor setting is primarily responsible for the experience of crowding and the relatively negative interpersonal affect that inhibits maintenance of positive and intimate social ties with neighbors.

A recent locational analysis of user behavior in corridor and suite residential environments reveals differential patterns of space use (Davis & Baum, Note 3). The architectural features of each dormitory type bring users into face-to-face contact under different levels of social stimulation. When engaged in social interaction, corridor residents are most frequently found in the long undifferentiated hallways that serve as transit areas, and they very seldomly socialize in end-hall lounges. In contrast, suite residents do the majority of their socializing in their individual suite lounges and are rarely noted in corridor areas that connect suites. When polled, people in corridor-style housing report they most prefer interacting with friends and neighbors in their bedrooms, whereas suite residents prefer the suite lounge (Baum & Valins, 1977). The discrepancy between corridor residents' locational preferences and the manner in which they actually maintain local social contacts reflects a lack of behavior-environment congruence. The features of hallways in corridor dormitories do not provide behavioral supports for comfortable socializing and casual interaction.

Although hallways in corridor-style dormitories and suite lounges in suite-style housing fulfill similar latent functions, the manifest function of corridor hallways precludes efficient regulation of interpersonal behavior. Because this zone's manifest function is primarily one of access to a large number of residential units, common bath, lounge, and other floors, it is very difficult for users to predict in advance *who* or *how many others* they will find there and whether those others are in the hallway for social purposes or are merely passing through. Casual neighboring and more intensive socializing in corridor hallways are very likely to suffer behavioral interference and disruption. These factors and the difficulty of conducting one's social interactions in private render hallways inadequate for positive social encounter. Additional behavior mapping data (Davis & Baum, Note 3) indicate that lounges and individual bedrooms in corridor housing are rarely utilized for social purposes. I believe these findings are also related to problems of control and privacy. Like hallway transit areas, corridor lounges assume the characteristics of public rather than semiprivate space. Lounges must be potentially shared with a large group of others, and their relative functional isolation from a large proportion of individual units reduces surveillance opportunities in advance of use. Thus, access to lounge areas is largely uncontrolled by the local population. Minimal use of corridor bedrooms for socializing may be related to the relative difficulty of coordinating their use as a private area for one's own social purposes with roommates' activities and privacy requirements.

The formation of social groups by residents surrounding common suite lounges is the most important condition differentiating the local social lives of corridor and suite residents. Circumstances under which local social contacts occur in suite housing are less stressful, because the clustering of residents into smaller units around adequate semiprivate interaction areas makes interaction more manageable. Suite residents encounter acceptable levels of social stimulation, and lounges have the requisite amenities to support casual interaction. The spatial relations between public hallways, the semiprivate lounge, and private bedroom areas enhance the evolution of local social ties. Because the suite lounge serves as a transit area for a relatively small group of immediate associates, behavioral disruption and intrusions on social interaction in the lounge are minimized. Because the lounge is shared by only four to six persons who have come to know one another, behavioral coordination in lounge areas is probably accomplished without too much difficulty. The immediate proximity of private and semiprivate spaces ensures that the local residential environment will support casual socializing without jeopardizing others' privacy. These factors render more certain local social conditions than those found in corridor-style dormitories. It is fairly easy for suite residents to predict in advance who and how many others are in the lounge, because the area can be kept under aural and visual surveillance from private rooms, and suitemates can actively exert control over access to their lounge.

The suite lounges that I have characterized as semiprivate interaction loci have no counterpart in corridor-style housing. I believe it is the absence of such spaces in corridor dormitories that brings about negative experiential consequences for users and generalized patterns of interpersonal avoidance (Baum & Valins, 1977; Davis & Baum, Note 3). Based on this analysis of architecture and sociality, some specific design recommendations emerge.

The contradiction between manifest and latent functions of corridor dormitory hallways results in too much social stimulation at inappropriate times. Levels of excessive social encounter are also facilitated by the allocation of nonspatial resources and residential group size. Specifically, the provision of a single bath to be shared by a large group of local residents results in frequent face-to-face contact in circulation areas and baths when social contact may be undesirable and intrude on privacy. Designing residential settings to facilitate *optimal* levels of local social encounter is a desirable goal, but empirical evidence required to formulate guidelines about what constitutes too much or too little social interaction is not yet available. Nonetheless, observations of Yancey (1972) and Baum and Valins (1977) strongly suggest that aversive lower and upper limits of local social contact may exist.

The size of user groups clustered around shared semiprivate areas is obviously related to quantity of local interaction. Although estimates of optimal human group size have been calculated by Calhoun (1973a, 1973b), they are rather speculative and do not serve the immediate needs of designers and architects. If the local residential group is too large, social overload may come to characterize social conditions; however, if the group is too small, Freedman (1975) has suggested that people may feel isolated. Specific recommendations concerning the limits of residential group size must await better abstract analysis and understanding of the social and psychological implications of local group size for various user populations.

The habitability of the individual dwelling unit is not merely a function of interior amenities and spatial arrangement; it is a joint function of its ecological relations with both semiprivate and public areas. Yancey (1972, p. 129) has suggested that the lack of suitable semiprivate interaction loci may have an "atomizing effect" on local social networks, and his observations seem to be generally confirmed by Baum and Valins (1977). The architectural configuration of high-density housing should provide semiprivate spaces whose proximity to private areas will encourage use. However, the spatial and functional relationships among these three types of zones must be carefully considered to minimize potential conflicts between manifest and latent functions. Public areas serving as access routes for large numbers of residents should not immediately adjoin entrances to individual residences. Instead, access paths should lead into semiprivate areas to act as "buffer zones" between public and private spaces (Newman, 1973). Small groups of residential units should be clustered around and have immediate entry to these semiprivate interaction loci if they are to serve as focal points for the development of local social networks.

Territoriality

Human territoriality has recently emerged as a distinct area of social-psychological research and theorizing (e.g., Altman, 1975; Altman & Haythorn, 1967; Edney, 1974, 1976; Sommer & Becker, 1969). Spaces with which people identify and over which they exert some measure of individual or collective social control have been termed *territories* (Lyman & Scott, 1967). Altman (1975, p. 114) has suggested that there are three types of human territories: (1) primary territories characterized by exclusive individual or group ownership or use; (2) secondary territories that are less exclusive in this sense; and (3) public territories marked by "almost free" access and use. Human territoriality is a complex phenomenon, and as Freedman (1975) has noted, the blithe assumption that it is a biologically induced drive in humans is unwarranted. Nevertheless, the literature devoted to human territoriality should be of interest to planners and architects for two reasons. Historically speaking, according to Skaburskis (1974), the neighborhood unit as a town-planning principle implicitly assumes that a sense of home, belonging, and community develop if "people are put in the same place and share the same amenities [p. 39]." Second, the concept of territoriality seems to allude to design interventions that can promote residents' identification with others in the local residential environment.

In terms of our previous discussion of college residences, suite lounges and the hallways and lounges in corridor-style dormitories seem to correspond, respectively, to secondary and public territories. Entrance into suite lounges is controllable by those who share the setting. Intensive use of suite lounges by surrounding residents and personal decorations supplied by users reflect the territorial characteristics of the lounges. Entry to corridor hallways is less controllable, because they are extensions of access routes from other floors and exterior areas. The lack of naturally forming social groups in corridor-style housing precludes group control and conversion of public hallways and lounges into semiprivate territories despite the fact that hallways, at least, serve a mixture of private and public functions.

In his study of architecture and crime in New York City public-housing projects, Newman (1973) concluded that the lack of semiprivate or secondary territorial spaces was one of the major design variables associated with high vandalism and criminal victimization rates. Although methodological and theoretical critiques of *Defensible Space* (e.g., Adams, 1973; Hillier, 1973) render its conclusions less certain, I agree with Altman (1975) that Newman's point of view deserves careful attention. The suggestion that physical design can create the *impression* that certain areas are under local proprietary influence and, thus, can deter criminal entry is an interesting hypothesis and may represent a tenable alternative to "hardening the target" (Patterson, Note 4, p. 6). However, I would propose that the implication of territorial prerogatives through symbolic design may have little substantive impact on residents' or strangers' perception of who is in control of a particular area. Secondary territories are not created by perceptual features alone but are effected through territorial behavior and intensive space use. The differentiation of double-loaded corridors, breaking up long corridors into smaller groups of apartments by unlocked swinging doors, and the perceptual grading of public into semiprivate spaces may help to facilitate the perceptual correlates of territory but do not ensure that hallways will come to serve a mixture of private and public activities. Physical grouping of residences around shared zones that enter into public areas, as in the case of suite dormitories, would seem to be a more direct and effective facilitator of territorial behavior.

Visual Stimuli and Behavioral Props

In a previous section, evidence indicated that designs that promote excessive levels of unwanted local social input lead to the experience of crowding. Although decreasing the number of residents who share access routes and local circulation areas addresses the problems of social overload and crowding stress rather directly, data from a small group of experimental studies suggest ways in which alterations of visual features of settings reduce high levels of social stimulation.

In an early study of human crowding, Desor (1972) asked people to place as many miniature figures as possible in a scaled-down model room without "overcrowding them [p. 80]." Her basic hypothesis was that architectural features that diminish the number of others in one's visual field (and by implication reduce olfactory and tactile cues associated with others' presence) result in increased room capacity. By systematically varying certain design variables and descriptions of ongoing behavior in the setting, she found evidence in support of this hypothesis. One result from this study is of particular interest for our purposes. By increasing the number of doors leading into the model room, crowding thresholds were substantially reduced; that is, fewer "people" were placed in the setting. This result is intriguing, because it suggests that the number of opportunities for access into a space is positively related to expected intensity of social stimulation. If this interpretation is correct, Desor's finding has implications for grouping local dwelling units and the design of interconnecting semiprivate spaces consistent with earlier recommendations. The sheer number of individual units that have direct entry to semiprivate spaces may serve as a cue for levels of anticipated social encounters. Large groups of units around semiprivate zones may induce expectations of relatively high levels of unavoidable local contact. This expectation may be sufficient to induce the perception of crowding and inhibit casual use of that space for social purposes. The number of access paths leading from public into semiprivate areas may serve similar cue functions and reduce the capacity of semiprivate zones to support informal socializing.

The results of two related studies (Baum & Davis, 1976; Worchel & Teddlie, 1976) have further implications for the interior design of residential environments. Using an experimental procedure and model room very similar to Desor's (1972), Baum and I assessed the influence of color, visual complexity, and behavioral orientation on setting capacity.

Light-colored rooms were found to have greater perceived capacity than dark rooms, because heightened color intensity and luminosity increase *apparent* spatial extent. Visual complexity (pictures on walls), on the other hand, had no effect on the number of miniature figures placed in light-colored rooms. When room color was dark, the provision of pictures on walls increased perceived room capacity under social interaction conditions and reduced room capacity when the nature of ongoing activities in the setting were nonsocial. This finding and the fact that subjects placed themselves near pictures when pictures were available strongly support the hypothesis that visually interesting design features fulfill two important functions. First, the level of social stimulation met in a setting can be reduced by diverting attention away from other people and toward nonsocial stimuli. Perhaps more important, however, visual complexity provides an opportunity for users to engage in alternative nonsocial behaviors (e.g., scanning decorations) not considered inappropriate by others present. Therefore, in addition to the provision of additional loci of person-environment interaction, the complexity variable may act as a behavioral prop enriching the variety of behaviors a setting will support. The reasons visual complexity produced different effects in dark rooms under nonsocial orientations are twofold. Since the primary concern of subjects considering this setting was availability of space rather than social input, pictures did not serve as distractors. Also, since the apparent space available was already reduced by room color, further increases in nonsocial stimulation provided by complexity may have resulted in too much sensory input. It is important to note that the design factors varied in this study had no systematic effects on esthetic ratings of the rooms.

Although it may be argued that the generalizability of these findings is limited by the task's projective nature, which obviated real experience in the setting, data provided by Worchel and Teddlie (1976) in a study involving people interacting at various distances reveal similar phenomena. When subjects were interacting at close distances, as would be the case under high-density conditions in nonlaboratory environments, the presence of pictures on the walls significantly reduced reported discomfort and the perception of crowding.

The results of these last studies provide empirical data that can be employed in the interior design of public and semiprivate spaces. Interior public spaces used by a large number of residents should be decorated in light hues to maximize perceived spatial extent. Also, the comfort of semiprivate interaction loci used for casual socializing will be enhanced if lightly colored and decorated. I would urge, however, that user decoration be permitted and encouraged, because it may more effectively promote satisfaction with the setting than professional design schemes. Users personalizing semiprivate spaces will foster casual interaction, promote identification with the local environment, and facilitate a sense of ownership. Like the ancient Assyrian, Gilgamesh, who journeyed into the wilderness to stamp his name on a brick, local residents can signify proprietorship of their environment.

SUMMARY DISCUSSION

The general intent of this paper has been (1) an analysis of how physical and perceptual characteristics of man-made environments interact with the behavior of people who live in them, and (2) the formulation of design goals that will foster a positive social climate in the face of an inevitably high-density human habitat. I have reviewed in detail some recent studies of human crowding to delineate different physical features of residential environments that mediate neighbor relations and either promote or impede development of positive local social conditions. An ecological approach to the design of high-density residential settings has been suggested as a general approach that may help to alleviate the potentially aversive impact of high density and reduce the likelihood of crowding stress. By designing residential environments that facilitate local social contact under positive environmental conditions, the quality of local social life and social organization may be enhanced.

It should be kept in mind, however, that the data base from which I have extrapolated design recommendations is limited in scope. The populations that served as subjects in these crowding studies were university students living in high-density dormitories. Inferences made from these data cannot necessarily be assumed to hold for other user groups in other types of residential environments. Although the studies reviewed show clearly how architectural factors can mediate social experience and play an important role in the formation of qualitatively different local affiliation patterns and social networks, the generalizability of these phenomena needs to be addressed through implementing behavioral studies in other residential settings.

Although I believe that the study of human-crowding phenomena has provided insight into the general problem of designing high-density residential environments, it is clear that a general theory of behavioral design does not exist that can both integrate existing data and predict how people and their habitats modify each other. The lack of theory may be due to the intrinsic difficulty of our task, but the inability of architects, designers, and social scientists to understand one another's specialized language impedes the theory building that is required. An implicit assumption of this chapter is that categorical distinctions among the roles of interior designers, architects, planners, and social scientists are counterproductive. Each group possesses specialized skills, and the coordination of these different types of expertise will facilitate the development of a general theory of behavioral design.

The potential of such a cooperative enterprise can only be measured against the possible consequences of not acting in concert. Although a behavioral theory of environmental design is not a panacea for the ills of urban civilization, we may be in the unique position of being able to help direct the social evolution of *homo sapiens* into *homo urbanis*.

ACKNOWLEDGMENTS

The author wishes to express appreciation to Andrew Baum, Donald J. Conway, Yakov M. Epstein, and Stuart Valins for their comments on an earlier version of this chapter.

REFERENCE NOTES

1. Aiello, J. R., Epstein, Y. M., & Karlin, R. A. Field experimental research on human crowding. In A. Baum (Chair), *Human response to crowding.* Symposium presented at the meeting of the Eastern Psychological Association, New York, April 1975.
2. Reichner, R. *On being ignored: The effects of residential group size on social interaction.* Unpublished master's thesis, State University of New York at Stony Brook, 1974.
3. Davis, G. E., & Baum, A. Role of social interaction in tall buildings. In S. Margalis (Chair), *Social-psychological research on high rise residential environments.* Symposium presented at the meeting of the American Psychological Association, Chicago, August 1975.
4. Patterson, A. H. Social control, density, and tall buildings. In S. Margulis (Chair), *Social psychological research on high rise residential environments.* Symposium presented at the meeting of the American Psychological Association, Chicago, August 1975.

REFERENCES

Adams, J. R. Defensible space. *Man-Environment Systems,* 1973, *3*(4), 267-268.
Altman, I. Some perspectives on the study of man-environment phenomena. *Representative Research in Social Psychology,* 1973, *4* (1), 109-126.
Altman, I. *The environment and social behavior.* Monterey, Calif.: Brooks/Cole, 1975.
Altman, I., & Haythorn, W. W. The ecology of isolated groups. *Behavioral Science,* 1967, *12* (3), 169-182.

Athanasiou, R., & Yoshioka, G. A. The spatial character of friendship formation. *Environment and Behavior*, 1973, *5* (1), 43-65.

Baum, A., & Davis, G. E. Spatial and social aspects of crowding perception. *Environment and Behavior*, 1976, *8* (4), 527-544.

Baum, A., Harpin, R. E., & Valins, S. The role of group phenomena in the experience of crowding. *Environment and Behavior*, 1975, *7* (2), 185-198.

Baum, A., & Valins, S. *Architecture and social behavior: Psychological studies of social density*. Hillsdale, N.J.: Lawrence Erlbaum Associates, 1977.

Bryce-Laporté, R. S. Urban relocation and family adaptation in Puerto Rico. In W. Mangin (Ed.), *Peasants in cities: Readings in the anthropology of urbanization*. Boston: Houghton Mifflin, 1970.

Calhoun, J. B. What sort of box? *Man-Environment Systems*, 1973, *3* (1), 3-30. (a)

Calhoun, J. B. R_x Evolution, tribalism, and the Cheshire Cat: Three paths from now. *Technological Forecasting and Social Change*, 1973, *4*, 263-282. (b)

Caplow, T., & Foreman, R. Neighborhood attraction in a homogeneous community. *American Sociological Review*, 1950, *15*, 357-366.

Davis, K. The urbanization of the human population. *Scientific American*, 1965, *213* (3), 40-53.

DeLong, A. J. The scientist and the sorcerer: Creating man-environment systems. *Architectural Student*, 1974, *24*, 15-18.

Desor, J. A. Toward a psychological theory of crowding. *Journal of Personality and Social Psychology*, 1972, *21* (1), 79-83.

Edney, J. J. Human territoriality. *Psychological Bulletin*, 1974, *81*(12), 959-975.

Edney, J. J. Human territories: Comments on functional properties. *Environment and Behavior*, 1976, *8*, (1), 31-47.

Epstein, Y. M., & Karlin, R. A. Effects of acute experimental crowding. *Journal of Applied Social Psychology*, 1975, *5*, (1), 34-53.

Festinger, L., Schachter, S., & Back, K. *Social pressures in informal groups*. New York: Harper & Row, 1950.

Freedman, J. *Crowding and behavior*. San Francisco: Freeman, 1975.

Freedman, J., Klevansky, S., & Ehrlich, P. The effect of crowding on human task performance. *Journal of Applied Social Psychology*, 1971, *1* (1), 7-25.

Freedman, J., Levy, A., Buchanan, R. W., & Price, J. Crowding and human aggression. *Journal of Experimental Social Psychology*, 1972, *8*, 528-548.

Galle, O. R., Gove, W. R., & McPherson, J. M. Population density and pathology: What are the relations for man? *Science*, 1972, *176*, 23-30.

Gans, H. J. Planning and social life. *Journal of the American Institute of Planners*, 1961, *27* (2), 134-140. (a)

Gans, H. J. The balanced community. *Journal of the American Institute of Planners*, 1961, *27* (3), 176-184. (b)

Gans, H. J. *The Levittowners*. New York: Pantheon, 1967.

Griffitt, W., & Veitch, R. Hot and crowded: Influences of population density and temperature on interpersonal affective behavior. *Journal of Personality and Social Psychology*, 1971, *17* (1), 92-98.

Hillier, B. In defense of space. *RIBA Journal*, 1973, *80*, 539-544.

Jacobs, J. *The economy of cities*. New York: Random House, 1969.

Lang J., & Moleski, W. A behavioral theory of design? *Design and Environment*, Winter 1973, *4* (4), 33-47.

Lee, T. Urban neighborhood as a socio-spatial schema. *Human Relations*, 1968, *21* (3), 241-267.

Loo, C. The effects of spatial density on the social behavior of children. *Journal of Applied Social Psychology,* 1972, *2* (4), 372-381.

Lyman, S. M., & Scott, M. B. Territoriality: A neglected sociological dimension. *Social Problems,* 1967, *12* (4), 236-249.

Milgram, S. The experience of living in cities. *Science,* 1970, *167* (3924), 1461-1468.

Nahemow, L., & Lawton, M. P. Similarity and propinquity in friendship formation. *Journal of Personality and Social Psychology,* 1975, *32* (2), 205-213.

Newcomb, T. M. The prediction of interpersonal attraction. *American Psychologist,* 1956. *11,* 575-586.

Newman, O. *Defensible space.* New York: Macmillan, 1973.

Osmond, H. Some psychiatric aspects of design. In L. B. Holland (Ed.), *Who designs America?* Garden City, N.Y.: Doubleday, 1966.

Proshansky, H. M. Theoretical issues in environmental psychology. *Representative Research in Social Psychology,* 1973, *4* (1), 93-107.

Schmitt, R. C. Implications of density in Hong Kong. *Journal of the American Institute of Planners,* 1963, *29* (3), 210-217.

Schmitt, R. C. Density, health, and social disorganization. *Journal of the American Institute of Planners,* 1966, *32* (1), 38-40.

Skaburskis, J. V. Territoriality and its relevance to neighborhood design: A review. *Journal of Architectural Research,* 1974, *3,* 39-45.

Sommer, R., & Becker, F. D. Territorial defense and the good neighbor. *Journal of Personality and Social Psychology,* 1969, *11,* 85-92.

Smith, J., Form, W. H., & Stone, G. P. Local intimacy in a middle-sized city. *American Journal of Sociology,* 1954, *60,* 276-284.

Valins, S., & Baum, A. Residential group size, social interaction, and crowding. *Environment and Behavior,* 1973, *5* (4), 421-439.

Weick, K. E. *The social psychology of organizing.* Reading, Mass.: Addison-Wesley, 1969.

Wirth, L. Urbanism as a way of life. *American Journal of Sociology,* 1938, *44,* 3-24.

Worchel, S., & Teddlie, C. Factors affecting the experience of crowding: A two-factor theory. *Journal of Personality and Social Psychology,* 1976, *34* (1), 30-40.

Yancey, W. Architecture, interaction, and social control: The case of a large-scale housing project. In J. Wohlwill & D. Carson (Eds.), *Environment and social science: Perspectives and applications.* Washington, D.C.: American Psychological Association, 1972.

Zeisel, J. *Sociology and architectural design.* New York: Russell Sage Foundation, 1975.

Zimbardo, P. The human choice: Individuation, reason, and order versus deindividuation, impulse and chaos. In W. J. Arnold & D. Levine (Eds.), *Nebraska Symposium on Motivation* (Vol. 17). Lincoln, Neb.: University of Nebraska Press, 1969.

13

Density, Crowding, and Preschool Children

Chalsa M. Loo
University of California, Santa Cruz

This chapter is a descriptive summary of a series of three recent research studies aimed at understanding how children are affected by crowding or high density and whether individual differences can be identified that account for differential effects of high density. The findings presented represent a portion of a larger research project underway. These findings are described in a sequence that allows the reader to examine the ways in which our research methodology, research questions, and instruments or measures became progressively more refined.

Study I was an investigation of the differential effects of spatial density on low and high scorers on behavior problem indexes. The major question addressed in this study was, "Are there differential effects of spatial density on normal versus behaviorally disturbed children?".

My dissatisfaction with prior research designs that investigated only single variables caused me to explore other analyses and designs that would allow for a more comprehensive analysis of density effects. This aim led to Study II, an investigation of the effects of spatial density on five clusters of single variables. These clusters were combined on the basis of observations made in a pilot test of the research and from a factor analysis run on the dependent variables. In keeping with my interest in individual differences, Study II also examined the differential effects of spatial density on boys versus girls and on far versus close personal space children. Study II also represented the first attempt to obtain the perceptions of children regarding the density conditions; these were obtained through a post-experimental interview questionnaire.

Study III was a collaborative endeavor with Denise Kennelly. It both refined the measures and procedures used in Study II and investigated the effects of social density (four-versus eight-person groups) on preschool children. In this study the five factors were obtained directly from the factor analysis of a combination of the rated dependent variables and the perceptions obtained from the post-experimental questionnaire. We continued the investigation into sex and personal space differences in regard to high density, this time looking at the effects of different sized groups of people on boys versus girls and on far versus close personal space children.

In summary, two types of densities were investigated: social and spatial density. Social density research compares the effects of larger and smaller groups of persons in the same-sized space, whereas spatial density studies compare the effects of larger or smaller rooms for the same number of people. In addition, three dimensions of individual differences were investigated: degree of behavioral normalcy, degree of personal space needs, and sex.

Educators, housing officials, sociologists, and psychologists have been concerned with the consequences of crowding on children in home, classroom, and neighborhood settings. Yet there has been very little research on the effects of crowding on children, probably owing to the fact that most researchers of crowding and density are social psychologists, who rely largely on the use of undergraduate students as participants for laboratory experimental settings. Although there are considerably more studies on the effects of density on adults, I was hesitant to generalize these findings to children, because coping capacity, normal range and mode of activity, need for personal space, and structure of normal activities are different for adults and children. This chapter begins with a brief review of the literature on the effects of density on children. Since Evans has extensively reviewed the research on developmental aspects of crowding in Chapter 9 of this volume, I mention only those studies most pertinent to our program of research.

DENSITY AND SOCIAL BEHAVIOR

Prior to age 5, children usually engage in parallel play in which two or more children are engaged in similar activity without interacting or reciprocally responding to one another. Beginning at about ages 4 to 5, parallel play decreases in frequency and social interaction develops. Such social play consumes a great deal of the child's waking hours and is an important contributor to the development of social maturity and communication skills. Let us examine the literature on the effects of density on various forms of social behavior.

Negative Social Behavior

The one social behavior that has received the most attention in the literature on crowding effects on children is aggression. Findings on the effects of high density on aggression are neither consistent nor conclusive. Aggressive/destructive behavior was found to increase with increasing social density (Hutt & Vaizey, 1966). Comparing behaviors evidenced in a classroom allowing less than 30 square feet per child to one allowing more than 50 square feet per child, Shapiro (1975) found more disruptive, aggressive, and otherwise unacceptable behavior in the high spatial density condition. Aggression for boys was found to be less in a high spatial density condition than in a low spatial density condition although no effects were found for girls (Loo, 1972). Smith and Connelly (1972) found no effect for density on aggression of children but found an effect for amount of play equipment on aggression. As amount of play equipment decreased, there was a consistent increase in aggression. Since Smith and Connelly (1972) confounded indoors/outdoors with density, their results should be treated as suggestive but not definitive. Rohe and Patterson (1974) found an interactive effect of density and equipment abundance on aggression. High density and low resources resulted in increased aggressive and destructive behavior, whereas high density and high resources did not.

Inconsistencies in findings regarding the effect of density on aggression may be due to a variety of factors: differing number and type of toys, different definitions of aggression, different sized density conditions, different effects of social and spatial density, or a curvilinear relationship between density and aggression (Loo, 1972). Aggression might be more frequent in very abundant space and in extremely constricted space and less frequent in somewhat crowded space that still allows enough room for gross motor behavior and retreat. Regarding definitions of aggression, the inclusion or exclusion of playful aggression in the definition of aggression may be another source of variance in findings.

A second type of behavior that may be considered as negative or at least as nonpositive social behavior includes noninvolvement in social interaction. Research on the effects of density on the extent of interaction of children suggests that social interaction decreases in a high density condition, although the issue is complex and unresolved. Social interaction decreased for 5-year-old children in a high social density condition (Hutt & Vaizey, 1966), and 5-year-olds interacted with fewer children in a high spatial density condition (Loo, 1972). Density had no effect on the extent of social interaction in Smith and Connelly's study (1972), but I contend that this was because of his subjects' ages (2½ to 4 years). Since social interaction has not yet fully developed at those ages, it is questionable to compare frequency of social interaction for such children. Shapiro (1975) found more onlooking and Price (1971) found more solitary behavior in a high density condition. In the present study I investigated the effects of density on *extent* of interaction (noninteraction versus social interaction) and on *quality* of interaction. More specifically, I studied the effects of density on two types of noninteraction: solitary behavior and onlooker behavior; as well as two types of social interaction: aggression and positive social overtures.

Posture and Motoric Activity

In a previous paper (Loo, 1972), I suggested that the effects of density on social behavior may be mediated by the effects of density on motoric activity. Prior research studies, although few in number, suggested effects of density on postures and motoric activity. Smith and Connelly (1972) found that there was more gross motor activity (running, skipping, and rough-and-tumble play) in an out-doors-larger area than in an indoors-smaller area. Preiser (1972) studied children under two spatial density conditions and found that the standing posture was more frequently adopted in the reduced space condition.

Additionally, there is some anecdotal evidence that density influences activity level. Friends of mine who have lived in France for several years observed that in Parisian apartments, which provide minimal space, children's play seemed more controlled and less active than the play of children in more spacious American homes. Although differences in cultural patterns of child rearing and disciplining or cultural differences in children's play, toys, or use of space must be considered, it is still possible that density is either affecting the degree to which parents control their children's behavior or that children cope with more or less space by accommodating their activity to the requirements of their environment. In the present study, I predicted that activity would be greatest in a low density condition, where a larger area allows for greater amounts of activity than does a smaller area.

Instability of Activity

Another variable related to social behavior that has been almost completely neglected in the literature concerns the extent to which high density environments lead to a disruption and a lack of completion of play activities. The development of a sense of mastery and competence is essential to a normal child's development. Furthermore, mastery and competence are partly dependent on the child's ability to be engaged in an activity and to complete the process of that activity. Frequent interruptions would preclude any sense of closure or any consistent and prolonged play activity. For example, if a child was role playing, the involvement would be minimal if the child was frequently interrupted. If a child was engaged in an activity requiring serious concentration, interruptions might well limit his or her interest in the activity as a result of being unable to concentrate on it. As a consequence, the child might choose to engage in more superficial activities, cease to engage in any type of play, or change activities frequently. In a previous study (Loo, 1972), I found a trend toward a greater frequency of interruptions in a high density condition, with girls being more frequently interrupted than boys. I posited that an interruption of behavior could have one of two general effects. An interruption could produce a brief pause in an activity, after which the child immediately resumes the interrupted activity; or the interruption could serve to end a particular activity than to be followed by some other behavior, such as observing others' activities ("nontoy" behavior) or a change in the toy played with.

Distancing Behavior

One way of coping with the problems of high density is to distance oneself from others. Distancing can be attained either physically or symbolically. Physically, the individual can move farther away from others when interacting with them. In some cases, however, physical distancing is difficult to attain, and the individual must instead resort to symbolic distancing, such as avoidance of eye contact and changing his or her axis of orientation (Argyle, 1967; Argyle & Dean, 1965; Liebman, 1970). Physical closeness has been found to be attenuated psychologically by such symbolic distancing behaviors (Pellegrini & Empey, 1970).

Research on symbolic distancing among children as a function of crowding is minimal. Escape behaviors and facing out positions are considered to be strategies for avoiding interaction. Escape behaviors include trying to open the door to a playroom, looking out of a window, or prolonged gazing into a mirror. Facing out can be operationalized by noting when a child's body faced a corner or the wall of a room in the first two rows of floor squares along a wall, without another child being located between the child and the wall. In the present program of research, we investigated the frequency of these symbolic distancing behaviors as a function of density.

SEX DIFFERENCES

Although the primary thrust of our research was to provide a more comprehensive examination of the effects of crowding on children, we were also interested in investigating individual differences in response to low and high spatial density conditions. These variables are of considerable interest and have been studied by a variety of investigators.

Sex differences found in crowding studies using adult subjects (Freedman, Levy, Buchanan, & Price, 1972; Ross, Layton, Erickson, & Schopler, 1973) suggest that females react more positively to a high-density condition than do males. Furthermore, Freedman's (1975) density-intensity hypothesis asserts that high density will intensify normal predispositions. He maintains that since males are more predisposed to competitiveness, a high-density condition will lead to an increase in competitiveness and that since females are more predisposed to cooperativeness, a high-density condition will lead to an increase in cooperativeness.

My 1972 findings demonstrated that whereas density had a negligible effect on frequency of interruptions for boys, girls were more interrupted in the high-density condition than in the low-density condition. Also, density had a negligible effect on aggression in girls, but there was a significant effect on aggression in boys. Sex differences in relation to symbolic distancing behaviors have been found. Males were found to sit farther from male accomplices than females sat from females; however, female interactants had significantly larger angular orientations between themselves than did male dyads (Pellegrini & Empey, 1970). Female adults were found to engage in more facial regard in the crowded room than in the uncrowded room whereas males were found to do the opposite (Ross et al., 1973). In the present study, sex differences were investigated by observing groups of children in mixed-sex composition.

STUDY I

The only published research on the effects of density on normal versus disturbed children is that of Hutt and Vaizey (1966), who found that brain-damaged children became increasingly more aggressive with increasing social density (both the medium and large groups), whereas normal children became significantly more aggressive only in the large group. Furthermore, brain-damaged children were 1.7 to 4 times more aggressive in the medium- and high-density conditions than were normals. With increasing density, autistic children spent significantly more time on the boundary of the room. Since the symptoms of pathology for autistic children include social isolation and resistance to interaction, increasing density appears to intensify the pathological symptoms of social withdrawal. In the present study I expected that children with behavior problems would have a lower tolerance for crowding stress and fewer strategies to cope adaptively with such a condition.

Five dimensions of behavior problems were examined: hyperactivity-distractability, anxiety, hostility-aggressiveness, behavior disturbance, and motor impulsivity. The Behavior Rating Scale for the Preschool Child, developed by Behar and Stringfield (1974) to assist educators and psychologists in the identification of preschool children with behavior problems, was used as the index for hyperactivity-distractability, anxiety, hostility-aggressiveness, and behavior disturbance. This scale consists of a check list of specific behaviors, weighted in terms of frequency of occurrence, which the teachers were asked to fill out for each participating child. Motor impulsivity was measured by administering the Draw-A-Line-Slowly Test (Maccoby, Dowley, Hagen, & Dagerman, 1965), which consists of asking the child to draw a line between two points as slowly as possible and recording the length of time taken for the child to draw the line.

Because my study was exploratory, many dependent variables were examined that were subsumed conceptually under the general areas of (1) extent and quality of social interaction, (2) activity mode and level, (3) instability of activity, (4) avoidance behaviors, and (5) affect. For extent of social interaction, children were rated for frequency of solitary play, onlooking, and social interaction. For quality of interaction, frequency of aggression and helpfulness-sharing were rated. For activity level and mode, frequency of lying down, sitting, standing, and walking were rated as well as the number of time intervals that the child remained on the same floor square as in the previous interval (defined as "inactivity"). The floor was divided into squares measuring approximately 2' X 2' each. For instability of activity, frequency of interruptions and number of toy changes were rated. Avoidance behaviors included frequency of facing out and escape behaviors. As already mentioned, facing out was defined as a child's facing a corner or wall in the first two rows of squares along the wall with no person being located between the child and the wall. Escape behaviors were rated as the frequency of trying to open the door, looking out of the window, or prolonged gazing into the mirror. Last, affect was rated for frequency of bored, distressed, angry affect (which together constituted total negative affect) and contented/happy expressions.

Participants in this study were 72 children, comprising 12 groups of six children each, three girls and three boys. All children in each group were from the same classroom. After the teachers had filled out a Preschool Behavior Questionnaire for each child and the Draw-A-Line-Slowly Test had been administered, the children were taken to a playroom and left there for about 1 hour, during which time six research assistants rated the children's behavior through a one-way mirror. An unfurnished room measuring 19'5" X 13'5" (a total area of 260.5 square feet) constituted the low spatial density condition. The high spatial density condition measured 9'9" X 13'5" (constituting an area of 130.8 square feet). The low density condition allowed 43.4 square feet per person, whereas the high density condition allowed 21.8 square feet per person. A wide variety of attractive toys was provided for both conditions and was identical for both conditions. Since a repeated measures design was used, each group came for two sessions (low and high density), separated by a few days to a week. A median split was performed on the scores for the behavior problem dimensions. Those children who scored below the median on each dimension were designated as "low," and those who scored above the median were designated as "high." The mean for low-hyperactive children was 0.25, for high-hyperactive children it was 4.78. The mean for low-anxiety children was 0.28, for high-anxiety children it was 4.83. The mean for low-hostile-aggressive children was 0.11; for high-hostile-aggressive children it was 7.00. The mean for low behaviorally disturbed children was 1.94; for high behaviorally disturbed children it was 18.22. The mean for impulsive children was 9.08 seconds, for high-motor inhibitors it was 30.90 seconds. All scales on the teacher ratings were highly correlated, but motor inhibition was not correlated with any of the other behavior problem dimensions.

An analysis of variance with unequal cell sizes was performed for density, sex, and each of the behavior problem indexes. The analyses yielded the following findings and implications. High-anxiety children were those whom teachers rated as evidencing worry, unhappiness, distress, fearfulness of new things or situations, fussiness, low tolerance for crying, a tendency to give up easily, staring into space, or speech difficulties. The analyses indicated that high-anxiety children expressed more negative affect and liked others less in the high-density condition compared to the low-density condition, whereas no density effect was found for the low-anxiety children for these variables. Negative affect consisted of a sum of scores for anger, distress, and boredom. Looking at a separate frequency count for each of these emotions, I found that in the high-density condition, 49 percent of the negative affect expressed by the high-anxiety children was anger, 34 percent was distress, and 17 percent was boredom. These findings demonstrate that children who are predisposed toward fearfulness and distress respond to a crowded condition through emotional avenues; their anxiety is intensified through expressions of anger and distress, which in turn are related to their decreased attraction to the other children.

If the low-anxiety children did not show increases in negative affect, what did they do? The difference between low- and high-anxiety children is fascinating. High-anxiety children responded to high density with expressions of emotional helplessness, but low-anxiety children responded with motoric coping behaviors consisting of a reduction in walking and increased facing out positions. Children with no anxiety symptoms (or very few) responded to high density through motoric channels that were more functionally adaptive to stress reduction. These differences warn us that very anxious children may need assistance in developing more adaptive means of stress reduction. Anger may be an expression of frustration that only makes a crowding state less bearable for others. Anger may well have a social-facilitative effect in making others in the situation angry as well. Crying may lead to adult intervention, but again this is not a coping strategy that would serve any useful function if no intervention is possible.

I also found that high-motor inhibitors, those who can control their movements and actions most effectively, altered their motor behaviors in the high-density condition in ways that were stress-reducing. High-motor inhibitors stood more, attempted to escape more, and were located on the fringes of the room more in the high-density condition than in the low-density condition, whereas the impulsive children showed no such behavioral differences. Rather, the impulsive children showed more negative affect in the high-density condition than did the high-motor inhibitors. In this case, motoric impulsivity relates to emotional impulsivity. An emotionally helpless response was demonstrated by both anxious and impulsive children, whereas behavioral alterations in motoric activity and positioning occurred for both nonanxious and motorically controlled children.

High-hyperactive-distractible children were those whom teachers rated as restless, squirmy, inattentive, and having poor concentration or a short attention span. Hyperactive-distractible children, particularly boys, were more active in the high density condition than in the low density condition; that is, they sat less and walked more. Low-hyperactive-distractible children showed no significant differences in sitting. Since sitting is associated with prolonged toy play or toy involvement, my findings suggest that hyperactive children are unable to play in a sedentary and prolonged manner in the high density condition, which is less the case with normal children. The stress of a crowded condition resulted in nervous pacing for hyperactive boys or simply intensified an already existing predisposition.

There was no significant effect for density on hostility-aggressiveness. Children whom teachers described as being aggressive, socially unpopular, irritable, disobedient, liars, blamers, and unsharing were not affected by density any differently from normal children.

Children given high ratings on behavior disturbance were those who showed signs of anxiety, hostility-aggressiveness, and hyperactivity-distractibility. Children who had no or few signs of behavior disturbance reduced their physical activity in the high-density condition, whereas the high-behaviorally-disturbed children generally showed no significant differences in behavior as a function of density. The low-behaviorally-disturbed children reduced their activity by playing less frequently with toys and by walking less. The only effect density had on high behaviorally disturbed children was on liking of the room. High behaviorally disturbed children disliked the high-density condition more than low behaviorally disturbed children. Since low behaviorally disturbed children altered their behavior in a functional manner to reduce crowding stress, it follows that they would not dislike the room as much as the high behaviorally disturbed children did.

Given all the dependent variables possible, I noted that differential effects of density were found for activity mode and level, avoidance behaviors, affect, and the children's reported liking of others. Differential effects were not found for any of the dependent variables that measured extent of social interaction (solitary play, onlooking, social interaction), quality of social interaction (aggression, positive social overtures), and instability of activity (frequency of interruptions, number of toy changes).

This study confirmed in my mind that crowding, or for that matter any environmental stress, will differentially affect certain types of people. An environmental psychologist should be a clinical psychologist as well in terms of commitment of one's roles to mental and physical health. The environmental diagnostician should identify those persons who are unable to escape from crowded living or working conditions and who are most stressed and distressed by such conditions. The environmental clinician should seek intervention strategies that reduce this stress. These strategies may be physical, environmental, social, psychological, economic, or political in focus, and may be direct, consultative, or catalytic in nature.

Study I identified certain "high-risk" types of children as well as provided information as to exactly which behaviors and perceptions differentiated the normal from the "high-risk" child. One of the unfortunate problems facing teachers, parents, planners, and administrators is that society expects and builds for the normal person. The child who deviates from the norm can be expected to experience frustration and distress when his or her environment cannot be flexible enough to accommodate to individual needs, weaknesses, or predispositions in ways that strengthen strategies, provide support systems, or supply opportunities to escape from unbearable situations.

As researchers of a phenomenon having potentially serious consequences on certain portions of the population, it behooves us to avoid an egocentric or ethnocentric orientation that justifies generalizations made to all persons based on the individual predilections of the researcher or on what does or does not occur among normally functioning undergraduate students. Crowding comes in many shapes and forms, just as the people who occupy such conditions. Jonathan Freedman lives in New York City and is a publicly proclaimed lover of crowded cities, or at least of New York. On the other hand, I lived in Chinatown, San Francisco, for 4 months, and due to the intermeshing of residential and commercial units crowded together, I was forced to move out of that community in order to achieve the peace and quiet I need to think and write. The sounds of a Chinese-owned lumber supply store located under my bedroom, electrically sawing wood at 8 a.m. every morning including Sundays, and the traffic noises that are not screened by the distance of front yards or sound housing construction were unbearable at times. Moreover, people have varied tolerance levels for stress and bombardment of stimuli and I tend to be on the "high risk" end of the scale. As such, I am very concerned about the plight of the environmental-high-risk person who lives in crowded conditions. If a person who is predisposed to anxiety, hyperactivity, and impulsivity has such behaviors intensified or expresses emotional distress and anger when crowded, what effect might this have on those family members who must live with him or her? Although we do not know if there is any direct relationship between crowding and child abuse, we do know that some of the reasons parents give for why they abuse their child focus on behaviors related to anger, distress, resistance, or anxiety on the part of their child.

STUDY II

The purposes of the second study were threefold: to study the effects of spatial density on clusters of behaviors, to investigate personal space differences in response to density, and to investigate sex differences in response to density. Research findings based on laboratory experimental work on density effects on humans had lacked a comprehensive scope of analysis with regard to crowding consequences. The analysis of single variables—aggression, task performance, social interaction—was a meager representation of the complexity of human behavior. In my search for a more comprehensive strategy for the study of density effects, I focused on patterns or clusters of behaviors that represented various dimensions of behaviors, and I utilized multivariate statistics for the data analysis.

Five clusters of behaviors were selected for analysis that represented combinations of social or nonsocial behaviors, motoric levels and types of activity, quality of play, and various types of interactions and responses. These factors were called (1) negative and nonsocial interaction, (2) onlooking while standing, (3) self-involved toy play, (4) avoidance, and (5) interrupted activity. These factors were derived from two sources: (1) observational impressions of global behaviors evidenced in a pilot study; and (2) a factor analysis of 30 specific dependent variables that represented ratings of the children's behavior in the density conditions.

Negative and nonsocial interaction consisted of frequency scores on physical aggression plus playful aggression minus positive social overtures. Playful aggression included rough-and-tumble play in which hurt was not intended; positive social overtures were acts of sharing, cooperation, conversation, or verbal overtures. Onlooking while standing consisted of frequency scores for standing plus scores for onlooking. Self-involved toy play consisted of scores for sitting plus solitary play minus nontoy intervals. Nontoy intervals were the number of 30-second intervals in which the child did not touch or engage in play with a toy. Avoidance consisted of frequency scores for escape attempts plus scores for facing out. Escape attempts included trying to open the door, looking out of the window, statements indicating a desire to leave like "Let me out of here!" or "I want to pee!" and gazing into the mirror for a prolonged time. Interrupted activity consisted of frequency scores for interruptions plus scores for toy changes.

The second purpose of this study was to investigate the differential effects of density on far and close personal space children. The relationship between personal space and density has been explored with adults (Cozby, 1973; Dooley, 1975; Rawls, Trego, McGaffey, & Rawls, 1972), but until this study it had not been explored with children. Studies on adults have found that in a high social density condition, far personal space men felt more unfriendly toward others and more negative and irritable than close personal space men (Dooley, 1975). The far personal space men also showed a deterioration in arithmetic and psychomotor task performance in the high-density condition as compared to their performance in the low-density condition (Rawls et al., 1972). Cozby (1973) found that close personal space adults preferred a high-density room more than a low-density room, whereas far personal space adults showed the opposite preference. Although individual differences in response to density in personal space and situational influences have been found for adults, the literature on children is neither as extensive nor as systematic (Whalen, Flowers, Fuller, & Jernigan, 1975).

Clearly, these findings of studies on adults cannot be directly applicable to the present study, since ways of defining and measuring density differ among other studies and between my own and others. However, prior research does provide some suggestive directions. The relationship between personal space and density was explored in the present study because interpersonal distance differences have been found to be present in a rudimentary form at age five (Bass & Weinstein, 1971; Guardo, 1969; Meisels & Guardo, 1969) and because the importance of personal space needs in relation to density effects is unknown for children.

Personal space was determined by adapting Horowitz, Duff, and Stratton's (1964) measures of body buffer zone for use with younger children. Each child was instructed to stand on a fixed spot and told that the female experimenter would walk toward him or her and that he or she should say "stop" as soon as the adult was getting "too close" (we had found a significant correlation between adult approach scores and peer approach scores in a pilot study). The mean score for eight angles of approach was calculated. In each classroom of volunteering children, the three highest-scoring boys and the three highest-scoring girls comprised a far personal space group; the three lowest-scoring boys and the three lowest-scoring girls comprised a close personal space group. There were six far personal space groups and six close personal space groups. The mean for far personal space children was 24.1 inches per approach; the mean for close personal space children was 8.4 inches per approach.

The same subjects, room size, and procedures were used in this study as in Study I but the data were analyzed differently. An analysis of variance was performed for the five clusters instead of for specific single variables and no analysis was done for behavior problem measures.

In the high density condition there were more negative and nonpositive interactions, onlooking while standing, avoidance, and interrupted activity than in the low density condition. There was more self-involved toy play in the low-density condition than in the high-density condition. A discriminant analysis revealed that negative and nonpositive interactions had the greatest weight as a predictor of the density conditions. Five-year-old children showed more aggressiveness and rough play and fewer positive social overtures in the high-density condition than in the low-density condition.

Less space leads to less constructive and more negative interactions among 5-year-olds. Less space increases the frequency of negative interactions while also slightly reducing the total frequency of social interactions. Onlooking while standing and avoidance clusters, which represent nonsocial or antisocial activities, occurred more frequently in a high-density condition. These findings make intuitive sense. If one experiences stress from crowding, it is likely that one will either reduce interaction or express frustration through aggressive or motoric channels. Which of these two responses is taken may depend on the age, personality, sex, or prior experience of the individual.

In addition, there was a significant Sex X Density interaction for negative and nonpositive-interactions. Girls showed smaller density differences than did boys, confirming my previous finding (Loo, 1972). Boys showed more negative and nonpositive interactions than did girls in both the high- and low-density conditions, but in the high-density condition, the differences between boys and girls were twice that in the low-density condition. High density was associated with an increase in aggressiveness and a decrease in positive overtures for girls; for boys, this effect was twice as strong.

There was also a significant Sex X Density interactive effect for self-involved toy play. Again, the effect of density on the frequency of self-involved toy play was greater for boys than for girls. The high-density condition reduced the frequency of self-involved toy play in boys to a greater extent than it did for girls.

Finally, a Sex X Density interactive effect was found for avoidance, demonstrating that the effects of density on avoidance were greater for boys than for girls. In the low-density condition, boys displayed almost half as much avoidance as girls, but in the high-density condition, the frequency of avoidance for boys doubled. In summary, for three of the five clusters there were consistent sex differences in response to spatial density conditions in a repeated measures design using mixed-sex groups. For negative and nonpositive interactions, self-involved toy play, and avoidance boys were affected by spatial density to a greater degree than were girls. These findings suggest that boys react to crowding with greater activity and aggressiveness than do girls. Under normal (low-density) conditions, girls act more avoidantly, but under high-density conditions, boys and girls display similar amounts of avoidance. It is possible that boys may be more sensitive to crowding or environmental stimuli than girls are, or it may be possible that there is no sex difference in reference to sensitivity to crowding. Rather, there are sex differences in *reactivity* to crowding. The need for answers to these questions led to the development of the post-experimental questionnaire to be discussed in Study III.

The main effects for sex found in the present study, which showed boys to be more aggressive than girls and girls to show more avoidance than boys, are consistent with prior research on sex differences (Maccoby & Jacklin, 1974).

Personal space was a weak differentiating variable in terms of density. Far personal space children displayed more negative and nonsocial interactions and less self-involved toy play than did close personal space children in the high-density condition, but these effects were not large.

To assess perceptions of the density conditions, we asked several questions in a post-experimental interview. On a scale of 1 to 5 (1 = disliked a lot, 5 = liked a lot), children liked both density conditions, but they liked the low-density condition ($\bar{X}$ = 4.26) significantly more than the high-density condition ($\bar{X}$ = 3.88). The high-density condition was experienced as being neutral or slightly positive. When given a choice of "too big," "too small," or "just the right size," 50 percent of the children reported that the high-density condition was "too small," and 76 percent of the children reported that the low-density condition was the "right size." When asked whether the room was crowded or not crowded, 28 percent said the high-density condition was crowded, whereas 8 percent in the low-density condition reported the room to be crowded. Although this difference is significant, it still leaves 72 percent who did not perceive the high-density condition as being crowded. Responses may have been invalid due to children's desire to please or to a response set of a "field trip" associated with the experiment. It is also possible that responses were valid—that the high-density condition did not constitute crowding for the majority of these children. It is also possible that 5-year-olds may not even conceptually grasp the definition of crowding or that their definition may differ from that of adults. In Study III we refined our questionnaire to explore how 5-year-olds define crowding and whether they have an accurate conceptual understanding of the term.

STUDY III

Study III, unlike Studies I and II, examined the effects of social density on 5-year-old children. Four-child groups were compared to eight-child groups in a room of 130.8 square feet. The four-child groups, termed the *uncrowded condition,* allowed for 32.70 square feet per child. The eight-child groups, termed the *crowded condition,* allowed for 16.35 square feet per child.

A few studies have compared social and spatial density effects. McGrew (1970) studied 5-year old children and found that social density was more potent than spatial density in eliciting adjustments in spacing behavior of preschoolers. Studies on adults have also shown that social density had more potent effects than spatial density (Baum & Koman, 1976; Nogami, 1976). Comparing area per person and group size, Marshall and Haslin (1975) found group size to be a more potent factor than area per person. Since prior research suggests that social density effects are stronger than spatial density effects, I expected that there would be greater effects of density on aggression and social interaction in this study than were found in my 1972 study.

In Study III, we refined the post-experimental questionnaire in several ways. First, we added the item, "Do you know what crowding means?", and found that most of the children answered "no" to that question, suggesting that the response to the Study II question regarding crowding perception was not totally valid. In Study III we asked the children what crowding meant to them. Of those who could give a response, most of the responses were "pushing and shoving," suggesting that adults and children may define crowding differently. After being told that "crowding is where there are either too many people or not enough space to do what you want to do or to feel comfortable" and being shown pictures of comparatively low and high social and spatial density diagrams for which they were required to select the "crowded" diagram, the children were asked how crowded the room was. On a 3-point scale (1 = not crowded, 2 = kind of crowded, 3 = very crowded), children in the high-density condition ($\bar{X}$ = 1.85) felt significantly more crowded than did children in the low-density condition ($\bar{X}$ = 1.50), validating our experimental manipulation. In the high-density condition, 25 percent said the room was "not crowded" and 75 percent said the room was either "kind of crowded" or "very crowded." In addition to these questions, we asked other questions that posed alternative ways of defining crowding. The high-density condition was reported to be a situation in which 77 percent of the children wanted fewer children in the room, 75 percent considered it crowded, 50 percent said others were too close, 46 percent said that others got in their way, and 35 percent wished others would leave. There were no differences between the two density conditions in terms of liking the room or liking others. The children in both density conditions liked one another and the rooms "a little." Some of these variables plus other variables on the post-experimental questionnaire showed up as factors in the factor analysis.

Twenty-two variables were rated in the low- and high-density conditions; these variables related to social and nonsocial behavior, activity level, body positions, perceptions, emotional reactions, coping strategies, quality of play, and quality of interactions. The subjects were 72 5-year-old children, who were observed in mixed-sex groups composed of an equal number of girls and boys. A nonrepeated measures design was used. Half of the groups were far personal space groups, and the other half were close personal space groups. The mean approach distance was 23.3 inches for the far personal space children and 7.5 inches for the close personal space children. There was no sex difference for personal space, which is consistent with Bass and Weinstein's (1971) findings that children ages 5 to 9 showed no sex differences in their preference for interpersonal distance.

A factor analysis of the rated behaviors and self-reported perceptions revealed five factors. Factor 1, called *activity-aggression-anger,* was composed of physical aggression, nonsitting, running, playful aggression, activity, and angry expressions. Factor 2, called *negative feelings,* was composed of five interview items: feeling bad from being the target of someone's aggression, feeling sad, angry, crowded, and being the target of someone's anger. Factor 3, called *avoidance,* was composed of escape attempts, facing out, and being bored or tired. Factor 4, called *social interactions,* was composed of positive social overtures. group interaction, and nonsolitary behavior. Factor 5, called *distress and fear* was composed of distress, no toy changes, no toy play, and feeling scared (an interview item). Apparently distress and fearfulness preclude any toy play.

Analyzing by group scores, the multivariate analysis of variance revealed a significant effect for density. A univariate analysis of variance was then performed on each separate factor. There was significantly more activity-aggression-anger demonstrated in the crowded condition than in the uncrowded condition. The findings on aggression are consistent with those of Hutt and Vaizey (1966) and Shapiro (1975). Although the present findings may seem inconsistent with those of my 1972 study, a closer analysis dispels this conclusion. The high social and high spatial density conditions were nearly identical in terms of area per person *and* in terms of frequency of aggression demonstrated. However, the frequency of aggression in the two low-density conditions differed along with the area per person. The low *social* density condition (32.70 square feet per person) had *fewer* aggressive acts than did the high social density condition, whereas the low *spatial* density condition (44.2 square feet per person) had *more* aggressive acts than the high spatial density condition. This finding argues for a curvilinear relationship between density and aggression, which has been suggested earlier (Loo, 1972).

In addition, there was a significant Density X Sex interaction. In the uncrowded condition, sex differences in activity-aggression-anger were not significant, but in the crowded condition boys showed significantly more activity-aggression-anger than did girls.

More negative feelings were reported in the crowded condition than in the uncrowded condition. There were no Sex X Density interactions, contrary to findings on adults, suggesting that sex differences in affective responses to crowding may develop over time.

There was no significant density effect for avoidance, and no Sex X Density effect. Apparently the strategy used to respond to crowding is to increase activity, be more aggressive, reduce interactions, reduce toy play, and feel more negatively rather than to attempt to escape. There were significantly more social interactions in the uncrowded condition than in the crowded condition and significantly more distress and fear in the crowded condition than in the uncrowded condition. This latter finding demonstrates that when crowding causes emotional reactions of distress and fear, it also results in failure to engage in normal task behavior for five-year-olds (which consists of toy or social play).

Personal space did not prove to be an important individual characteristic that predicted differential responses to social density. The findings on personal space for Studies II and III suggest that personal space is a weak differentiating variable for social or spatial density for 5-year-old children.

The findings for activity-aggression-anger, social interaction, and distress and fear shed doubt on Freedman's repeated statement (1971, 1975; Freedman, Heshka, & Levy, 1975) that crowding has no negative consequences for humans. The findings of the three studies presented argue strongly against generalization from studies on undergraduate students to children. More generally, the findings of the three studies presented argue for exploring greater individual differences in terms of behavior disturbance, age, and sex. The magnitude of the effects of social density was greater than that for spatial density, which supports prior research findings in which social density (group size) was found to have a more potent effect on behavior and perceptions than spatial density (room size).

Studies II and III demonstrated that a factor-analytic approach to determining the dependent variables to be studied leads to a more comprehensive understanding of crowding effects. Moreover, the eventual refinement of the questionnaire indicated that children's perceptions of the density conditions and their emotional responses can be determined and can add significantly to our understanding of the consequences of crowding on children.

ACKNOWLEDGMENTS

The research projects described in this chapter were funded by Grant MH 25522 from the National Institute of Mental Health, Applied Research Branch, and by Faculty Research Funds and a Summer Faculty Fellowship granted by the University of California at Santa Cruz.

I would like to acknowledge the assistance of Denise Kennelly in organizing the experimental sessions for Study III, Tom Wickens and Jeanne Tschann for their statistical and computer assistance, the principals and teachers of Bay View Elementary School, Natural Bridges School, and Westlake Elementary School for their cooperation, Laurie Kiguchi for her typing assistance, Werner Feibel for his contributions on the personal space measure, and all those who served as raters.

Results from Study I were presented at the Western Psychological Association Convention in Seattle, Washington, April 1977. A more detailed description of Study I is in press with *Environment and Behavior.* Results from Study II were presented at the American Psychological Association Convention in Washington, D.C., September 1975.

REFERENCES

Argyle, M. *The psychology of interpersonal behavior.* Baltimore: Penguin Books, 1967.
Argyle, M., & Dean, J. Eye-contact, distance, and affiliation. *Sociometry,* 1965, *28,* 289-304.
Bass, M., & Weinstein, M. Early development of interpersonal distance in children. *Canadian Journal of Behavior Science,* 1971, *3,* 368-375.
Baum, A., & Koman, S. Differential response to anticipated crowding: Psychological effects of social and spatial density. *Journal of Personality and Social Psychology,* 1976, *34,* 526-536.
Behar, L., & Stringfield, S. Behavior rating scale for the preschool child. *Developmental Psychology,* 1974, *10,* 601-610.
Cozby, P. C. Effects of density, activity, and personality on environmental preferences. *Journal of Research in Personality,* 1973, *7,* 45-60.
Dooley, B. *Crowding stress: The effects of social density on men with close or far personal space.* Unpublished doctoral dissertation, University of California at Los Angeles, 1974; presented at the Western Psychological Association Convention, Sacramento, 1975.
Freedman, J. A positive view of population density. *Psychology Today,* September 1971, pp. 58-86.
Freedman, J. *Crowding and behavior.* San Francisco, Calif.: Freeman & Co., 1975.
Freedman, J., Heshka, S., & Levy, A. Population density and pathology: Is there a relationship? *Journal of Experimental Social Psychology,* 1975, *11,* 539-552.
Freedman, J., Levy, A., Buchanan, R., & Price, J. Crowding and human aggressiveness. *Journal of Experimental Social Psychology,* 1972, *8,* 528-548.
Guardo, C. Personal space in children. *Child Development,* 1969, *40,* 143-151.
Horowitz, M., Duff, D., & Stratton, L. Personal space and the body buffer zone. *Archives of General Psychology,* 1964, *11,* 651-656.

Hutt, C., & Vaizey, M. J. Differential effects of group density on social behavior. *Nature,* 1966, *209,* 1371-1372.

Liebman, M. The effects of sex and race norms on personal space. *Environment and Behavior,* 1970, *2,* 208-246.

Loo, C. The effects of spatial density on the social behavior of children. *Journal of Applied Social Psychology,* 1972, *2,* 372-381.

Maccoby, E. E., Dowley, E. M., Hagen, J. W., & Dagerman, R. Activity level and intellectual functioning in normal preschool children. *Child Development,* 1965, *36,* 761-770.

Maccoby, E. E., & Jacklin, C. N. *The psychology of sex differences.* Stanford, Calif.: Stanford University Press, 1974.

Marshall, J., & Heslin, R. Boys and girls together: Sexual competition and the effect of density and group size on cohesiveness. *Journal of Personality and Social Psychology,* 1975, *31,* 952-961.

McGrew, P. L. Social and spatial density effects on spacing behavior in preschool children. *Journal of Child Psychology and Psychiatry,* 1970, *11,* 197-205.

Meisels, M., & Guardo, C. J. Development of personal space schematas. *Child Development,* 1969, *40,* 1167-1178.

Nogami, G. Crowding: Effects of group size, room size or density? *Journal of Applied Social Psychology,* 1976, *6,* 105-125.

Pellegrini, R. J., & Empey, J. Interpersonal spatial orientation in dyads. *Journal of Psychology,* 1970, *76,* 67-70.

Preiser, W. Behavior of nursery school children under different spatial densities. *Man-Environment Systems,* 1972, *2,* 247-250.

Price, J. *The effect of crowding on the social behavior of children.* Unpublished doctoral dissertation, Columbia University, 1971.

Rawls, J. R., Trego, R. E., McGaffey, C. N., & Rawls, D. J. Personal space as a predictor of performance under close working conditions. *Journal of Social Psychology,* 1972, *86,* 261-267.

Rohe, W., & Patterson, A. The effects of varied levels of resources and density on behavior in a day care center. In D. Carson (Ed.), *EDRA V convention proceedings,* 1974.

Ross, M., Layton, B., Erickson, B., & Schopler, J. Affect, facial regard and reactions to crowding. *Journal of Personality and Social Psychology,* 1973, *28,* 69-76.

Shapiro, S. Some classroom ABC's: Research takes a closer look. *Elementary School Journal,* 1975, *75,* 437-441.

Smith, P., & Connelly, K. Patterns of play and social interaction in preschool children. In N. B. Jones (Ed.), *Ethological studies of child behavior.* Cambridge: Cambridge University Press, 1972.

Whalen, C., Flowers, J., Fuller, M., & Jernigan, T. Behavior studies of personal space during early adolescence. *Man-Environment Systems,* 1975, *5,* 289-297.

14

Crowding and Helplessness: Potential Consequences of Density and Loss of Control

Judith Rodin
Yale University

Andrew Baum
Trinity College

A potential feature of residential experience in socially dense environments appears to be a general loss of control over social outcomes. As a result of the arrangement of social and spatial resources in these settings and the number and nature of interactions it fosters, residents seem to have fewer outcomes that are contingent on their own responding. This kind of social dysfunction was discussed by Calhoun (1962, 1970) in explaining the severe behavioral disruption and social disorganization observed in rat and mouse colonies, and it has been offered as a link between the physical conditions of density and the stressful experience of crowding. Zlutnick and Altman (1972), for example, proposed that high density may engender the "kinds of interpersonal events where people are unable to control their interactions with others and/or where the psychological costs for interaction are high, and produce subjective feelings of an inability to control interpersonal exchange [p. 50]." In other words, regulatory control essential for positive social experience (the ability of each individual to control when and with whom he or she will interact) is impaired when too many people are present, and overload, unwanted interaction, and stress are potential products.

High-density living may also undermine one's feelings of choice. Under these conditions, for example, residents cannot always have quiet when they would like it and may have to adapt to conditions beyond their control. When too many people are forced to use certain areas in a residential setting, choice on a number of dimensions may be curtailed as residents reluctantly relinquish the notion that they can choose whom they may talk to and pass in the hallways, or when they can use the shower, telephone, and so on. Thus, features of the environment—especially a primary environment such as one's home—can restrict actual or potential social outcomes and freedom of choice (Baron & Rodin, 1978). Behavioral constraint, perceived loss of regulatory control, and diminished feelings of choice are likely consequences of living in high-density settings.

Although objective control is important when considering response to density, we feel that there is greater heuristic value in considering perceived control as the crucial variable. The implicit assumption is frequently made that outcome control and a reasonably high number of choices are good and valuable; however, this is not always so. Circumstances may result in negative response to choice as the number available becomes confusing or options are not easily distinguished from one another. Therefore, in order to assume that the restriction of control (i.e., outcome-behavior contingencies) is negative, we must assume that control is valued or valuable for that person at the particular point in time. To do this, a distinction between objective and perceived control is necessary.

A second reason for considering perceived rather than objective control derives from the imperfect relationship between the two concepts. Increases in objective features of environmental control, such as the availability of response options, do not necessarily increase perceived control. If residents do not recognize these increases, or if they have learned that their behavior and outcomes are not contingent, there is no reason to assume that people will perceive an increase in control. By the same token, it is possible to obtain increases in perceived control that have no basis in reality; that is, specific environmental conditions that provide the "illusion" of greater control will increase perceived control while not affecting objective control (Langer, 1975).

PERCEIVED CONTROL IN RESIDENTIAL SETTINGS

The dynamics of control in high-density residential settings, then, involve a number of regulatory and choice-related variables. At the most basic level, we can consider the impact of behavioral constraint, disruption, and blocking of goal-oriented behavior. In addition, the ability to regulate social interaction and to choose the frequency and duration of selected interpersonal contacts may be considered. Finally, the unpredictability of interaction, which seems to increase with social density, contributes to loss of control in these settings. When people are forced to live together in large numbers and to occupy spaces that are undifferentiated and not easily divided among residents, interaction becomes more likely and the number of different people with whom interaction is possible increases. As a result, residents may interact more frequently with neighbors not known to them. And as interactions with spatially distant neighbors increase, the predictability of each encounter decreases. Because specific modes of interaction are difficult to develop among so many individuals, the range of social inputs becomes less predictable, and effective social behaviors may be harder to develop. Moreover, since the behavior of others may change, even those interaction strategies that have been effective can, over time, become dysfunctional.

These relationships have been studied in a number of residential settings (e.g., college dormitories, prisons, housing projects, high-rise apartment buildings) and have been verified using samples of children, college students, and adults (Baum & Valins, 1977; McCarthy & Saegert, in press; Paulus, Cox, McCain, & Chandler, 1975; Rodin, 1976). Despite rather unique resident populations, these studies have yielded interesting data. Because of the economics of construction, the interior design of residential units often fails to provide suitable proximate space that can be used by developing residential groups and converted to semi-private territory (e.g., Yancey, 1972). As a result, interaction occurring in public hallway space is not regulated by the evolution of group norms, and the impact of the large numbers of other residents is exacerbated. When large numbers of residents are forced to share public living areas that are not suitable for use as group territory, the high frequency of unwanted and inconvenient interactions with unknown or unfamiliar others can make effective regulation of social interactions difficult. In support of this assertion, Baum and Valins (1977) demonstrated that when freshmen dormitory residents were grouped around common living areas in relatively large numbers and interaction with others was more frequent, the residents felt that regulation of social contact was more difficult, that their dormitories were crowded, and that the quality of residential interaction had become increasingly negative.

Of greater interest here, these studies revealed that factors leading to diminished feelings of social control were associated with crowding, withdrawal, and lack of persistence on problem-solving tasks. Questionnaire data obtained from freshman residents of dormitories, the design of which grouped large numbers of residents (34 to 40) around undifferentiated but shared living space, suggested that these students entered the dormitories with expectations and needs regarding regulation of interaction but that these needs were not being met. Residents of dormitories requiring smaller groups (6 to 20) to share living spaces did not complain of this; the arrangment of interior space in these dormitories more adequately supported preferred modes of social contact and control, fulfilling expectations by facilitating group formation and individual ability to regulate social interaction. Although all dormitories housed students in comparable densities and provided for basic residential needs, the long-corridor dormitories appeared to be associated with crowding, because the large number of residents sharing common areas inhibited groups development and effective utilization of public space in the dormitory. Unable to regulate the social interaction on their floor and unable to fully withdraw from it, these residents perceived their dormitories as being crowded and experienced stress and a loss of control (Baum & Valins, 1977).

Because a primary feature of the residential experience in these socially dense environments appears to be a loss of control or regulation of social contact, it is possible that repeated failure to control environmental and social outcomes in these settings may lead to a sense of helplessness. As Seligman (1975) has noted, when people learn that their outcomes are independent of responses and are therefore uncontrollable, they are less apt to behave adaptively, even when control over outcomes is offered or restored. Among residents of the long-corridor dormitories, helplessness training may begin when residents recognize their inability to regulate social encounters on their floors. Their ineffectiveness in predicting or controlling the nature and frequency of their social contacts may become associated with perceived independence of behavior and outcomes, and helplessness conditioning may begin. Repeated exposure to this lack of regulatory control may lead residents to give up more readily and to stop trying to control or make active choices (Rodin, 1976).

Two experiments were conducted comparing residents of long- and short-corridor designs (Baum & Valins, 1977) that allow us to begin to evaluate these hypotheses. Resident freshmen, randomly assigned to dormitory units, were first observed in an experimental setting in which they waited by themselves or with a same-sex confederate. Thus, the effects of an architectural manipulation of social density were assessed in the laboratory, where experimental conditions were designed to reveal the ways in which these variations influenced mood and behavior.

Of the long- and short-corridor dormitory residents, 48 were randomly selected from the housing lists for freshmen. Subjects arrived at the laboratory alone, expecting to participate in a study of "impression formation." After greeting the subject, the experimenter related the purpose of the experiment, adding that the experiment was running late and that it would be a little while before everything was ready. Subjects were asked to wait in an adjoining room until the experiment was ready to begin. It was here that the experimental manipulation was introduced. In one condition, subjects encountered five empty chairs lined up against one wall of the room. In the second condition, there were five chairs and there was a same-sex confederate in seat No. 1 who was introduced as another subject waiting for the same experiment. Confederates remained responsive during the waiting session but did not initiate eye contact or conversation.

Once subjects had selected a seat, an observer began continuous observation of facial regard and conversation initiation. Mood and background questionnaires were given after three and 10 minutes. When the subject completed the second set of forms, the experimenter asked him or her to come to another room. Once outside the waiting room, the experimenter glanced at a clipboard with notes on it, turned to the subject, and indicated that the subject could now participate in either of two conditions in the actual experiment. The nature of the conditions was left vague, and Baum and Valins were interested first in whether subjects asked for further information before choosing, and second, in whether they made a choice. After a pause (for any questions by subjects regarding the two conditions), subjects were taken to another room and thoroughly debriefed.

As predicted, long- and short-corridor residents responded to the waiting-room situation in comparable ways when waiting alone. However, with the introduction of the confederate as a potential interactor, responses of long- and short-corridor residents diverged. Long-corridor residents sat significantly farther from the confederate than did short-corridor residents and spent less time looking at and talking to the confederate than did short-corridor residents.

Questionnaire responses reflecting subjects' discomfort also conformed to prediction: Although long- and short-corridor respondents reported comparable levels of comfort while alone, long-corridor residents felt significantly more uncomfortable following three and 10 minutes of waiting.

Most relevant to the present hypotheses, significantly more short-corridor residents asked questions about the possible choice of the two vaguely described conditions. Although the finding was not widespread or overwhelming, more long-corridor residents seemed to exhibit some behaviors and attitudes in the laboratory that were symptomatic of the helplessness syndrome. Questionnaire data about experience in their dormitories revealed that long-corridor residents did express significantly greater feelings of helplessness than did short-corridor residents in that setting. Furthermore, when asked about the value of trying to change things and trying to make things better, long-corridor residents indicated that they more often believed that such attempts were worthless than did short-corridor residents. These findings suggest that ineffective regulation of interaction in the dormitory may reduce residents' general feelings of choice and control, and it is likely that some helplessness conditioning occurs.

In summary, long-corridor residents on the average report feelings of helplessness and fail to question and choose between experimental conditions when they are given the option to do so. It appears, then, that long-corridor residents do exhibit some symptoms of helplessness, which we believe is the result of a socially mediated inability to control outcomes and exercise full decision freedom in their residential settings. However, thus far, experimental tests were limited to situations with low potential for true social interaction. In the next study, the possibility for high or low levels of social interaction was explicitly varied.

Of freshmen residents of long- and short-corridor dormitories, 40 were randomly selected from the housing lists for the two residential environments, with the exception that half were male and half female. They were tested with same-sex experimenters.

Subjects arrived at the laboratory alone, expecting to participate in a "social bargaining game." After greeting the subject, the experimenter asked that he or she be seated, explaining that a second subject would be playing the game as well. After approximately one minute, a same-sex confederate arrived, and the experimenter began to explain the experimental procedures. In all conditions, subjects were told that they would be playing a prisoners' dilemma game, and the probability of interaction was manipulated as follows: Half of the subjects were told that they were not allowed to talk with each other (no interaction), and half were told that they could talk with each other as long as they did not specifically discuss their game plan (interaction). Once the "probability of interaction" manipulation was completed, the game was explained and subjects moved to their game positions.

The game was a modified, three-choice prisoner's dilemma game similar to that used by Kurlander, Miller, and Seligman (1975). In the modified version of this experimental task, a player could make any of three responses, reflecting cooperative, competitive, or withdrawal strategies. Withdrawal was viewed as being most reflective of helplessness, because it represented an inability to arrive at decisions or an unwillingness to participate in and meaningfully influence the game's outcome.

Participants were told that the object of the game was simply to score as many points as possible. Subjects were not told to maximize the differences between their scores and their partner's, nor were they asked to cooperate. Instead, they were told that at the end of the experiment (after all subjects had participated) those players scoring in the highest 25% of all participants would share a monetary reward. In this way, the possibility of both players in a given session winning a postexperimental prize was made clear. This was done to standardize subject goals and to assure that subjects did not perceive the game as a maximizing-difference exercise.

The primary behavioral indexes were subjects' responses during the 25-trial game. The mean proportions of cooperative, competitive, and withdrawal responses are presented in Table 1. First, it is clear that the long-corridor residents were considerably less cooperative than short-corridor residents. The nature of the noncooperative strategy was different, however, depending on whether interaction was permitted. For long-corridor residents, competition was greater when interaction was permitted and withdrawal was greater when it was not permitted, relative to the short-corridor subjects. High rates of competition may have been used as a technique to minimize potential involvement with the confederate, because he or she was presumably informed of each choice the subject made. The desire for minimal involvement may also be seen in the fact that only two long-corridor residents spoke to the confederate when permitted, whereas eight short-corridor residents initiated conversation. Unlike competition, the withdrawal evidenced in the long interaction situation seemed to represent giving up, because subjects failed to exert any control at all.[1]

Additional data suggest that frequent competition or withdrawal responding led to a failure to accumulate points. Long-corridor residents did not do as well

[1]Subsequent research with this modified PD game has suggested that the competitive strategy is viewed by students as the best strategy for communicating to their partner that they did not like him or her or that they did not wish to interact. Similarly, students reported that the cooperative strategy was best for trying to get to know one's partner, and the withdrawal strategy was best when the game "did not matter" and participants did not care what happened.

TABLE 1
Mean Percentage of Cooperative, Competitive, and Withdrawal Responses

Dormitory design	Cooperative		Competitive		Withdrawal	
	Interaction	No interaction	Interaction	No interaction	Interaction	No interaction
Long corridor	13	11	78	54	9	35
Short corridor	40	40	49	48	11	12

at the game ($\overline{X}$ point total = --26.9) as did short-corridor residents ($\overline{X}$ = +16.9). Long-corridor residents did particularly poorly on the task when participants were allowed to talk ($\overline{X}$ = −58.5), scoring more points when they were not allowed to talk with the other participant.

McConahay and Rodin (Note 1) found similar data for junior high school students who played a game in which there was also potential for competition. Subjects played the game in a small space and were allowed to talk. When the residential density of these randomly selected subjects was entered as a factor in a regression analysis with competitive choice as the dependent variable, McConahay and Rodin found that the more crowded children were more likely to choose competitive than cooperative responses, even when (in 50% of the cases) the competitive strategy actually minimized their own outcomes as well as the other subject's. For example, in a choice between three for him and one for the other subject or five for each of them, the crowded child more often chose the first option.

At the present time, we can only speculate about the meaning of these data, but there are several intriguing possibilities. Although high density per se is not viewed as a stressor, uncontrollability fostered by associated environmental conditions is (Baron & Rodin, 1978). Let us suppose that, as Glass and Singer (1972) have argued, there are postadaptational consequences for repeated exposure to uncontrollable and/or unpredictable features of the environment. Indeed, Sherrod (1974) has demonstrated that the inability to terminate interaction in a highly dense setting does have negative aftereffects. When considering dormitory residents who lack such control, one might expect negative aftereffects and some helplessness, but not in all situations. First, helplessness conditioning is clearly incomplete, because residents apparently learn to avoid interaction as a means of coping with crowding stress. To some extent this avoidance is effective, but it appears to become a response that is emitted in a highly stereotyped fashion regardless of the specific features of the situation. Whenever there is the anticipation of, or actual occurrence of, social interaction, these residents try to avoid it. Although this clearly is a behavioral response and therefore not helplessness, it is one that is maladaptive in most situations outside the dormitory and is frequently unrelated to specific outcomes available to the individual.

When there is no possibility for interaction and/or when other people are not present, the stereotyped response to social stimuli is not elicited, and some helplessness-like behavior can be observed.

Alternatively, it may be that the competitive responding of long-corridor residents represents reactance, a stage presumed to occur during a sequential process involving loss of control as the first stage and the emergence of helplessness as the final stage (Wortman & Brehm, 1975). If we assume that students came to live in the dormitories expecting to be able to regulate their social experience and that they brought with them previously developed modes of achieving and maintaining control, it can be argued that the frustration of attempts to regulate interaction in the long-corridor dormitory aroused reactance among these residents. Because other students may be seen as being responsible for this reduction of behavioral choice and for frustration of coping responses, attempts to reassert control may be directed toward them in a variety of situations. When these social cues for reactance are not salient, the long-corridor residents simply withdraw.

Although these studies are consistent with a general "helplessness" formulation, they were not explicitly designed to test the relationships between environmental restrictions of control and a resultant failure to engage in control-relevant behaviors. Rather, they sought to test the generality of response styles developed as a result of certain residential experiences. It is also possible that these college-age students had sufficient prior effectance training to innoculate them against the full effects of helplessness conditioning (Seligman, Maier, & Geer, 1968). By contrast, the consequences of environment-derived uncontrollability should be more observable among young children for whom a major portion of social learning will occur under these conditions. Both physical and social settings exert their influence early in development and may deprive children of the experiences necessary to develop expectancies for outcome control and choice or to learn that they are valuable.

Rodin (1976) considered this hypothesis in two experiments designed to test the effects of chronically high residential density on responses to choice and control of outcomes. In the first study, children pressed a lever to earn candy as a reinforcement and, in certain phases of the experiment, were able to press a second lever if they chose, which allowed them to pick their own candy rather than having the experimenter select candy for them. Controlling for socioeconomic status, Rodin found that children who lived in high residential density were significantly less likely than children from less-dense homes to choose to control the administration of available outcomes themselves.

Why should it be the case that the more crowded children did not choose to control their own outcomes? First, they may have already learned that they have little control over most outcomes and thus do not even try to exercise control over them. Or, rather than having learned that they are unable to exercise control in general, they may have been exposed to a more specific type of learning as the result of residential density. It has been suggested that children who do not have adequate privacy at home will lack some of the cognitive skills necessary for self-initiated behavior (Altman, 1975; Laufer, Proshansky, & Wolfe, 1976). Children from high-density backgrounds who do not choose self-mediated rewards in preference to rewards administered by the experimenter may be exhibiting poor acquisition of self-regulation skills (Bandura, 1971). By this line of reasoning, they simply have not been able to develop the necessary skills for exercising a self-regulation kind of control. This would suggest, however, that despite their failure to exert control when self-regulation is required, these children may still try to exercise control over other people, which should be consistent with competitive behavior in highly interactive situations (Baum & Valins, 1977; McConahay & Rodin, Note 1) while failing to exert control when self-regulation is required (Rodin, 1976).

One can also explain the failure of children from high-density apartments to work for the self-administration of rewards when the alternative was to be rewarded by the experimenter by assuming that (1) chronically high room density establishes a potential for overload by providing excessive and often unpredictable stimulation, thus it may require excessive vigilance; (2) when outcomes are equal, persons who have experienced uncontrollable overload will prefer the less effortful of alternative activities; (3) self-selection of rewards may be avoided simply because self-selection is a more effortful way of obtaining the same outcomes (Baron & Rodin, 1978). Exercising control, as varied in this experiment, may not have been useful or adaptive for the subjects.

Because the results of the first experiment are consistent with several interpretations, a second study was conducted to examine more directly the effects of high density on responses to controllable and uncontrollable outcomes. In this study, a randomly selected sample of junior high school students was tested. No social interaction was permitted throughout the task. Subjects were first asked to solve a series of either solvable or unsolvable problems, and then all were given a second, solvable series. As Hiroto and Seligman (1975) have pointed out, unsolvability in a cognitive task is formally analogous to inescapability of shock, because in both, the probability of reinforcement (correct or incorrect, or shock or no shock) is independent of responding. It was predicted that control-relevant experiences due to high residential density would influence expectancies formed in an experimental situation that made uncontrollability between response and outcome salient. Specifically, Rodin expected that for all subjects, experience with uncontrollable outcomes would interfere with the acquisition of a subsequent response that could control relevant outcomes but that crowded children would be more strongly affected by uncontrollability.

Subjects participated in a series of experiments for 3 hours in either crowded or uncrowded same-sex four-person groups. At the conclusion of the experiment, each child was interviewed extensively, using both oral and written questionnaires to accumulate demographic information relevant to family structure and residential density.

The results indicated that subjects had fewer correct answers on solvable puzzles if they were living in high-density environments or had just been asked to solve an unsolvable puzzle. Other factors such as race and parents' education level also explained significant portions of the variance in performance, but short-term crowding in the laboratory did not. The interaction of high home density and pretreatment with an unsolvable puzzle also contributed to the variance in performance on solvable puzzles (see Figure 1).

These findings are in some ways similar to those reported by Goeckner, Greenough, and Mead (1973), who found that rats reared under conditions of high density showed poorer performance on complex appetitive and avoidance tasks. In explaining why many animals reared in high-density settings failed to respond at all in a complex and stressful discrimination task, these researchers used a helplessness-training framework. Thus, rats raised in high-density conditions entered into these tasks with a prior learning history that emphasized the noncontingency of response and outcome. Rodin suggested that, when the features of the present experiment made the noncontingency of response and solution of puzzles salient, high-density subjects were slower to solve puzzles. Since their learning histories included extensive helplessness conditioning, these subjects may have come to the laboratory with strong expectations regarding the noncontingency of their responding and the consequent outcomes. Thus, they began working on the first task with expectancies of noncontingency or uncontrollability, and their performance was inhibited.

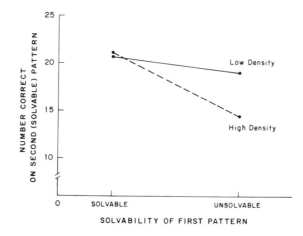

FIG. 1   (From Rodin, J. Density, perceived choice and response to controllable outcomes. *Journal of Experimental and Social Psychology*, 1976, *12*, 575. Reprinted with permission of *Journal of Experimental and Social Psychology*, Academic Press.)

To consider the hypothesis regarding expectancies of noncontingency in another way, learning on the *first* solvable task was also examined. Children from high-density housing took significantly longer than low-density children to learn the solvable pattern. Consequently, they did appear to have greater difficulty learning the contingent response. Nonetheless, once given pretraining with a solvable series, they did almost as well on the second solvable task as did low-density children. Having seen that their responses on this type of task were effective, they were better able to learn a similar task.

All these experiments support the view that chronic high-density living may reduce one's feelings of choice and control. To summarize the line of reasoning that the experiments support, we have argued that high density may have negative consequences because it fosters conditions in which both negative and positive events may be unpredictable and/or uncontrollable. Predictability and perceived control have been shown often to reduce the aversiveness of noxious stimuli (Glass & Singer, 1972; Pervin, 1963; Staub, Tursky, & Schwartz, 1971). Although less well investigated, prediction and control probably have an equally important effect on response to positive outcomes (Lauzetta & Driscoll, 1966; Wortman, 1975). Adaptation to lack of prediction and control may lead to cognitive and motivational deficits (Glass & Singer, 1972), expectancies for a lack of control, and subsequent helplessness (Seligman 1975; Wortman & Brehm, 1975). Although this interpretation of our data is speculative, it provides an interface to a growing body of literature on the importance of predictability and control for human and animal behavior.

For several reasons, however, we caution against a straightforward application of the helplessness formulation proposed by Seligman and his associates (Seligman, 1975) to the effects of physical density and crowding in a naturalistic environment. First, at the antecedent level, it is not entirely clear which specific features of the residential setting produced these effects. Although we would argue that they derive from the kinds of interpersonal interactions resulting from the density, rather than spatial arrangements per se, we have no *direct* evidence that supports this view. Architectural arrangements of residential space may increase the impact of high density and decrease residents' ability to regulate their social experience, but it is doubtful that these spatial arrangements have comparable effects when density is low. Second, we do not believe that our subjects feel or have become generally helpless as a result of this presumed "helplessness conditioning." Rather, we hold that situational factors make control-relevant contingencies more or less salient, and that these elicit expectancies and/or behaviors as a result of residential density variables are sensitive to issues of control. Third, the studies we have described range from helplessness conditioning that arises from a presumed disparity between expected and actual control to helplessness conditioning that may derive from a lack rather than a loss of control. Specifying the differential implications of these mediating variables that we have presumed to affect other control-relevant behaviors and clarifying their limiting conditions are intriguing directions for future research.

REFERENCE NOTE

1. McConahay, J., & Rodin, J. *Interactions of long and short term density on task performance.* Unpublished manuscript, Yale University, 1976.

REFERENCES

Altman, I. *The environment and social behavior.* Monterey, Calif.: Brooks/Cole, 1975.

Bandura, A. *Social learning theory.* New York: General Learning Press, 1971.

Baron, R., & Rodin, J. Perceived control and crowding stress. In A. Baum, J. Singer, & S. Valins (Eds.), *Advances in environmental psychology* (Vol. 1). Hillsdale, N.J.: Lawrence Erlbaum Associates, 1978.

Baum, A., & Valins, S. *Architecture and social behavior: Psychological studies of social density.* Hillsdale, N.J.: Lawrence Erlbaum Associates, 1977.

Calhoun, J. Population density and social pathology. *Scientific American,* 1962, *206,* 139-148.

Calhoun, J. Space and strategy of life. *Ekistics,* 1970, *29,* 425-437.

Glass, D., & Singer, J. *Urban stress: Experiments on noise and social stressors.* New York: Academic Press, 1972.

Goeckner, D., Greenough, W., & Mead, W. Deficits in learning tasks following chronic overcrowding in rats. *Journal of Personality and Social Psychology,* 1973, *28,* 256-261.

Hiroto, D., & Seligman, M. Generality of learned helplessness in man. *Journal of Personality and Social Psychology,* 1975, *31,* 311-327.

Kurlander, H., Miller, W., & Seligman, M. Learned helplessness, depression, and prisoner's dilemma. In M. Seligman (Ed.), *Helplessness.* San Francisco: Freeman, 1975.

Langer, E. The illusion of control. *Journal of Personality and Social Psychology,* 1975, *32,* 311-328.

Lanzetta, J., & Driscoll, J. Preference for information about an uncertain but unavoidable outcome. *Journal of Personality and Social Psychology,* 1966, *3,* 96-102.

Laufer, R., Proshansky, H., & Wolfe, M. Some analytic dimensions of privacy. In H. Proshansky, W. Ittelson, & L. Rivlin (Eds.), *Environmental psychology.* New York: Holt, Rinehart & Winston, 1976.

McCarthy, D., & Saegert, S. Residential density, social overload, and social withdrawal. *Human Ecology,* in press.

Paulus, P., Cox, V., McCain, G., & Chandler, J. Some effects of crowding in a prison environment. *Journal of Applied Social Psychology,* 1975, *5,* 86-91.

Pervin, L. The need to predict and control under conditions of threat. *Journal of Personality,* 1963, *31,* 570-585.

Rodin, J. Density, perceived choice and response to controllable and uncontrollable outcomes. *Journal of Experimental and Social Psychology,* 1976, *12,* 564-578 (fig. 1, p. 575).

Seligman, M. *Helplessness.* San Francisco: Freeman, 1975.

Seligman, M., Maier, S., & Geer, J. The alleviation of learned helplessness in the dog. *Journal of Abnormal and Social Psychology,* 1968, *73,* 256-262.

Sherrod, D. Crowding, perceived control, and behavioral effects. *Journal of Applied Social Psychology,* 1974, *4,* 171-186.

Staub, E., Tursky, B., & Schwartz, G. Self-control and predictability: Their effects on reactions to aversive stimulation. *Journal of Personality and Social Psychology,* 1971, *18,* 157-162.

Wortman, C. Some determinants of perceived control. *Journal of Personality and Social Psychology,* 1975, *31,* 282-294.

Wortman, C., & Brehm, J. Responses to uncontrollable outcomes: An integration of reactance theory and the learned helplessness model. In L. Berkowitz (Ed.), *Advances in experimental social psychology* (Vol. 8). New York: Academic Press, 1975.

Yancey, W. Architecture, interaction, and social control: The case of a large-scale housing project. In J. Wohlwill & D. Carson (Eds.), *Environment and the social sciences: Perspectives and applications.* Washington, D.C.: American Psychological Association, 1972.

Zlutnick, S., & Altman, I. Crowding and human behavior. In J. Wohlwill & D. Carson (Eds.), *Environment and the social sciences: Perspectives and applications.* Washington, D.C.: American Psychological Association, 1972.

Author Index

Subject Index